INTERMEDIATE
GREEK
GRAMMAR

INTERMEDIATE GREEK GRAMMAR

SYNTAX FOR STUDENTS OF THE NEW TESTAMENT

DAVID L. MATHEWSON

AND

ELODIE BALLANTINE EMIG

Baker Academic

a division of Baker Publishing Group
Grand Rapids, Michigan

Published by Baker Academic
a division of Baker Publishing Group
P.O. Box 6287, Grand Rapids, MI 49516-6287
www.bakeracademic.com

Printed in the United States of America

Library of Congress Cataloging-in-Publication Data
Names: Mathewson, David L., 1963– author. | Emig, Elodie Ballantine, 1956– author.
Title: Intermediate Greek grammar : syntax for students of the New Testament / David L.
    Mathewson and Elodie Ballantine Emig.
Description: Grand Rapids, MI : Baker Academic, 2016. | Includes bibliographical references and
    indexes.
Identifiers: LCCN 2016010357 | ISBN 9780801030727 (cloth)
Subjects: LCSH: Greek language, Biblical—Grammar. | Greek language, Biblical—Syntax. | Bible.
    New Testament—Language, style.
Classification: LCC PA817 .M37 2016 | DDC 487/.4—dc23
LC record available at https://lccn.loc.gov/2016010357

16   17   18   19   20   21   22   7   6   5   4   3   2   1

We dedicate this book to the glory of God
and with love to our children:

Caleb & Kara, Jordan, and Ally Mathewson
Peter and Alex & Mackenzie Emig

THE NEW JERUSALEM

*We believe that the study of biblical Greek is,
among other things, a spiritual journey, so the drawing
is of a path to the new Jerusalem.*

CONTENTS

ACKNOWLEDGMENTS

We wish to express our gratitude to those who have helped us with this grammar. Our colleagues at Denver Seminary have been nothing but encouraging and supportive; in particular we thank Bill Klein, Craig Blomberg, Erin Heim, Danny Carroll R., Rick Hess, and Hélène Dallaire. We are also grateful for our students, without whom we would not have taken on such a task. Much of the material in this book has been tested in our Greek exegesis courses, and we are grateful for the input and overwhelmingly positive response of our many students who interacted with this material. We thank our graders who freed us up to do research and write: Joe Terracina, Jon Groce, Emmanuel Engulu, and Spencer Trefzger.

It is also important to acknowledge our debt to those who read any or all of the drafts of our manuscript: Ben Crenshaw, Sue Bailey, Erin Heim, Craig Blomberg, Hélène Dallaire, Don Payne, and Roy Ciampa. Their careful attention to the manuscript and helpful comments saved us from several mistakes. But as it is customary to acknowledge, any shortcomings are not to be attributed to them but to us!

We are also extremely grateful to Jim Kinney and James Ernest for their initial interest in our book and the invitation to publish it with Baker Academic. This volume would not be what it is without the stellar editorial work of Wells Turner. The entire staff at Baker Academic has been a joy to work with throughout the entire process!

I (Elodie) thank my New Song Church family (especially Beth & Loren, Iris, Josh & Jen, Sarah & Brett, and Sue), my BBB women's group (Hélène, Lori, Ramona, Su, and Sue), and Austin & Robyn for tons of prayers along the way.

I (Dave) would like to thank my small group at Aspen Ridge Church in Evergreen, Colorado, for their interest in this book and continual prayers.

Finally, we thank our children, Caleb & Kara, Jordan, and Ally Mathewson; Peter and Alex & Mackenzie Emig. They have encouraged, inspired, and loved us all along the way. It is to them that we lovingly dedicate this book. But above all, we give God the glory for sustaining us for the duration!

ABBREVIATIONS

General and Bibliographic

acc.	accusative case
BCE	before the Common Era
BDAG	Walter Bauer, Frederick W. Danker, William F. Arndt, and F. Wilbur Gingrich. *A Greek-English Lexicon of the New Testament and Other Early Christian Literature*. Chicago: University of Chicago Press, 2000.
BDF	Friedrich Blass and Albert Debrunner. *A Greek Grammar of the New Testament and Other Early Christian Literature*. Translated and edited by Robert A. Funk. Chicago: University of Chicago Press, 1961.
Black	David Alan Black. *It's Still Greek to Me: An Easy-to-Understand Guide to Intermediate Greek*. Grand Rapids: Baker, 1998.
Brooks and Winbery	J. A. Brooks and C. L. Winbery. *Syntax of New Testament Greek*. Lanham, MD: University Press of America, 1979.
CE	Common Era
chap(s).	chapter(s)
Dana and Mantey	H. E. Dana and Julius Mantey. *A Manual Grammar of the Greek New Testament*. New York: Macmillan, 1955.
dat.	dative case
ESV	English Standard Version
gen.	genitive case

JSNTSup	Journal for the Study of the New Testament Supplement Series
KJV	King James Version
LXX	Septuagint, Greek translation of the Hebrew Bible
Moule	C. F. D. Moule. *An Idiom Book of New Testament Greek*. 2nd ed. Cambridge: Cambridge University Press, 1959.
Mounce	William D. Mounce. *The Basics of Biblical Greek Grammar*. 3rd ed. Grand Rapids: Zondervan, 2009.
NA[28]	Eberhard and Erwin Nestle, Barbara and Kurt Aland, et al., eds. *Novum Testamentum Graece*. 28th rev. ed. Stuttgart: Deutsche Bibelgesellschaft, 2012.
NICNT	New International Commentary on the New Testament
NIV	New International Version
NRSV	New Revised Standard Version
NT	New Testament
OT	Old Testament
PNTC	Pillar New Testament Commentary
Porter	Stanley E. Porter. *Idioms of the Greek New Testament*. 2nd, corrected ed. Sheffield: JSOT Press, 1994.
Robertson	A. T. Robertson. *A Grammar of the Greek New Testament in the Light of Historical Research*. 4th ed. Nashville: Broadman, 1934.
SBLGNT	*The Greek New Testament: SBL Edition*. Edited by Michael W. Holmes. Atlanta: SBL Press, 2010.
Turner	Nigel Turner. *Syntax*. Vol. 3 of *A Grammar of New Testament Greek*. By James Hope Moulton, Wilbert Francis Howard, and Nigel Turner. Edinburgh: T&T Clark, 1963.
UBS[5]	Barbara and Kurt Aland, et al., eds. *The Greek New Testament*. 5th rev. ed. Stuttgart: United Bible Societies, 2014.
Wallace	Daniel B. Wallace. *Greek Grammar beyond the Basics*. Grand Rapids: Zondervan, 1996.
Young	Richard A. Young. *Intermediate New Testament Greek: A Linguistic and Exegetical Approach*. Nashville: Broadman & Holman, 1994.
Zerwick	Maximilian Zerwick. *Biblical Greek: Illustrated by Examples*. Rome: Pontificio Istituto Biblico, 1963.

Old Testament

Gen.	Genesis		Song	Song of Songs
Exod.	Exodus		Isa.	Isaiah
Lev.	Leviticus		Jer.	Jeremiah
Num.	Numbers		Lam.	Lamentations
Deut.	Deuteronomy		Ezek.	Ezekiel
Josh.	Joshua		Dan.	Daniel
Judg.	Judges		Hosea	Hosea
Ruth	Ruth		Joel	Joel
1–2 Sam.	1–2 Samuel		Amos	Amos
1–2 Kings	1–2 Kings		Obad.	Obadiah
1–2 Chron.	1–2 Chronicles		Jon.	Jonah
Ezra	Ezra		Mic.	Micah
Neh.	Nehemiah		Nah.	Nahum
Esther	Esther		Hab.	Habakkuk
Job	Job		Zeph.	Zephaniah
Ps(s).	Psalm(s)		Hag.	Haggai
Prov.	Proverbs		Zech.	Zechariah
Eccles.	Ecclesiastes		Mal.	Malachi

New Testament

Matt.	Matthew		1–2 Thess.	1–2 Thessalonians
Mark	Mark		1–2 Tim.	1–2 Timothy
Luke	Luke		Titus	Titus
John	John		Philem.	Philemon
Acts	Acts		Heb.	Hebrews
Rom.	Romans		James	James
1–2 Cor.	1–2 Corinthians		1–2 Pet.	1–2 Peter
Gal.	Galatians		1–3 John	1–3 John
Eph.	Ephesians		Jude	Jude
Phil.	Philippians		Rev.	Revelation
Col.	Colossians			

INTRODUCTION

Why This Book?

I.1. We love Greek. We want our students to love Greek or, falling short of that, to be committed to using it (and Hebrew) in life and ministry. Loving a language and teaching it, however, are insufficient reasons to write a new intermediate Greek grammar. After we started this project, we became aware that Andreas Köstenberger, Benjamin Merkle, and Robert Plummer were working on *Going Deeper with New Testament Greek* (B&H, 2016) and perhaps doing so for reasons similar to ours. The last substantial intermediate grammar, Dan Wallace's *Greek Grammar beyond the Basics* (Zondervan), was published in 1996, preceded in 1994 by Richard Young's *Intermediate New Testament Greek* (Broadman & Holman) and followed in 1998 by Black's much shorter offering, *It's Still Greek to Me* (Baker). All of these were preceded by Stanley Porter's grammar, *Idioms of the Greek New Testament* (Sheffield, 1992), which is closest in perspective to what we have attempted to write. And while we acknowledge again our incalculable debt to all of them and the many others who have paved our way, much has shifted or changed in the world of NT Greek studies since the 1990s. The vastly increased availability of Accordance, BibleWorks, and Logos software along with modern linguistic developments and advances in specific areas of Greek grammar have necessitated some reassessments of our approach to grammar.[1] One specific area yet to be integrated sufficiently into grammars is verbal aspect theory (the exception being Porter's work mentioned above). These advances make

---

1. For some of these advances, see Constantine R. Campbell, *Advances in the Study of Greek: New Insights for Reading the New Testament* (Grand Rapids: Zondervan, 2015).

the time ripe for an intermediate-level grammar that integrates them. We have written this grammar to be an accessible textbook for students and professors alike but also to be useful to pastors and anyone involved in teaching the NT. In short, it is intended for all who need an intermediate-level Greek grammar that incorporates insights from some of the most recent developments in the study of NT Greek.

1.2. What are the distinctive features of this grammar? First, as already mentioned, without trying to be comprehensive we have attempted to incorporate some of the most recent linguistic insights into the study of Koine Greek. We have particularly endeavored to make accessible to students advances in the areas of verbal aspect theory, the voice system, conjunctions, as well as linguistic and discourse studies. In a number of areas, we think that we are unique in the way we have categorized or "labeled" grammatical constructions. Second, we have attempted to keep grammatical categories and labels to a minimum, focusing on the most important or the most common usages. Third, we have tried to illustrate the different grammatical points with examples taken from across the entire spectrum of NT texts. That is, where possible, we have culled illustrations of each grammatical feature from the Gospels, Acts, the Pauline Letters, the General Epistles, and Revelation to expose the student to different literary genres and the Greek styles of various authors. We have also made a point of locating fresh examples, whenever possible, that have not been used by other grammars, though some conventional examples are just too good to pass up. Fourth, we have intentionally avoided writing an exegetical grammar; however, we often include discussion of illustrative texts to demonstrate the exegetical value of the application of Greek grammar. A final feature is the use of larger chunks of text for practice. Rather than following the custom of many grammars in choosing verse-length examples isolated from their contexts, in most instances we have chosen to include larger stretches of NT text. These come at the end of the discussion of each major grammatical point, or sometimes at the end of the chapter, and are labeled "For Practice." Our hope is that students will be encouraged to move beyond looking at isolated grammatical features to considering their function within a larger context.

Though we would be thrilled if all Bible students shared our passion for reading Scripture in the original languages, we count it a blessing to live in an age of multiple translations. We affirm that God's words should be made available to all people in every possible language. (We acknowledge that not everyone is called to study Hebrew and Greek and that among the great cloud of witnesses are multitudes who are not.) As any of us who have ever tried to learn a foreign language know, translation involves varying degrees of interpretation. There is no one-to-one correspondence between any two languages, and it is not always possible to bring out the fullest, most nuanced meaning of a particular text in translation. Therefore, in this grammar we do not rely on translation to bring out all the subtleties of the grammatical features that are illustrated with Greek examples. Our English translation may or may not fully capture the grammar being illustrated; that is, the goal of exegesis is not to produce an ideal translation. Rather, the focus should be on grammatical analysis and on knowing the importance of grammatical analysis for interpreting the biblical text.

The following reflect some of the broader and most basic commitments of this grammar. We have tried to keep these commitments firmly in mind as we have written each section. One important insight that has emerged from the application of linguistics to Greek grammar is the realization that Greek should be treated like any other language. Many mistreatments of NT Greek come down to a misunderstanding of how language actually works. The point is, we do not write and speak in our own language the way we often treat NT Greek.

Minimalistic Grammar

I.3. A very common approach, which gives unwarranted attention to individual grammatical units and their meanings, is what could be called a *maximalist* approach to grammar, or the "exegetical nuggets" approach.[2] The goal of maximalist NT grammar and exegesis is to uncover the most meaning possible in each grammatical form or construction. This is often accompanied by the multiplication of categories, labels, and rules for their usage. The focus is on individual words and grammatical forms, often at the expense of sensitivity to the broader context in which they occur. Such individual elements of NT Greek are thought to be "rich" in meaning. This can be seen, for example, in approaches that read theological significance out of verb tenses. So we are told that the perfect tense (ἐγήγερται) in 1 Cor. 15:4 is theologically significant because it portrays Christ's resurrection as a reality based on a past action that continues into the present. This theological insight may be valid (in fact, we would insist that it is!), but it is not dependent on a single linguistic unit, the perfect tense-form (nor are we convinced that this is a correct understanding of the perfect tense-form itself). Rather, such insight comes from the broader context of Paul's discussion of the resurrection in 1 Cor. 15. Or how often

2. Moisés Silva, *God, Language, and Scripture: Reading the Bible in the Light of General Linguistics* (Grand Rapids: Zondervan, 1990), 144.

have we heard the aorist tense, or the genitive case, or prepositions "milked" for theological purposes? We think here of the weight that has sometimes been given to the debate between the "objective" and "subjective" genitive in the expression πίστις Ἰησοῦ Χριστοῦ. It is not that it is unimportant whether we think in terms of faith placed in Jesus Christ or of Jesus' own faithfulness; it is just that our decision in many cases is primarily theological rather than grammatical and should not be based solely on isolated elements such as tenses, cases, or prepositions. Once more, our focus should be on the larger context as the bearer of theology. Any major theological points worth affirming and arguing for will certainly not be nuanced in small grammatical subtleties or fine distinctions between case uses. Rather, they will be clear from their entire contexts.[3] At the heart of this is the failure to recognize how language actually works. According to Rodney Decker, too much grammatical analysis is characterized by the efforts of preachers or teachers

> to find nuggets that support an emphasis that they want to make in the text, . . . even in some commentaries that attempt to focus only on the Greek text. We do not understand our own language in this way even though a grammarian can dissect such texts and assign appropriate taxonomical labels to the individual elements. Grammatical study of ancient texts in "dead" languages (i.e., those no longer spoken by a community of native speakers) is of value. It helps us understand what is being said and enables us to grasp the alternative possibilities in a written text. More often it facilitates *eliminating* invalid possibilities of meaning. But when all is said and done, all the grammatical and syntactical data are important only in that they enable us to grasp the meaning of the statements in their context.[4]

A maximalist approach to Greek grammar is often an outgrowth of a view of Scripture as the inspired Word of God. Certainly if the NT is God's Word, each grammatical expression must be semantically weighty and bursting with import! As Moisés Silva describes this perspective, "Surely an inspired text must be full of meaning: we can hardly think that so much as a single word in the Bible is insignificant or dispensable."[5] We agree with Silva that this overlooks that God has spoken to his people in normal language. As authors,

---

3. Ibid., 115: "But we can feel confident that no reasonable writer would seek to express a major point by leaning on a subtle grammatical distinction—especially if it is a point not otherwise clear from the whole context (and if it *is* clear from the context, then the grammatical subtlety plays at best a secondary role in exegesis)."

4. Rodney J. Decker, *Mark 1–8: A Handbook on the Greek Text* (Waco: Baylor University Press, 2014), xxii–xxiii.

5. Silva, *God, Language, and Scripture*, 13.

we are committed to the authority and inspiration of Scripture. However, this does not necessitate taking the Greek language in an unnatural or artificial way. Inspiration does not somehow transform the language into something more than it was before. Therefore, we are committed to a minimalistic view of grammar, where maximal meaning is not attributed to the individual linguistic units but is found in their broader context.[6] Also, we have kept categories and labels to a minimum. This does not mean that grammar is unimportant or that precise grammatical analysis should be avoided, but we must understand the role it plays in contributing meaning to the overall context. There is danger in reading far more from the grammar than is justified. A minimalist approach also has an andragogical benefit: it relieves the student from the burden of learning an unwieldy list of case or tense labels. It greatly streamlines the choices and the categories for which students are responsible, thereby freeing them up to focus on entire texts instead of isolated details.

Realistic View of Language

I.4. In a similar vein is the assessment of the overall character of the Greek language, especially as it relates to other languages. Many maintain a superior status for Greek. In their grammar Dana and Mantey claim that in comparison with others, "the Greek language, with scarcely an exception, proves to be the most accurate, euphonious, and expressive."[7] More recently, Chrys Caragounis has concluded that in its history and development Greek is "unique" and "unparalleled."[8] He also states that in the Classical (Attic) period

> the Greek language reaches its highest degree of perfection: the verb attains 1,124 forms, expressing 1,602 ideas; the noun signals fifteen meaning-units, the great variety of subordinate conjunctions, along with the infinitive and participle, facilitate an almost infinite diversity of hypotactical clauses, the wealth of particles makes possible the expression of the finest of nuances, and the sentence becomes the paragon of complete thought expressed in balanced grammatical relations.[9]

However, such an assessment surely overestimates Greek as a language and its place within the development of language. Moreover, it can easily lead to

6. Decker, *Mark 1–8*, xxii.
7. Dana and Mantey 268.
8. Chrys Caragounis, *The Development of Greek and the New Testament* (Grand Rapids: Baker Academic, 2006), 21.
9. Ibid., 33.

the grammatical maximalism referred to above. In our view, Greek should be treated just like any other language. This means that it is not more precise, more expressive, more wonderfully accurate and intricate than any other language, as if it were the only language in which God could have possibly revealed his Second Testament. Greek is no better or worse than any other language. All languages have their unique features, but a general principle of linguistics is that what can be said in one language can be approximated (since we have said that there is no one-for-one correspondence) in any other. No one language is or was more suitable to communicate God's revelation of himself to his people than any other. Greek has strengths and limitations, just like any other language.

Descriptive Grammar

I.5. Almost the opposite of the previous observation is found in many older grammars, such as BDF, that compared the Koine Greek of the NT to earlier Classical Greek. NT Greek grammar was judged by how well it measured up to Classical Greek standards. The general consensus was that the Greek of the NT was poorer or deficient, or that its users were less competent, or the like. Even today one still hears or reads statements such as, "the writers were careless in their use of Greek," or claims that this or that construction is "sloppy," "bad," or "improper" Greek. Instead, throughout the pages of this grammar we have avoided making judgments as to the correctness or incorrectness of the grammar used by NT authors. It is our conviction that the job of grammar is to be descriptive of how language is actually used, not to be prescriptive and make judgments about how it "ought to be" used. Languages change and evolve, so it is illegitimate to hold up one period of the Greek language's use as superior to another and then to judge a given usage to be "poor" or "incorrect." The "correct" grammar is that upon which language users agree. A corollary of this approach to grammar is that the study of language should be primarily *synchronic* (describing the use of language at a given point in time) rather than *diachronic* (describing the historical development of a language through time).[10] Therefore, although we occasionally make some diachronic observations, our study of Greek grammar has as its primary goal the (synchronic) description of usage at the time of the writing under consideration, the Koine Greek used in the NT, though the focus

10. Stanley E. Porter, "Studying Ancient Language from a Modern Linguistic Perspective: Essential Terms and Terminology," *Filologia Neotestamentaria* 2 (1989): 153–54; Silva, *God, Language, and Scripture,* 41–44.

will be on the Greek of the NT. For example, an overreliance on diachronic (historical) study was partly responsible for the use by some grammarians of an eight-case system for Greek nouns. Based on a descriptive and synchronic approach to grammar, we will side with those who advocate a five-case approach (see chap. 1, on the cases).

Semantics versus Pragmatics

I.6. One important principle that this grammar has tried to keep in mind is the distinction between semantics and pragmatics. That is, there is a difference between the semantics (meaning) of a given grammatical unit and its pragmatic function in various contexts. For example, a participle is a specific grammatical form with specific meaning, but it can function in a variety of ways in a sentence: as adjective, substantive, adverb, or main verb. This distinction can be seen especially in the discussion on verbal aspect. Each aspect has a distinct meaning (semantics) but can function in a variety of temporal and "kind-of-action" contexts (pragmatics).

Realistic View of Software

I.7. Biblical language software (e.g., Logos, BibleWorks, and Accordance) is a boon to just about everyone, from serious scholars to interested laypeople. Word and grammar searches can now be conducted in seconds, saving us valuable time and energy. Statistics for a given grammatical feature are easier to compile accurately and effortlessly. Corpus studies can be executed with greater facility and thoroughness.[11] We have relied heavily on such software in writing this grammar. From our perspective, though, the greatest software in the world still lacks the ability to ensure that people use it sensibly. Access to Hebrew and Greek versions (with every word parsed) and almost countless translations does not guarantee that one understands these texts.

We find ourselves at a pivotal point in history; at least in the West, theological education is in decline in terms of both duration and scope. There is a growing trend among seminaries either to discontinue courses in the biblical languages altogether or to replace them with courses on how to use Bible software. We believe that students need to develop a solid working knowledge of and feel for the biblical languages if they are to have any chance of using

11. Matthew Brook O'Donnell, *Corpus Linguistics and the Greek of the New Testament* (Sheffield: Sheffield Phoenix, 2005).

the tools well. We seem to be facing the opposite but equivalent problem to what was on Martin Luther's mind when he penned his famous (at least among teachers of the biblical languages) letter on education to councilmen in Germany. In the sixteenth century the access problem was the reverse of ours: Greek and Hebrew manuscripts were available to very few, and the reformers were just beginning to displace Latin in favor of Hebrew and Greek. Nearly half a millennium later, biblical manuscripts are almost universally accessible, the two standard Greek texts by Nestle-Aland and the UBS are in their 28th and 5th editions respectively,[12] standard lexical tools continue to be updated, biblical language computer programs continue to increase and develop, and Greek grammars are now plentiful. Yet the study of Greek has fallen on hard times in current theological education. With Martin Luther, we believe there is a spiritual battle underway.

> For the devil smelled a rat, and perceived that if the languages were revived a hole would be knocked in his kingdom which he could not easily stop up again. Since he found he could not prevent their revival, he now aims to keep them on such slender rations that they will of themselves decline and pass away. . . . Although the gospel came and still comes to us through the Holy Spirit alone, we cannot deny that it came through the medium of languages, was spread abroad by that means, and must be preserved by the same means. . . . In proportion then as we value the gospel, let us zealously hold to the languages. . . . And let us be sure of this: we will not long preserve the gospel without the languages. . . . The Holy Spirit is no fool. He does not busy himself with inconsequential or useless matters. He regarded the languages as so useful and necessary to Christianity that he ofttimes brought them down with him from heaven. This alone should be a sufficient motive for us to pursue them with diligence and reverence and not to despise them. . . . When our faith is . . . held up to ridicule, where does the fault lie? It lies in our ignorance of the languages; and there is no other way out than to learn the languages. . . . Since it becomes Christians then to make good use of the Holy Scriptures as their one and only book and it is a sin and a shame not to know our own book or to understand the speech and words of our God, it is a still greater sin and loss that we do not study languages, especially in these days when God is giving us men and books and every facility and inducement to this study, and desires his Bible to be an open book. . . . The preacher or teacher can expound the Bible from beginning to end as he pleases, accurately or

12. Although the two standard editions differ in format (the UBS edition presents only a small selection of the textual variants presented in the Nestle-Aland edition), they represent the same edited Greek text. The SBLGNT, edited by Michael W. Holmes, represents an alternative edition of the Greek text that differs from the Nestle-Aland / United Bible Societies text in more than 540 variation units.

inaccurately, if there is no one there to judge whether he is doing it right or wrong. But in order to judge, one must have a knowledge of the languages; it cannot be done any other way.[13]

We believe Martin Luther's words need to be heard again in our seminaries, colleges, and Christian universities today!

13. Martin Luther, "To the Councilmen of All Cities in Germany That They Establish and Maintain Christian Schools," in *The Christian in Society II*, vol. 45 of *Luther's Works*, ed. Walther I. Brandt (Philadelphia: Muhlenberg, 1962), 358–65.

1

THE CASES

1.1. As an inflected language, Greek uses a system called "case" to mark a group of words, nominals (nouns, pronouns, adjectives, adjectival participles, and articles), in order to indicate their grammatical function and relationship to other words within a sentences (e.g., subject, predicate nominative, direct object, indirect object). In English we primarily follow word order to determine grammatical function. If we change the order of "The player hit the ball" to "The ball hit the player," the grammatical function (subject, object) of "player" and "ball" changes. In Greek it is the inflected endings, not word order, that indicate such things. If we follow the formal endings of the Greek case system, there are at most five cases: nominative, accusative, genitive, dative, vocative.[1]

The choice of a case ending by an author communicates a specific meaning, which is refined by how it relates to its broader context. A common approach to the cases is to create multiple labels (such as nominative of appellation, possessive genitive, instrumental dative) to name the various ways they function in representative contexts. So, for example, Wallace (72–175) provides

---

1. An eight-case system was argued for by several older grammarians. See Robertson 446–543; Dana and Mantey 65–68. There are still some supporters of the eight-case system for Koine Greek (i.e., nominative, genitive, ablative, dative, locative, instrumental, accusative, vocative): see Brooks and Winbery 2–3. However, based on the formal evidence that at most there are only five case endings and that advocates of the eight-case system rely too much on a historical approach to the cases (diachronic) rather than on the evidence from Koine Greek (synchronic), this view is becoming less common in grammars and will not be discussed any further.

some thirty-three labels for the genitive case and twenty-seven for the dative. Analyzing the cases in NT interpretation, then, sometimes consists of simply attaching the correct label or category to each occurrence of a Greek case (a method we call "pin the label on the grammatical construction"). The following points are meant to introduce our treatment of cases in the rest of this chapter.

1.2. It is helpful to distinguish, as Porter (81–82) does, between (a) the meaning contributed by the semantics of the case itself, (b) the meaning contributed by other syntactical features, and (c) the meaning contributed by the broader context. Thus the interpreter must consider all three of these in arriving at the meaning of a given case construction: the case (e.g., a genitive), other syntactical features (e.g., the genitive follows a noun that semantically communicates a verbal process), and the broader context (e.g., this construction occurs in a given context of one of Paul's Letters).

1.3. This grammar will follow a "minimalist" approach to the cases. That is, it focuses on the basic, more common, or exegetically significant usages of the cases rather than multiplying numerous categories with their respective labels. This is not to suggest that there are no other valid usages or categories than those listed below. But it is important to remember that "these names are *merely appellations* to distinguish the different *contextual variations* of usage, and that they do not serve to *explain the case itself*."[2] It is important to distinguish the semantics of the case forms from the pragmatic usage of the cases in different contexts. These different labels (appellations) are not the *meanings* of the cases, but reflect the different contextual realizations of the meanings of the case forms. This approach also allows for ambiguity in the case functions. Sometimes more than one potential label will "fit" when there is not enough evidence to select a specific category with confidence. In such cases the interpreter should refrain from feeling the need to pin down a given case function. The focus should be on the meaning the case contributes to the context. Many grammars often illustrate different case functions with the clearest examples they can find. The problem is that students may think that in every case they must discover "the correct label." But ambiguous examples often prove more fruitful for teaching exegesis in that they resist so easily pinning a category or label on a given case. At times NT authors may have been ambiguous as to the exact function of the case, or a single label may not capture the function of the case in a given context. At other times there is simply not enough evidence to confidently label a given case usage.

1.4. Although we hope that a "minimalist" approach to case usage will free students of the Greek NT to give their full attention to the forest rather

---

2. J. P. Louw, "Linguistic Theory and the Greek Case System," *Acta Classica* 9 (1966): 73.

than the trees, we acknowledge our great debt to those who have created and refined case labels. Labels help us think logically and systematically about language. There is obvious value in the discipline of considering the many ways in which one might understand, for example, τὴν πίστιν τοῦ θεοῦ (subjective genitive, objective genitive, possessive genitive, or genitive of source come to mind for τοῦ θεοῦ). Problems can and do arise, however, when we think language usage is always logical and systematic rather than intuitive—as if case endings were themselves inflected for further meaning, or as if the authors worked from a list of genitive usages. Perhaps for the majority of students of biblical Greek, labels are both intimidating and seen as ends in themselves. Our goal is to encourage students to make their goal the explanation of entire texts, not just to pick the right label for individual elements in those texts.

The Nominative Case

1.5. Defining the Greek nominative case has posed a challenge for grammars. Sometimes it is described in terms of one of its primary functions, to indicate the subject of a sentence (Dana and Mantey 68–69). Though this is one of its common uses, the description is too narrow and does not account for all of the nominatives. As frequently recognized, the Greeks themselves designated it as the "naming case" (Robertson 456). The nominative is the case that *designates, or specifies, a nominal idea*. It simply names or designates an entity rather than specifying a relationship (as with the genitive or dative).[3] The various syntactic functions explained below may be understood in this light. Furthermore, in relation to the other cases, the nominative is the unmarked case and carries the least semantic weight (but perhaps sometimes more marked than the accusative; see below), although at times it can have important functions in a discourse.

Subject

1.6. One of the most common functions of the nominative case is to designate or name the grammatical subject of a verb in any voice (S + V). The nominative subject often indicates the topic of the sentence.[4]

3. Gary A. Long, *Grammatical Concepts 101 for Biblical Greek* (Peabody, MA: Hendrickson, 2006), 38.
4. Joseph E. Grimes, "Signals of Discourse Structure in Koine," in *Society of Biblical Literature 1975 Seminar Papers* (Missoula, MT: Society of Biblical Literature, 1975), 1:151–64.

Τότε παραγίνεται ὁ Ἰησοῦς ἀπὸ τῆς Γαλιλαίας (Matt. 3:13)	Then **Jesus** arrived from Galilee.
Πέτρος δὲ καὶ Ἰωάννης ἀνέβαινον εἰς τὸ ἱερὸν ἐπὶ τὴν ὥραν τῆς προσευχῆς τὴν ἐνάτην (Acts 3:1)	And **Peter** and **John** went up into the temple at the ninth hour of prayer.
νόμος δὲ παρεισῆλθεν ἵνα πλεονάσῃ τὸ παράπτωμα· οὗ δὲ ἐπλεόνασεν ἡ ἁμαρτία, ὑπερεπερίσσευσεν ἡ χάρις (Rom. 5:20)	But the **law** came in, in order that **trespass** might increase. But where **sin** increases, **grace** increases more.

Since Greek verbs indicate person and number through their inflected endings and therefore do not require the mention of an explicit subject, "when the subject is expressed it is often used either to draw attention to the subject of discussion or to mark a shift in the topic, perhaps signaling that a new person or event is the center of focus" (Porter 295–96). Sometimes an expressed subject is needed to indicate a change of speakers in a dialogue or to reintroduce a character who has been offstage for some time (see chap. 13, on discourse considerations).

ἕτερος δὲ τῶν μαθητῶν εἶπεν αὐτῷ. . . . ὁ δὲ Ἰησοῦς λέγει αὐτῷ . . . (Matt. 8:21–22)	And **another** of the disciples said to him. . . . And **Jesus** said to him. . . . (*a change of speakers in a dialogue*)
Ἄγγελος δὲ κυρίου ἐλάλησεν πρὸς Φίλιππον λέγων (Acts 8:26)	And an **angel** of the Lord spoke to Philip, saying. . . . (*introduces a new subject*)
Παρακαλῶ οὖν ὑμᾶς ἐγὼ ὁ δέσμιος ἐν κυρίῳ ἀξίως περιπατῆσαι τῆς κλήσεως ἧς ἐκλήθητε (Eph. 4:1)	Therefore, **I**, the prisoner in the Lord, exhort you to walk worthily of the calling with which you were called.

In a discourse in which the author has already identified himself, as here (Eph. 1:1), the explicit first-person reference to the author is emphatic.

διὸ καὶ ὁ θεὸς αὐτὸν ὑπερύψωσεν, καὶ ἐχαρίσατο αὐτῷ τὸ ὄνομα τὸ ὑπὲρ πᾶν ὄνομα (Phil. 2:9)	Therefore, **God** also highly exalted him and gave him the name above every name. (*a switch to a new subject; from Christ to God*)

In Phil. 2:6–7 the subject of the finite verbs is Jesus Christ.

4

Οὕτως καὶ ὁ **Χριστὸς** οὐχ ἑαυτὸν ἐδόξασεν γενηθῆναι ἀρχιερέα (Heb. 5:5)

So also **Christ** did not glorify himself in order to become a high priest.

In the midst of the author's discussion of the qualifications of a high priest, the nominative indicates a shift to the topic of Jesus Christ.

Καὶ οἱ ἑπτὰ **ἄγγελοι** οἱ ἔχοντες τὰς ἑπτὰ σάλπιγγας ἡτοίμασαν αὐτοὺς ἵνα σαλπίσωσιν. (Rev. 8:6)

And the seven **angels** who have the seven trumpets prepared them, in order that they might blow them.

The nominative resumes reference to or brings back onstage the seven angels after their introduction in Rev. 8:2 was interrupted by two other angelic figures in verses 3–5.

Predicate

1.7. Another frequent usage of the nominative case is to complete a "linking verb" (S + LV + **PN**) that links it to the subject. The most common verbs are εἰμί and γίνομαι (and ὑπάρχω).

ἀποκριθεὶς ὁ Πέτρος λέγει αὐτῷ· Σὺ εἶ ὁ **χριστός**. (Mark 8:29)

Answering, Peter said to him, "You are the **Christ**."

οὗτός ἐστιν ὁ **Μωϋσῆς** ὁ εἴπας τοῖς υἱοῖς Ἰσραήλ· (Acts 7:37)

This is **Moses**, who spoke to the children of Israel.

οὐ γάρ ἐστιν ἡ βασιλεία τοῦ θεοῦ **βρῶσις** καὶ **πόσις** (Rom. 14:17)

For the kingdom of God is not **food** and **drink**.

Γίνεσθε δὲ **ποιηταὶ** λόγου καὶ μὴ **ἀκροαταὶ** μόνον (James 1:22)

Become **doers** of the word and not **hearers** only.

Οὗτοι οἱ περιβεβλημένοι τὰς στολὰς τὰς λευκὰς **τίνες** εἰσὶν καὶ πόθεν ἦλθον; (Rev. 7:13)

These who are clothed with white robes, **who** are they and from where did they come?

One problem emerges with the predicate use of the nominative: since this construction often involves two substantives in the nominative case, one the subject and the other the predicate nominative (S + LV + **PN**), and since word order cannot be the deciding factor in Greek for grammatical function, how is the reader of Greek to distinguish the subject from the predicate nominative?

The main issue is with third-person examples. With first- or second-person pronouns or verbs (e.g., ἐστέ) the decision is not difficult: "I," "we," "you" will be the subject. The following guidelines may prove useful for third-person examples. They are also arranged in order of importance (that is, 1 trumps all the others), though 2 and 3 seem to operate on the same level (in that case, 4 comes into effect).[5]

1. If only one of the words in the nominative is a pronoun, it will be the subject.[6]

   αὕτη δέ ἐστιν ἡ αἰώνιος ζωή   And **this** is eternal life.
   (John 17:3)

2. If only one of the words in the nominative has an article, it will be the subject.[7]

   Καὶ ὁ **λόγος** σὰρξ ἐγένετο καὶ   And the **Word** became flesh and
   ἐσκήνωσεν ἐν ἡμῖν (John 1:14)   lived among us.

3. If only one of the words in the nominative is a proper name, it will be the subject.

   Ἠλίας ἄνθρωπος ἦν ὁμοιοπαθὴς   **Elijah** was a man with the same
   ἡμῖν (James 5:17)   nature as ours.

4. If both have the article or are proper names, the one that comes first will be the subject.

   ἡ **ἐντολὴ** ἡ παλαιά ἐστιν ὁ   The old **commandment** is the
   λόγος ὃν ἠκούσατε. (1 John   word that you heard.
   2:7)

---

5. See Wallace 42–45 (Wallace calls this the "pecking order"); Porter 109. The standard work on this is Lane McGaughy, *Toward a Descriptive Analysis of EINAI as a Linking Verb in New Testament Greek*, SBL Dissertation Series 6 (Missoula, MT: Society of Biblical Literature, 1972).
6. McGaughy, *Toward a Descriptive Analysis*, 46–48, 55–61.
7. Ibid., 55–56.

With Names (Appellation)

1.8. Sometimes names or titles in Greek will occur in the nominative case, even when another case might be expected (BDF §143). Many of these have a grammatical explanation, such as being a subject or predicate nominative of a verbless clause or being in apposition to a noun in the nominative case.

Ἐγένετο ἄνθρωπος ἀπεσταλμένος παρὰ θεοῦ, ὄνομα αὐτῷ Ἰωάννης· (John 1:6)	There came a man, sent from God; his name [was] **John.**

It is possible to understand this as an example of an elided verb: "His name was John."

ὑμεῖς φωνεῖτέ με Ὁ **διδάσκαλος** καὶ Ὁ **κύριος** (John 13:13)	You call me **teacher** and **Lord.**

It is possible to treat this example as a direct quotation of what they called him: "Teacher and Lord."

καὶ ἀπὸ Ἰησοῦ Χριστοῦ, **ὁ μάρτυς ὁ πιστός, ὁ πρωτότοκος** τῶν νεκρῶν καὶ **ὁ ἄρχων** τῶν βασιλέων τῆς γῆς (Rev. 1:5)	And from Jesus Christ, **the faithful witness, the firstborn** from the dead, and **the ruler** of the kings of the earth. (*three titles in the nominative in apposition to the genitive* Ἰησοῦ Χριστοῦ)

καὶ ἐν τῇ Ἑλληνικῇ ὄνομα ἔχει Ἀπολλύων. (Rev. 9:11)	And in Greek he has the name **Apollyon.**

Here we might expect the accusative case. This could also be understood as the predicate nominative of a verbless parenthetical clause: "He has a name—[it is] Apollyon."

Independent

1.9. A word in the nominative case can sometimes form its own clause. This is consistent with its meaning: to designate or specify a nominal idea. The usage is common in titles or salutations of letters, for example, and may sometimes explain its use with names above.

χάρις ὑμῖν καὶ **εἰρήνη** ἀπὸ θεοῦ πατρὸς ἡμῶν. (Col. 1:2)	**Grace** to you and **peace** from God our Father.

αὐτῷ ἡ **δόξα** ἐν τῇ ἐκκλησίᾳ καὶ ἐν Χριστῷ Ἰησοῦ εἰς πάσας τὰς γενεάς (Eph. 3:21)

To him [be] the **glory** in the church in Christ Jesus unto all generations.

Ἀποκάλυψις Ἰησοῦ Χριστοῦ, ἣν ἔδωκεν αὐτῷ ὁ θεός (Rev. 1:1)

The **revelation** of Jesus Christ, which God gave to him.

Absolute, or "Hanging"

1.10. Here the nominative is grammatically unrelated to the clause to which it is linked, though it is connected conceptually. This use of the nominative often occurs with a participle or a relative clause, which then gets picked up by a pronoun in another case in the following main clause (Zerwick 10). This is also known as a "left dislocation," whereby an entity is detached from and placed outside and in front of the main clause (see chap. 13, on discourse considerations). The "dislocated" nominative then is usually resumed in the main clause with a pronoun.[8] Such a construction often draws attention to the element in the nominative or serves to introduce or shift to a new topic (Porter 86).

πᾶν **ῥῆμα** ἀργὸν ὃ λαλήσουσιν οἱ ἄνθρωποι, ἀποδώσουσιν περὶ αὐτοῦ λόγον ἐν ἡμέρᾳ κρίσεως· (Matt. 12:36)

Every useless **word** that people speak, they will give an account concerning *it* in the day of judgment.

Here the nominative ῥῆμα is picked up with the genitive pronoun αὐτοῦ in the main clause.

ὅσοι δὲ ἔλαβον αὐτόν, ἔδωκεν αὐτοῖς ἐξουσίαν τέκνα θεοῦ γενέσθαι (John 1:12)

But **as many as** received him, *to them* he gave the right to become children of God.

ὁ γὰρ **Μωϋσῆς** οὗτος, ὃς ἐξήγαγεν ἡμᾶς ἐκ γῆς Αἰγύπτου, οὐκ οἴδαμεν τί ἐγένετο αὐτῷ. (Acts 7:40)

For this **Moses**, who led us out of Egypt, we do not know what happened *to him*.

---

8. Steven E. Runge, *Discourse Grammar of the Greek New Testament: A Practical Introduction for Teaching and Exegesis* (Peabody, MA: Hendrickson, 2010), 289.

καὶ ὁ **νικῶν** καὶ ὁ **τηρῶν** ἄχρι τέλους τὰ ἔργα μου, δώσω αὐτῷ ἐξουσίαν ἐπὶ τῶν ἐθνῶν (Rev. 2:26)

And the **one who overcomes** and **who keeps** my works until the end, I will give *to him/her* authority over the nations.

Apposition

1.11. As with all the other cases, a substantive in the nominative case can stand in apposition to another nominative substantive. Both substantives sit side by side, "residing in the same syntactic slot in the clause," and *refer* to the same entity.[9]

Ἰωσὴφ δὲ ὁ **ἀνὴρ** αὐτῆς, δίκαιος ὢν καὶ μὴ θέλων αὐτὴν δειγματίσαι, ἐβουλήθη λάθρα ἀπολῦσαι αὐτήν. (Matt. 1:19)

But Joseph, her **husband**, being righteous and not wanting to expose her publicly, decided to divorce her in secret.

Παῦλος **ἀπόστολος** Χριστοῦ Ἰησοῦ διὰ θελήματος θεοῦ καὶ Τιμόθεος ὁ **ἀδελφὸς** (2 Cor. 1:1)

Paul, an **apostle** of Christ Jesus through the will of God, and Timothy, the **brother**.

Οὗτος γὰρ ὁ Μελχισέδεκ, **βασιλεὺς** Σαλήμ, **ἱερεὺς** τοῦ θεοῦ τοῦ ὑψίστου (Heb. 7:1)

For this Melchizedek, **king** of Salem, **priest** of the most high God. . . .

καὶ ἐπὶ τὸ μέτωπον αὐτῆς ὄνομα γεγραμμένον, **μυστήριον**, **Βαβυλὼν** ἡ μεγάλη, ἡ **μήτηρ** τῶν πορνῶν καὶ τῶν βδελυγμάτων τῆς γῆς. (Rev. 17:5)

And upon her forehead was a name written: **Mystery, Babylon** the great, the **mother** of harlots and of the abominations of the earth.

The Vocative Case

1.12. The vocative case is utilized when someone (e.g., the reader) or something is addressed directly. There is some debate as to whether the vocative should be considered a separate case from the nominative, since it has separate forms

9. Long, *Grammatical Concepts*, 42.

only in the singular.[10] Its function was being taken over by the nominative case.[11] The presence of the vocative seems to be emphatic, since it directly brings the addressees into the discourse. It is often used to draw attention to upcoming material and to indicate breaks in the discourse.

ὁ δὲ Ἰησοῦς στραφεὶς καὶ ἰδὼν αὐτὴν εἶπεν· Θάρσει, **θύγατερ**· (Matt. 9:22)	And Jesus turned, and seeing her, he said: "Take heart, **daughter**."
Ὦ ἀνόητοι **Γαλάται**, τίς ὑμᾶς ἐβάσκανεν; (Gal. 3:1)	O foolish **Galatians**, who has bewitched you?

This is a rare occurrence (17× in the NT) of Ὦ before the vocative.[12]

μὴ πλανᾶσθε, **ἀδελφοί** μου ἀγαπη- τοί. (James 1:16)	Do not be deceived, my beloved **brothers and sisters**.
Τεκνία μου, ταῦτα γράφω ὑμῖν ἵνα μὴ ἁμάρτητε. (1 John 2:1)	My **little children**, I write these things to you in order that you may not sin.

For Practice

1.13. Analyze the nominatives (in bold) in the following texts, paying attention to the function of each as well as to how you determine the function.

[9]Καὶ ἐγένετο ἐν ἐκείναις ταῖς ἡμέραις ἦλθεν Ἰησοῦς ἀπὸ Ναζαρὲτ τῆς Γαλιλαίας καὶ ἐβαπτίσθη εἰς τὸν Ἰορδάνην ὑπὸ Ἰωάννου. [10]καὶ εὐθὺς ἀναβαίνων ἐκ τοῦ ὕδατος εἶδεν σχιζομένους τοὺς οὐρανοὺς καὶ τὸ πνεῦμα ὡς περιστερὰν καταβαῖνον εἰς αὐτόν· [11]καὶ **φωνὴ** ἐγένετο ἐκ τῶν οὐρανῶν· Σὺ εἶ ὁ **υἱός** μου ὁ **ἀγαπητός**, ἐν σοὶ εὐδόκησα. [12]Καὶ εὐθὺς τὸ **πνεῦμα** αὐτὸν ἐκβάλλει εἰς τὴν ἔρημον. [13]καὶ ἦν ἐν τῇ ἐρήμῳ τεσσεράκοντα ἡμέρας πειρα- ζόμενος ὑπὸ τοῦ Σατανᾶ, καὶ ἦν μετὰ τῶν θηρίων, καὶ οἱ **ἄγγελοι** διηκόνουν αὐτῷ. (Mark 1:9–13)

---

10. Porter 87–88. Cf. Wallace 66–67, who argues for a separate vocative case.
11. Moule 32; Turner 34.
12. See Zerwick 35–36, who notes that ὦ before the vocative was usual in Classical Greek, and that when it occurs in the Greek of the NT, "one is justified in supposing that there is some reason for its use" (36). BDF §146.1.b says that it expresses emotion, and Dana and Mantey (71) say that it carries more force.

¹Ἀποκάλυψις Ἰησοῦ Χριστοῦ, ἣν ἔδωκεν αὐτῷ ὁ θεὸς δεῖξαι τοῖς δούλοις αὐτοῦ, ἃ δεῖ γενέσθαι ἐν τάχει. . . . ⁴Ἰωάννης ταῖς ἑπτὰ ἐκκλησίαις ταῖς ἐν τῇ Ἀσίᾳ· **χάρις** ὑμῖν καὶ **εἰρήνη** (Rev. 1:1, 4a)

The Genitive Case

1.14. A syntactically versatile case, the genitive has a broad range of usage, including uses that we often express with the English prepositions *of* and *from*. (Please note that *of* is not the meaning of the genitive case; it is the English preposition used sufficiently variously, and often ambiguously, to represent some but not all of the case's uses in translation.) Traditional grammars refer to the genitive case as descriptive, defining, specifying, or even adjectival;[13] more linguistically orientated grammars prefer the term "restrictive."[14] The genitive is most often employed in constructions in which one substantive (in the genitive, N_{gen}) *particularizes*, or *restricts*, another (the head noun, or substantive, N). Regardless of the genitive subcategory chosen in a given context to fine-tune one's understanding of a phrase like ἡ ἀγάπη τοῦ θεοῦ ("the love of God"), θεοῦ restricts "love" to love associated with God. Moreover, "restriction" is definitely the preferable term to account for uses such as genitives that modify verbs or function as direct objects. We agree with Porter, then, that *"the essential semantic feature of the genitive case is restriction."*[15] The common order is for the noun in the genitive to follow its head term, the noun it modifies. When this is reversed, more prominence is given to the word in the genitive.

Moisés Silva provides a partial analogy to the Greek genitive case from English usage.[16] Instead of the gloss "of," a better aid is a specialized construction found in English where, like Greek, two nouns are juxtaposed but, unlike typical Greek, the first one modifies the second:

spring picnic   stone wall   fire rescue   tree removal

In each of these English examples, the first noun describes or restricts the second noun. Upon closer inspection, we can even describe the relationship between them based on our understanding of the contexts in which they are used. The first one indicates a temporal relationship, the time when the picnic

13. Porter 92; Wallace 78; Long, *Grammatical Concepts*, 52.
14. Porter 92; Louw, "Linguistic Theory," 83–84; Long, *Grammatical Concepts*, 50.
15. Porter 92, italics original.
16. Moisés Silva, *Interpreting Galatians*, 2nd ed. (Grand Rapids: Baker Academic, 2001), 65n2.

occurs. The second exemplifies a relationship of content or makeup of the wall. In the third example the first noun describes the setting of the second, or it may carry the sense of "rescue from fire." In the fourth example the first noun is the object of the action implied in the second noun ("I remove the tree"). Greek does something similar to this, but rather than relying on word order, it indicates which noun is doing the restricting by placing it in the genitive.

Because of the versatility of the genitive case, there are scholars who understand it as having upward of thirty distinct uses (Wallace 72–136). Some of these seem to have more to do with the vagaries of English translation than with anything inherent in Greek (either encoded in the genitive formal ending or obvious from context); others split already-fine theological hairs. Therefore, we will limit our discussion to a manageable number of uses of the genitive that helpfully illustrate the most common or most exegetically significant uses of the case in the NT. We also encourage our readers not to assume that every use of the genitive will fit neatly into a given subcategory. In other words, it is not always clear just how a genitive restricts. Some NT genitives are rather clear as to their function in given contexts; some are too ambiguous to be labeled; others are strung together in chains for emphasis; still others are probably intended to be understood in a particular way that, because of the passage of time and our distance from the original context, will not be obvious to today's interpreter. The genitive's function is to restrict, and only context can indicate exactly how it does so. Our task is to consider interpretive options as well as their theological and practical implications, not necessarily to arrive at *the* one "correct" label. Even in the study of grammar, the journey can be the destination.

Genitive Constructions Restricting Substantives

Below are genitives in constructions in which they restrict substantives $(N + N_{gen})$.

1.15. **Descriptive (attributive, qualitative).** As mentioned above, some grammars view the genitive case as being essentially descriptive. In such systems the term *descriptive genitive* is almost redundant; hence the category "descriptive genitive" has been used as a catchall of "last resort" for genitive uses that cannot be otherwise classified (Wallace 79). We will consider descriptive genitives to be those $(N + N_{gen})$ that restrict the head noun as an adjective ("a thing of beauty," i.e., a beautiful thing) or another noun ("ant farm") might. The genitive of description "might well be considered the essential *use* of the genitive case."[17]

---

17. Porter 92, italics added.

ἀποδώσουσιν περὶ αὐτοῦ λόγον ἐν
ἡμέρᾳ **κρίσεως·** (Matt. 12:36)

They will give an account for it
on **judgment** day.

καθὼς γέγραπται ὅτι Ἕνεκεν σοῦ
θανατούμεθα ὅλην τὴν ἡμέραν,
ἐλογίσθημεν ὡς πρόβατα **σφαγῆς.**
(Rom. 8:36)

Just as it is written, "For your
sake we are put to death the
whole day, we are counted as
sheep **for slaughter.**"

ὁ δὲ θεὸς τῆς **εἰρήνης** μετὰ πάντων
ὑμῶν· ἀμήν. (Rom. 15:33)

And the God **of peace** [be] with
you all. Amen.

> Wallace (106) calls this a genitive of product, which may be an unneces-
> sary refinement. God does produce peace, but nothing in the genitive
> case itself or the context of Romans requires that we see more than a
> description of God here.

ἐν τῇ ἀποκαλύψει τοῦ κυρίου
Ἰησοῦ ἀπ' οὐρανοῦ μετ' ἀγγέλων
δυνάμεως αὐτοῦ ἐν φλογὶ **πυρός**
(2 Thess. 1:7–8)

At the revelation of the Lord Jesus
from heaven with his **powerful** angels in **fiery** flame.

τῷ νικῶντι δώσω αὐτῷ φαγεῖν ἐκ
τοῦ ξύλου τῆς **ζωῆς** (Rev. 2:7)

To the one who overcomes, I will
grant to him/her to eat from the
tree **of life.**

1.16. Possessive and source (relationship, origin). We will examine these
functions of the genitive together because they are semantically related. The
fact that we often pair possession with the preposition *of* and source with
from in our translations obscures that relationship; moreover, it focuses our
attention more on English than on Greek. The genitive may be used to indicate
possession, source/origin, or relationship because in all of these instances
a head noun is restricted by a genitive noun or pronoun in terms of "some
sort of" dependence or derivation (Porter 93). In the phrase ἡ μαρτυρία τοῦ
Ἰωάννου (John 1:19), "John's testimony," we may correctly understand John
as the source or origin as well as the possessor of his own testimony.

Τοῦ δὲ Ἰησοῦ χριστοῦ ἡ γένεσις
οὕτως ἦν. (Matt. 1:18)

Now the birth **of Jesus Christ** was
like this.

> Note that the genitives precede the head noun for emphasis.

τῶν δὲ δώδεκα ἀποστόλων τὰ
ὀνόματά ἐστιν ταῦτα· πρῶτος
Σίμων ὁ λεγόμενος Πέτρος
καὶ Ἀνδρέας ὁ ἀδελφὸς αὐτοῦ,
Ἰάκωβος ὁ τοῦ Ζεβεδαίου καὶ
Ἰωάννης ὁ ἀδελφὸς αὐτοῦ
(Matt. 10:2)

Now the names **of the twelve
apostles** are these: first, Simon
called Peter and Andrew **his**
brother, James the [son] **of
Zebedee** and John **his** brother.

> Here we see four genitives that are all basically possessive; the third
> could also be labeled a genitive of relationship, a subcategory in which
> a particular relationship between the head noun and the genitive is as-
> sumed rather than stated.

Καὶ μετὰ δὲ τὸ παραδοθῆναι
τὸν Ἰωάννην ἦλθεν ὁ Ἰησοῦς
εἰς τὴν Γαλιλαίαν κηρύσσων τὸ
εὐαγγέλιον τοῦ θεοῦ (Mark 1:14)

And after John was arrested,
Jesus went into Galilee, preaching
the good news **of God.**

> How should we understand τοῦ θεοῦ? Is it possessive, source, or does
> it belong in the section below ("Subjective and Objective")?

καὶ ἡ εἰρήνη τοῦ Χριστοῦ βραβευ-
έτω ἐν ταῖς καρδίαις ὑμῶν, εἰς ἣν
καὶ ἐκλήθητε ἐν ἑνὶ σώματι· καὶ
εὐχάριστοι γίνεσθε. (Col. 3:15)

And let peace **from Christ** rule in
your hearts, to which you were
indeed called in one body, and be
thankful.

καὶ ἔπλυναν τὰς στολὰς αὐτῶν καὶ
ἐλεύκαναν αὐτὰς ἐν τῷ αἵματι τοῦ
ἀρνίου. (Rev. 7:14)

And they washed their robes and
made them white in the blood **of
the Lamb.** (*possession*)

1.17. Subjective and objective. When a genitive restricts a noun that can be
construed to indicate a verbal process (often it has a cognate verb, e.g., ἀγάπη
and ἀγαπάω), it may be subjective or objective. If the genitive is the agent of
the verbal process, we can label it as *subjective.* If the genitive is the object
or patient of the verbal process, we can label it as *objective.* In some biblical
contexts both categories, and perhaps others, make good sense and we must
entertain the possibility that the author was purposely ambiguous, and/or
that we just don't know enough to make the correct call.

διὰ τοῦτο λέγω ὑμῖν, πᾶσα
ἁμαρτία καὶ βλασφημία
ἀφεθήσεται τοῖς ἀνθρώποις, ἡ δὲ
τοῦ **πνεύματος** βλασφημία οὐκ
ἀφεθήσεται. (Matt. 12:31)

Because of this I tell you, every sin
and blasphemy will be forgiven
people, but blasphemy **against** the
Spirit will not be forgiven.

Πνεύματος is objective; that the Holy Spirit does not blaspheme goes
without saying, and the presence of κατὰ τοῦ πνεύματος τοῦ ἁγίου
in Matt. 12:32 makes the conclusion unassailable.

τίς ἡμᾶς χωρίσει ἀπὸ τῆς ἀγάπης
τοῦ **Χριστοῦ**; (Rom. 8:35a)

Who will separate us from the
love **of Christ**?

Here the context makes clear that Paul has Christ's love for us in mind,
since any or all of the items on the list in 8:35b might be misconstrued
by some as contradicting his love for us. Because love is a verbal process, most would label Χριστοῦ a subjective genitive, but it would not
be incorrect to think of love as being either an attribute or a possession
of Christ. Nor would it be misleading to speak of Christ as being the
source of love. In other words, Χριστοῦ is considered to be subjective
(context makes it subjective rather than objective) because of the verbal nature of ἀγάπης, not because Christ isn't the source or possessor
of love. There is sometimes considerable overlap between the standard
genitive subcategories. We do well to keep this in mind when debating
fine shades of meaning.

ἡ γὰρ ἀγάπη τοῦ **Χριστοῦ** συνέχει
ἡμᾶς, κρίναντας τοῦτο ὅτι εἷς ὑπὲρ
πάντων ἀπέθανεν· ἄρα οἱ πάντες
ἀπέθανον· (2 Cor. 5:14)

For the love **of Christ** compels us,
having decided this: that one died
for all; therefore, all died.

Most take this instance of Χριστοῦ as being subjective also, but the
context is not as definitive. Héring argues that the genitive is objective,[18]
and a few think that Paul might have intended it to do double-duty.[19]
    In order to account for unclear instances such as this, Wallace (119–20)
has included the category "plenary genitive" (both objective and subjective), which seems only to compound the problem. This is more a matter

18. Jean Héring, *The Second Epistle of Saint Paul to the Corinthians* (London: Epworth,
1967), 50.
    19. Zerwick is representative. Of 2 Cor. 5:14 he says,
    The objective genitive (Paul's love for Christ) does not suffice for, apart from the fact that
    Paul usually renders the objective-genitive sense by εἰς (cf. Col. I,4), the reason which he
    adds speaks of the love which Christ manifested for us in dying for all men; nor is the
    subjective genitive (Christ's love for us) fully satisfactory by itself, because the love in

of ambiguity in the context than a legitimate grammatical category. It is not that we have too few categories for the genitive or even, as we think, too many, but that we sometimes treat them as objective and inviolable realities rather than mere tools of our trade that should not obscure our focus on the biblical text itself. In 2 Cor. 5:14 Χριστοῦ could be either subjective or objective, but not both. We should probably avoid the "plenary" category and simply admit ambiguity.

οὐ δικαιοῦται ἄνθρωπος ἐξ ἔργων νόμου ἐὰν μὴ διὰ πίστεως Ἰησοῦ Χριστοῦ (Gal. 2:16)	A person is not justified by works of the law, but through faith **in/of Jesus Christ.**

Much ink has been spilled over the use of the genitive Ἰησοῦ Χριστοῦ here and in Rom. 3:22, where Paul uses the same prepositional phrase. (Each should, of course, be considered separately in its own context, as nothing requires the conclusion that the same word or group of words is always used the same way.) The debate centers on whether Ἰησοῦ Χριστοῦ is an objective genitive (faith *in* Jesus Christ) or a subjective genitive (faithfulness *of* [i.e., produced by] Jesus Christ). Both are certainly coherent in the context. Paul could be affirming that Christian Jews have realized that their right standing before God is based not on their keeping of the law but on Jesus' faithfulness in fulfilling all of its demands and their full trust in him (subjective gen.). Paul could also be stating quite emphatically (διὰ *πίστεως* Ἰησοῦ Χριστοῦ, καὶ ἡμεῖς εἰς Χριστὸν Ἰησοῦν *ἐπιστεύσαμεν*) that Christian Jews know that their right standing with God is based solely on faith in Jesus Christ (objective gen.). Grammar and lexical range alone cannot solve the problem. Any solution must depend on broader contextual and theological considerations.

Ἀποκάλυψις Ἰησοῦ Χριστοῦ, ἣν ἔδωκεν αὐτῷ ὁ θεὸς δεῖξαι τοῖς δούλοις αὐτοῦ, ἃ δεῖ γενέσθαι ἐν τάχει (Rev. 1:1)	The revelation **of Jesus Christ,** which God gave him to show to his servants what things must happen quickly.

Given the chain of command, most commentators think Ἰησοῦ Χριστοῦ is subjective or source: God gave the revelation to Jesus, who in turn gives it to his servants.[20]

---

question is a living force working in the spirit of the apostle. In other words, we cannot simply classify this genitive under either heading without neglecting a part of its value. (13)

20. David L. Mathewson, *Revelation: A Handbook on the Greek Text* (Waco: Baylor University Press, 2016), 1.

Ὧδε ἡ ὑπομονὴ τῶν **ἁγίων** ἐστίν,
οἱ τηροῦντες τὰς ἐντολὰς τοῦ **θεοῦ**
καὶ τὴν πίστιν Ἰησοῦ. (Rev. 14:12)

Here is the endurance **of the saints**,
the ones who keep the command-
ments **of God** and faith **in/of Jesus**.

There is general consensus regarding the first two (subjective), but John
may be as misunderstood as Paul is concerning the third. Is Ἰησοῦ subjective or objective?

σύνδουλός σού εἰμι καὶ τῶν
ἀδελφῶν σου τῶν ἐχόντων
τὴν μαρτυρίαν Ἰησοῦ· τῷ θεῷ
προσκύνησον· ἡ γὰρ μαρτυρία
Ἰησοῦ ἐστιν τὸ πνεῦμα τῆς
προφητείας. (Rev. 19:10)

I am your fellow servant and of
your brothers and sisters who
have the testimony **of Jesus**. Worship God. For the testimony **of
Jesus** is the spirit of prophecy.

Both instances of Ἰησοῦ are ambiguous, though one could make a case
for objective.[21]

1.18. Epexegetical/appositional. Although simple apposition can occur in
any case (the nominal and the appositive must be in the same case; e.g., Παῦλος
ἀπόστολος, "Paul, an apostle" [1 Tim. 1:1]), the genitive in particular may be
used to restate, define, or explain a nominal that is usually in a different case.

Πέτρος δὲ πρὸς αὐτούς·
Μετανοήσατε, καὶ βαπτισθήτω
ἕκαστος ὑμῶν ἐπὶ τῷ ὀνόματι Ἰησοῦ
Χριστοῦ εἰς ἄφεσιν τῶν ἁμαρτιῶν
ὑμῶν, καὶ λήμψεσθε τὴν δωρεὰν
τοῦ **ἁγίου πνεύματος**· (Acts 2:38)

And Peter [said] to them, "Repent
and each of you must be baptized
in the name of Jesus Christ for
forgiveness of your sins, and you
will receive the gift **of the Holy
Spirit**."

Among the many intriguing elements of this verse is the final genitive.
There is agreement among modern commentators that the genitive is

---

21. See Mathewson, *Revelation*, 263:
It is possible that this should be understood as a subjective genitive (the testimony that
Jesus bore). However, the fact that the testimony is something that they have (ἐχόντων)
along with the clear references elsewhere (6:9; 11:7; 12:11; 17:6) to the saints as testifying/
having testimony as a cause for their death, suggests that the genitive Ἰησοῦ here should
be taken as objective (the testimony about Jesus). G. K. Beale opts for both a subjective
and objective genitive reading (*The Book of Revelation: A Commentary on the Greek
Text*, New International Greek Testament Commentary [Grand Rapids: Eerdmans, 1999],
947; see also Stephen S. Smalley, *The Revelation to John: A Commentary on the Greek
Text of the Apocalypse* [Downers Grove, IL: IVP Academic, 2005], 487). However, this
confuses grammatical ambiguity with semantic "fullness" of interpretation.

epexegetical; baptized believers will receive the Holy Spirit as a gift ("the gift that is the Holy Spirit" is clearer than "the gift of the Holy Spirit"). However, there may be options other than taking ἁγίου πνεύματος as epexegetical. Δωρεάν is after all a verbal noun, so ἁγίου πνεύματος could be construed as subjective or source (the gift given by the Holy Spirit). Few would dispute that the Holy Spirit gives gifts, but the focus of Acts 2:38 seems to be not on the gifts that the Holy Spirit gives but on the Holy Spirit himself as the gift that believers receive. The decision comes down primarily to context and theology.[22]

καὶ σημεῖον ἔλαβεν **περιτομῆς**, σφραγῖδα τῆς δικαιοσύνης τῆς πίστεως τῆς ἐν τῇ ἀκροβυστίᾳ (Rom. 4:11)	And he received the sign **of circumcision** as a seal of the righteousness of the faith that he had while uncircumcised.

Although the genitives τῆς δικαιοσύνης τῆς πίστεως might be debated, περιτομῆς is a straightforward example of an epexegetical genitive: the sign *is* circumcision.

τὸ δὲ Ἀνέβη τί ἐστιν, εἰ μὴ ὅτι καὶ κατέβη εἰς τὰ κατώτερα μέρη τῆς **γῆς**; (Eph. 4:9)	But what is "He ascended" if not that he also descended to the lower [parts] **of the earth?**

How should we understand the genitive γῆς? Is it possessive, is it epexegetical, or does it belong in the next section (partitive)?

γίνου πιστὸς ἄχρι θανάτου, καὶ δώσω σοι τὸν στέφανον τῆς **ζωῆς**. (Rev. 2:10)	Be faithful until death, and I will give you the crown **of life**. (*the crown that* is *life*)

1.19. Partitive. The noun in the genitive indicates the whole of which the noun it modifies is a part: "some [i.e., a part] **of our students** [i.e., the whole]." The label of this category may be counterintuitive, but partitive genitives are common in Greek and English. In English we might say that a bite **of chocolate** is rarely enough. "**Of chocolate**" is the whole of which "a bite" is a part. Once we get past the fact that the whole, not its parts, is in the genitive, the idiom is easily recognized.

---

22. Peter is making a momentous theological statement that can only be fully grasped in the context of both Testaments of Scripture.

Τότε ἀπεκρίθησαν αὐτῷ τινες τῶν **γραμματέων** καὶ **Φαρισαίων** λέγοντες· Διδάσκαλε, θέλομεν ἀπὸ σοῦ σημεῖον ἰδεῖν. (Matt. 12:38)	Then some **of the scribes** and **Pharisees** answered him, saying, "Teacher, we want to see a sign from you."
καὶ αὐτὸς φωνήσας εἶπεν· Πάτερ Ἀβραάμ, ἐλέησόν με καὶ πέμψον Λάζαρον ἵνα βάψῃ τὸ ἄκρον τοῦ **δακτύλου** αὐτοῦ ὕδατος καὶ καταψύξῃ τὴν γλῶσσάν μου (Luke 16:24)	And calling out, he said, "Father Abraham, have mercy on me and send Lazarus that he may dip the tip **of** his **finger** in water and cool my tongue."

> "In water" (ὕδατος) may also be loosely construed as partitive but is taken as a genitive with a verb of filling (in this case, dipping: the object dipped is in the accusative, and the entity into which it is dipped is in the genitive) in BDF§172.

κατὰ μίαν **σαββάτου** ἕκαστος **ὑμῶν** παρ᾽ ἑαυτῷ τιθέτω θησαυρίζων ὅ τι ἐὰν εὐοδῶται, ἵνα μὴ ὅταν ἔλθω τότε λογεῖαι γίνωνται. (1 Cor. 16:2)	On the first day **of the week** each **of you** individually should put something aside, saving as you prosper, so that there be no collections when I come.
οἱ λοιποὶ τῶν **νεκρῶν** οὐκ ἔζησαν ἄχρι τελεσθῇ τὰ χίλια ἔτη. (Rev. 20:5)	The rest **of the dead** did not come to life until the thousand years were finished.

Genitive Constructions Restricting Adjectives or Verbs

Below are genitives in constructions in which they restrict adjectives or verbs ($A + N_{gen}$ or $V + N_{gen}$).

1.20. With adjectives (and occasionally adverbs). Genitives that restrict the comparative forms of adjectives or adverbs often express comparison and require "than" in English translation. There are also some adjectives and adverbs whose meanings are fine-tuned or restricted by the genitive case.

μὴ σὺ μείζων εἶ τοῦ **πατρὸς** ἡμῶν Ἀβραάμ, ὅστις ἀπέθανεν; (John 8:53)	You aren't greater [comparative adjective] **than** our **father** Abraham who died, are you?

εὐχαριστῶ τῷ θεῷ, **πάντων** ὑμῶν μᾶλλον γλώσσαις λαλῶ· (1 Cor. 14:18)

I thank God, I speak in tongues more [comparative adverb] **than all** of you.

πιστὸς ὁ λόγος καὶ πάσης **ἀποδοχῆς** ἄξιος (1 Tim. 4:9)

This saying is trustworthy and worthy [adjective] **of all acceptance.**

ὅστις γὰρ ὅλον τὸν νόμον τηρήσῃ, πταίσῃ δὲ ἐν ἑνί, γέγονεν **πάντων** ἔνοχος. (James 2:10)

For whoever keeps the whole law but stumbles in one thing is guilty [adjective] **of all** [of it].

ὀφθαλμοὺς ἔχοντες μεστοὺς **μοιχαλίδος** καὶ ἀκαταπαύστους **ἁμαρτίας** (2 Pet. 2:14)

Having eyes full [adjective] **of adultery,** and unceasing [adjective] **from sin.**

οἳ ἐμαρτύρησάν σου τῇ ἀγάπῃ ἐνώπιον ἐκκλησίας, οὓς καλῶς ποιήσεις προπέμψας **ἀξίως** τοῦ **θεοῦ**· (3 John 6)

Who testified to your love before the church; by sending whom on their way in a manner worthy [adverb, lit. "worthily"] **of God,** you will do well.

1.21. With verbs. Genitive nouns can directly modify or restrict verbs and thus function as adverbs. Truly adverbial genitives are not widely used in the NT. Under this category we would include two functions of the genitive that are often treated separately by other grammars: time and price.

1. *Genitive expressing time*

ἦλθεν δὲ καὶ Νικόδημος, ὁ ἐλθὼν πρὸς αὐτὸν **νυκτὸς** τὸ πρῶτον (John 19:39)

And Nicodemus, who had first come **at night,** also came.

> Functioning as an adverbial genitive of time, νυκτός restricts Nicodemus's previous visit to the nighttime. Temporal genitives are most often employed to designate the time within which something occurs as opposed to a specific point, short or long, at which something occurs (dative, e.g., "Nicodemus came on that night"), or an extent of time (accusative, e.g., "Nicodemus came for the night").

2. *Genitive expressing price*

τιμῆς ἠγοράσθητε· μὴ γίνεσθε δοῦλοι ἀνθρώπων. (1 Cor. 7:23)	You were bought **for a price**; do not become people's slaves.

Here the genitive answers the question "How much?" and thus restricts the meaning of the verb "bought."

1.22. As objects of verbs. Some verbs, especially those expressing perception/sensation (e.g., ἀκούω, ἅπτω, κρατέω), volition/acquisition (e.g., ἐπιθυμέω, τυγχάνω), emotion (e.g., ἀνέχω, ἐπιμελέομαι), memory (e.g., ἐπιλανθάνομαι, μιμνήσκομαι, μνημονεύω), and governing (e.g., ἄρχω, κυριεύω), as well as certain verbs with prepositional prefixes (especially verbs prefixed by ἀπό, ἐκ, and κατά), may take their direct objects in the genitive case (S + V + DO$_{gen}$). If you are unsure whether a particular verb can take a complement (direct object) in the genitive case, consult BDAG.

ἀκούσας δὲ ὄχλου διαπορευομένου ἐπυνθάνετο τί εἴη τοῦτο· (Luke 18:36)	And having heard **a crowd** passing by, he asked what this might be/mean.

There is some debate concerning the fact that ἀκούω can take either the accusative or genitive as its direct object. The traditional understanding is that ἀκούω with the genitive means to hear without understanding, while ἀκούω with the accusative means to hear with comprehension (Robertson 506). This distinction is not always observed in the NT, however. We agree with Wallace (133) that Koine Greek writers did not follow strict rules when deciding to use the genitive or accusative case with ἀκούω.

οὐχ ὅτι κυριεύομεν ὑμῶν τῆς πίστεως, ἀλλὰ συνεργοί ἐσμεν τῆς χαρᾶς ὑμῶν (2 Cor. 1:24)	Not that we rule your **faith,** but we are fellow workers for your joy.

1.23. Genitive absolute. This genitive construction will be covered in chapter 10, on participles.

For Practice

1.24. Analyze the genitives (in bold) in the following texts from Rom. 8 and 2 Pet. 2, identifying their various possible functions. We have not included genitive objects of prepositions.

¹Οὐδὲν ἄρα νῦν κατάκριμα τοῖς ἐν Χριστῷ Ἰησοῦ· ²ὁ γὰρ νόμος τοῦ
πνεύματος τῆς **ζωῆς** ἐν Χριστῷ Ἰησοῦ ἠλευθέρωσέν σε ἀπὸ τοῦ νόμου
τῆς **ἁμαρτίας** καὶ τοῦ **θανάτου**. ³τὸ γὰρ ἀδύνατον τοῦ **νόμου**, ἐν ᾧ ἠσθένει
διὰ τῆς σαρκός, ὁ θεὸς τὸν **ἑαυτοῦ** υἱὸν πέμψας ἐν ὁμοιώματι **σαρκὸς**
ἁμαρτίας καὶ περὶ ἁμαρτίας κατέκρινε τὴν ἁμαρτίαν ἐν τῇ σαρκί, ⁴ἵνα τὸ
δικαίωμα τοῦ **νόμου** πληρωθῇ ἐν ἡμῖν τοῖς μὴ κατὰ σάρκα περιπατοῦσιν
ἀλλὰ κατὰ πνεῦμα· (Rom. 8:1–4)

¹³ἀδικούμενοι μισθὸν **ἀδικίας**· ἡδονὴν ἡγούμενοι τὴν ἐν ἡμέρᾳ τρυφήν,
σπίλοι καὶ μῶμοι ἐντρυφῶντες ἐν ταῖς ἀπάταις **αὐτῶν** συνευωχούμε-
νοι ὑμῖν, ¹⁴ὀφθαλμοὺς ἔχοντες μεστοὺς **μοιχαλίδος** καὶ ἀκαταπαύστους
ἁμαρτίας, δελεάζοντες ψυχὰς ἀστηρίκτους, καρδίαν γεγυμνασμένην
πλεονεξίας ἔχοντες, **κατάρας** τέκνα, ¹⁵καταλιπόντες εὐθεῖαν ὁδὸν ἐπλα-
νήθησαν, ἐξακολουθήσαντες τῇ ὁδῷ τοῦ **Βαλαὰμ** τοῦ **Βοσὸρ** ὃς μισθὸν
ἀδικίας ἠγάπησεν ¹⁶ἔλεγξιν δὲ ἔσχεν ἰδίας **παρανομίας**· ὑποζύγιον ἄφωνον
ἐν **ἀνθρώπου** φωνῇ φθεγξάμενον ἐκώλυσεν τὴν τοῦ **προφήτου** παρα-
φρονίαν. (2 Pet. 2:13–16)

The Dative Case

1.25. The dative case is often described as the case of personal interest, loca-
tion, and means.[23] However, this does not necessarily convey its meaning.
More comprehensively, the dative case may be defined as conveying *relation*.[24]
This seems to account for its various usages. A very common use of the da-
tive is to indicate the indirect object, though this is only one of its functions.
Also common is the function of the dative as an adjunct modifying the verb.

Indirect Object (Advantage, Disadvantage)

1.26. A substantive in the dative case may be used to specify the indirect
object in a sentence, that is, the person or thing toward which the action of
a verb form is directed ("I gave authority *to him*"). This also includes what
grammarians label the dative of *advantage* or *disadvantage*: the dative indicates
the person or thing for whose benefit (advantage) or detriment (disadvantage)
the action occurs, depending on the broader context.

23. Dana and Mantey 84; Black 52; James Allan Hewett, *New Testament Greek*, rev. C. Michael Robbins and Steven R. Johnson (Grand Rapids: Baker Academic, 2009), 254.
24. Louw, "Linguistic Theory," 81, 83; followed by Porter 97.

Ἀμὴν λέγω ὑμῖν ὅτι εἰσίν τινες
τῶν ὧδε ἑστηκότων οἵτινες οὐ μὴ
γεύσωνται θανάτου (Mark 9:1)

Truly I say **to you** that there are
some of those who stand here
who will not taste death.

καθὼς ἔδωκας **αὐτῷ** ἐξουσίαν
πάσης σαρκός (John 17:2)

Just as you gave **to him** authority
over all flesh.

δεῖξόν **μοι** τὴν πίστιν σου χωρὶς
τῶν ἔργων, κἀγώ **σοι** δείξω ἐκ τῶν
ἔργων μου τὴν πίστιν.
(James 2:18)

Show **to me** your faith without
works, and I will show **to you** my
faith by my works.

ὥστε μαρτυρεῖτε **ἑαυτοῖς** ὅτι υἱοί
ἐστε τῶν φονευσάντων τοὺς
προφήτας (Matt. 23:31)

So then, you witness **against yourselves**, that you are descendants of
those who murdered the prophets.
(*disadvantage*)

καὶ τὴν πόλιν τὴν ἁγίαν
Ἰερουσαλὴμ καινὴν εἶδον
καταβαίνουσαν ἐκ τοῦ οὐρανοῦ
ἀπὸ τοῦ θεοῦ, ἡτοιμασμένην ὡς
νύμφην κεκοσμημένην τῷ **ἀνδρὶ**
αὐτῆς. (Rev. 21:2)

I saw the holy city, the new Jerusalem, coming down out of
heaven from God, prepared like
a bride adorned **for** her **husband**.
(*advantage*)

Reference or Respect (Possession)

1.27. In this use, an action is done more generally "with reference to" or
"with respect to" something or someone, indicated by the dative. This usage
may be closest to the dative's fundamental meaning. We have also included
the *dative of possession* here.

Μακάριοι οἱ πτωχοὶ τῷ **πνεύματι**,
ὅτι αὐτῶν ἐστιν ἡ βασιλεία τῶν
οὐρανῶν. (Matt. 5:3)

Blessed are the poor **in spirit /
with respect to spirit**, for theirs is
the kingdom of heaven. (*limiting
an adjective*)

σοὶ ἦσαν κἀμοὶ αὐτοὺς ἔδωκας,
καὶ τὸν λόγον σου τετήρηκαν.
(John 17:6)

They were **yours** and you gave
them to me, and they have kept
your word. (*possession*)

οἵτινες ἀπεθάνομεν τῇ **ἁμαρτίᾳ**, πῶς ἔτι ζήσομεν ἐν αὐτῇ; (Rom. 6:2)	We who have died [with respect] **to sin**, how shall we still live in it?

This is a classic example of reference or respect cited by most grammars.

οὐχ ὁ θεὸς ἐξελέξατο τοὺς πτωχοὺς τῷ **κόσμῳ** πλουσίους ἐν πίστει; (James 2:5)	Has not God chosen the poor **in** [with respect to or in the world's view] **the world** to be rich in faith?

Instrumental (Agent, Cause, Manner, Means)

1.28. Though most grammars tend to separate these usages, they are frequently difficult and/or unnecessary to distinguish.[25] In the sentence "She killed him *with a sword*," is "sword" the means, the instrument, or the manner (the way) in which the killing takes place? (English "with" is itself ambiguous.) The dative specifies that someone brings about an action in relation to something else (e.g., a sword).

καὶ νῦν δόξασόν με σύ, πάτερ, παρὰ σεαυτῷ τῇ **δόξῃ** ᾗ εἶχον πρὸ τοῦ τὸν κόσμον εἶναι παρὰ σοί. (John 17:5)	And now you glorify me, Father, in your presence **with the glory** that I had with you before the world was. (*Is this instrument or manner?*)
τῇ **ἀπιστίᾳ** ἐξεκλάσθησαν, σὺ δὲ τῇ **πίστει** ἕστηκας. (Rom. 11:20)	They were cut off **on account of** their **unbelief**, but you stand **on account of** your **faith**. (*causal;* BDF §196)
πίστει νοοῦμεν κατηρτίσθαι τοὺς αἰῶνας **ῥήματι** θεοῦ (Heb. 11:3)	**By faith** we know that the universe was created **by the word** of God.
Καὶ εἶδον ἕνα ἄγγελον ἑστῶτα ἐν τῷ ἡλίῳ, καὶ ἔκραξεν **φωνῇ** μεγάλῃ (Rev. 19:17)	And I saw an angel standing in the sun, and he cried out **with a** great **voice**.

25. Porter 98–99. For the distinction between these usages, see Wallace 158–69; Dana and Mantey 89–91; Brooks and Winbery 42–49.

24

Association

1.29. This usage could easily fall under the instrumental dative or even the dative of respect. The dative indicates that an action is performed in association with someone or something else.

καὶ πολλοὶ τελῶναι καὶ ἁμαρτωλοὶ συνανέκειντο τῷ Ἰησοῦ καὶ
τοῖς **μαθηταῖς** αὐτοῦ (Mark 2:15)

And many tax collectors and sinners sat at the table **with Jesus**
and his **disciples.**

Association is suggested by the verb with the συν- prefix.

διὸ καὶ πυκνότερον αὐτὸν μετα-
πεμπόμενος ὡμίλει **αὐτῷ.** (Acts
24:26)

Therefore, also summoning him
very often, he conversed **with
him.**

εἰ γὰρ τοῖς **πνευματικοῖς** αὐτῶν
ἐκοινώνησαν τὰ ἔθνη, ὀφείλουσιν
καὶ ἐν τοῖς σαρκικοῖς λειτουργῆσαι
αὐτοῖς. (Rom. 15:27)

For if the nations shared **in** their
spiritual blessings, they ought to
minister to them also in material
things.

Location (Place, Sphere)

1.30. The dative case specifies the location, either physical (place) or meta-phorical (sphere or realm), where an action takes place. "Sphere" could also fit under the dative of respect.

καὶ οἱ στρατιῶται πλέξαντες
στέφανον ἐξ ἀκανθῶν ἐπέθηκαν
αὐτοῦ τῇ **κεφαλῇ** (John 19:2)

And the soldiers, having woven
together a crown of thorns,
placed it **on his head.** (*physical
location*)

τῇ **δεξιᾷ** οὖν τοῦ θεοῦ ὑψωθείς
(Acts 2:33)

Therefore, having been exalted **to**
the **right hand** of God. (*spatial
location*)

εἴ γε ἐπιμένετε τῇ **πίστει** (Col. 1:23)

If indeed you remain **in faith.**
(*sphere*)[a]

[a] Constantine R. Campbell, *Colossians and Philemon: A Handbook on the Greek Text*
(Waco: Baylor University Press, 2013), 19.

ἵνα ὑμᾶς προσαγάγῃ τῷ θεῷ, θανατωθεὶς μὲν σαρκὶ ζῳοποιηθεὶς δὲ **πνεύματι·** (1 Pet. 3:18)	In order that he might offer you to God, having been put to death in the flesh, but being made alive **in the spirit.**

The dative πνεύματι seems to indicate metaphorical location (sphere), though it could also be classified as respect or manner (again showing how difficult it sometimes is to sharply distinguish these functions of the dative).

Time

1.31. As an extension of the category of location, the dative also indicates a particular place or point in time (cf. the genitive and accusative of time).[26]

δεῖ αὐτὸν εἰς Ἱεροσόλυμα ἀπελθεῖν καὶ . . . ἀποκτανθῆναι καὶ τῇ τρίτῃ **ἡμέρᾳ** ἐγερθῆναι. (Matt. 16:21)	It is necessary for him to depart into Jerusalem and . . . to be put to death and to be raised **on the third day.**
καὶ αὐτῇ τῇ **ὥρᾳ** ἐπιστᾶσα ἀνθωμολογεῖτο τῷ θεῷ (Luke 2:38)	And **at that very hour** she came and was praising God.
Οὐαὶ οὐαί, ἡ πόλις ἡ μεγάλη, Βαβυλὼν ἡ πόλις ἡ ἰσχυρά, ὅτι μιᾷ **ὥρᾳ** ἦλθεν ἡ κρίσις σου. (Rev. 18:10)	Woe, woe, the great city, Babylon the strong city, for **in one hour** your judgment has come.

Direct Object

1.32. Some verbal processes are completed (i.e., take a direct object) not with a noun in the accusative case but with one in the dative case (S + V + DO$_{dat}$). That is, the meanings of some verbs seem to lend themselves to the notion of *relation* communicated by the dative.[27]

---

26. This is irrespective of the actual duration of the action, whether short or long. The dative simply indicates a specific time.

27. The following are some verbs that can take an object in the dative case: ἀκολουθέω, ἀνίστημι, ἀπειθέω, βοηθέω, διακονέω, διατάσσω, δουλεύω, ἐξομολογέω, ἐπιτάσσω, ἐπιτιμάω, εὐχαριστέω, λατρεύω, ὀργίζω, παραγγέλλω, πείθω, πιστεύω, προσκυνέω, συμβουλεύω, ὑπακούω, ὑπηρετέω, χαρίζομαι.

οἱ δὲ εὐθέως ἀφέντες τὰ δίκτυα
ἠκολούθησαν **αὐτῷ**. (Matt. 4:20)

And immediately leaving their
nets they followed **him**.

καὶ πῶς ἐπεστρέψατε πρὸς τὸν θεὸν
ἀπὸ τῶν εἰδώλων δουλεύειν **θεῷ**
ζῶντι καὶ ἀληθινῷ (1 Thess. 1:9)

And how you turned to God from
idols to serve the living and true
God.

The verb προσκυνέω (to worship) frequently takes the dative case (e.g.,
Matt. 2:11; 4:9; John 4:21; Heb. 1:6; Rev. 4:10), but it also can take the accusative (Matt. 4:10; Rev. 9:20; 13:8; 14:9, 11).

After Certain Adjectives

1.33. Some adjectives, especially belonging to the word group of "likeness"
(e.g., ὅμοιος), or adjectives compounded with συν- (e.g., σύμμορφος) are commonly accompanied by a noun in the dative (BDF §194[2]). Some examples
might be classified as datives of reference (Wallace 174).

Ὁμοία ἐστὶν ἡ βασιλεία τῶν
οὐρανῶν **κόκκῳ** σινάπεως
(Matt. 13:31)

The kingdom of heaven is likened
to a mustard **seed**.

ὃς μετασχηματίσει τὸ σῶμα τῆς
ταπεινώσεως ἡμῶν **σύμμορφον τῷ**
σώματι τῆς δόξης αὐτοῦ
(Phil. 3:21)

Who will transform our humble
bodies in conformity **to his body**
of glory.

καὶ ὁ καθήμενος ὅμοιος ὁράσει
λίθῳ ἰάσπιδι καὶ σαρδίῳ, καὶ ἶρις
κυκλόθεν τοῦ θρόνου ὅμοιος
ὁράσει **σμαραγδίνῳ**. (Rev. 4:3)

And the one seated on the
throne [was] like in appearance
to a jasper and ruby **stone**, and
[there was] a rainbow around the
throne like in appearance **to an**
emerald.

The dative ὁράσει (appearance) in both instances is probably a dative
of means or manner ("in appearance") or respect ("with respect to
appearance").

For Practice

1.34. Analyze the datives (in bold) in the following texts from Rom. 8, identifying their various possible functions. We have not included datives that occur with prepositions.

⁷διότι τὸ φρόνημα τῆς σαρκὸς ἔχθρα εἰς θεόν, τῷ γὰρ **νόμῳ** τοῦ θεοῦ οὐχ ὑποτάσσεται, οὐδὲ γὰρ δύναται. . . . ¹²Ἄρα οὖν, ἀδελφοί, ὀφειλέται ἐσμέν, οὐ τῇ **σαρκὶ** τοῦ κατὰ σάρκα ζῆν. . . . ¹⁴ὅσοι γὰρ **πνεύματι** θεοῦ ἄγονται, οὗτοι υἱοί εἰσιν θεοῦ. . . . ¹⁶αὐτὸ τὸ πνεῦμα συμμαρτυρεῖ τῷ **πνεύματι** ἡμῶν ὅτι ἐσμὲν τέκνα θεοῦ. . . . ²⁰τῇ γὰρ **ματαιότητι** ἡ κτίσις ὑπετάγη, οὐχ ἑκοῦσα ἀλλὰ διὰ τὸν ὑποτάξαντα. . . . ²⁴τῇ γὰρ **ἐλπίδι** ἐσώθημεν· ἐλπὶς δὲ βλεπομένη οὐκ ἔστιν ἐλπίς, ὃ γὰρ βλέπει τίς ἐλπίζει; . . . ²⁶Ὡσαύτως δὲ καὶ τὸ πνεῦμα συναντιλαμβάνεται τῇ **ἀσθενείᾳ** ἡμῶν· . . . ἀλλὰ αὐτὸ τὸ πνεῦμα ὑπερεντυγχάνει **στεναγμοῖς ἀλαλήτοις**. . . . ²⁸Οἴδαμεν δὲ ὅτι τοῖς **ἀγαπῶσι** τὸν θεὸν πάντα συνεργεῖ εἰς ἀγαθόν, τοῖς κατὰ πρόθεσιν **κλητοῖς** οὖσιν. (Rom. 8:7, 12, 14, 16, 20, 24, 26, 28)

The Accusative Case

1.35. In Classical Greek the accusative case, thought by some to be the oldest case (Robertson 466), was employed more than any other, including the nominative. By the Koine period, though the accusative still was the most used of the oblique cases, its range had diminished. Its predominant uses in the NT are as the object of verbs and prepositions and as the "subject" of infinitives. Some grammars call it the case of limitation or extent;[28] Louw labels it "the indefinite case."[29] Porter says that it *expresses an idea without defining it.*[30] Since the meanings of *limitation* (as expressed by the accusative case) and restriction (as expressed by the genitive) significantly overlap, it might be helpful to repeat that the accusative frequently limits the action of verbs as the default case for their direct objects, whereas the genitive more often restricts substantives. Verbs in general take accusative direct objects; verbs of specific types or with particular nuances can take their objects in the genitive or dative cases. Adverbial accusatives are more frequent and flexible than adverbial genitives.

---

28. For example, Dana and Mantey 91; Young 9; Zerwick 23; Wallace 178.
29. Louw, "Linguistic Theory," 78.
30. Porter 88, italics original.

Direct Object

1.36. Most verbs take their direct object in the accusative case: S + V + DO$_{acc}$

Ἑτοιμάσατε τὴν **ὁδὸν** κυρίου (Mark 1:3)	Prepare the Lord's **way**.
ἠγάπησας **δικαιοσύνην** καὶ ἐμίσησας **ἀνομίαν·** (Heb. 1:9)	You have loved **righteousness** and hated **lawlessness**.
Καὶ ὅτε ἤνοιξεν τὴν **σφραγῖδα** τὴν δευτέραν, ἤκουσα τοῦ δευτέρου ζῴου λέγοντος· Ἔρχου. (Rev. 6:3)	And when he opened the second **seal**, I heard the second living creature saying, "Come."

Cognate

1.37. This is really just a type of direct object. As the label suggests, the construction involves a verb taking its cognate (same-root) noun as an object or as an adverbial modifier. In English we also have cognate direct objects (we can sing songs, pray prayers, and fight good fights) and adverbs (we can pray prayerfully and rejoice joyfully). In both languages cognate constructions are sometimes used for emphasis.

καὶ μὴ δυνάμενοι προσενέγκαι αὐτῷ διὰ τὸν ὄχλον ἀπεστέγασαν τὴν **στέγην** ὅπου ἦν (Mark 2:4)	And being unable to bring [him] to him [i.e., to Jesus] because of the crowd, they un**roof**ed the **roof** where he [i.e., Jesus] was.

> This awkward translation preserves the cognate accusative, but "they made a hole in the roof" would certainly be more accurate English, since there is no indication that they removed the entire roof.

εἰ οὖν τὴν ἴσην **δωρεὰν ἔδωκεν** αὐτοῖς ὁ θεὸς ὡς καὶ ἡμῖν πιστεύσασιν ἐπὶ τὸν κύριον Ἰησοῦν Χριστόν, ἐγὼ τίς ἤμην δυνατὸς κωλῦσαι τὸν θεόν; (Acts 11:17)	Therefore if God **gave** them the same **gift** as [he gave] also to us who believed in the Lord Jesus Christ, who was I, that I could hinder God?

> This time the cognates "gave" and "gift" work well in English.

ἀγωνίζου τὸν καλὸν ἀγῶνα τῆς πίστεως, ἐπιλαβοῦ τῆς αἰωνίου ζωῆς, εἰς ἣν ἐκλήθης καὶ ὡμολόγησας τὴν καλὴν ὁμολογίαν ἐνώπιον πολλῶν μαρτύρων. (1 Tim. 6:12)

Fight the good **fight** of faith, take hold of the eternal life to which you were called and [about which] you **confessed** your good **confession** before many witnesses.

The second of these cognate pairs is usually rendered in English as "you made your good confession"; alas, this seems to blunt Paul's force.

ἐάν τις ἴδῃ τὸν ἀδελφὸν αὐτοῦ **ἁμαρτάνοντα ἁμαρτίαν** μὴ πρὸς θάνατον (1 John 5:16)

If anyone sees his/her brother or sister **sinning a sin** not [leading] to death.

ὃς **ἐμαρτύρησεν** τὸν λόγον τοῦ θεοῦ καὶ τὴν **μαρτυρίαν** Ἰησοῦ Χριστοῦ, ὅσα εἶδεν. (Rev. 1:2)

Who **testifies** to the word of God and the **testimony** of Jesus Christ, as much as he saw.

Double

1.38. Some verbs may have two objects in the accusative case that are not joined by a coordinating conjunction such as καί. In these cases we can have (1) a **personal** (remote/indirect) and <u>impersonal</u> (direct) object (e.g., Alex gave **Mack** a <u>book</u>) or (2) an <u>object</u> (direct) and **predicate complement** (e.g., Peter also gave a <u>book</u> as a **present**). At first glance, all of the examples below seem to involve objects that are personal (ὑμᾶς, τοὺς προφήτας, and αὐτὸν refer to persons) and impersonal (ἅ, γάλα, ὑπόδειγμα, and στῦλον are things). The distinction between the two types of double accusative depends not solely on the personal nature of one of the accusatives but rather on whether or not both accusatives in a doublet refer to the same person or entity. If they *do*, they make up an object/complement double accusative (in the English example above, "book" and "present" have the same referent). If they *do not*, they make up a personal/impersonal double accusative ("Mack" and "book" have different referents).

τὸ γὰρ ἅγιον πνεῦμα διδάξει ὑμᾶς ἐν αὐτῇ τῇ ὥρᾳ <u>ἅ</u> δεῖ εἰπεῖν. (Luke 12:12)

For the Holy Spirit will teach **you** at that time <u>what things</u> are necessary to say. (**personal**/*impersonal*) γάλα <u>ὑμᾶς</u> ἐπότισα (1 Cor. 3:2)   I gave **you** <u>milk</u> to drink. (**personal/** *impersonal*)

ὑπόδειγμα λάβετε, ἀδελφοί, τῆς κακοπαθίας καὶ τῆς μακροθυμίας τοὺς <u>προφήτας</u>, οἳ ἐλάλησαν ἐν τῷ ὀνόματι κυρίου. (James 5:10)   Take the <u>prophets</u>, brothers and sisters, who spoke in the name of the Lord, as **an example** of suffering and endurance. (*object/* **complement**)

> In this example, we reversed the word order in English translation so that the articular τοὺς προφήτας is the direct object and the anarthrous (without the article) ὑπόδειγμα is the predicate complement.

ὁ νικῶν ποιήσω <u>αὐτὸν</u> στῦλον ἐν τῷ ναῷ τοῦ θεοῦ μου (Rev. 3:12)   The one who overcomes, I will make <u>him/her</u> a **pillar** in the temple of my God. (*object/***complement**)

> The personal pronoun αὐτόν is the direct object, and the impersonal noun στῦλον is the predicate complement. We could add "to be" ("I will make him/her to be a pillar") to our English translation, but it is not necessary.

Adverbial

1.39. As the label suggests, nominals or adjectives in the accusative case can function as adverbs. An accusative can indicate *how* and *how long, how far* or *to what extent* (manner/measure), *when* (time), and *with respect/reference to what* an action occurs.

1. *Manner*

ὁ δὲ Ἰησοῦς παρακούσας τὸν λόγον λαλούμενον λέγει τῷ ἀρχισυναγώγῳ· Μὴ φοβοῦ, **μόνον** πίστευε. (Mark 5:36)   But Jesus, overhearing what was being said, said to the synagogue ruler, "Don't be afraid; **only** believe."

> The adjective μόνον cannot modify anything but the verb in this sentence. We have an unambiguous adverbial accusative here, which answers the question "To what extent . . . ?"

οὐδὲ **δωρεὰν** ἄρτον ἐφάγομεν παρά τινος (2 Thess. 3:8)   Neither **as a gift** [i.e., without paying] did we eat bread from anyone.

καὶ ἐκαυματίσθησαν οἱ ἄνθρωποι **καῦμα** μέγα· (Rev. 16:9)

And the people were scorched
with great **heat.** (*this could
also be an example of respect/
reference*)

2. Measure

καὶ αὐτὸς ἀπεσπάσθη ἀπ᾽ αὐτῶν
ὡσεὶ λίθου **βολὴν,** καὶ θεὶς τὰ
γόνατα προσηύχετο (Luke 22:41)

And he drew away from them
about a stone's **throw,** and,
having gotten to his knees, he
prayed.

Here the extent ("How far . . . ?") of Jesus' withdrawal is indicated by
accusative βολήν, which is further restricted by the genitive λίθου.

3. Time

λέγει αὐτοῖς· Ἔρχεσθε καὶ
ὄψεσθε. ἦλθαν οὖν καὶ εἶδαν
ποῦ μένει, καὶ παρ᾽ αὐτῷ
ἔμειναν τὴν **ἡμέραν** ἐκείνην·
(John 1:39)

He said to them, "Come and
you will see." So they went and
saw where he was staying and
stayed with him that **day.**

In this example, extent of time, rather than extent of space, is indicated
by the accusatives τὴν ἡμέραν ἐκείνην.

4. Respect/reference

ἀληθεύοντες δὲ ἐν ἀγάπῃ αὐξήσω-
μεν εἰς αὐτὸν τὰ **πάντα,** ὅς ἐστιν ἡ
κεφαλή, Χριστός (Eph. 4:15)

But speaking the truth in love, let
us grow **in all respects** into him
who is the head, Christ.

With Infinitives

1.40. Infinitives can take both a subject and direct object in the accusative
case. When, as is often the case, the subject of the infinitive is different from
that of the main verb, the infinitive's subject will be in the accusative case.
Some older grammars explained the accusative subject of the infinitive as
the accusative of general reference.[31] We will simply refer to the accusative
functioning as the subject of the infinitive. And although infinitives have a

---

31. E.g., Robertson 490; Dana and Mantey 93; Brooks and Winbery 56.

wider range of usage in Greek than in English, we do have at least a partial equivalent for accusatives functioning as subjects. In the sentence "God enables us to love them," the word *us* is both the direct object of "enables" and also the functional subject of "to love." Subjects and complements of *infinitives of being* in Greek will also usually be in the accusative case (but note an exception below). When a Greek infinitive has both a subject and an object in the accusative case, word order or context almost always clarifies which is which.

λέγει αὐτοῖς· Ὑμεῖς δὲ τίνα με λέγετε εἶναι; (Matt. 16:15)	He said to them, "But **whom** do you claim **me** to be?"

> This translation preserves the somewhat awkward infinitive clause and takes με as the subject and τίνα as the predicate accusative of εἶναι, despite the Greek word order.

Οὐ γὰρ θέλω ὑμᾶς ἀγνοεῖν, ἀδελφοί, τὸ μυστήριον τοῦτο (Rom. 11:25)	For I do not want **you** to be ignorant, brothers and sisters, of this **mystery**.

> In this instance, sense and word order point in the same direction: ὑμᾶς is the subject of the infinitive and τὸ μυστήριον τοῦτο is its object.

καὶ γὰρ ὀφείλοντες εἶναι διδάσκαλοι διὰ τὸν χρόνον, πάλιν χρείαν ἔχετε τοῦ διδάσκειν ὑμᾶς τινά τὰ στοιχεῖα τῆς ἀρχῆς τῶν λογίων τοῦ θεοῦ, καὶ γεγόνατε χρείαν ἔχοντες γάλακτος, οὐ στερεᾶς τροφῆς. (Heb. 5:12)	For [although] you ought to be *teachers* by now, you have need for *someone* to teach *you* the elementary principles of the oracles of God again, and you have become ones having need of milk, not solid food.

> Both the participle ὀφείλοντες and the predicate noun διδάσκαλοι are nominative (rather than accusative) around the first infinitive, εἶναι, because they agree with "you," the subject of the main verb ἔχετε. With the shift in subject from "you" to "someone," we also see a shift in case from the nominative to the accusative τινά used with the second infinitive διδάσκειν. Additionally, διδάσκειν is complemented by a double accusative: the personal object is ὑμᾶς and the impersonal object is τὰ στοιχεῖα. The presence of three accusatives with one infinitive demonstrates at least that the author thought his readers had mastered the elementary principles of grammar!

ἀλλὰ ἔχω κατὰ σοῦ ὅτι ἀφεῖς τὴν γυναῖκα Ἰεζάβελ, ἡ λέγουσα ἑαυτὴν προφῆτιν, καὶ διδάσκει καὶ πλανᾷ τοὺς ἐμοὺς **δούλους** πορνεῦσαι καὶ φαγεῖν **εἰδωλόθυτα**. (Rev. 2:20)	But I have against you that you permit the woman Jezebel, who calls herself a prophet and teaches and deceives my **servants** to commit sexual immorality and to eat **meat offered to idols**.

The first accusative is the subject of both πορνεῦσαι and φαγεῖν, and the second is the object of φαγεῖν alone.

For Practice

1.41. Analyze the accusatives (in bold) in the following texts, identifying their various possible functions. We have not included accusatives that occur with prepositions.

²¹κἀκεῖθεν ᾐτήσαντο **βασιλέα**, καὶ ἔδωκεν αὐτοῖς ὁ θεὸς τὸν **Σαοὺλ υἱὸν** Κίς, **ἄνδρα** ἐκ φυλῆς Βενιαμίν, **ἔτη** τεσσεράκοντα· ²²καὶ μεταστήσας **αὐτὸν** ἤγειρεν τὸν **Δαυὶδ** αὐτοῖς εἰς βασιλέα, ᾧ καὶ εἶπεν μαρτυρήσας· Εὗρον **Δαυὶδ** τὸν τοῦ Ἰεσσαί, **ἄνδρα** κατὰ τὴν καρδίαν μου, ὃς ποιήσει **πάντα** τὰ **θελήματά** μου. ²³τούτου ὁ θεὸς ἀπὸ τοῦ σπέρματος κατ᾽ ἐπαγγελίαν ἤγαγεν τῷ Ἰσραὴλ **σωτῆρα Ἰησοῦν** (Acts 13:21–23)

¹Καὶ εἶδον **ἄγγελον** καταβαίνοντα ἐκ τοῦ οὐρανοῦ, ἔχοντα τὴν **κλεῖν** τῆς ἀβύσσου καὶ **ἅλυσιν** μεγάλην ἐπὶ τὴν χεῖρα αὐτοῦ. ²καὶ ἐκράτησεν τὸν **δράκοντα**, ὁ ὄφις ὁ ἀρχαῖος, ὅς ἐστιν Διάβολος καὶ ὁ Σατανᾶς, καὶ ἔδησεν **αὐτὸν** χίλια **ἔτη**, ³καὶ ἔβαλεν **αὐτὸν** εἰς τὴν ἄβυσσον, καὶ ἔκλεισεν καὶ ἐσφράγισεν ἐπάνω αὐτοῦ, ἵνα μὴ πλανήσῃ ἔτι τὰ **ἔθνη**, ἄχρι τελεσθῇ τὰ χίλια **ἔτη**· μετὰ ταῦτα δεῖ λυθῆναι **αὐτὸν** μικρὸν **χρόνον**. ⁴Καὶ εἶδον **θρόνους**, καὶ ἐκάθισαν ἐπ᾽ αὐτούς, καὶ κρίμα ἐδόθη αὐτοῖς, καὶ τὰς **ψυχὰς** τῶν πεπελεκισμένων διὰ τὴν μαρτυρίαν Ἰησοῦ καὶ διὰ τὸν λόγον τοῦ θεοῦ, καὶ οἵτινες οὐ προσεκύνησαν τὸ **θηρίον** οὐδὲ τὴν **εἰκόνα** αὐτοῦ καὶ οὐκ ἔλαβον τὸ **χάραγμα** ἐπὶ τὸ μέτωπον καὶ ἐπὶ τὴν χεῖρα αὐτῶν· καὶ ἔζησαν καὶ ἐβασίλευσαν μετὰ τοῦ Χριστοῦ χίλια **ἔτη**. (Rev. 20:1–4)

2

PRONOUNS

2.1. A common understanding of a pronoun is that it is a word that substitutes for another noun, known as its antecedent (when the antecedent *follows* the pronoun, it is labeled a postcedent). Thus Richard Young defines pronouns as "words that take the place of nouns while pointing to a place in the text where the noun occurs."[1] Robertson says that pronouns "avoid the repetition of the substantive."[2] Examples of a pronoun standing in place of another substantive are not hard to come by in the NT. In John 1:3 (πάντα δι' αὐτοῦ ἐγένετο, καὶ χωρὶς αὐτοῦ ἐγένετο οὐδὲ ἕν) the two instances of the pronoun αὐτοῦ have as their antecedent the single word λόγος in verse 1.

However, this understanding of pronouns is too limited. Sometimes the pronoun is a substitute not for a single word but for a group of words or an even larger unit of discourse (e.g., an entire paragraph). In Rom. 5:12 Paul begins a new section with Διὰ τοῦτο (for this reason, because of this). While there is disagreement as to the antecedent of the pronoun τοῦτο (is it 5:11? 5:9–10? 5:1–11? 3:21–5:11? the entire Letter of Romans so far?),[3] most agree that the antecedent is not just a single word. In 1 John 2:3 (Καὶ ἐν τούτῳ γινώσκομεν ὅτι ἐγνώκαμεν αὐτόν, ἐὰν τὰς ἐντολὰς αὐτοῦ τηρῶμεν, "And in *this* we know that we know him, if we keep his commands") the postcedent of

1. Young 71. So Brooks and Winbery 74.
2. Robertson 676. Also Dana and Mantey 122.
3. See Douglas Moo, *The Epistle to the Romans*, NICNT (Grand Rapids: Eerdmans, 1996), 316–17.

the pronoun τούτῳ is the entire clause introduced by ἐάν. In view of this, we will define the pronoun as *a word that functions as a substitute for a variety of linguistic units*, whether a word, a group of words, or something larger (paragraphs or even larger units of discourse). Consequently, pronouns play an important role in creating cohesion in discourse by linking units of text together (see chap. 13, on discourse considerations).

In the English example "The student liked the professor; he enrolled for every course she taught," the pronouns "he" and "she" substitute for "student" and "professor" in the first part of the clause. That is, "student" and "professor" are the antecedents of "he" and "she." But in the sentence "We took a trip across Europe; we had been planning it for a long time," the pronoun "it" in the second clause has as its antecedent at least the entire word group "a trip across Europe" in the first clause. The antecedent of the pronoun "we" is left unidentified linguistically in this sentence.

Before considering the different categories of pronouns in Greek, it will be helpful to review three general observations.

1. Like nouns, pronouns can be inflected for case, gender, and number. While the pronoun generally agrees in gender and number with its antecedent (the linguistic entity for which the pronoun is a substitute), the case of the pronoun is generally determined by how it functions within its clause. Therefore, almost everything discussed regarding Greek cases in chapter 1 applies to pronouns. That is, pronouns can do the same things other substantives can and should also be analyzed according to the various case functions (nominative subject, objective genitive, dative of means, accusative direct object, etc.).

2. Some pronoun forms are employed as both pronouns and adjectives (e.g., αὐτός, οὗτος/ἐκεῖνος, τίς, τις). When standing in the place of a substantive, they function as pronouns. When modifying another substantive, they serve as adjectives.

3. A very important part of analyzing pronouns is identifying their antecedents/postcedents. Sometimes it is rather obvious from the context; at other times it is ambiguous and requires a decision on the part of the interpreter (see the discussion of Rom. 5:12 above). *Frequently, neuter pronouns have as their antecedent a linguistic unit larger than a single word.* So what are we to make of the antecedent of τοῦτο in Eph. 2:8b (καὶ τοῦτο οὐκ ἐξ ὑμῶν)? Is it χάριτι or πίστεως from 8a? Or is it the entire clause "for by grace you are saved through faith"? The latter is more likely, since the neuter gender of τοῦτο does not match the gender of any of the individual words in 8a. To take another example:

ἀπεκδυσάμενος τὰς ἀρχὰς καὶ   Stripping off the rulers and
τὰς ἐξουσίας ἐδειγμάτισεν ἐν   authorities, he disgraced them
παρρησίᾳ, θριαμβεύσας αὐτοὺς   publicly, triumphing over them
ἐν αὐτῷ. (Col. 2:15)   by **him/it.**

> What is the antecedent of αὐτῷ? It could be the cross (τῷ σταυρῷ)
> in verse 14. However, it could also be Christ (τοῦ Χριστοῦ in verse
> 11), reflecting Paul's well-known "in Christ" language.[4] Both nouns
> are masculine and singular, so gender and number do not help with
> identifying the correct antecedent.

Consequently, students of NT Greek should pay careful attention to each pronoun and also the broader context and not assume that they necessarily know what the antecedent is. How one determines the antecedent of a pronoun can have important interpretive consequences.

The following treatment of pronouns will adhere to a fairly standard system of classification and discuss nine different classes of pronouns.[5]

Personal Pronoun (ἐγώ, ἡμεῖς, σύ, ὑμεῖς, αὐτός)

2.2. Personal pronouns in the Greek NT are used to refer to various persons and entities. This class of pronouns is the most common in the NT (occurring around 10,780 times) and comprises first-, second-, and third-person forms. In Koine Greek the intensive pronoun αὐτός has also taken over the function of the third-person personal pronoun (Dana and Mantey 122; see below). As mentioned above, personal pronouns frequently take on many of the case functions discussed in our presentation of the cases (nominative, genitive, dative, accusative) in chapter 1. In addition to their case functions, a number of usages should be identified.

Subject Specifier

2.3. The personal pronoun can be used to specify the subject of a clause. Some grammars claim that it is emphatic, since an explicit subject is not required.[6] While this is often true, especially with first- and second-person

4. Constantine R. Campbell, *Colossians and Philemon: A Handbook on the Greek Text* (Waco: Baylor University Press, 2013), 41.
5. Compare the categories found in Robertson 676–753; Dana and Mantey 122–35; BDF §§277–306; Wallace 315–51; Porter 129–38; Young 71–80; Black 67–73; Gary A. Long, *Grammatical Concepts 101 for Biblical Greek* (Peabody, MA: Hendrickson, 2006), 133–57.
6. Dana and Mantey 123; Young 72.

pronouns, pronouns can be used for other purposes in discourse. For the function of the pronouns in discourse, see chapter 13, on discourse considerations.

| μακάριοι οἱ πενθοῦντες, ὅτι **αὐτοὶ** παρακληθήσονται. (Matt. 5:4) | Blessed are those who mourn, for **they** will be comforted. |

> Αὐτοί is likely emphatic; the specification of the subject is not necessary, since it already is clear from the first part of the sentence and the ending of παρακληθήσονται.

| ὥστε τὸ πλοῖον καλύπτεσθαι ὑπὸ τῶν κυμάτων, **αὐτὸς** δὲ ἐκάθευδεν. (Matt. 8:24) | So that the boat was overtaken by the waves, but **he** slept. |

> The pronoun probably is used to "reactivate" Jesus as a main character (see chap. 13).

| γνῶσιν ὅτι **ἐγὼ** ἠγάπησά σε. (Rev. 3:9) | They will know that **I** love you. |

> The pronoun further emphasizes Christ's love for the hearers.

Contrast

2.4. Sometimes personal pronouns highlight a contrast.

| Ἠκούσατε ὅτι ἐρρέθη τοῖς ἀρχαίοις. . . . **ἐγὼ** δὲ λέγω ὑμῖν (Matt. 5:21–22) | You have heard that it was said to those of old, . . . but **I** say to you. |

| **Ὑμεῖς** δὲ οὐκ ἐστὲ ἐν σαρκὶ ἀλλὰ ἐν πνεύματι (Rom. 8:9) | But **you** are not in the flesh but in the Spirit. |

> Ὑμεῖς contrasts with the οἱ ἐν σαρκί in the previous verse (v. 8).

Emphasis

2.5. See the intensive use of αὐτός below, under "Intensive Pronoun."

Reflexive

2.6. Although rare, there appear to be a few occasions when the personal pronoun αὐτός functions similarly to a reflexive pronoun (see the discussion of reflexive pronouns later in this chapter), though this may be more a matter of English translation. Dana and Mantey (124) think there are at least two clear examples of this in the NT and that there may be others.

Μὴ θησαυρίζετε **ὑμῖν** θησαυροὺς ἐπὶ τῆς γῆς (Matt. 6:19)	Do not store up **for yourselves** treasures on the earth.

This could also be analyzed as a dative of advantage (see also Matt. 6:20).

ὅσα ἐδόξασεν **αὐτὴν**ᵃ καὶ ἐστρη-νίασεν, τοσοῦτον δότε αὐτῇ βασανισμὸν καὶ πένθος. (Rev. 18:7)	As much as she glorified **herself** and lived in luxury, give her as much torment and grief.

ᵃThe reflexive pronoun ἑαυτήν is found in several manuscripts (א² 1006 1841 1854).

Possession

2.7. The most common way of expressing possession is by a personal pronoun in the genitive case.

ποιῆσαι ὅσα ἡ χείρ **σου** καὶ ἡ βουλὴ προώρισεν γενέσθαι. (Acts 4:28)	To do as much as **your** hand and will determined to happen.
τὰ γὰρ ἀόρατα **αὐτοῦ** ἀπὸ κτίσεως κόσμου τοῖς ποιήμασιν νοούμενα καθορᾶται (Rom. 1:20)	For **his** invisible attributes from the creation of the world are clearly seen, being perceived by what was made.

Intensive Pronoun (αὐτός)

2.8. This is the most commonly found pronoun form in the NT. We have already encountered one important function of αὐτός: as the third-person personal pronoun (see above). There are two others to consider.

Identical

2.9. When αὐτός stands in the attributive position (article + αὐτός + substantive), it functions adjectivally in an identifying manner and can be translated "same."

| ἀπελθὼν προσηύξατο ἐκ τρίτου τὸν αὐτὸν λόγον εἰπὼν πάλιν. (Matt. 26:44) | Having gone away, he prayed a third time, saying **the same** thing again. |

| ἄλλῳ δὲ λόγος γνώσεως κατὰ τὸ αὐτὸ πνεῦμα (1 Cor. 12:8) | But to another a word of knowledge [is given] according to **the same** Spirit. |

| ἐκ τοῦ αὐτοῦ στόματος ἐξέρχεται εὐλογία καὶ κατάρα. (James 3:10) | From **the same** mouth come blessing and cursing. |

Intensive

2.10. When αὐτός stands in the predicate position (without the article), it exhibits its intensive meaning and can be translated "self" (himself, herself, itself, themselves, myself, ourselves, yourself, yourselves). That is, the pronoun shares the same syntactic slot as the substantive it accompanies.[7] In these instances αὐτός is emphatic and focuses attention on the noun it goes with; this is why Gary Long labels it a "focus pronoun."[8] It is used not only with third-person references but also with first and second person to also mean "self" (Moule 121).

| ὁ δὲ Πέτρος ἤγειρεν αὐτὸν λέγων· Ἀνάστηθι· καὶ ἐγὼ αὐτὸς ἄνθρωπός εἰμι. (Acts 10:26) | And Peter raised him saying, "Get up; I **myself** am also a man." (*used with first person*) |

| αὐτοὶ γὰρ οἴδατε πῶς δεῖ μιμεῖσθαι ἡμᾶς, ὅτι οὐκ ἠτακτήσαμεν ἐν ὑμῖν (2 Thess. 3:7) | For you **yourselves** know how it is necessary to imitate us, because we were not lazy among you. (*used with second person*) |

| καὶ αὐτὸς ὁ θεὸς μετ' αὐτῶν ἔσται (Rev. 21:3) | And God **himself** will be with them. |

---

7. Long, *Grammatical Concepts*, 139.
8. Ibid., 138.

Possessive Pronoun/Adjective
(ἐμός, σός, ἡμέτερος, ὑμέτερος)

2.11. The possessive "pronoun" is actually a possessive adjective. As an adjective it agrees with the substantive it modifies in case, gender, and number and can fill an attributive modifying slot. But in a few instances it acts as a possessive pronoun (i.e., a substantive) rather than modifying another substantive. There is no third-person form for possessive pronouns/adjectives; this function is performed by the genitive of αὐτός. As we already stated, the most common way of expressing possession is with the genitive of the personal pronouns.

καὶ τὰ ἐμὰ πάντα σά ἐστιν καὶ τὰ σὰ ἐμά (John 17:10)	And all **my things** are **yours**, and **your things** are **mine**.

> The first- and second-person possessive pronouns/adjectives function substantivally as subjects and predicate nominatives. Also, the articles indicate which pronouns are the subjects.

οὐ περὶ τῶν ἡμετέρων δὲ μόνον ἀλλὰ καὶ περὶ ὅλου τοῦ κόσμου. (1 John 2:2)	Not concerning **ours** only but also concerning the entire world's.

> Here the possessive τῶν ἡμετέρων stands in place of a noun, referring back to ἁμαρτιῶν in the first part of the verse.

καὶ διδάσκει καὶ πλανᾷ τοὺς ἐμοὺς δούλους πορνεῦσαι καὶ φαγεῖν εἰδωλόθυτα. (Rev. 2:20)	And she [i.e., Jezebel] teaches and deceives **my** servants to commit adultery/sexual immorality and to eat meat offered to idols. (*attributive usage*)

> This is the only place in Revelation where a possessive adjective occurs.

Demonstrative Pronoun (οὗτος, ἐκεῖνος, ὅδε)

2.12. The demonstrative pronoun specifies a relationship of nearness (οὗτος, ὅδε, "this" [or "these" when plural])[9] or remoteness (ἐκεῖνος, "that" [or "those" when plural]) from the perspective of the speaker/writer. It points to things that are near or far. The notion of nearness or remoteness indicated

---

9. Ὅδε is used only 10× in the Greek NT: Luke 10:39; Acts 21:11; James 4:13; Rev. 2:1, 8, 12, 18; 3:1, 7, 14.

by the demonstrative pronoun may refer to spatial, temporal, mental, or even textual proximity. Sometimes the entity referred to with a demonstrative is not near or far spatially or textually but near or far only from the perspective of the author. The demonstrative can function either as a substantive (a true pronoun) or as a modifier (a demonstrative adjective). As a modifier it stands in predicate position (without the article) in relation to what it modifies, though it is translated as an attributive modifier (Matt. 13:1, Ἐν τῇ ἡμέρᾳ ἐκείνῃ, "in *that* day"). As a pronoun the demonstrative can be either *anaphoric*, pointing back to something mentioned previously, or *cataphoric*, pointing forward to something to be mentioned later (Porter 134). However, it is not always easy to determine which it is. One important pragmatic effect of the use of the two demonstratives is that the "near" demonstrative (οὗτος) can be used to indicate participants (persons or entities) that are thematic or the center of attention, while the "remote" demonstrative (ἐκεῖνος) indicates participants that are not the center of attention (also called "backgrounded").[10]

1. *Nearness* (οὗτος, ὅδε)

Ταῦτα ἐλάλησεν Ἰησοῦς, καὶ ἐπάρας τοὺς ὀφθαλμοὺς αὐτοῦ εἰς τὸν οὐρανὸν εἶπεν· (John 17:1)	Jesus spoke **these things**, and lifting his eyes to heaven, he said. (*pronoun*)

The demonstrative anaphorically refers back to what Jesus spoke in chapter 16.

Διὰ τοῦτο παρέδωκεν αὐτοὺς ὁ θεὸς εἰς πάθη ἀτιμίας· (Rom. 1:26)	Because of **this**, God gave them over to dishonorable passions. (*pronoun*)

The neuter demonstrative refers anaphorically back to at least all of verse 25.

---

10. Stephen H. Levinsohn, "Towards a Unified Linguistic Description of οὗτος and ἐκεῖνος," in *The Linguist as Pedagogue: Trends in the Teaching and Linguistic Analysis of the Greek New Testament*, ed. Stanley E. Porter and Matthew Brook O'Donnell (Sheffield: Sheffield Phoenix, 2009), 204–16.

| παντὸς ὀνόματος ὀνομαζομένου οὐ μόνον ἐν τῷ αἰῶνι **τούτῳ** ἀλλὰ καὶ ἐν τῷ μέλλοντι· (Eph. 1:21) | Every name being named not only in **this** age but in the coming [age]. (*adjective*) |
| **Τάδε** λέγει ὁ κρατῶν τοὺς ἑπτὰ ἀστέρας ἐν τῇ δεξιᾷ αὐτοῦ (Rev. 2:1) | The one who grasps the seven stars in his right hand says **these things**. (*pronoun*) |

The demonstrative τάδε cataphorically points forward to the content of Christ's speech in verses 2–6.

2. *Remoteness* (ἐκεῖνος)

πολλοὶ ἐροῦσίν μοι ἐν **ἐκείνῃ** τῇ ἡμέρᾳ· Κύριε κύριε (Matt. 7:22)	Many will say to me in **that** day, "Lord, Lord." (*remote time; adjective*)
ἐκεῖνον δεῖ αὐξάνειν, ἐμὲ δὲ ἐλαττοῦσθαι. (John 3:30)	It is necessary for **him / that one** to increase but for me to decrease. (*pronoun*)
βλέπω ὅτι ἡ ἐπιστολὴ **ἐκείνη** εἰ καὶ πρὸς ὥραν ἐλύπησεν ὑμᾶς (2 Cor. 7:8)	I see that **that** epistle, if even for a time, grieved you. (*adjective*)
εἰ ἀπιστοῦμεν, **ἐκεῖνος** πιστὸς μένει· (2 Tim. 2:13)	If we are unfaithful, **that one** remains faithful. (*pronoun*)

2.13. Sometimes the demonstrative appears to be used with the sense of a personal pronoun and can be translated "she," he," or "they." Several grammars conclude that in these instances the force of the demonstrative has been weakened.[11] While this is possible, one must be careful not to conclude too quickly that the sense of the demonstrative has been diminished in all instances. We cannot allow our English translation to determine whether the demonstrative has lost its force, and sometimes good sense can still be made by retaining the demonstrative thrust, as the examples below illustrate.

| **οὗτος** ἦν ἐν ἀρχῇ πρὸς τὸν θεόν. (John 1:2) | **He / this one** was in the beginning with God. |

---

11. Black 73; Wallace 328.

οὗτος ἦλθεν εἰς μαρτυρίαν (John 1:7)	He / this one came as a witness.
οὐκ ἦν ἐκεῖνος τὸ φῶς (John 1:8)	He / that one was not the light.

It could be argued that the demonstratives retain their force here, with Jesus and then John the Baptist being introduced in verses 2 and 7 and then contrasted in verse 8 with the remote demonstrative used of John.

οὗτος ἦλθεν πρὸς αὐτὸν νυκτός (John 3:2)	He / this one [i.e., Nicodemus] came to him at night.

Interrogative Pronoun (τίς, ποῖος, ποσός)

2.14. "Interrogative pronouns replace a nominal and introduce a question"[12] that is meant to elicit a response in the form of specific information. They can also be used as either pronouns or adjectives. The interrogative pronoun τίς should be distinguished from the indefinite pronoun τις, which is an enclitic (i.e., it does not have its own accent; see below).

1. Interrogative pronouns can introduce direct ("She asked me, '*Who* are you?'") or indirect ("She asked *who* I was") questions.

Τίνα λέγουσιν οἱ ἄνθρωποι εἶναι τὸν υἱὸν τοῦ ἀνθρώπου; (Matt. 16:13)	**Who** do people say the Son of Man is?
εἰς τὸ εἰδέναι ὑμᾶς **τίς** ἐστιν ἡ ἐλπὶς τῆς κλήσεως αὐτοῦ, **τίς** ὁ πλοῦτος τῆς δόξης τῆς κληρονομίας αὐτοῦ ἐν τοῖς ἁγίοις, καὶ **τί** τὸ ὑπερβάλλον μέγεθος τῆς δυνάμεως αὐτοῦ (Eph. 1:18–19)	That you might know **what** is the hope of his calling, **what** are the riches of his glorious inheritance in the saints, and **what** is the surpassing greatness of his power. (*indirect questions*)
Τίς ἄξιος ἀνοῖξαι τὸ βιβλίον καὶ λῦσαι τὰς σφραγῖδας αὐτοῦ; (Rev. 5:2)	**Who** is worthy to open the scroll and to loose its seals?

12. Long, *Grammatical Concepts*, 140.

2. Interrogatives can also be used adjectivally (as interrogative adjectives) to modify another substantive (e.g., "*Which* book did you mean?").

ἐὰν γὰρ ἀγαπήσητε τοὺς ἀγαπῶντας ὑμᾶς, **τίνα** μισθὸν ἔχετε; (Matt. 5:46)	For if you love those who love you, **what** reward do you have?
τί ἀγαθὸν ποιήσω ἵνα σχῶ ζωὴν αἰώνιον; (Matt. 19:16)	**What** good must I do in order that I might have eternal life?

3. The neuter τί can sometimes be translated "why." In these instances it is in the accusative case and technically may be an adverbial accusative of respect ("with respect to what," i.e., "why"; Porter 136).

Τί με λέγεις ἀγαθόν; (Mark 10:18)	**Why** do you call me good?
τί ὡς ζῶντες ἐν κόσμῳ δογματίζεσθε; (Col. 2:20)	**Why**, as though living in the world, do you submit to its decrees?

4. Greek also can ask two other kinds of questions: ποῖος introduces questions that are *qualitative* in nature (What sort of? What kind of?), and πόσος introduces questions that are *quantitative* in nature (How much? How many?).

Οὐκ ἀκούεις **πόσα** σου καταμαρτυροῦσιν; (Matt. 27:13)	Do you not hear **how many things** they are accusing you of? (*quantitative interrogative*)
οἵτινες οὐκ ἐπίστασθε τὸ τῆς αὔριον **ποία** ἡ ζωὴ ὑμῶν· (James 4:14)	You who do not know what will happen tomorrow; **what sort of thing** is your life? (*qualitative interrogative*)

5. Sometimes πόσος occurs along with μᾶλλον in quantitative comparisons ("how much more").

πόσῳ μᾶλλον ὁ πατὴρ ὑμῶν ὁ ἐν τοῖς οὐρανοῖς δώσει ἀγαθὰ τοῖς αἰτοῦσιν αὐτόν. (Matt. 7:11)	**How much more** will your Father who is in heaven give good things to those who ask him.

εἰ γὰρ ἐχθροὶ ὄντες κατηλλάγημεν τῷ θεῷ διὰ τοῦ θανάτου τοῦ υἱοῦ αὐτοῦ, **πολλῷ μᾶλλον** καταλλαγέντες σωθησόμεθα ἐν τῇ ζωῇ αὐτοῦ· (Rom. 5:10)	For if while being enemies we were reconciled to God through the death of his Son, **how much more**, having been reconciled, will we be saved by his life.

Reflexive Pronoun (ἐμαυτοῦ, σεαυτοῦ, ἑαυτοῦ, ἑαυτῶν)

2.15. Reflexive pronouns reflect the verbal process back on the subject of the verb or highlight the subject in some way ("He dressed *himself*"). A reflexive notion is communicated more commonly with a reflexive pronoun than with a middle-voice verb. Reflexives are often employed as objects/complements of verbs, but sometimes they play other grammatical roles. In Eph. 5:28 (ὡς τὰ ἑαυτῶν σώματα, "as *their own* bodies") the reflexive ἑαυτῶν is a genitive indicating possession. Since they primarily refer back to the subject of verbs, they cannot themselves be the subject, so there is no nominative case.

ἀλλὰ ὕπαγε **σεαυτὸν** δεῖξον τῷ ἱερεῖ (Mark 1:44)	But go and show **yourself** to the priest.
μετὰ φόβου καὶ τρόμου τὴν **ἑαυτῶν** σωτηρίαν κατεργάζεσθε (Phil. 2:12)	With fear and trembling, work out **your own** salvation.
ἡ πίστις, ἐὰν μὴ ἔχῃ ἔργα, νεκρά ἐστιν καθ᾽ **ἑαυτήν.** (James 2:17)	Faith, if it does not have works, is dead by **itself.** (*object of a preposition*)
καὶ ἐπείρασας τοὺς λέγοντας **ἑαυτοὺς** ἀποστόλους, καὶ οὐκ εἰσίν (Rev. 2:2)	And you tested those who call **themselves** apostles, and they are not.

Reciprocal Pronoun (ἀλλήλων)

2.16. The reciprocal pronoun expresses a mutual relationship or an interchange of action between or among two or more members of a group ("each other, one another"). Naturally, it only exhibits plural forms and does not occur in the nominative case.

ἔλεγον οὖν οἱ μαθηταὶ πρὸς ἀλλήλους· (John 4:33)	Therefore, the disciples said to **one another.**
Ἄνδρες, ἀδελφοί ἐστε· ἱνατί ἀδικεῖτε ἀλλήλους; (Acts 7:26)	Men, you are brothers; why are you harming **one another?**
μόνον μὴ τὴν ἐλευθερίαν εἰς ἀφορμὴν τῇ σαρκί, ἀλλὰ διὰ τῆς ἀγάπης δουλεύετε ἀλλήλοις· (Gal. 5:13)	Only do not use your freedom as an occasion for the flesh, but through love serve **each other.**
ἐδόθη αὐτῷ λαβεῖν τὴν εἰρήνην ἐκ τῆς γῆς καὶ ἵνα ἀλλήλους σφάξουσιν (Rev. 6:4)	[The ability] to take peace from the earth was given to him so that [people] would slaughter **one another.**

Relative Pronoun (ὅς, ὅστις)

2.17. A relative pronoun introduces its own clause and relates to another clause by means of an antecedent, or *head*. According to Wallace (335), relatives "are 'hinge' words in that they . . . refer back to an antecedent in the previous clause and also function in some capacity in their own clause." In the sentence "Ally waited on the customer, who was standing impatiently at the register," the relative pronoun *who* has as its antecedent "customer" and functions to connect the two clauses. Greek also has an indefinite relative pronoun, ὅστις (whoever, anyone who), though its usage is restricted in the NT to the nominative case.[13] In Greek, relative pronouns generally agree in gender and number with their antecedent, or head. Their case is determined by how they function within their own clauses. However, exceptions to both of these rules will be considered below. Some relative pronouns do not have an antecedent located in another clause. This section will cover only the grammar of the relative pronoun. For a treatment of the syntax of relative clauses, see chapter 11.

The following examples conform to the standard practice of relative pronouns agreeing with their antecedent in gender and number, with their case being determined by their grammatical function within the relative clause.

---

13. Ὅτου, standing for οὗτινος and following ἕως five times in the NT, might be considered an exception.

ἰδοὺ ἄνδρες φέροντες ἐπὶ κλίνης ἄνθρωπον **ὃς** ἦν παραλελυμένος (Luke 5:18)

Look, men carrying upon a bed a man **who** was paralyzed.

The antecedent "man" is accusative, but the relative ὃς is nominative because it is the subject of ἦν in its own clause.

οὐ κατὰ τὴν διαθήκην **ἣν** ἐποίησα τοῖς πατράσιν αὐτῶν (Heb. 8:9)

Not according to the covenant **that** I made with their fathers.

ἀπὸ τοῦ πατρὸς τῶν φώτων, παρ' **ᾧ** οὐκ ἔνι παραλλαγὴ ἢ τροπῆς ἀποσκίασμα. (James 1:17)

From the Father of lights, with **whom** there is no variation or shadow of change.

The antecedent of ᾧ is the genitive πατρός. The relative is dative because it is the object of the preposition παρά.

τὸ μέρος αὐτῶν ἐν τῇ λίμνῃ τῇ καιομένῃ πυρὶ καὶ θείῳ, **ὅ** ἐστιν ὁ θάνατος ὁ δεύτερος. (Rev. 21:8)

Their share is in the lake that burns with fire and sulfur, **which** is the second death.

The relative pronoun is neuter and has as its antecedent at least the entire phrase "the lake that burns with fire and sulfur." As explained earlier, neuter pronouns often have an antecedent of more than one word.

There are exceptions (by now the Greek student should not be shocked at this!) to the general rule that relatives agree with their antecedent in gender and number, with case determined by function within the relative clause.

Case Deviation

2.18. The most common pattern of deviation occurs when the case of the relative pronoun is "attracted" to that of its antecedent (often known as *direct attraction*). That is, the relative pronoun takes on the case of its antecedent, irrespective of its role in its own clause. This is usually found with what otherwise would be an accusative relative pronoun being attracted to the dative or genitive case.[14]

14. K. L. McKay, *A New Syntax of the Verb in New Testament Greek: An Aspectual Approach*, Studies in Biblical Greek 5 (New York: Peter Lang, 1994), 149.

δόξασόν με σύ, πάτερ, παρὰ
σεαυτῷ τῇ δόξῃ ᾗ εἶχον πρὸ τοῦ
τὸν κόσμον εἶναι παρὰ σοί.
(John 17:5)

And now you glorify me, Father,
in your presence with the glory
that I had with you before the
world was.

> The relative here should be in the accusative case, since it is the direct
> object of εἶχον, but because of attraction to its antecedent "glory," it
> is in the dative case.

καὶ ἐν τούτῳ γινώσκομεν ὅτι μένει
ἐν ἡμῖν, ἐκ τοῦ πνεύματος **οὗ** ἡμῖν
ἔδωκεν. (1 John 3:24)

And by this we know that he remains in us, by the Spirit **whom**
he gave to us.

> Though one would expect οὗ to be in the accusative case since it is the
> direct object of ἔδωκεν, here it is in the genitive case because of attrac-
> tion to its antecedent, τοῦ πνεύματος.

περὶ πάντων τῶν ἔργων ἀσεβείας
αὐτῶν **ὧν** ἠσέβησαν καὶ περὶ
πάντων τῶν σκληρῶν **ὧν**
ἐλάλησαν κατ' αὐτοῦ ἁμαρτωλοὶ
ἀσεβεῖς. (Jude 15)

Concerning all the works of their
ungodliness **that** they have committed in an ungodly manner and
concerning all the harsh things
that ungodly sinners have spoken
against him.

> In both cases we would expect the accusative case, but both relatives
> are genitive by attraction to ἔργων.

Less commonly, the reverse occurs, and the antecedent is attracted to the
case of the relative pronoun. This is known as *indirect* or *inverse attraction*.

ἀκούσας δὲ ὁ Ἡρῴδης ἔλεγεν· Ὃν
ἐγὼ ἀπεκεφάλισα Ἰωάννην, οὗτος
ἠγέρθη. (Mark 6:16)

And when Herod heard, he said,
"**John, whom** I beheaded, this
one is raised."

> The postcedent Ἰωάννην should be in the nominative case, corresponding
> to οὗτος, which picks it up in the following clause; it has been attracted
> to the accusative of ὅν.

Gender Deviation

2.19. There are also cases where the relative pronoun does not agree in
gender with its antecedent. This can often be explained by the sense (rather
than the grammar) of the antecedent. One common pattern is for the relative

pronoun to take its gender from the predicate nominative to which it is linked by εἰμί in its own clause.[15]

Ἔστιν παιδάριον ὧδε ὃς ἔχει πέντε ἄρτους κριθίνους καὶ δύο ὀψάρια· (John 6:9)	There is a child here **who** has five barley loaves and two fish.

Although the antecedent is neuter (παιδάριον), the relative pronoun is masculine to reflect the physical gender of the child, the sense overriding grammatical gender agreement.

Καὶ τῷ σπέρματί σου, ὅς ἐστιν Χριστός. (Gal. 3:16)	"And to your seed," **who** is Christ.

The masculine gender of the pronoun, rather than the neuter following σπέρματι, is due to the masculine predicate, Χριστός, to which the pronoun is linked by ἐστίν.

πᾶς πόρνος ἢ ἀκάθαρτος ἢ πλεονέκτης, ὅ ἐστιν εἰδωλολάτρης (Eph. 5:5)	Every immoral person, or unclean person, or greedy person, **who** is an idolater.

The neuter ὅ could refer back to all three vices (Moule 130); however, in light of the parallel with Col. 3:5, it is more likely that the neuter is used to refer to the idea or abstract quality of greed. Again the sense overrides the expected grammatical gender agreement.[16]

καὶ ἑπτὰ λαμπάδες πυρὸς καιόμεναι ἐνώπιον τοῦ θρόνου, ἅ εἰσιν τὰ ἑπτὰ πνεύματα τοῦ θεοῦ (Rev. 4:5)	And seven lamps of fire burning before the throne, **which** are the seven spirits of God.

The neuter relative ἅ has as its antecedent the feminine "lamps," but it is attracted to the gender of the predicate nominative τὰ ἑπτὰ πνεύματα.

---

15. A. T. Robertson and W. Hersey Davis, *A New Short Grammar of the Greek Testament*, 10th ed. (Grand Rapids: Baker, 1977), 270.

16. Peter T. O'Brien, *The Letter to the Ephesians*, PNTC (Grand Rapids: Eerdmans, 1999), 362n13.

ποιῆσαι εἰκόνα τῷ θηρίῳ, ὃς ἔχει
τὴν πληγὴν τῆς μαχαίρης καὶ
ἔζησεν. (Rev. 13:14)

To make an image to the beast,
who has the blow from the sword
and yet lives.

While the antecedent θηρίῳ is neuter, the relative is masculine, probably
due to sense: the beast refers (metaphorically) to a person.

Disconnected Relative Pronouns

2.20. In some instances the relative pronoun is not connected to an antecedent, or head, in another clause.

1. When a relative pronoun does not have an antecedent in the text itself, its clause is known as a *headless relative clause*. In such cases the entire clause introduced by the relative functions as a noun element within a larger clause (also known as an embedded clause; see chap. 11, on clauses).

   Ὃ ἦν ἀπ' ἀρχῆς, ὃ ἀκηκόαμεν,
   ὃ ἑωράκαμεν τοῖς ὀφθαλμοῖς
   ἡμῶν, ὃ ἐθεασάμεθα καὶ αἱ
   χεῖρες ἡμῶν ἐψηλάφησαν, περὶ
   τοῦ λόγου τῆς ζωῆς (1 John 1:1)

   What was from the beginning,
   what we have heard, **what** we
   have seen with our eyes, **what**
   we have beheld and our hands
   have touched, concerning the
   word of life.

   These entire relative clauses, summarized by ὃ ἑωράκαμεν καὶ
   ἀκηκόαμεν in verse 3 after the digression of verse 2, may be understood as direct objects of ἀπαγγέλλομεν in verse 3. They are
   fronted for prominence.

   Ὃ βλέπεις γράψον εἰς
   βιβλίον καὶ πέμψον ταῖς ἑπτὰ
   ἐκκλησίαις (Rev. 1:11)

   What you see, write [it] in a
   scroll and send [it] to the seven
   churches.

   The entire relative clause functions as the direct object of γράψον.

2. At other times, the antecedent of the relative pronoun is not in another clause but is inside of, or internal to, the relative clause itself. This is known as an *internally headed relative clause* or an *incorporated antecedent*.[17] In these cases it is usually the object of a preposition.

---

17. McKay, *New Syntax*, 149–50. Cf. BDF §294(5).

ἐν ᾧ γὰρ κρίματι κρίνετε κριθή-
σεσθε (Matt. 7:2)

For by **which** judgment you
judge, you will be judged.

> The relative pronoun has as its postcedent κρίματι within the rela-
> tive clause itself; hence, it is internally headed, incorporated into
> the relative clause.

Διὰ τοῦτο καὶ ἡμεῖς, ἀφ᾽ **ἧς**
ἡμέρας ἠκούσαμεν, οὐ παυόμεθα
ὑπὲρ ὑμῶν προσευχόμενοι καὶ
αἰτούμενοι (Col. 1:9)

For this reason we also, from
which day we heard, do not
cease praying on your behalf
and asking.

3. The relative pronoun may occur without a specific referent and in combination with a preposition to serve as a *connective*.

Μὴ δύνανται οἱ υἱοὶ τοῦ
νυμφῶνος **ἐν ᾧ** ὁ νυμφίος μετ᾽
αὐτῶν ἐστιν νηστεύειν;
(Mark 2:19)

The sons of the bridal chamber
are not able to fast **while** the
bridegroom is with them, are
they?

ὁ θάνατος διῆλθεν **ἐφ᾽ ᾧ** πάντες
ἥμαρτον (Rom. 5:12)

Death entered **in which** /
because all sinned.

> While the pronoun ᾧ could have a specific antecedent (Adam?
> Death? Law?), it could function as a conjunction meaning "for the
> reason that," "because" (BDAG 727; i.e., ἐπὶ τούτῳ ὅτι). If the latter
> is the case, ἐφ᾽ ᾧ (because) gives the reason why death entered. The
> interpretation of this connection has important exegetical implica-
> tions for how one understands the relationship between Adam's sin,
> our sin, and death. See also the ἐφ᾽ ᾧ construction in 2 Cor. 5:4.[18]

2.21. Sometimes the function of the relative pronoun is unclear, which in
turn can have important exegetical implications.

μηδεὶς ὑμᾶς καταβραβευέτω
θέλων ἐν ταπεινοφροσύνῃ καὶ
θρησκείᾳ τῶν ἀγγέλων, **ἃ** ἑόρακεν
ἐμβατεύων (Col. 2:18)

Let no one disqualify you, de-
lighting in humility and worship
of angels, going into detail about
what they have seen.

---

18. Wallace 342–43; Moo, *Romans*, 320–29.

> *or* Let no one disqualify you, de-
> lighting in humility and worship
> of angels, **which** they have seen
> upon entering.

The precise meaning of several words in this verse is debated—such as
ταπεινοφροσύνη, θρησκεία, and ἐμβατεύω (either "go into detail"
or "enter")—as is the use of the genitive τῶν ἀγγέλων (is it subjective
or objective?). But part of the issue has to do with the antecedent of the
relative pronoun ἅ. It could lack an antecedent and introduce a clause
that functions as the direct object of ἐμβατεύων (going into detail). If
this is the case, the first rendering above would be followed: "going
into detail about **what** [left unspecified] they have seen." However, the
relative pronoun could have as its antecedent ἐν ταπεινοφροσύνῃ καὶ
θρησκείᾳ τῶν ἀγγέλων (humility and worship of angels; note that ἅ
is neuter). In this case, the second rendering above would be followed:
"humility and worship of angels, **which** they have seen upon entering,"
giving ἅ a specific referent. The latter could find support from the fact
that other instances of the neuter relative pronouns in this section clearly
refer back to an antecedent (see Col. 2:17, 22, 23).

Ὅστις and Ὅς

2.22. Though there appears to have been a distinction in Classical Greek,
there is some debate as to whether the indefinite relative ὅστις (from ὅς +
τις; whoever) and the relative ὅς (who) possess distinct meanings in Koine
Greek. Blass, Debrunner, and Funk (BDF §293) claim that "the definite relative ὅς and the indefinite relative ὅστις are no longer clearly distinguished in
the NT." This is due in large part to the almost complete limitation of the
indefinite relative to the nominative case and its use in seemingly parallel
fashion with ὅς. In Luke 2:4 ὅστις has a definite referent (εἰς πόλιν Δαυὶδ
ἥτις καλεῖται Βηθλέεμ, "into the city of David, **which** is called Bethlehem").
However, there appear to be a number of examples where a distinction in
meaning does makes sense. The so-called indefinite relative pronoun can be
used in two different senses: *generic* ("whoever, anyone who, which as other
like things") or *essential* ("which by its very nature").[19]

ἀλλ' **ὅστις** σε ῥαπίζει εἰς τὴν δεξιὰν σιαγόνα, στρέψον αὐτῷ καὶ τὴν ἄλλην· (Matt. 5:39)	But **whoever** strikes you on the right cheek, turn to him also the other. (*generic*)

---

19. Moule 124; Porter 133; Long, *Grammatical Concepts*, 156.

| οἵτινες ἀπεθάνομεν τῇ ἁμαρτίᾳ, πῶς ἔτι ζήσομεν ἐν αὐτῇ; (Rom. 6:2) | We **who** [are of such a nature][a] died to sin, how shall we still live in it? (*essential*) |

[a] See also Moo, *Romans*, 357n24.

| οἵτινες οὐκ ἐπίστασθε τὸ τῆς αὔριον ποία ἡ ζωὴ ὑμῶν· (James 4:14) | You **who** [are of such a nature] do not know what will happen tomorrow, what sort of thing is your life? (*essential*) |

An indefinite relative pronoun can also be formed by combining the relative with ἄν or ἐάν. In these instances we should probably understand an assumed condition ("if").

| ὃς ἐὰν οὖν λύσῃ μίαν τῶν ἐντολῶν τούτων τῶν ἐλαχίστων καὶ διδάξῃ οὕτως τοὺς ἀνθρώπους . . . · ὃς δ' ἂν ποιήσῃ καὶ διδάξῃ . . . (Matt. 5:19) | Therefore **whoever** breaks [i.e., if anyone breaks] one of the least of these commandments and teaches people [to do] likewise . . . , but **whoever** does and teaches [i.e., if anyone does and teaches]. |

| ὃς ἐὰν ὁμολογήσῃ ὅτι Ἰησοῦς ἐστιν ὁ υἱὸς τοῦ θεοῦ (1 John 4:15) | **Whoever** confesses [i.e., if anyone confesses] that Jesus is the Son of God. |

Correlative Pronouns

2.23. Two additional important classes of relative pronouns are the *qualitative correlative pronoun* (οἷος, "such as, what kind") and the *quantitative correlative pronoun* (ὅσος, "as much, as many").

| καθὼς οἴδατε **οἷοι** ἐγενήθημεν ἐν ὑμῖν δι' ὑμᾶς· (1 Thess. 1:5) | Just as you know **what manner** [i.e., what sort of men] we were among you on your account. |

| **ὅσα** ἐδόξασεν αὐτὴν καὶ ἐστρηνίασεν, τοσοῦτον δότε αὐτῇ βασανισμὸν καὶ πένθος. (Rev. 18:7) | **As much as** she glorified herself and lived in luxury, give her as much torment and grief. |

Indefinite Pronoun (τις)

2.24. An indefinite pronoun refers to a person or entity that is unidentified or unspecified. It should be distinguished from the interrogative pronoun, which has its own accent (τίς, see above).[20] The indefinite pronoun can serve either as a substantive (i.e., as a pronoun) or as an adjective modifier.

εἴ τις ἔχει ὦτα ἀκούειν ἀκουέτω.
(Mark 4:23)

If **anyone** has ears to hear, he/she should hear.

> The indefinite acts as a substantive, as the subject of ἔχει.

Ἄνθρωπος δέ τις ἦν πλούσιος
(Luke 16:19)

And a **certain** man was rich.

> Here the indefinite is an adjectival modifier of ἄνθρωπος.

εἰ δέ τι ἠδίκησέν σε ἢ ὀφείλει,
τοῦτο ἐμοὶ ἐλλόγα· (Philem. 18)

And if he has wronged you in **anything** or owes you, charge this to me.

εἴ τις ἔρχεται πρὸς ὑμᾶς καὶ
ταύτην τὴν διδαχὴν οὐ φέρει, μὴ
λαμβάνετε αὐτὸν (2 John 10)

If **someone** comes to you and does not bring this teaching, do not receive him.

Occasionally, εἷς (one) functions in an indefinite manner. As Chrys Caragounis observes, in the "NT the cardinal numbers, εἷς, μία, ἕν, are losing their numerical value and are being reduced to an indefinite pronoun,"[21] though they still often retain their numerical property in the NT (see chap. 4, on the article).

Καὶ ἰδοὺ εἷς προσελθὼν αὐτῷ
εἶπεν· (Matt. 19:16)

And look, **a certain person** / **someone** came to him and said.

καὶ ἤκουσα ἑνὸς ἀετοῦ πετομένου
ἐν μεσουρανήματι (Rev. 8:13)

And I heard **an** eagle flying in midheaven.

---

20. James Allan Hewett, *New Testament Greek*, rev. C. Michael Robbins and Steven R. Johnson (Grand Rapids: Baker Academic, 2009), 133–34.
21. Chrys Caragounis, *The Development of Greek and the New Testament* (Grand Rapids: Baker Academic, 2006), 113.

For Practice

2.25. Analyze the pronouns (in bold) according to their kind, their antecedent (or postcedent), and function in the following NT texts.

²**οὗτος** ἦν ἐν ἀρχῇ πρὸς τὸν θεόν. ³πάντα δι᾽ **αὐτοῦ** ἐγένετο, καὶ χωρὶς **αὐτοῦ** ἐγένετο οὐδὲ ἕν. ὃ γέγονεν ⁴ἐν **αὐτῷ** ζωὴ ἦν, καὶ ἡ ζωὴ ἦν τὸ φῶς τῶν ἀνθρώπων· ⁵καὶ τὸ φῶς ἐν τῇ σκοτίᾳ φαίνει, καὶ ἡ σκοτία **αὐτὸ** οὐ κατέλαβεν. ⁶Ἐγένετο ἄνθρωπος ἀπεσταλμένος παρὰ θεοῦ, ὄνομα **αὐτῷ** Ἰωάννης· ⁷**οὗτος** ἦλθεν εἰς μαρτυρίαν, ἵνα μαρτυρήσῃ περὶ τοῦ φωτός, ἵνα πάντες πιστεύσωσιν δι᾽ **αὐτοῦ**. ⁸οὐκ ἦν **ἐκεῖνος** τὸ φῶς, ἀλλ᾽ ἵνα μαρτυρήσῃ περὶ τοῦ φωτός. . . . ¹⁵(Ἰωάννης μαρτυρεῖ περὶ **αὐτοῦ** καὶ κέκραγεν λέγων· Οὗτος ἦν ὃν εἶπον· Ὁ ὀπίσω **μου** ἐρχόμενος ἔμπροσθέν **μου** γέγονεν, ὅτι πρῶτός **μου** ἦν·) ¹⁶ὅτι ἐκ τοῦ πληρώματος **αὐτοῦ** **ἡμεῖς** πάντες ἐλάβομεν, καὶ χάριν ἀντὶ χάριτος· ¹⁷ὅτι ὁ νόμος διὰ Μωϋσέως ἐδόθη, ἡ χάρις καὶ ἡ ἀλήθεια διὰ Ἰησοῦ Χριστοῦ ἐγένετο. ¹⁸θεὸν **οὐδεὶς** ἑώρακεν πώποτε· μονογενὴς θεὸς ὁ ὢν εἰς τὸν κόλπον τοῦ πατρὸς **ἐκεῖνος** ἐξηγήσατο. (John 1:2–8, 15–18)

¹·⁴καὶ **ταῦτα** γράφομεν **ἡμεῖς** ἵνα ἡ χαρὰ **ἡμῶν** ᾖ πεπληρωμένη. ⁵Καὶ ἔστιν **αὕτη** ἡ ἀγγελία ἣν ἀκηκόαμεν ἀπ᾽ **αὐτοῦ** καὶ ἀναγγέλλομεν **ὑμῖν**, ὅτι ὁ θεὸς φῶς ἐστιν καὶ σκοτία ἐν **αὐτῷ** οὐκ ἔστιν **οὐδεμία**. ⁶ἐὰν εἴπωμεν ὅτι κοινωνίαν ἔχομεν μετ᾽ **αὐτοῦ** καὶ ἐν τῷ σκότει περιπατῶμεν, ψευδόμεθα καὶ οὐ ποιοῦμεν τὴν ἀλήθειαν· ⁷ἐὰν δὲ ἐν τῷ φωτὶ περιπατῶμεν ὡς **αὐτός** ἐστιν ἐν τῷ φωτί, κοινωνίαν ἔχομεν μετ᾽ **ἀλλήλων** καὶ τὸ αἷμα Ἰησοῦ τοῦ υἱοῦ **αὐτοῦ** καθαρίζει **ἡμᾶς** ἀπὸ πάσης ἁμαρτίας. ⁸ἐὰν εἴπωμεν ὅτι ἁμαρτίαν οὐκ ἔχομεν, **ἑαυτοὺς** πλανῶμεν καὶ ἡ ἀλήθεια οὐκ ἔστιν ἐν **ἡμῖν**. . . . ²·⁴ὁ λέγων ὅτι Ἔγνωκα **αὐτὸν** καὶ τὰς ἐντολὰς **αὐτοῦ** μὴ τηρῶν ψεύστης ἐστίν, καὶ ἐν **τούτῳ** ἡ ἀλήθεια οὐκ ἔστιν· ⁵**ὃς** δ᾽ ἂν τηρῇ **αὐτοῦ** τὸν λόγον, ἀληθῶς ἐν **τούτῳ** ἡ ἀγάπη τοῦ θεοῦ τετελείωται. ἐν **τούτῳ** γινώσκομεν ὅτι ἐν **αὐτῷ** ἐσμεν· ⁶ὁ λέγων ἐν **αὐτῷ** μένειν ὀφείλει καθὼς **ἐκεῖνος** περιεπάτησεν καὶ **αὐτὸς** περιπατεῖν. (1 John 1:4–8; 2:4–6)

3

ADJECTIVES AND ADVERBS

Adjectives

3.1. The primary function of an adjective is to modify or describe (limit or qualify) a substantive or nominal (noun or noun equivalent). But this is not the only way adjectives can function. They can also be employed as substantives and adverbs. Regardless of their role, adjectives have gender, number, and case. Most adjectives have first- and second-declension endings, though some have third-declension endings, and two appear to be hybrids (μέγας and πολύς).[1] All distinctly feminine adjectives (i.e., adjectives that have separate feminine forms) use first-declension endings (e.g., δίκαιος, -αία, -ον and πᾶς, πᾶσα, πᾶν). Most masculine and masculine/feminine (338) adjectives follow the second declension (e.g., ἄδικος, -ον and διάβολος, -ον), but there is still a significant group that follows the third (e.g., ἀληθής, -ές and ἄφρων, -ον). Likewise, most neuter adjectives use second-declension endings, but a significant minority of adjectives use the third (e.g., ἀληθές and ἄφρον). Adjectives agree with what they modify in gender, number, and case. If an adjective is being used substantivally, it agrees with its referent in gender and number, but its case is determined by its own grammatical function.

We will discuss adjectives below according to four primary functions: attributive, predicate, substantival, and adverbial usages.

1. Approximations ("most," "some," etc.) are derived from William D. Mounce, *The Morphology of Biblical Greek* (Grand Rapids: Zondervan, 1994).

Attributive Adjectives

3.2. Attributive adjectives modify substantives by attributing descriptors (qualities/characteristics/limitations) to them. Attributive adjectives are frequently articular, or arthrous (this is true of almost 75 percent of NT adjectives; Wallace 309), and if a substantive is articular, an attributive adjective modifying it will almost always be articular also. If there is only one article present, the adjective will be between the article and the substantive. There are at least five configurations for the relationship of the adjective to the article and/or the substantive it modifies.

3.3. Arthrous constructions

1. *Article + adjective + substantive.* This is a common attributive word order, or structure, and helpfully can be translated word for word into English. The adjective and substantive share the same article. But because the adjective precedes the noun, it may be considered to be more prominent than the head noun or substantive in a majority of NT contexts.[2]

    τὴν μακαρίαν ἐλπίδα (Titus 2:13)   the blessed hope (*with emphasis on blessedness*)

2. *Article + substantive + article + adjective.* In another attributive structure the adjective follows the substantive (according to Levinsohn, this is the default order).[3] Because the article is repeated, some grammarians have followed Robertson in thinking that this structure emphasizes

---

2. Wallace (306), following Robertson (776), seems to indicate that in this structure (his first attributive position) the adjective is always emphatic. There is a significant minority of exceptions, however, according to Levinsohn:

When this Principle [i.e., the principle of natural information flow, which states that "information that has already been established in the immediate context precedes information that is new to the context and, more generally, more established information precedes less established information" (p. 1)] is violated, then the adjective is indeed emphasised. When the Principle is adhered to, in contrast, it is often the case that the noun or some other element of the clause is emphasised. (Stephen H. Levinsohn, "A Fresh Look at Adjective-Noun Ordering in Articular Noun Phrases" [July 2011]: 8, http://www-01.sil.org/~levinsohns/Greek-Adjective-Noun-Ordering.pdf)

In other words, when an adjective gives new information and precedes the noun, it is emphatic. However, when an adjective repeats information established in the previous context and precedes the noun, it is not emphatic.

3. Levinsohn, "Fresh Look," 2.

both adjective and substantive with climactic focus on the adjective.[4] Levinsohn, however, argues that the structure gives equal or less weight to the adjective.[5] Therefore, the wooden translation (which is in keeping with Robertson's description of an addition of an appositive) of the example below, "I am the shepherd, the good [one]," overstates the force of the word order.[6]

> ἐγώ εἰμι ὁ ποιμὴν ὁ καλός (John 10:14)

> I am **the good shepherd.**

3. *Substantive* + *article* + *adjective*. In the NT this structure is most often found with proper names in the substantive slot (e.g., ἀσπάσασθε Ἐπαίνετον τὸν ἀγαπητόν μου, "Greet my **beloved** Epaenetus" [Rom. 16:5]) and participles in the adjective slot (e.g., παιδίοις τοῖς ἐν ἀγορᾷ καθημένοις, "**children sitting** in the marketplace" [Luke 7:32]). But it is also found, albeit infrequently, with common nouns and adjectives (e.g., εἰρήνην τὴν ἐμὴν δίδωμι ὑμῖν, "**My peace** I give to you" [John 14:27]).

3.4. Anarthrous constructions. As mentioned above, more than 25 percent of attributive adjectives are anarthrous and modify anarthrous substantives.

1. *Adjective* + *substantive*

> μόνῳ σοφῷ θεῷ (Rom. 16:27)

> To the **only wise God.**

> In the doxology of Rom. 16, "only" and "wise" contribute additional attributes to "the eternal God" (v. 26). They precede θεῷ and thus should be considered emphatic.[7]

2. *Substantive* + *adjective*

> λόγοις πονηροῖς φλυαρῶν ἡμᾶς (3 John 10)

> Talking nonsense against us with **evil words.**

---

4. "Both substantive and adjective receive emphasis and the adjective is added as a sort of climax in apposition with a separate article" (Robertson 776). Wallace (306), Young (81), and Black (59–60) note the emphatic nature of this structure.

5. Levinsohn, "Fresh Look," 2.

6. Jesus introduced the shepherd metaphor in John 10:2, so the principle of natural information flow is not violated in verse 14. "Good" and "shepherd" are equally emphasized.

7. Romans 16:25–27 is placed in brackets in NA[28] and UBS[5].

Predicate Adjectives

3.5. Predicate adjectives do not simply modify substantives; they add assertions or predicate qualities to them. To translate them into English, one can supply a form of the verb *to be*, if no form of εἶναι is present in the Greek text. In predicate structures lacking a form of εἶναι, the adjectives are *anarthrous*, regardless of whether or not the substantives have articles. This also means that some adjectives in the NT may be either attributive or predicative, because their substantives are also anarthrous. In such cases, one should have significant contextual warrant to consider an adjective as predicative (e.g., when there is no verb present in the adjective's clause).

1. *Adjective + article + substantive*

ἄξιος γὰρ ὁ ἐργάτης τῆς τροφῆς αὐτοῦ. (Matt. 10:10)

For **the worker** [is] **worthy** of his food.

> The idea of worthiness, repeated in verse 13 (ἡ οἰκία ἀξία), is introduced in verse 10 in the most prominent position in its clause. The combination of anarthrous adjective, arthrous noun, and no verb requires that we supply the verb *is* in English translation.

2. *Article + substantive + adjective*

οὐ γὰρ οἱ ἀκροαταὶ νόμου δίκαιοι παρὰ τῷ θεῷ (Rom. 2:13)

For not **the hearers** of the law [are] **righteous** before God.

3. *Adjective + substantive*

μακάριος ἀνὴρ οὗ οὐ μὴ λογίσηται κύριος ἁμαρτίαν. (Rom. 4:8)

Blessed [is] the **person** whose sin the Lord never counts.

> Context requires a verb before the relative clause, and word order places some emphasis on blessedness.

4. *Substantive + adjective*

χωρὶς γὰρ νόμου ἁμαρτία νεκρά (Rom. 7:8)

For without the law, **sin** [is] **dead.**

> Because there is no verb in the clause, νεκρά must be a predicate adjective, and we can supply "is" in our English translation.

Substantival Adjectives

3.6. Substantival adjectives designate persons, places, or things; that is, they fill the slot of a noun in a clause. Therefore, they can function any way a noun can: subject, direct object, predicate complement, and the like. Substantival adjectives are usually arthrous/articular, but occasionally they appear without preceding articles. As explained above, substantival adjectives agree with that to which they refer in gender and number, but their case is determined by how they are used in a particular clause.

Πορνεία δὲ καὶ ἀκαθαρσία πᾶσα ἢ πλεονεξία μηδὲ ὀνομαζέσθω ἐν ὑμῖν, καθὼς πρέπει **ἁγίοις** (Eph. 5:3)	But sexual immorality and all impurity or greediness must not be named among you, just as it is proper among **saints / holy ones.**

Although anarthrous, it is clear from the context that ἁγίοις refers to people (ἐν ὑμῖν).

πάντα δὲ δοκιμάζετε, **τὸ καλὸν** κατέχετε (1 Thess. 5:21)	But test all things; hold on to **the good.**

The articular adjective "good" fills a noun slot (direct object/complement), viewed as a whole entity expressed by the neuter singular.

Adverbial Adjectives

3.7. Adverbial adjectives, which modify verbs rather than substantives, are usually in the accusative case and may be arthrous/articular. Certain adjectives fill an adverbial slot as a natural extension of their meaning (e.g., λοιπόν, μόνον, πρῶτον). As stated in chapter 1, nominals in the accusative case may indicate how (and how long, how far, or to what extent), when, and with respect/reference to what an action occurs.

πολὺ πλανᾶσθε. (Mark 12:27)	You are **greatly/much** mistaken. (*to what extent*)
καὶ εἰς πάντα τὰ ἔθνη **πρῶτον** δεῖ κηρυχθῆναι τὸ εὐαγγέλιον. (Mark 13:10)	And to all the nations, **first** it is necessary for the good news to be preached. (*when*)

ὁ δὲ Ἰησοῦς ἀκούσας ἀπεκρίθη αὐτῷ· μὴ φοβοῦ, **μόνον** πίστευσον, καὶ σωθήσεται. (Luke 8:50)	And Jesus, having heard, answered him, "Don't be afraid, **only** believe, and she will be healed." (*to what extent*)
τὸ λοιπὸν ἐκδεχόμενος ἕως τεθῶσιν οἱ ἐχθροὶ αὐτοῦ ὑποπόδιον τῶν ποδῶν αὐτοῦ (Heb. 10:13)	**From then on** [i.e., for the remaining time] waiting until his enemies are placed as a footstool for his feet. (*how long*)

Comparison of Adjectives

3.8. Comparison of adjectives was a carryover from Classical Greek to Koine Greek. As with English, comparatives in Greek normally compare two items, while superlatives compare three or more. Yet, as Porter (122–23) says, scholars disagree regarding the fluidity of or interchangeability among each of the three degrees of comparison (positive [simple adjective], comparative, and superlative; e.g., "quick, quicker, quickest" or "good, better, best" in English) in NT usage. For example, it is generally accepted that the superlative forms were giving way to the comparative. Along the same lines, Moulton suggests, "Practically we may say that in the vernacular documents the superlative forms are used to express the sense of our 'very'" (known as the elative use).[8] We agree with Porter's conclusion that the interpreter must carefully examine and consider context when "deciding the force of the adjective" (123). There are NT examples of (1) the positive being used for both the comparative and superlative (in English, "good" for "better" and "best"), (2) the comparative being used for the superlative ("better" for "best") and as an elative ("better" for "very good" or possibly just "good"), (3) and the superlative being used as an elative ("best" for "very good"). It is possible that, along with changes in Greek usage, Hebrew's lack of formal comparative and superlative adjectives had some influence on the NT writers.[9] The table presents the comparative and superlative forms of some common adjectives.

8. James Hope Moulton, *Prolegomena*, vol. 1 of *A Grammar of New Testament Greek*, by James Hope Moulton, Wilbert Francis Howard, and Nigel Turner, 3rd ed. (Edinburgh: T&T Clark, 1908), 78.

9. In Hebrew the comparative is expressed by the positive + מִן. Superlative constructions are too numerous to mention here but also employ positive adjectives.

	← Elative ("very . . .") →	
Positive	Comparative ("-er"; "more") Often ending in -τερος or -ιων	Superlative ("-est"; "most") Often ending in -τατος or -ιστος
δίκαιος, -α, -ον (just)	δικαιότερος, -α, -ον	δικαιότατος, -η, -ον
ταχύς, -εῖα, -ύ (fast)	ταχίων, -ον	τάχιστος, -η, -ον
ἀγαθός, -ή, -όν (good)	κρείσσων/κρείττων, -ον	κράτιστος, -η, -ον
κακός, -ή, -όν (bad)	χείρων, -ον	χείριστος, -η, -ον
μέγας, -άλη, -α (great)	μείζων, -ον	μέγιστος, -η, -ον
μικρός, -ά, -όν (small)	μικρότερος, -α, -ον / ἐλάσσων, ἔλασσον	ἐλάχιστος, -η, -ον

3.9. Positive degree. This is the "standard" use of the adjective to modify a noun.

ὁ δὲ Ἰησοῦς ἀφεὶς φωνὴν **μεγάλην** ἐξέπνευσεν. (Mark 15:37)	And Jesus, having let out a **great** cry, expired.
ὥστε ὁ μὲν νόμος **ἅγιος**, καὶ ἡ ἐντολὴ **ἁγία** καὶ **δικαία** καὶ **ἀγαθή**. (Rom. 7:12)	So indeed the law is **holy**, and the commandment is **holy** and **just** and **good**.

3.10. Comparative degree. When stated comparisons are made in the NT, either the particle ἤ ("or," but in comparisons "than"), the genitive of comparison (see also chap. 1), or the prepositions παρά or ὑπέρ with the accusative case are employed.

μείζων τούτων ἄλλη ἐντολὴ οὐκ ἔστιν. (Mark 12:31)	**Greater than these** there is no other commandment.
ὅτι οἱ υἱοὶ τοῦ αἰῶνος τούτου **φρονιμώτεροι ὑπὲρ** τοὺς υἱοὺς τοῦ φωτὸς (Luke 16:8)	Because the children of this age are **more shrewd than** the children of light.
Ἰησοῦς **πλείονας** μαθητὰς ποιεῖ καὶ βαπτίζει **ἤ** Ἰωάννης (John 4:1)	Jesus was making and baptizing **more** disciples **than** John.

καὶ διαθήκης νέας μεσίτῃ Ἰησοῦ
καὶ αἵματι ῥαντισμοῦ **κρεῖττον**
λαλοῦντι **παρὰ** τὸν Ἄβελ.
(Heb. 12:24)

And to Jesus, the mediator of the
new covenant, and to the sprin-
kled blood speaking **something
better than** that of Abel.

3.11. Superlative degree. There are not many superlative adjectives in the
NT (about forty), and most of these can be easily understood as elatives
(with the sense of "very, exceedingly"). Although Wallace (298n13; following
Robertson [280] and Zerwick [50]) treats πρῶτος and ἔσχατος as superlative
forms, we will not, since both adjectives are incapable of formally changing
degree (though we agree that they *are* superlative in sense). Moreover, both
of these adjectives—πρῶτος more often than ἔσχατος—are used to compare
two entities (Wallace 303; the comparative πρότερος occurs only 11 times in
the NT and was being replaced by πρῶτος).[10]

Τότε ἤρξατο ὀνειδίζειν τὰς
πόλεις ἐν αἷς ἐγένοντο **αἱ
πλεῖσται** δυνάμεις αὐτοῦ, ὅτι οὐ
μετενόησαν· (Matt. 11:20)

Then he began to denounce the
cities in which **most** of his mira-
cles happened, because they did
not repent.

3.12. Mixed Usages

1. *Positive for comparative*

καλόν σέ ἐστιν μονόφθαλμον
εἰσελθεῖν εἰς τὴν βασιλείαν τοῦ
θεοῦ **ἢ** δύο ὀφθαλμοὺς ἔχοντα
βληθῆναι εἰς τὴν γέενναν
(Mark 9:47)

It is **better** for you to enter the
kingdom of God with one eye
than, having two eyes, to be
thrown into hell.

The presence of ἤ makes it obvious that a comparison is being made
and that καλόν fills the slot of καλλίων.

καὶ οὐδεὶς πιὼν παλαιὸν θέλει
νέον· λέγει γάρ· ὁ παλαιὸς
χρηστός ἐστιν. (Luke 5:39)

And no one drinking old [wine]
desires new, for he/she says,
"The old is **better**."

Here the comparison between "old" and "new wine" is assumed
rather than made explicit, so one could translate χρηστός as "good."

10. Moulton, *Prolegomena*, 79.

2. Positive for superlative

διδάσκαλε, ποία ἐντολὴ **μεγάλη**
ἐν τῷ νόμῳ; (Matt. 22:36)

Teacher, what is the **greatest**
commandment in the law?

The Pharisee was testing Jesus, so we may conclude that the task
was to elevate one commandment above all others.

εὐλογημένη σὺ ἐν γυναιξὶν
καὶ **εὐλογημένος** ὁ καρπὸς τῆς
κοιλίας σου. (Luke 1:42)

You are **most blessed** among
women, and **most blessed** [is]
the fruit of your womb.

The addition of "most" is not strictly necessary, but it is clear that
Elizabeth is comparing Mary to all women and her baby to all babies.

3. Comparative for superlative

ὁ δὲ **μείζων** ὑμῶν ἔσται ὑμῶν
διάκονος. (Matt. 23:11)

But the **greatest** of you will be
your servant.

Since Jesus was addressing both his disciples and a crowd, a superlative understanding of μείζων is warranted.

οἱ δὲ ἐσιώπων· πρὸς ἀλλήλους
γὰρ διελέχθησαν ἐν τῇ ὁδῷ τίς
μείζων. (Mark 9:34)

But they were silent, for on
the way they had argued with
one another about who was
greatest.

We agree with Moule (97) that the disciples were more likely discussing who was the greatest of all of them rather than discussing the
relative greatness of any two of them.

4. *Comparative as elative*

Ἀθηναῖοι δὲ πάντες καὶ οἱ ἐπιδημοῦντες ξένοι εἰς οὐδὲν ἕτερον ηὐκαίρουν ἢ λέγειν τι ἢ ἀκούειν τι **καινότερον**. (Acts 17:21)	And all the Athenians and the foreigners staying there had time for nothing other than to tell or to hear something **[brand] new**.

News is not being explicitly compared,[11] and though "brand" is not necessary in English here, something more than the simple positive but less than the superlative represents what is going on in the Greek.[12]

Σταθεὶς δὲ ὁ Παῦλος ἐν μέσῳ τοῦ Ἀρείου πάγου ἔφη· ἄνδρες Ἀθηναῖοι, κατὰ πάντα ὡς **δεισιδαιμονεστέρους** ὑμᾶς θεωρῶ. (Acts 17:22)	And Paul, standing in the middle of the Areopagus, said, "Athenians, I see that in all respects you are **very religious**."

Following on the heels of verse 21, Luke/Paul employs the same idiom to highlight another characteristic of Athenians.[13]

5. *Superlative as elative*

ἢ οὐκ οἴδατε ὅτι οἱ ἅγιοι τὸν κόσμον κρινοῦσιν; καὶ εἰ ἐν ὑμῖν κρίνεται ὁ κόσμος, ἀνάξιοί ἐστε κριτηρίων **ἐλαχίστων**; (1 Cor. 6:2)	Or don't you know that the saints will judge the world, and if the world is judged by you, are you unworthy of **trivial** cases?

It is possible that Paul actually meant the "smallest" cases literally, but it is more likely that he intended very small or trivial cases.

---

11. But Robertson (665) says that καινότερον "means, of course, something newer than what they had recently heard," but also that "the elative comparative is still comparative."

12. Contra Zerwick (50), who thinks the comparative is equivalent to a positive.

13. "When [ἄνδρες, used "as a formal opening to a speech"] is followed by another vocative noun identifying the referents, it should be left untranslated." Martin M. Culy and Mikeal C. Parsons, *Acts: A Handbook on the Greek Text* (Waco: Baylor University Press, 2003), 11.

δι᾽ ὧν τὰ τίμια καὶ **μέγιστα** ἡμῖν
ἐπαγγέλματα δεδώρηται
(2 Pet. 1:4)

Through which he has given
us valuable and **very great**
promises.

Paired as it is with the positive τίμια, μέγιστα makes better sense
when translated as the elative "very great" rather than as a true
superlative.

For Practice

3.13. Analyze the adjectives (in bold) in the following text, paying attention
to the function as well as to how you determine the function of each one.

³³"Η ποιήσατε τὸ δένδρον **καλὸν** καὶ τὸν καρπὸν αὐτοῦ **καλόν**, ἢ ποιήσατε
τὸ δένδρον **σαπρὸν** καὶ τὸν καρπὸν αὐτοῦ **σαπρόν**· ἐκ γὰρ τοῦ καρποῦ τὸ
δένδρον γινώσκεται. ³⁴γεννήματα ἐχιδνῶν, πῶς δύνασθε **ἀγαθὰ** λαλεῖν
πονηροὶ ὄντες; ἐκ γὰρ τοῦ περισσεύματος τῆς καρδίας τὸ στόμα λαλεῖ.
³⁵ὁ **ἀγαθὸς** ἄνθρωπος ἐκ τοῦ **ἀγαθοῦ** θησαυροῦ ἐκβάλλει **ἀγαθά**, καὶ ὁ
πονηρὸς ἄνθρωπος ἐκ τοῦ **πονηροῦ** θησαυροῦ ἐκβάλλει **πονηρά**. ³⁶λέγω
δὲ ὑμῖν ὅτι **πᾶν** ῥῆμα **ἀργὸν** ὃ λαλήσουσιν οἱ ἄνθρωποι ἀποδώσουσιν περὶ
αὐτοῦ λόγον ἐν ἡμέρᾳ κρίσεως· ³⁷ἐκ γὰρ τῶν λόγων σου δικαιωθήσῃ, καὶ
ἐκ τῶν λόγων σου καταδικασθήσῃ. (Matt. 12:33–37)

Adverbs

3.14. Adverbs are indeclinable forms primarily employed to modify verbs,
but they may also modify adjectives, other adverbs, or even substantives. In
fact, "adverbs are old case forms of nouns (substantive and adjective) and
pronouns."[14] Thus an adverb with the article can fill a substantive slot. Adverbs are sometimes classified as particles, since both are indeclinable, and
yet many adverbs have retained dormant[15] case endings (e.g., genitive: ποῦ,
ἑξῆς; dative: ἐκεῖ, πρωΐ; and accusative: σήμερον, λίαν). We will treat adverbs
as a discrete subcategory of particles because, like adjectives, at least adverbs
of manner and extent can have degree and be compared (cf. "quickly, more
quickly, most quickly," or "well, better, best" in English). Also the only hard-
and-fast distinction between an adverb and an adverbial preposition is that

---

14. William Watson Goodwin, *Greek Grammar*, rev. Charles Burton Gulick (Boston: Ginn,
1930), 90.

15. That is, these case endings are present but nonfunctional.

"the preposition . . . is only an adverb specialized to define a case usage."[16] Moreover, some prepositions are related to adverbs ending in -ω, such as ἐκ and ἔξω, εἰς and ἔσω, ἀνά and ἄνω, and κατά and κάτω.

Frequently, adverbs of manner end in -ως (most adjectives can be made adverbs by replacing their genitive plural case ending with -ως), and adverbs of location/direction end in -θεν (e.g., ἄνωθεν and μακρόθεν). Quite a few adverbs of time end in -οτε. By itself, ὅτε may be considered a particle, a conjunction, or an adverb of time, but τότε and πότε, for example, are usually classified as adverbs. Numerical adverbs, with the exception of ἅπαξ, end in -ις (e.g., πολλάκις and ἑπτάκις). Because they introduce indications of time, manner, location, direction, extent, and frequency, adverbs provide essential information that the careful interpreter must not minimize.

Function of Adverbs

3.15. Adverbs in the NT demonstrate a diversity of functions.

1. *Modifying a* verb

πλὴν **καλῶς** *ἐποιήσατε* συγκοι-νωνήσαντές μου τῇ θλίψει. (Phil. 4:14)	Nevertheless, you *did* **well** sharing in my affliction.

2. *Modifying an* adjective

ἰδόντες δὲ τὸν ἀστέρα ἐχάρησαν χαρὰν μεγάλην **σφόδρα**. (Matt. 2:10)	And having seen the star, they rejoiced with **extremely** *great* joy.

3. *Modifying another* adverb

οἱ δὲ καθιστάνοντες τὸν Παῦλον ἤγαγον ἕως Ἀθηνῶν, καὶ λαβόντες ἐντολὴν πρὸς τὸν Σιλᾶν καὶ τὸν Τιμόθεον ἵνα **ὡς τάχιστα** ἔλθωσιν πρὸς αὐτὸν ἐξῄεσαν. (Acts 17:15)	And those escorting Paul brought him as far as Athens and left, having taken a command for Silas and Timothy to come to him **as** *quickly as possible*.

---

16. Peter Giles, *A Short Manual of Comparative Philology for Classical Students* (London: Macmillan, 1895), 299.

4. *Modifying a* substantive

> τὸ δὲ Ἁγὰρ Σινᾶ ὄρος ἐστὶν ἐν
> τῇ Ἀραβίᾳ· συστοιχεῖ δὲ τῇ **νῦν**
> Ἰερουσαλήμ, δουλεύει γὰρ μετὰ
> τῶν τέκνων αὐτῆς. (Gal. 4:25)

> Now Hagar is Mount Sinai in
> Arabia, and she corresponds to
> *the* **current** *Jerusalem*, for she is
> in slavery with her children.

5. *Functioning as a substantive*

> **τὰ ἄνω** φρονεῖτε, μὴ τὰ ἐπὶ τῆς
> γῆς. (Col. 3:2)

> Think about **the things above,**
> not the things on earth.

The article functions as a "nominalizer," indicating that the adverb
acts as a noun (nominal).

Categories of Adverbs

3.16. The following summarizes the main semantic categories for adverbs.

1. *Time*

> **τότε** οἱ ἐν τῇ Ἰουδαίᾳ
> φευγέτωσαν εἰς τὰ ὄρη
> (Matt. 24:16)

> **Then** those in Judea must flee
> to the mountains.

2. *Manner*

> ἰδόντες τὴν Μαριὰμ ὅτι **ταχέως**
> ἀνέστη καὶ ἐξῆλθεν
> (John 11:31)

> Having seen Mary rise **quickly**
> and leave.

3. *Location*

> ὁ δὲ εἶπεν· Φέρετέ μοι **ὧδε**
> αὐτούς. (Matt. 14:18)

> And he said, "Carry them **here**
> to me."

4. *Direction*

> Ὁ **ἄνωθεν** ἐρχόμενος **ἐπάνω**
> πάντων ἐστίν· (John 3:31)

> The one coming **from above** is
> **above** all.

5. *Extent*

οἱ δὲ **περισσῶς** ἐξεπλήσσοντο
λέγοντες πρὸς ἑαυτούς· Καὶ τίς
δύναται σωθῆναι; (Mark 10:26)

They were **exceedingly** amazed,
saying to each other, "Then
who is able to be saved?"

6. *Frequency*

νηστεύω **δὶς** τοῦ σαββάτου,
ἀποδεκατῶ πάντα ὅσα κτῶμαι.
(Luke 18:12)

I fast **twice** a week; I tithe on
all that I acquire.

Comparison of Adverbs

3.17. Like adjectives, adverbs can indicate degrees of comparison.

Positive (cf. English forms ending in "-ly")	Comparative ("-er"; "more") Neuter accusative singular of the comparative adjective	Superlative ("-est"; "most") Neuter accusative plural of the superlative adjective
ταχέως (quickly)	τάχιον	τάχιστα
ὀλίγως (barely)	ἔλασσον	ἐλάχιστα
πολύ (greatly)	πλεῖον	πλεῖστα
μάλα (much)	μᾶλλον	μάλιστα
ἡδέως (gladly)	ἥδιον	ἥδιστα

1. *Positive degree*

Σπούδασον ἐλθεῖν πρός με
ταχέως· (2 Tim. 4:9)

Hurry to come to me **quickly**.

2. *Comparative degree.* The genitive of comparison may be used with adverbs.

ἔτρεχον δὲ οἱ δύο ὁμοῦ· καὶ ὁ
ἄλλος μαθητὴς προέδραμεν **τάχιον**
τοῦ Πέτρου καὶ ἦλθεν πρῶτος εἰς
τὸ μνημεῖον. (John 20:4)

And they were both running
together, and the other disciple
ran **faster than Peter** and arrived first at the tomb.

This is a true comparative, but τάχιον can also be elative.[17]

17. Zerwick (49–50) cites John 13:27 as an example.

3. *Superlative degree.* Like superlative adjectives, superlative adverbs are rare in Koine Greek.

οἱ δὲ καθιστάνοντες τὸν Παῦλον ἤγαγον ἕως Ἀθηνῶν, καὶ λαβόντες ἐντολὴν πρὸς τὸν Σιλᾶν καὶ τὸν Τιμόθεον ἵνα ὡς **τάχιστα** ἔλθωσιν πρὸς αὐτὸν ἐξῄεσαν. (Acts 17:15)	And those escorting Paul brought him as far as Athens and left, having taken a command for Silas and Timothy to come to him as **quickly as possible** [i.e., the quickest way].

For Practice

3.18. Analyze the adverbs (in bold) in the following text.

[8]**Πρῶτον** μὲν εὐχαριστῶ τῷ θεῷ μου διὰ Ἰησοῦ Χριστοῦ περὶ πάντων ὑμῶν, ὅτι ἡ πίστις ὑμῶν καταγγέλλεται ἐν ὅλῳ τῷ κόσμῳ. [9]μάρτυς γάρ μού ἐστιν ὁ θεός, ᾧ λατρεύω ἐν τῷ πνεύματί μου ἐν τῷ εὐαγγελίῳ τοῦ υἱοῦ αὐτοῦ, ὡς **ἀδιαλείπτως** μνείαν ὑμῶν ποιοῦμαι [10]**πάντοτε** ἐπὶ τῶν προσευχῶν μου, δεόμενος εἴ **πως ἤδη ποτὲ** εὐοδωθήσομαι ἐν τῷ θελήματι τοῦ θεοῦ ἐλθεῖν πρὸς ὑμᾶς. [11]ἐπιποθῶ γὰρ ἰδεῖν ὑμᾶς, ἵνα τι μεταδῶ χάρισμα ὑμῖν πνευματικὸν εἰς τὸ στηριχθῆναι ὑμᾶς, [12]τοῦτο δέ ἐστιν συμπαρακληθῆναι ἐν ὑμῖν διὰ τῆς ἐν ἀλλήλοις πίστεως ὑμῶν τε καὶ ἐμοῦ. [13]**οὐ** θέλω δὲ ὑμᾶς ἀγνοεῖν, ἀδελφοί, ὅτι **πολλάκις** προεθέμην ἐλθεῖν πρὸς ὑμᾶς, καὶ ἐκωλύθην ἄχρι τοῦ **δεῦρο**, ἵνα τινὰ καρπὸν σχῶ καὶ ἐν ὑμῖν **καθὼς** καὶ ἐν τοῖς λοιποῖς ἔθνεσιν. [14]Ἕλλησίν τε καὶ βαρβάροις, σοφοῖς τε καὶ ἀνοήτοις ὀφειλέτης εἰμί· [15]**οὕτως** τὸ κατ' ἐμὲ πρόθυμον καὶ ὑμῖν τοῖς ἐν Ῥώμῃ εὐαγγελίσασθαι. (Rom. 1:8–15)

4

THE ARTICLE (ὁ, ἡ, τό)

4.1. The Greek article occurs more frequently than any other word in the NT (19,867×), more than twice as many times as the next in line, καί (9,018×). Not only is the article numerous, it is also important, supremely so because it is used in a variety of ways that the English definite article is not. Technically, the term *definite article* is inaccurate in the case of Koine Greek. Greek has only one article, so there is no simple opposition between definite ("the") and indefinite ("a, an") articles as there is in English.[1] In Koine Greek both εἷς, μία, ἕν (one) and τίς, τί (someone/something) are sometimes employed to indicate that someone or something is indefinite.[2] Similarly, the article ὁ, ἡ, τό may—but does not have to—indicate definiteness. In other words, the presence of the article in Greek does not require that it be translated as the definite article in English, nor does the absence of the article in Greek require that an indefinite article be added to an English translation. The Greek article is not primarily used to make definite what would otherwise be indefinite. Probably because the article traces its origin to the demonstrative pronoun, its essential function is deictic; that is, *it points*.[3]

1. Those grammars that designate ὁ, ἡ, τό as "the definite article" are misleading.
2. In Modern Greek the number "one" is used in the singular, and the word for "some" (μερικοί, -ές, -ά) is used in the plural.
3. Robertson (755) claims that the article isn't deictic because it "does not point out the object as far and near" but later says that it "aids in pointing out like an index finger. It is a pointer" (756).

The article points in various ways,
many of which can be translated into English:

the, a, this, these, that, those, who, which, whose, my, our, your, his, her, their,   Substantive

As a pointer, the article precedes its head term and must agree with it in gender, number, and case. Occasionally the article will take the place of its referent (just as a pronoun would), but it can still be said to point to that referent (e.g., καὶ ἐπέθηκεν αὐτῇ τὰς χεῖρας, "and he laid **his** hands" [Luke 13:13]). An important distinctive of the Greek article is its ability to point to parts of speech other than nouns in such a way that it nominalizes, or assigns "nominal status" to, them.[4] Thus articles may nominalize entire phrases and clauses as well as individual adjectives, adverbs, and participles.

4.2. Carson and Porter have more than adequately demonstrated that the presence and absence of the Greek article are not easily codified.[5] Indeed, Carson is correct when he concludes, "I suspect that some uses are determined more by the 'feel' of the speaker or writer of the language than by unambiguous principles."[6] However much we might like it to be, it is not always true that the presence of the article indicates identity and its absence indicates quality. For example, as Levinsohn observes, when an anarthrous noun that "has unique referential identity" is used to signal discontinuity (point of departure) in a discourse, it indicates special prominence.[7] As Carson and Porter have shown, there is significant overlap between arthrous and anarthrous categories of usage.[8] Some articular nouns represent qualitative categories (e.g., Αἱ ἀλώπεκες φωλεοὺς ἔχουσιν καὶ τὰ πετεινὰ τοῦ οὐρανοῦ κατασκηνώσεις, "**foxes** have dens and **birds** of the sky, nests" [Matt. 8:20]), and some anarthrous nouns refer to particular, individual entities (e.g., καὶ πύλαι ᾅδου οὐ κατισχύσουσιν αὐτῆς, "and **the gates** of Hades will not overpower it" [Matt. 16:18]). Porter (104) states, "Matters of particularity and

---

4. Haiim B. Rosén, *Early Greek Grammar and Thought in Heraclitus* (Jerusalem: Israel Academy of Sciences and Humanities, 1988), 45, quoted in Wallace 209.

5. D. A. Carson, *Exegetical Fallacies*, 2nd ed. (Grand Rapids: Baker, 1996), 79; Porter 104. Generic articles and articles with abstract nouns challenge the widely held notion that "a noun *cannot* be *in*definite when it has the article" (Wallace 243, emphasis original).

6. Carson, *Exegetical Fallacies*, 79.

7. Stephen H. Levinsohn, *Discourse Features of New Testament Greek: A Coursebook*, 2nd ed. (Dallas: Summer Institute of Linguistics, 2000), 165.

8. See Porter 103–4; Carson, *Exegetical Fallacies*, 79–80.

individuality are established not on the basis of whether the article is present, but on the basis of the wider context." For example, articles are often absent before definite nouns in prepositional phrases (e.g., Ἐν ἀρχῇ ἦν ὁ λόγος, "in **the beginning** was the Word" [John 1:1]) and in some genitive constructions (e.g., ἀπ᾽ ἀρχῆς **κόσμου** ἕως τοῦ νῦν, "from the beginning of **the world** until now" [Matt. 24:21]) or when a participant or object is introduced for the first time in narrative (e.g., εἶδον . . . **βιβλίον**, "I saw . . . a **scroll**" [Rev. 5:1], which becomes τὸ βιβλίον, "the scroll," in 5:2).

We offer Robertson's dictum as both hortatory and cautionary: "The vital thing is to see the matter from the Greek point of view and find the reason for the use of the article" (756–57). The stark reality is that we must try to find reasons for the articles we encounter without being able to see NT matters from the first-century Greek point of view. Fortunately, there are enough interesting and idiosyncratic articular uses to keep students occupied for a long time. As you consider articles, you will probably notice their absence in places where you might include them in English translation, but this book will not undertake to explain those absences. Not only does the presence of the article provide more than sufficient challenge for us who are far removed temporally and linguistically from the NT documents; we are also not convinced that its absence is a necessary grammatical category. The presence or absence is notoriously elusive of concrete explanation. "It is sometimes claimed that an important theological issue is involved in the use or non-use of the article . . . ; but each instance needs to be discussed on its own merits, and in some instances it is hard to avoid the impression that usage is arbitrary" (Moule 111–12).

Particular

4.3. Although we maintain that the practice is misleading, discussion of ὁ, ἡ, τό as the "definite article" is not without some reason. The Greek article was indeed employed to distinguish one or more particular persons, places, or things from others. It was also variously used to point forward or back to particular items in discourse. Consequently, the Greek article can be said to fill the grammatical slot of an *identifier*. The basic function of the article is to point out; how it does so is capable of more than one interpretation or English translation.

With Nouns

4.4. The following examples serve to illustrate the wide range of ways in which the article can point at particular nouns, including proper nouns and abstract nouns.

ἀποκριθεὶς δὲ ὁ Ἰησοῦς εἶπεν αὐτοῖς· (Matt. 21:21)	And answering, *Jesus* said to them.

> The article points to the person identified by the name "Jesus," very likely to indicate the shift of subject back to Jesus from the disciples (v. 20). This takes some getting used to because we do not use definite articles with personal names in English (though we do, for example, with rivers [the Mississippi, the Nile, etc.]) and because Koine Greek may seem inconsistent in its use of articles with proper nouns. In other words, we are dealing with an idiom we don't quite "get" and therefore can't always explain adequately (Wallace 246). Sometimes, as above, articles with proper nouns appear to bring someone or some place back into a story line (functioning anaphorically, i.e., pointing back), sometimes they seem to lend emphasis to a name or designate a title, and sometimes they may serve solely to identify the case of an indeclinable name (Porter 107). But none of these provide for any hard-and-fast rules. In the end we will agree with Robertson (759) that "it seems needless to make extended observations about the presence or absence of the Greek article with names of countries, cities, rivers, persons."

Καὶ περιῆγεν *τὰς κώμας* κύκλῳ διδάσκων. (Mark 6:6)	And he was going around *the villages* on a circuit teaching.
πλὴν ὁ υἱὸς τοῦ ἀνθρώπου ἐλθὼν ἆρα εὑρήσει *τὴν πίστιν* ἐπὶ τῆς γῆς; (Luke 18:8)	However, the Son of Man having come, will he find *faith* upon the earth?

> "Faith" is an abstract noun, and abstract nouns (e.g., ἀγάπη, ἀλήθεια, εἰρήνη, χάρις) are often articular in Greek, perhaps to particularize them (Porter 107). We could certainly make the case that a particular type of faith evidenced by the widow in the preceding parable (vv. 2–5) is in view here.

Ἴδε ὁ ἀμνὸς τοῦ θεοῦ. (John 1:36)	Behold, *the Lamb* of God.

> The first article points to a definite lamb, and the second points to a definite God, but only the former is translated into English. John had particular, individual beings in mind; thus the English definite article is required to translate ὁ ἀμνός, and an uppercase G is required in the translation of

τοῦ θεοῦ. This further demonstrates that the English article functions differently from the Greek article; here the Greek articles simply point at ἀμνός and θεοῦ to distinguish them from other lambs and gods.[9]

εἰς τὸ μὴ ταχέως σαλευθῆναι ὑμᾶς ἀπὸ *τοῦ* νοὸς μηδὲ θροεῖσθαι (2 Thess. 2:2)	So that you not be quickly shaken from *your* [rather than "the"] *composure* nor disturbed.
ὁ γὰρ θέλων ζωὴν ἀγαπᾶν καὶ ἰδεῖν ἡμέρας ἀγαθὰς παυσάτω *τὴν* γλῶσσαν ἀπὸ κακοῦ καὶ χείλη τοῦ μὴ λαλῆσαι δόλον (1 Pet. 3:10)	For the one wishing to love life and to see good days must keep *his/her tongue* from evil and his/her lips from speaking deceit.

With Adjectives

4.5. The article may be used as a nominalizer with an adjective to mark it as substantival or to distinguish it as being in either the predicate or attributive position (see chap. 3).

τὸν ἄρτον ἡμῶν *τὸν ἐπιούσιον* δὸς ἡμῖν σήμερον· (Matt. 6:11)	Our *daily* bread give to us today.

The first article is present probably because of the possessive pronoun ἡμῶν.[10] The second article marks ἐπιούσιον as an attributive adjective.

οἵτινες ἐνδείκνυνται *τὸ* ἔργον τοῦ νόμου γραπτὸν ἐν ταῖς καρδίαις αὐτῶν (Rom. 2:15)	Who show *the* work of the law [is] *written* on their hearts.

The article's position before the noun and that it is not repeated before the adjective make the latter predicative.

---

9. Wallace labels the article before ἀμνός in ὁ ἀμνὸς τοῦ θεοῦ (at least in John 1:29) as monadic (i.e., unique) because only Jesus is designated this way in the NT. Taken without τοῦ θεοῦ, it could also fit his category of lamb par excellence: the best of all lambs (Wallace 222–24). We would be more inclined to label both *nouns*, not the articles, as either monadic (there is only one true God and one Lamb of God) or par excellence (Jesus is the best of all possible lambs, and God is the best of all possible gods). Both categories tell us more about the mind of the interpreter than what can be known about the NT author's use of the article.

10. Nouns modified by possessive pronouns are almost always articular in the NT. This idiom is carried over from Attic Greek. William Watson Goodwin, *Greek Grammar*, rev. Charles Burton Gulick (Boston: Ginn, 1930), 206.

Παῦλος καὶ Τιμόθεος δοῦλοι Χριστοῦ Ἰησοῦ πᾶσιν *τοῖς ἁγίοις* ἐν Χριστῷ Ἰησοῦ τοῖς οὖσιν ἐν Φιλίπποις σὺν ἐπισκόποις καὶ διακόνοις· (Phil. 1:1)	Paul and Timothy, servants of Christ Jesus, to all *the saints / holy ones* in Christ Jesus who are in Philippi with overseers and deacons.

Because it is before the adjective ἁγίοις, the article both particularizes and nominalizes it.

With Other Parts of Speech

4.6. As with adjectives, articles can nominalize other parts of speech (participles, adverbs, and prepositional phrases). So too, they can "adjectivize" certain parts of speech.

1. *Nominalizing.* In the following examples the articles nominalize various parts of speech or turn them into noun equivalents or nominals.

ὁ *ἐπὶ τοῦ δώματος* μὴ καταβάτω ἆραι *τὰ ἐκ τῆς οἰκίας* αὐτοῦ (Matt. 24:17)	*The one on the roof* must not go down to take *things from his/her house.* (*prepositional phrases*)
καὶ ἀφεὶς αὐτοὺς πάλιν ἐμβὰς ἀπῆλθεν εἰς *τὸ πέραν.* (Mark 8:13)	And having left them and having embarked again, he went away to *the other side.* (πέραν *is an adverb that normally means "beyond"*)
ἀπὸ *τοῦ νῦν* δὲ ἔσται ὁ υἱὸς τοῦ ἀνθρώπου καθήμενος ἐκ δεξιῶν τῆς δυνάμεως τοῦ θεοῦ. (Luke 22:69)	And from *now* [on] the Son of Man will be seated at the right hand of the power of God. (*adverb*)
τὸ γὰρ *τί προσευξώμεθα καθὸ δεῖ* οὐκ οἴδαμεν (Rom. 8:26)	For we do not know *what to pray* as we ought.

The article marks the entire clause τί προσευξώμεθα καθὸ δεῖ as the direct object of οἴδαμεν.

ὁ γὰρ εἰπών Μὴ μοιχεύσῃς εἶπεν
καί Μὴ φονεύσῃς· (James 2:11)

For *the one who said*, "Do not commit adultery," also said, "Do not murder." (*participle*)

2. *Adjectivizing.* In the following examples the articles either turn various parts of speech into adjectival modifiers or clarify what they modify (in the case of participles).

οἱ δὲ ὄχλοι *οἱ προάγοντες* αὐτὸν
καί *οἱ ἀκολουθοῦντες* ἔκραζον
λέγοντες· (Matt. 21:9)

And the crowds *that* went before him and *that* followed [or *those who followed*] were crying out, saying.

> Since participles are technically verbal adjectives, the boldface Greek articles do not make προάγοντες and ἀκολουθοῦντες adjectival, but they certainly indicate that both participles are in agreement with ὄχλοι, are functioning adjectivally, and should be considered separately from the adverbial λέγοντες. The first participle is an attributive modifier of ὄχλοι; the second could be either another modifier of ὄχλοι (referring to the crowds behind as well as in front of Jesus) or a separate substantive (referring separately to those following Jesus).

εἴ πως καταντήσω εἰς τὴν
ἐξανάστασιν *τὴν ἐκ νεκρῶν.*
(Phil. 3:11)

If somehow I may attain the resurrection *from the dead.*

> The article τήν marks the prepositional phrase ἐκ νεκρῶν as adjectival, modifying τὴν ἐξανάστασιν. Similarly employed articles could be *translated* as relative pronouns (e.g., the resurrection **that** is from the dead), but their function remains to demonstrate that a prepositional phrase is adjectival.

δικαιούμενοι δωρεὰν τῇ αὐτοῦ
χάριτι διὰ τῆς ἀπολυτρώσεως *τῆς*
ἐν Χριστῷ Ἰησοῦ· (Rom. 3:24)

Being justified as a gift by his grace through the redemption *that is in Christ Jesus.* (*adjective modifier*)

Τοῖς πλουσίοις ἐν *τῷ νῦν* αἰῶνι
παράγγελλε μὴ ὑψηλοφρονεῖν
(1 Tim. 6:17)

Instruct the rich in *the present* age not to be arrogant. (*the articular adverb functions like an adjective*)

δι᾽ ὧν ὁ τότε κόσμος ὕδατι
κατακλυσθεὶς ἀπώλετο·
(2 Pet. 3:6)

Through which **the** *then*
world, having been flooded
with water, perished. (*with an
adverb*)

Anaphoric Use

4.7. This can be seen as a specialized function of the use of the article with
nouns, which was discussed above. Some grammars call this the article of
previous reference. A common pattern is for the introduction of an item to
be anarthrous and then for subsequent references to the same item to have
the anaphoric article, pointing back to its first (anarthrous) mention.

καὶ συνήχθησαν πρὸς αὐτὸν ὄχλοι
πολλοί, ὥστε αὐτὸν εἰς πλοῖον
ἐμβάντα καθῆσθαι, καὶ πᾶς ὁ ὄχλος
ἐπὶ τὸν αἰγιαλὸν εἱστήκει.
(Matt. 13:2)

And large *crowds* gathered to
him so that he, having gone into
a boat, sat and **the**/**that** whole
crowd stood on the shore.

> Despite the shift from plural to singular, the same crowd of people seems
> to be in view.

ὃ ἐθεασάμεθα καὶ αἱ χεῖρες ἡμῶν
ἐψηλάφησαν, περὶ τοῦ λόγου
τῆς ζωῆς—καὶ ἡ ζωὴ ἐφανερώθη
(1 John 1:1–2)

What we saw and our hands
touched concerning the word
of *life*—and **this**/**that** *life* was
manifested.

> The article before the second occurrence of ζωή is anaphoric, referring
> back to the particular life just mentioned. Anaphoric articles are often
> used after an anarthrous noun has been introduced (the introduction of
> τῆς ζωῆς is arthrous likely because it modifies the arthrous τοῦ λόγου;
> see §4.12, on Apollonius's canon, below).

Τί ὄφελος, ἀδελφοί μου, ἐὰν
πίστιν λέγῃ τις ἔχειν ἔργα δὲ μὴ
ἔχῃ; μὴ δύναται ἡ πίστις σῶσαι
αὐτόν; (James 2:14)

What is the profit, my brothers
and sisters, if someone claims to
have *faith* but has no deeds? Is
that *faith* able to save him/her?

> The article is anaphoric, referring back to the first mention of faith (with-
> out the article).

| ἰδοὺ θρόνος ἔκειτο ἐν τῷ οὐρανῷ, καὶ ἐπὶ *τὸν* θρόνον καθήμενος (Rev. 4:2) | Look, a *throne* was placed in heaven, and there was one seated upon *the/that* *throne*. |

The introduction of the throne is anarthrous (even though it is a specific throne that John sees). All the remaining mentions of the throne in Rev. 4:2–11 contain anaphoric articles that point back to its first mention (vv. 2, 3, 4, 5, 6, 9, 10) in the pericope.

Categorical/Generic Use

4.8. Articles point out categories or classes. Where the particular article distinguishes one or more individual entities from others, the categorical article designates one or more entities as representative (when the substantive is singular) or definitive (when the substantive is plural) of an entire class/category. We can sometimes translate singular, categorical articles with the indefinite "a"/"an" in English.

| λέγει γὰρ ἡ γραφή· Βοῦν ἀλοῶντα οὐ φιμώσεις, καί· Ἄξιος ὁ ἐργάτης τοῦ μισθοῦ αὐτοῦ. (1 Tim. 5:18) | For Scripture says, "You shall not muzzle an ox treading grain," and "*A/the worker* is worthy of his/her wage." |

Although most English translations render the boldface article as "the," the translation "a" works just as well and avoids giving the impression that a particular worker is in view. "A worker" here represents the class of all working people.

| ἐν γὰρ τῷ Μωϋσέως νόμῳ γέγραπται· Οὐ κημώσεις βοῦν ἀλοῶντα. μὴ *τῶν* βοῶν μέλει τῷ θεῷ, (1 Cor. 9:9) | For in the law of Moses is written, "You shall not muzzle an ox treading grain." God isn't concerned about *oxen*, is he? |

"Oxen" defines a class.

Other Uses

4.9. Articles can stand alone as substantives, indicate case for indeclinable or partially declinable words (proper nouns, infinitives, and adverbs), bracket units of thought, distinguish a subject from a predicate nominative (see chap.

1, on case), and introduce genitives and indirect speech or quotations. Some of the examples below also fit the categories above; that is, the article often serves more than one purpose.

οἱ δὲ λέγουσιν αὐτῷ· Οὐκ ἔχομεν ὧδε εἰ μὴ πέντε ἄρτους καὶ δύο ἰχθύας. (Matt. 14:17)

And *they* said to him, "We have here only five loaves and two fish."

> The article, standing alone, is the subject of the finite verb λέγουσιν. In narrative, οἱ δέ often acts as a "switch reference" device to indicate a shift to a new subject (see chap. 13, on discourse considerations).

ὥσπερ γὰρ ἡ ἀστραπὴ ἀστράπτουσα ἐκ *τῆς* ὑπὸ τὸν οὐρανὸν *εἰς τὴν* ὑπ' οὐρανὸν λάμπει (Luke 17:24)

For as lightning flashing *from one part* of the sky shines *into another part* of the sky.

> Both articles are simple objects of prepositions (and in turn are modified by prepositional phrases).

Τῇ ἐπαύριον πάλιν εἱστήκει ὁ Ἰωάννης καὶ ἐκ τῶν μαθητῶν αὐτοῦ δύο (John 1:35)

On the next day again, John stood and two of his disciples.

> This time the article makes the indeclinable adverb ἐπαύριον dative as well as nominalizing it.

καὶ ἐμβλέψας *τῷ* Ἰησοῦ περιπατοῦντι λέγει· Ἴδε ὁ ἀμνὸς τοῦ θεοῦ. (John 1:36)

And having seen *Jesus* walking, he said, "Look, the Lamb of God."

> Whatever else it may be doing, the article indicates that the partially declinable proper noun Ἰησοῦ is dative.

καὶ *τὰ* νῦν λέγω ὑμῖν (Acts 5:38)

And concerning *present things* I tell you.

> Along with nominalizing and assigning a case to the adverb νῦν, the article makes it plural.

καὶ κρινεῖ ἡ ἐκ φύσεως ἀκροβυστία
τὸν νόμον τελοῦσα σὲ **τὸν** διὰ
γράμματος καὶ περιτομῆς *παρα-*
βάτην νόμου. (Rom. 2:27)

And *the* naturally *uncircumcised*
keeping the law will judge you,
who by letter and circumcision,
[are] a *transgressor* of the law.

In both uses the boldface article and the italic head noun "bracket" what
is between them, marking off a unit of thought.

τὸ γὰρ· Οὐ μοιχεύσεις, Οὐ
φονεύσεις, Οὐ κλέψεις, Οὐκ
ἐπιθυμήσεις (Rom. 13:9)

For "Do not commit adultery, do
not murder, do not steal, do not
covet."

or For *the* commandments "Do
not . . ."

The article probably introduces a quotation (τό functions like an opening
double quotation mark) and should not be translated, but it could be
shorthand for the second table of the law.[11]

τίς γὰρ οἶδεν ἀνθρώπων *τὰ* τοῦ
ἀνθρώπου εἰ μὴ τὸ πνεῦμα τοῦ
ἀνθρώπου *τὸ* ἐν αὐτῷ; (1 Cor. 2:11)

For who among persons knows *the*
things/thoughts of *a person* if not
the spirit of the person *that* [is] *in*
him/her?

The neuter plural article is substantival, filling the slot of a head noun
modified by a genitive. The last article τό functions as an "adjectivizer,"
which turns the prepositional phrase into an attributive modifier of τὸ
πνεῦμα.

εἰ δὲ αἰσχρὸν γυναικὶ *τὸ κείρασθαι*
ἢ *ξυρᾶσθαι*, κατακαλυπτέσθω.
(1 Cor. 11:6)

But if for a woman *to cut off* [her
hair] or *to shave* is disgraceful,
she should cover up.

Despite the word order, the placement of the article shows that the
infinitives are the subject and αἰσχρὸν is a predicate adjective.

---

11. Max Zerwick and Mary Grosvenor, *A Grammatical Analysis of the Greek New Testament* (Rome: Biblical Institute Press, 1981), 489.

καὶ ταύτην τὴν φωνὴν ἡμεῖς
ἠκούσαμεν ἐξ οὐρανοῦ ἐνεχθεῖσαν
(2 Pet. 1:18)

And we heard *this voice* carried
from heaven.

The article in one of the predicate positions is used with both near and
far demonstrative modifiers (see chap. 2, on pronouns).

ἐγὼ τὸ Ἄλφα καὶ τὸ Ὦ, ὁ πρῶτος καὶ
ὁ ἔσχατος, ἡ ἀρχὴ καὶ τὸ τέλος.
(Rev. 22:13)

I am *the Alpha* and *the Omega*,
the First and *the Last*, *the Beginning* and *the End*.

These articles not only nominalize a series of letters and adjectives but
also turn them into titles.

Granville Sharp's Rule

4.10. Sharp's rule can be simplified to state that the use of an article *only before
the first* of two or more singular, personal substantives (A [art.] + S + καί +
S) in the same case and joined by καί indicates that "the latter always relates
to the same person that is expressed or described by the first."[12] The rule, one
of six regarding articular use for which Sharp is responsible, "is in fact quite
complex, too complex to analyze here."[13] Because it has been misunderstood
and misapplied, it is imperative to recognize that Sharp's rule is conclusive
*only with singular, personal, common (not proper) nouns and substantival
adjectives or participles*. In cases where all of the above restrictions do not
obtain, there will still be some conceptual link between the substantives, but
they may or may not refer to the same entity.[14]

12. Granville Sharp, *Remarks on the Uses of the Definite Article in the Greek Text of the
New Testament*, ed. William David McBrayer (1774; repr., Atlanta: Original Word, 1995), 8,
italics removed.

13. Carson, *Exegetical Fallacies*, 81. For a more thorough treatment of Sharp's rule, see
Wallace 270–90.

14. The rule does not imply that two or more articular, singular, personal, common nouns
(A + S + καί + A + S) joined by καί *must* refer to different people.

| ἦν καιροῖς ἰδίοις δείξει ὁ μακάριος καὶ μόνος δυνάστης, ὁ βασιλεὺς τῶν βασιλευόντων καὶ κύριος τῶν κυριευόντων (1 Tim. 6:15) | Which the blessed and only Ruler will show in his own time, [that is] *the King* of kings *and Lord* of lords. |

The rule is followed: the King and Lord are the same person and further define the blessed and only Ruler.

| καὶ ἐποίησεν ἡμᾶς βασιλείαν, ἱερεῖς τῷ θεῷ καὶ πατρὶ αὐτοῦ— αὐτῷ ἡ δόξα καὶ τὸ κράτος εἰς τοὺς αἰῶνας τῶν αἰώνων· ἀμήν. (Rev. 1:6) | And he made us a kingdom, priests to his *God and Father*—to him [be] the glory and power for ever [and ever]. Amen. |

The rule is followed: "God" and "his [Jesus'] Father" are the same person.

| ἔλεγον τοῖς μαθηταῖς αὐτοῦ· Ὅτι μετὰ *τῶν τελωνῶν καὶ ἁμαρτωλῶν* ἐσθίει; (Mark 2:16) | They [scribes and Pharisees] said to his disciples, "[Why] does he eat with *tax collectors and sinners?*" |

The rule does not apply here, because the nouns in the phrase "tax collectors and sinners" are plural, and yet there definitely is a link between them: the two distinct groups are treated as united (Wallace 278–79).

Colwell's Rule

4.11. This rule pertains to nominatives joined by the copula εἶναι. The rule states, "A definite predicate nominative has the article when it follows the verb, [but] it does not have the article when it precedes the verb."[15] The rule, to which Colwell identifies exceptions (definite, arthrous predicate nominatives follow the verb in 90 percent of instances, and definite, anarthrous predicate nominatives precede the verb in 87 percent),[16] *assumes* the definiteness of the nouns under its rubric.[17] That is, *it is not a rule about determining*

15. E. C. Colwell, "A Definite Rule for the Use of the Article in the Greek New Testament," *Journal of Biblical Literature* 52 (1933): 13.
16. Ibid., 17.
17. "It is obvious that the significance of these figures rests upon the accuracy with which definite predicate nouns without the article have been identified. There are bound to be mistakes in the list of definite predicate nouns without the article, but an attempt has been made to exclude all nouns as to whose definiteness there could be any doubt" (ibid., 17).

definiteness but an observation of a pattern: predicate nominatives that are already determined to be definite tend to lack the article when they precede the verb εἶναι. Based on this pattern, Colwell predicts definiteness in more-ambiguous contexts. The opening verse of John's Gospel contains one of the many passages where this rule suggests the translation of a predicate as a definite noun. The noun θεός in the clause καὶ θεὸς ἦν ὁ λόγος is definite, it is suggested, because it precedes the verb and is anarthrous. The clause should be translated, "And the Word was God." Yet, as Carson points out, Colwell's statistics are insufficient to predict definiteness.[18] The sample size from which Colwell extrapolates is small (367 predicate nouns); he does not examine all anarthrous predicate nominatives that precede the verb nor all arthrous predicate nominatives that follow the verb. It is worth reiterating here that words without articles are not necessarily indefinite simply because they lack articles, nor are words definite simply because they have the article; word order, structure, or individual style may require articles or allow for their absence.

In the case of John 1:1, the article distinguishes the subject from the predicate nominative (because when two common nouns are joined by εἶναι and only one has the article, the one with the article is the subject regardless of word order; see chap. 1, on cases), and its absence is not a reliable predictor of indefiniteness. Wallace (269), for example, thinks θεός, rather than being definite, is probably qualitative (the focus is on the Word's divine *essence*), "for the largest proportion of pre-verbal anarthrous predicate nominatives fall into this category." This observation rests on an assumption similar to Colwell's, however; Wallace determines what constitutes a qualitative noun. And while we agree with his theology, that the Word "shared the *essence* of the Father, though they differed in person" (Wallace 269), we are not at all convinced that John's grammar was intended to reflect such fine trinitarian nuances. It is one thing to say that John 1:1 avoids various forms of modalism but quite another to say that it does so by John's conscious, grammatical choice. It seems more likely that John left θεός anarthrous to confirm that ὁ λόγος is the subject all three times that it appears in the verse (Ἐν ἀρχῇ ἦν ὁ λόγος, καὶ ὁ λόγος ἦν πρὸς τὸν θεόν, καὶ θεὸς ἦν ὁ λόγος) without disturbing the pattern of ὁ λόγος ending the first clause, beginning the second, and ending the third, and a form of θεός ending the second clause and beginning the third.

18. Carson, *Exegetical Fallacies*, 84.

Ἐν ἀρχῇ ἦν ὁ λόγος,

καὶ ὁ λόγος ἦν πρὸς τὸν θεόν,

καὶ θεὸς ἦν ὁ λόγος.

Apollonius's Canon and Corollary

4.12. As we mentioned above, in genitive constructions there is a tendency for an anarthrous head (governing) noun to be modified by an anarthrous genitive (governed) noun. The full rule is that when a head noun governs a genitive noun, both will either have the article or lack it (A + noun + A + noun$_{gen}$, or noun + noun$_{gen}$). The rule holds about 80 percent of the time in the NT, and most of its exceptions can be explained. Hull, who studied 461 exceptions, found that all but 32 could be explained by one or more of seven "conditions."[19] Five of these conditions have been neatly subsumed under two broader points by Young (67, italics added):

(1) The head noun may be anarthrous while the genitive qualifier is articular, especially if the head noun is the *object of a preposition*, a *predicate nominative*, or a *vocative*; (2) either may be anarthrous if it is a *proper name* (including κύριος) even though the other may be articular.

The final two conditions involve anarthrous head nouns that are modified by either anarthrous adjectives or genitives of apposition.[20]

ἤδη δὲ ἡ ἀξίνη πρὸς *τὴν* ῥίζαν *τῶν* δένδρων κεῖται· (Matt. 3:10)	And already the ax is laid to *the root of the trees*. (*preposition + A + noun + A noun$_{gen}$*)
Εἴτε οὖν ἐσθίετε εἴτε πίνετε εἴτε τι ποιεῖτε, πάντα εἰς δόξαν θεοῦ ποιεῖτε. (1 Cor. 10:31)	Therefore, whether you eat, whether you drink, whether you do anything, do all things to *the glory of God*. (*preposition + noun + noun$_{gen}$*)

19. Sanford D. Hull, "Exceptions to Apollonius' Canon in the New Testament: A Grammatical Study," *Trinity Journal*, n.s., 7 (1986): 5.
20. Ibid., 7–8.

καὶ ἔχω **τὰς** κλεῖς **τοῦ** θανάτου καὶ
τοῦ ᾅδου. (Rev. 1:18)

And I have *the keys of death* and *of Hades.* (*A + noun + A + noun*$_{gen}$ *+ καί + noun*$_{gen}$)

καὶ ἀνέβη καπνὸς ἐκ τοῦ φρέατος
ὡς καπνὸς καμίνου μεγάλης
(Rev. 9:2)

And smoke rose from the pit like *the smoke of a* great *furnace.* (*noun + noun*$_{gen}$)

4.13. A corollary to Apollonius's rule has been proposed by David Hedges, who observed of Paul's Greek that when both the nouns in a genitive construction are anarthrous, both will be definite, indefinite, or qualitative about 75 percent of the time.[21] Wallace (250) observes that Hedges's work with the Pauline corpus comports with that of scholars looking at other NT books. The corollary, like the canon, is merely an observation of a pattern. The former is incapable of predicting definiteness or other qualities, and the latter is incapable of predicting the presence or absence of the article. Therefore, neither canon nor corollary is of weighty exegetical significance.

For Practice

4.14. Analyze the articles (in bold) in the following texts.

¹Προσέχετε δὲ **τὴν** δικαιοσύνην ὑμῶν μὴ ποιεῖν ἔμπροσθεν **τῶν** ἀνθρώπων πρὸς **τὸ** θεαθῆναι αὐτοῖς· εἰ δὲ μή γε, μισθὸν οὐκ ἔχετε παρὰ **τῷ** πατρὶ ὑμῶν **τῷ** ἐν **τοῖς** οὐρανοῖς. ²Ὅταν οὖν ποιῇς ἐλεημοσύνην, μὴ σαλπίσῃς ἔμπροσθέν σου, ὥσπερ **οἱ** ὑποκριταὶ ποιοῦσιν ἐν **ταῖς** συναγωγαῖς καὶ ἐν **ταῖς** ῥύμαις, ὅπως δοξασθῶσιν ὑπὸ **τῶν** ἀνθρώπων· ἀμὴν λέγω ὑμῖν, ἀπέχουσιν **τὸν** μισθὸν αὐτῶν. ³σοῦ δὲ ποιοῦντος ἐλεημοσύνην μὴ γνώτω **ἡ** ἀριστερά σου τί ποιεῖ **ἡ** δεξιά σου, ⁴ὅπως ᾖ σου **ἡ** ἐλεημοσύνη ἐν **τῷ** κρυπτῷ· καὶ **ὁ** πατήρ σου **ὁ** βλέπων ἐν **τῷ** κρυπτῷ ἀποδώσει σοι. ⁵Καὶ ὅταν προσεύχη- σθε, οὐκ ἔσεσθε ὡς **οἱ** ὑποκριταί· ὅτι φιλοῦσιν ἐν **ταῖς** συναγωγαῖς καὶ ἐν **ταῖς** γωνίαις **τῶν** πλατειῶν ἑστῶτες προσεύχεσθαι, ὅπως φανῶσιν **τοῖς** ἀνθρώποις· ἀμὴν λέγω ὑμῖν, ἀπέχουσιν **τὸν** μισθὸν αὐτῶν. (Matt. 6:1–5)

¹⁴Ὅταν δὲ ἴδητε **τὸ** βδέλυγμα **τῆς** ἐρημώσεως ἑστηκότα ὅπου οὐ δεῖ, **ὁ** ἀναγινώσκων νοείτω, τότε **οἱ** ἐν **τῇ** Ἰουδαίᾳ φευγέτωσαν εἰς **τὰ** ὄρη,

---

21. David W. Hedges, "Apollonius' Canon and Anarthrous Constructions in Pauline Literature: An Hypothesis" (MDiv thesis, Grace Theological Seminary, 1983).

¹⁵ὁ ἐπὶ τοῦ δώματος μὴ καταβάτω μηδὲ εἰσελθάτω τι ἆραι ἐκ τῆς οἰκίας αὐτοῦ, ¹⁶καὶ ὁ εἰς τὸν ἀγρὸν μὴ ἐπιστρεψάτω εἰς τὰ ὀπίσω ἆραι τὸ ἱμάτιον αὐτοῦ. ¹⁷οὐαὶ δὲ ταῖς ἐν γαστρὶ ἐχούσαις καὶ ταῖς θηλαζούσαις ἐν ἐκείναις ταῖς ἡμέραις. ¹⁸προσεύχεσθε δὲ ἵνα μὴ γένηται χειμῶνος· ¹⁹ἔσονται γὰρ αἱ ἡμέραι ἐκεῖναι θλῖψις οἵα οὐ γέγονεν τοιαύτη ἀπ᾽ ἀρχῆς κτίσεως ἣν ἔκτισεν ὁ θεὸς ἕως τοῦ νῦν καὶ οὐ μὴ γένηται. (Mark 13:14–19)

²⁶ἐὰν οὖν ἡ ἀκροβυστία τὰ δικαιώματα τοῦ νόμου φυλάσσῃ, οὐχ ἡ ἀκροβυστία αὐτοῦ εἰς περιτομὴν λογισθήσεται; ²⁷καὶ κρινεῖ ἡ ἐκ φύσεως ἀκροβυστία τὸν νόμον τελοῦσα σὲ τὸν διὰ γράμματος καὶ περιτομῆς παραβάτην νόμου. ²⁸οὐ γὰρ ὁ ἐν τῷ φανερῷ Ἰουδαῖός ἐστιν, οὐδὲ ἡ ἐν τῷ φανερῷ ἐν σαρκὶ περιτομή· ²⁹ἀλλ᾽ ὁ ἐν τῷ κρυπτῷ Ἰουδαῖος, καὶ περιτομὴ καρδίας ἐν πνεύματι οὐ γράμματι, οὗ ὁ ἔπαινος οὐκ ἐξ ἀνθρώπων ἀλλ᾽ ἐκ τοῦ θεοῦ. (Rom. 2:26–29)

5

PREPOSITIONS

5.1. The Greek language boasts a rather full and fascinating system of prepositions. Probably having their origin as adverbs, prepositions are short, fixed words (they do not take inflected endings) that enable the Greek cases to express their force more clearly in relationship to other words in the sentence. According to Wallace (361), "Prepositions are used with cases either to clarify, strengthen, or alter the basic case usage." Or, in Porter's words, prepositions are to be seen as "in some way helping the case to manifest its meaning and to perform more precisely its various functions."[1] Most grammarians agree that prepositions were used more extensively by the time of the NT in comparison to earlier (Classical) Greek. This may have been due to changes taking place in the Greek case system that created a greater need for prepositions to help the cases express their meanings. Most prepositions occur with nouns in only one case (e.g., ἐκ with the genitive). Just six prepositions occur with nouns in two different cases, and only three with nouns in three cases (genitive, dative, and accusative),[2] as shown in the following tables.

1. Porter 140, italics removed.
2. In Classical Greek both περί and ὑπό also take the dative case. William Watson Goodwin, *Greek Grammar*, rev. Charles Burton Gulick (Boston: Ginn, 1930), 259, 261.

Prepositions Used with One Case

Preposition	Genitive	Dative	Accusative
ἀνά			X
ἀντί	X		
ἀπό	X		
εἰς			X
ἐκ	X		
ἐν		X	
πρό	X		
σύν		X	

Prepositions Used with Two Cases

Preposition	Genitive	Dative	Accusative
διά	X		X
κατά	X		X
μετά	X		X
περί	X		X
ὑπέρ	X		X
ὑπό	X		X

Prepositions Used with Three Cases

Preposition	Genitive	Dative	Accusative
ἐπί	X	X	X
παρά	X	X	X
πρός	X	X	X

5.2. The meaning of a preposition is influenced by the case of its object, that is, the nominal that it governs. Moreover, there is some inevitable overlap between the meanings of prepositions and the various independent case functions. In fact, some grammars (e.g., Brooks and Winbery) have treated prepositions along with the case system. However, "it is best to consider the prepositional phrase as a syntactical unit that must be analyzed as a whole"

(Young 85). The preposition followed by its object (and any modifiers it may have) together form what is known as a prepositional phrase (preposition + nominal + any modifiers constitute a prepositional phrase). In the sentence "Caleb placed the Ping-Pong paddle on the table," the prepositional phrase is "on the table," which consists of the preposition "on" and its object "the table." Prepositional phrases in Greek can modify verbs or nouns. In some instances they can function as substantives, as in the English sentence "*On the wooden table* is where he placed the book."

It is customary for Greek grammars to distinguish between "proper" and "improper" prepositions. "Proper" prepositions are those that can be prefixed to a verb (e.g., διά, εἰς; thus διέρχομαι and εἰσέρχομαι), whereas "improper" prepositions are not prefixed to verbs (e.g., ἔμπροσθεν, ἕνεκεν).[3] The so-called proper preposition is by far the most common type in the NT. For purposes of NT exegesis, however, we do not think that distinguishing between these two types of prepositions is helpful or necessary. There does not appear to be any difference in the way "proper" or "improper" prepositions function when part of a prepositional phrase.[4]

In first-year Greek you probably learned the basic meanings of prepositions, primarily through the various translation glosses associated with their uses with the cases. This grammar will expand your understanding of prepositions by introducing other important meanings.

Interpreting Greek Prepositions

5.3. Prepositions are important for the connections and relationships they convey. However, the interpreter must resist the temptation to "overinterpret" them. Prepositions are not carriers of theological meaning, though they are used in important theological contexts. Wallace (356) probably overstates their importance when, describing the connections that prepositions convey, he says, "The realities expressed by such connections are, at times, breathtaking." Murray Harris concludes that "prepositions in themselves do not carry theological meaning" but still claims that "the way they are used invests them with theological import."[5] But theology cannot merely be read off of prepositions; it must be derived from larger expressions of thought. Certainly, any important theological concept will be communicated and supported by

---

3. For lists of improper prepositions, see Murray J. Harris, *Prepositions and Theology in the Greek New Testament* (Grand Rapids: Zondervan, 2012), 241–42; Porter 179–80.

4. Harris, *Prepositions*, 27.

5. Ibid., 13.

sentences, paragraphs, and larger units of discourse rather than "nuanced" in prepositions. Prepositions at most allow for, support, or point to important theological teachings; they do not "prove" them or bear these theological concepts. This is not to suggest that prepositions are unimportant to our theology; it is just that we need to understand what role they play. The connections and relationships they convey are only part of the contextual information that contributes to our theological understanding.

The NT Greek grammars often report that there was a growing laxity in the use of prepositions in the Koine period.[6] In the Greek of the NT, prepositions are experiencing more overlap in meaning. The distinction between motion (traditionally expressed by the accusative case) and rest (traditionally expressed by the dative case) is sometimes neglected. The most common prepositions that show some semantic overlap are as follows:

ἐκ and ἀπό
εἰς and ἐν
εἰς and πρός
ὑπέρ and περί

Due to this overlap, the student should not always insist on precise distinctions and fine shades of meaning between prepositions. At the same time, we cannot too quickly dismiss any such distinctions, since no two prepositions overlap 100 percent. The context must determine whether a distinction is intended or not.

5.4. There has been some debate as to whether prepositions carry a basic sense that accounts for all their various usages. We find it helpful to begin with the basic or local meaning of the preposition and then to consider other meanings in relationship to it. This is not to commit a "root fallacy" or to suggest that NT writers necessarily used prepositions with a basic sense in mind or that there was always a clear connection between the basic sense of a preposition and its diverse uses.[7] But if only for purposes of helping us to grasp the various usages of prepositions, it is sometimes helpful to begin with the basic, local meaning of the preposition and then explore other extended meanings, fully aware that the connections between them are often unclear to us (and probably to the biblical authors). As with other words, the meaning of a preposition is determined by usage in context. At times it is difficult to distinguish the force of a preposition from the meaning contributed by its

6. Turner 249; Young 85–86; Moule 48.
7. Porter (142) adopts a similar approach.

context or the way it is *translated*. But we will resist the temptation to multiply categories unnecessarily. As Zerwick (40) helpfully concludes, prepositions "are in reality conventional signs whose sense is usually fairly general, the exact meaning in each case being determined by usage and above all by the subject matter."

The Function of Prepositions and Prepositional Phrases

Prefixed to Verbs

5.5. As we mentioned above, so-called proper prepositions are those that can be prefixed to verbs (e.g., ἐκ in ἐκβάλλω). When prefixed to a verb, a preposition can perform at least three functions.

1. A preposition can add its basic, local meaning to the verb. This often occurs with verbs indicating motion. The best example is ἔρχομαι, to which a number of prepositions can be prefixed to add their basic, local meanings: εἰσέρχομαι (I go/come in, I enter), ἐξέρχομαι (I go out), διέρχομαι (I go through), ἐπέρχομαι (I come upon/against), κατέρχομαι (I come down), παρέρχομαι (I go/pass by), προσέρχομαι (I go toward).

2. Prefixing a preposition to a verb can intensify the verb's meaning. A commonly cited example of this is the verb ἐσθίω. In its simple form ἐσθίω means "I eat," but κατεσθίω, with a prefixed preposition, means "I eat up, devour" (BDAG 531–32). The verb ἐργάζομαι means "I work," while κατεργάζομαι means "I work out" (see Phil. 2:12), emphasizing the carrying out of the work (Robertson 564). Γινώσκω means "I know," whereas the compound ἐπιγινώσκω can mean "I know fully" (BDAG 369; see 1 Cor. 13:12). Porter (141) argues that the verb ἀποκαταλλάσσω (to reconcile) in Eph. 2:16 and Col. 1:20, 22, with the preposition ἀπό prefixed to the already prefixed καταλλάσσω, may have an intensifying effect on the action of the verb in light of Paul's discussion of the work of Christ. The student will want to rely on works such as BDAG to determine when this happens.

3. Prefixing a preposition to a verb can change the meaning of the verb altogether. The verb γινώσκω means "I know," but ἀναγινώσκω, with the preposition ἀνά prefixed, means "I read" (see Luke 4:16). The compound form παρακαλέω could imply "I call alongside," but in the NT it often means "I urge, exhort, comfort" (see Eph. 4:1).

Adverbial

5.6. The entire prepositional phrase can modify the verbal element in a clause, probably its most common function. This is how we should understand prepositions with infinitives (preposition + article + infinitive): prepositions can take infinitives as their objects, and the entire construction functions adverbially (e.g., διὰ τὸ ἔχειν; see chap. 9, on infinitives).

Τί ποιήσω ὅτι ὁ κύριός μου ἀφαιρεῖται τὴν οἰκονομίαν **ἀπ᾽** ἐμοῦ; (Luke 16:3)	What shall I do, for my master has taken the stewardship **from** me?
πᾶσαν σπουδὴν ποιούμενος γράφειν ὑμῖν **περὶ** τῆς κοινῆς ἡμῶν σωτηρίας (Jude 3)	Making all diligence to write to you **concerning** our common salvation.
Μετὰ ταῦτα εἶδον ἄλλον ἄγγελον καταβαίνοντα **ἐκ** τοῦ οὐρανοῦ (Rev. 18:1)	**After** these things I saw another angel coming down **from** heaven. (*both prepositions modify verbs*)

Adjectival

5.7. The entire prepositional phrase can function as a substantive modifier, filling the slot of an adjective in a clause. Sometimes the prepositional phrase will be preceded by an article, which turns the prepositional phrase into an attributive modifier (see Matt. 7:3 below).

καὶ ἰδοὺ φωνὴ **ἐκ** τῶν οὐρανῶν λέγουσα· (Matt. 3:17)	And look, a voice **from** heaven, saying.

The prepositional phrase identifies the location or source of the voice.

τί δὲ βλέπεις τὸ κάρφος τὸ **ἐν** τῷ ὀφθαλμῷ τοῦ ἀδελφοῦ σου; (Matt. 7:3)	And why do you see the speck *that is* **in** the eye of your brother/sister?

The article signals that the prepositional phrase modifies κάρφος.

ποιμάνατε τὸ **ἐν** ὑμῖν ποίμνιον τοῦ θεοῦ (1 Pet. 5:2)	Shepherd the flock of God *that is* **among** you.

καὶ οὐδεὶς ἐδύνατο **ἐν** τῷ οὐρανῷ οὐδὲ **ἐπὶ** τῆς γῆς οὐδὲ **ὑποκάτω** τῆς γῆς ἀνοῖξαι τὸ βιβλίον οὔτε βλέπειν αὐτό. (Rev. 5:3)	And no one **in** heaven, or **on** earth, or **under** the earth was able to open the scroll or to look in it.

Substantival

5.8. Occasionally the entire prepositional phrase can function as a substantive. In this way it fills the noun slot in a clause (e.g., as subject or direct object). This usage most often occurs with an article that acts as a nominalizer, turning the prepositional phrase into a substantive (see chap. 4, on the article).

ὃς δ᾽ ἂν πίῃ **ἐκ** τοῦ ὕδατος οὗ ἐγὼ δώσω αὐτῷ, οὐ μὴ διψήσει εἰς τὸν αἰῶνα (John 4:14)	And whoever drinks **of** the water that I will give to him/her will never thirst, forever.

> The prepositional phrase ἐκ τοῦ ὕδατος functions as the direct object of πίῃ, though it may be considered to modify an understood "some" (see the partitive use of ἐκ below).

τοῖς **ὑπὸ** νόμον ὡς **ὑπὸ** νόμον (1 Cor. 9:20)	To those **under** the law [I became] as under the law.

> The article has a nominalizing effect, turning the prepositional phrase into an indirect object or dative of advantage.

Γινώσκετε ἄρα ὅτι οἱ **ἐκ** πίστεως, οὗτοι υἱοί εἰσιν Ἀβραάμ. (Gal. 3:7)	Therefore, know that those **of** [i.e., characterized by] faith, these are children of Abraham.

The Prepositions and Their Meanings

5.9. The following section treats all the so-called proper prepositions used in the NT. It does not attempt to be comprehensive or exhaustive but catalogs some major uses, occasionally mentioning less common but interesting or important ones. We will begin with the "basic," or local (spatial), meaning of the preposition, followed by other extended meanings.[8] For more nuances, as well as treatment of improper prepositions, the student should consult BDAG or Louw and Nida's *Greek-English Lexicon*.[9]

Ἀνά

5.10. *Case and frequency.* Ἀνά is used with the accusative case and occurs 13 times in the NT.[10]

Basic or local meaning. The preposition ἀνά suggests the notion of *motion upward* but primarily carries this meaning when prefixed to verbs (ἀναβαίνω, "I go up, ascend"; ἀνάγω, "I lead up, bring up"). More commonly, it occurs in combination with other words. Its opposite is κατά (down).

In combination with other words, the preposition ἀνά is used in the following two ways in the NT.

Positional. In combination with μέσον it can have a positional meaning, "in the midst." In Matt. 13:25 an enemy sows weeds **ἀνὰ μέσον** (**in** the midst) of the wheat. Likewise, the Lamb is described as being **ἀνὰ μέσον** (**in** the midst) of the throne in Rev. 7:17.

Distributive. Ἀνά can also carry a distributive sense in some contexts, meaning "each" or "apiece." With this usage the preposition is usually followed by a word expressing a numerical value. In Luke 10:1 Jesus sends his disciples out **ἀνὰ δύο δύο** (two **by** two; BDAG 58). In Rev. 4:8 John sees four living creatures that have **ἀνὰ πτέρυγας ἕξ** (six wings **apiece**).

Ἀντί

5.11. *Case and frequency.* Ἀντί is used with the genitive case and occurs 22 times in the NT.

Basic or local meaning. The basic meaning of ἀντί is "face to face" (Robertson 572) or "against." In the NT period its predominant sense is *substitution* ("instead of, in place of"). This was its prevailing sense in Classical and Hellenistic Greek. Ἀντί overlaps in meaning with ὑπέρ (on behalf of, for). The force of ἀντί has resulted in much debate because of its use in passages

---

8. The following list does not include ἀμφί (on both sides of; Goodwin, *Greek Grammar*, 254) since it never occurs independently in the NT but only as a prefix to certain verbs (e.g., ἀμφιβάλλοντας, "casting" [Mark 1:16]).

9. J. P. Louw and E. A. Nida, *Greek-English Lexicon of the New Testament Based on Semantic Domains*, 2nd ed., 2 vols. (New York: United Bible Societies, 1989).

10. The statistics for NT occurrences of this and all subsequent prepositions are taken from Wallace 357; the parenthetical statistics for prepositions taking more than one case are from BibleWorks 9.

that refer to the atonement of Christ. In Mark 10:45 Jesus describes his up-coming death as giving his life λύτρον ἀντὶ πολλῶν (a ransom **for/in place of** many; see also Matt. 20:28).[11] The debate concerns whether ἀντί should be given its substitutionary meaning, so that Christ's death is understood as a death *instead of* or *in place of* ours, or whether it only carries the notion *on behalf of*. In the NT and extrabiblical literature, there is strong evidence for taking it in a substitutionary sense: "instead of" or "in place of."[12] Therefore, the meaning of ἀντί in these two texts provides important support for and points to the substitutionary theory of Christ's atonement. At the same time, the preposition by itself does not "prove" or contain the entire doctrine of Christ's substitutionary atonement (Robertson 573–74). For similar issues, see ὑπέρ below.

Another important text that can turn on the meaning given to the preposition is John 1:16: χάριν ἀντὶ χάριτος (grace **instead of** grace). Though some (e.g., the NRSV) take this to mean that we have received grace upon grace or in addition to grace,[13] with the idea that one expression of grace has been added on top of another, the meaning of substitution should be read here as well: grace *in place of* grace.[14]

Exchange. The notion of "in place of" can sometimes suggest "something in exchange for something else." Matthew 5:38: Ὀφθαλμὸν ἀντὶ ὀφθαλμοῦ καὶ ὀδόντα ἀντὶ ὀδόντος (an eye **in exchange for** an eye and a tooth **in exchange for** a tooth).

Ἀπό

5.12. *Case and frequency.* Ἀπό is used with the genitive case and occurs 646 times in the NT.

Basic or local meaning. The basic meaning of ἀπό is *separation from* ("from, away from"). Ἀπό seems to enjoy substantial overlap with ἐκ (out of, from), though they can still sometimes be distinguished (away from vs. out of). Its antonyms are πρός (toward) and ἐπί (on, upon). Matthew 5:29: ἔξελε αὐτὸν καὶ βάλε ἀπὸ σοῦ (pluck it out and throw it **from** you); Rev. 20:11: οὗ ἀπὸ τοῦ προσώπου ἔφυγεν ἡ γῆ καὶ ὁ οὐρανός (**from** whose face the earth and heaven fled).

---

11. For a detailed discussion of these two texts, the history of treatment of the preposition ἀντί in them, and the theological implications, see Wallace (365–67) and Harris (*Prepositions*, 52–54), though both discussions range beyond the meaning of the preposition ἀντί.

12. See Wallace 365–67; Harris, *Prepositions*, 52–54.

13. Harris, *Prepositions*, 55.

14. D. A. Carson, *The Gospel according to John*, PNTC (Grand Rapids: Eerdmans, 1991), 132.

Time. Ἀπό can also convey a temporal sense, namely, the time from which something happens. Matthew 16:21: Ἀπὸ τότε ἤρξατο ὁ Ἰησοῦς (**From** then [on] Jesus began); 1 John 3:8: ἀπ' ἀρχῆς ὁ διάβολος ἁμαρτάνει (**from** the beginning the devil is / has been sinning).

Instrument, cause, agency, or source. We have included these notions together because they are closely related and sometimes difficult to distinguish. Some of these meanings show overlap with the preposition ἐκ. James 1:13: Ἀπὸ θεοῦ πειράζομαι ("I am being tempted **by** God": agency); Rev. 21:10: καταβαίνουσαν ἐκ τοῦ οὐρανοῦ ἀπὸ τοῦ θεοῦ ("coming down out of heaven **from** God": source).

Διά

5.13. *Case and frequency.* Διά is used with the genitive and accusative cases and occurs 667 times (387 with the gen.; 280 with the acc.) in the NT.

Basic or local meaning. The basic sense of διά seems to be *between* or *through.* The notion of "because of" (with the acc.) may derive from the idea of the *cause* of movement through or between,[15] though the relationship between the two senses is neither obvious nor certain.

Spatial (gen.). Διά is often used with its local or spatial meaning, "through." Mark 9:30: παρεπορεύοντο **διὰ** τῆς Γαλιλαίας (They passed **through** Galilee); Acts 13:49: διεφέρετο δὲ ὁ λόγος . . . **δι'** ὅλης τῆς χώρας (the word spread . . . **through** all the region).

Instrument, means (gen.). Διά frequently indicates the intermediate means or agent of an action. Ephesians 2:8: τῇ γὰρ χάριτί ἐστε σεσῳσμένοι **διὰ** πίστεως (For by grace you are saved **through** faith); Rev. 1:1: ἀποστείλας **διὰ** τοῦ ἀγγέλου αὐτοῦ (having sent **through** his angel). But sometimes it can denote the ultimate agent, as in Gal. 4:7: καὶ κληρονόμος **διὰ** θεοῦ (and an heir **through** God).

Temporal (genitive). As Porter (149) says, διά can be used of "time through which." Luke 5:5: **δι'** ὅλης νυκτὸς κοπιάσαντες (laboring **through** all the night); Acts 1:3: **δι'** ἡμερῶν τεσσεράκοντα (**through** [a period of] forty days).

Causal (accusative). With the accusative case, διά expresses a causal idea. Luke 5:19: μὴ εὑρόντες ποίας . . . **διὰ** τὸν ὄχλον (not finding any way . . . **because of** the crowd); Philem. 9: **διὰ** τὴν ἀγάπην μᾶλλον παρακαλῶ (I would rather appeal [to you] **because of** love).

Διά is often joined with the demonstrative τοῦτο to indicate a connection or with the interrogative τί to introduce a question. Both retain a causal sense. Hebrews 2:1: **Διὰ τοῦτο** δεῖ περισσοτέρως προσέχειν ἡμᾶς (**For this reason** [i.e.,

---

15. Porter 148; Robertson 583.

therefore] it is necessary for us all the more to pay attention); John 8:46: διὰ τί ὑμεῖς οὐ πιστεύετέ μοι; (**For what reason** [i.e., why] do you not believe me?).

Εἰς

5.14. *Case and frequency.* Εἰς is used with the accusative case and occurs 1,767 times in the NT; only ἐν is used more frequently.

Basic or local meaning. The basic sense of εἰς has to do with *direction toward and into* (Porter 151). In the NT it enjoys some overlap with ἐν, though we should not think that they are completely synonymous. It also partially overlaps in sense with πρός (to, toward). Its antonym is ἐκ (out of). Its local meaning can clearly be seen when it is prefixed to verbs of motion, such as εἰσέρχομαι (I go into, enter). Second John 10: μὴ λαμβάνετε αὐτὸν **εἰς** οἰκίαν (do not receive him **into** your house); Rev. 21:24: καὶ οἱ βασιλεῖς τῆς γῆς φέρουσιν τὴν δόξαν αὐτῶν **εἰς** αὐτήν (and the kings of the earth will bring their glory **into** it).

Location (in). Most grammars recognize that there is considerable overlap between εἰς and ἐν.[16] While it would be going too far to say that they are entirely synonymous, there are a number of instances where εἰς appears to indicate location or resting place and can be translated "in." Possible examples are John 1:18: μονογενὴς θεὸς ὁ ὢν **εἰς** τὸν κόλπον τοῦ πατρός (the only God, who is **in** the bosom of the Father); Luke 11:7: τὰ παιδία μου μετ' ἐμοῦ **εἰς** τὴν κοίτην εἰσίν (my children are with me **in** bed).

Mark 1:9: καὶ ἐβαπτίσθη **εἰς** τὸν Ἰορδάνην (and he was baptized **in/into** the Jordan). Should εἰς be understood in its local meaning, to be baptized "into," with a contrast to verse 10, where Jesus comes up out of the water (ἀναβαίνων ἐκ τοῦ ὕδατος)? Or should this be taken as an example of the interchangeability between εἰς and ἐν, so that Jesus is baptized "in" the Jordan? See the parallel statement in verse 5 (ἐν τῷ Ἰορδάνῃ).

Figurative direction or goal. This is a metaphorical application of the locative sense of εἰς. Matthew 6:13: καὶ μὴ εἰσενέγκῃς ἡμᾶς **εἰς** πειρασμόν (and do not lead us **into** temptation); Col. 1:16: τὰ πάντα δι' αὐτοῦ καὶ **εἰς** αὐτὸν ἔκτισται (all things through him and **for** him are created).

Purpose or result. Expanding on the previous category, direction or goal can indicate purpose or result. Romans 5:18: **εἰς** πάντας ἀνθρώπους **εἰς** κατάκριμα (to all people, **resulting in** condemnation), with εἰς used of both direction and result; 1 Cor. 9:18: **εἰς** τὸ μὴ καταχρήσασθαι τῇ ἐξουσίᾳ μου (**in order** not to make full use of my authority).

16. Harris, *Prepositions*, 84–88; Wallace 363; Zerwick 33–37; Young 86.

Acts 2:38: βαπτισθήτω . . . **εἰς** ἄφεσιν τῶν ἁμαρτιῶν ὑμῶν (be baptized . . . **for** the forgiveness of your sins). Many have avoided "purpose" as a description of the use of εἰς in this verse in order to avoid the implications that forgiveness of sins is conditioned upon baptism. However, it is difficult to avoid purpose (or result) as the meaning of εἰς here. Most likely baptism stood for the entire process of the conversion experience, so that Luke is not claiming that the physical rite of baptism in itself merits salvation.

Ἐκ

5.15. *Case and frequency.* Ἐκ is used with the genitive case and occurs 914 times in the NT.

Basic or local meaning. In its most basic sense ἐκ signals *movement out of*. As seen above, it enjoys semantic overlap with ἀπό (from, away from). Its antonym is εἰς (into). The local meaning of ἐκ is often seen when prefixed to verb forms: ἐκβάλλω (I cast out); ἐξέρχομαι (I go/come out of). Matthew 2:15: **Ἐξ** Αἰγύπτου ἐκάλεσα τὸν υἱόν μου (**out of** Egypt I called my son); Luke 2:4: Ἀνέβη δὲ καὶ Ἰωσὴφ ἀπὸ τῆς Γαλιλαίας **ἐκ** πόλεως Ναζαρὲθ εἰς τὴν Ἰουδαίαν εἰς πόλιν Δαυίδ (And Joseph also went up from Galilee **out of** the city of Nazareth into Judea into the city of David). Notice in the latter example the contrast between the three prepositions ἀπό, ἐκ, and εἰς.

Separation. Revelation 2:5: κινήσω τὴν λυχνίαν σου **ἐκ** τοῦ τόπου αὐτῆς (I will remove your lamp **from** its place).

Instrument, cause, agent, source. As with ἀπό, we have listed these senses together because they are closely related and not always easily distinguishable. Ephesians 2:9: οὐκ **ἐξ** ἔργων, ἵνα μή τις καυχήσηται (not **by** works, so that no one may boast); James 2:18: σοὶ δείξω **ἐκ** τῶν ἔργων μου τὴν πίστιν (I will show you my faith **by** my works); Rev. 1:16: **ἐκ** τοῦ στόματος αὐτοῦ ῥομφαία δίστομος ὀξεῖα ἐκπορευομένη (**from** his mouth proceeds a sharp two-edged sword).

Partitive. Ἐκ and its object can indicate the whole of which something is a part (see the discussion of the partitive genitive in chap. 1). Matthew 10:29: ἓν **ἐξ** αὐτῶν οὐ πεσεῖται ἐπὶ τὴν γῆν (one **of** them will not fall upon the earth); Rev. 2:7: φαγεῖν **ἐκ** τοῦ ξύλου τῆς ζωῆς (to eat **from** the tree of life).

Ἐν

5.16. *Case and frequency.* Ἐν is used with the dative case and occurs 2,752 times in the NT. It is the most frequent (and versatile) preposition in the NT.

Basic or local meaning. The basic meaning of ἐν is the static sense of *in* or *in the realm of.* It overlaps with the preposition εἰς, though as already stated, the overlap is partial and not absolute. The sense of "location in" is widespread in the NT. Luke 2:8: ποιμένες ἦσαν ἐν τῇ χώρᾳ τῇ αὐτῇ (shepherds were **in** the same country); Rev. 12:1: σημεῖον μέγα ὤφθη ἐν τῷ οὐρανῷ (a great sign was seen **in** heaven). Sometimes ἐν is used with a plural object and conveys the notion of "within" or "among" (Robertson 587). Colossians 1:27: γνωρίσαι τί τὸ πλοῦτος . . . ἐν τοῖς ἔθνεσιν (to make known what is the wealth . . . **among** the gentiles). See also 1 Pet. 1:11.

Sphere. This is not really a separate usage from the basic local meaning but a metaphorical application of it (Turner 262). Something takes place or is located within the sphere of influence or control of something else. Ephesians 6:10: ἐνδυναμοῦσθε ἐν κυρίῳ καὶ ἐν τῷ κράτει τῆς ἰσχύος αὐτοῦ (Be strong **in** the Lord and **in** the power of his strength).

Ἐν Χριστῷ. There are about 80 examples of this expression in Paul (e.g., Eph. 1:3), and its precise meaning is the subject of debate.[17] Young thinks that it should be understood as under the category of association, "as denoting a close, personal, life-enhancing relationship or union with Christ."[18] While this may be the force of this expression in some instances, it is better to understand it as indicating sphere. That is, Christ is the sphere in which Christians exist. Porter (159) correctly captures the sense: "One is in the sphere of Christ's control."

Instrument or means. Ἐν can indicate the instrument or impersonal means by which an action takes place. Mark 3:23: ἐν παραβολαῖς ἔλεγεν αὐτοῖς (he spoke to them **in/by** parables); Rev. 6:8: ἀποκτεῖναι ἐν ῥομφαίᾳ καὶ ἐν λιμῷ καὶ ἐν θανάτῳ (to kill **with** sword and **with** famine and **with** death).

Manner. Ἐν can refer to the manner by which an action takes place. Colossians 1:28: διδάσκοντες πάντα ἄνθρωπον ἐν πάσῃ σοφίᾳ (teaching every person **in** all wisdom); 1 Pet. 1:17: ἐν φόβῳ τὸν τῆς παροικίας ὑμῶν χρόνον ἀναστράφητε (conduct yourselves **in** fear during the time of your sojourning).

Accompaniment or attendant circumstances.[19] Ἐν can introduce something that accompanies an activity. First Thessalonians 4:16: ὁ κύριος ἐν κελεύσματι, ἐν φωνῇ ἀρχαγγέλου καὶ ἐν σάλπιγγι θεοῦ (The Lord, **with** a shout, **with** the voice of an archangel, and **with** the trumpet of God). However, this usage is often difficult to distinguish from that of manner.

---

17. The definitive study is now Constantine R. Campbell, *Paul and Union with Christ: An Exegetical and Theological Study* (Grand Rapids: Zondervan, 2012).

18. Young 96. See also Harris, *Prepositions*, 123.

19. See Moule 78; Young 97.

Time. Ἐν is used temporally in a number of contexts.[20] The primary use of the infinitive following ἐν belongs here. Luke 2:1: Ἐγένετο δὲ **ἐν** ταῖς ἡμέραις ἐκείναις (And it came about **in** those days); 1 Cor. 5:5: τὸ πνεῦμα σωθῇ **ἐν** τῇ ἡμέρᾳ τοῦ κυρίου (the spirit might be saved **on** the day of the Lord).

Ἐπί

5.17. *Case and frequency.* Ἐπί is used with the genitive, dative, and accusative cases and occurs 890 times (220 with the gen.; 187 with the dat.; 483 with the acc.) in the NT.

Basic or local meaning. The basic meaning of ἐπί is *location upon.* Its antonym is ὑπό (under).[21]

Spatial location (genitive, dative, accusative). Normally, with the accusative case ἐπί implies movement to a location upon, whereas the genitive and dative indicate position or specific location.[22] Matthew 3:16: ὡσεὶ περιστερὰν ἐρχόμενον **ἐπ'** αὐτόν (as a dove coming down **upon** him); Mark 2:10: **ἐπὶ** τῆς γῆς ἀφιέναι ἁμαρτίας (to forgive sins **upon** the earth); Eph. 2:20: ἐποικοδομηθέντες **ἐπὶ** τῷ θεμελίῳ τῶν ἀποστόλων καὶ προφητῶν (having been built **upon** the foundation of the apostles and prophets). However, the distinction between the three cases with ἐπί is often difficult, and sometimes unnecessary, to discern. For example, notice Paul's reference to building upon a foundation where 1 Cor. 3:12 has the accusative (ἐπὶ τὸν θεμέλιον) and Eph. 2:20 has the dative (ἐπὶ τῷ θεμελίῳ). In the repeated references to God seated on the throne in John's Apocalypse, there seems to be no detectable distinction in meaning between the cases used with ἐπί.[23]

Genitive:	ὁ καθήμενος ἐπὶ τοῦ θρόνου (Rev. 4:10; 5:1, 7; 6:16; 7:15)
Dative:	ὁ καθήμενος ἐπὶ τῷ θρόνῳ (Rev. 4:9; 5:13; 7:10; 19:4; 21:5)
Accusative:	ὁ καθήμενος ἐπὶ τὸν θρόνον (Rev. 4:2)

Used with the dative, ἐπί can be translated "at," specifying nearness in location. John 4:6: ἐκαθέζετο οὕτως **ἐπὶ** τῇ πηγῇ (he [i.e., Jesus] sat thus **at** the well). However, this sense is also present with the accusative: Rev. 3:20: ἕστηκα **ἐπὶ** τὴν θύραν (I stand **at** the door).

Time (accusative, genitive). Mark 2:26: εἰσῆλθεν . . . **ἐπὶ** Ἀβιαθὰρ ἀρχιερέως (he entered . . . **at** the time of Abiathar the high priest); Heb. 1:2: **ἐπ'** ἐσχάτου

20. This could be seen as an extension of the basic sense of "location in."
21. Harris, *Prepositions*, 137.
22. Moule 49–50; Dana and Mantey 106.
23. Harris, *Prepositions*, 137.

τῶν ἡμερῶν τούτων ἐλάλησεν ἡμῖν (**in** these last days he has spoken to us). With the accusative, ἐπί may imply movement or extension through time. Acts 17:2: ἐπὶ σάββατα τρία διελέξατο αὐτοῖς (he discussed with them **on** three Sabbaths).

Cause or basis (dative). As an extension of its local usage, ἐπί can point out the cause or basis of an action. It is often used to indicate "the grounds for emotional or other reactions" (Zerwick 42). Mark 1:22: ἐξεπλήσσοντο ἐπὶ τῇ διδαχῇ αὐτοῦ (they were amazed **at** his teaching); Rom. 5:2: καυχώμεθα ἐπ᾽ ἐλπίδι (we boast **because of** / **on the basis of** the hope).

Purpose or intention (accusative, dative). Ἐπί can also carry the notion of purpose. Matthew 3:7: ἐρχομένους ἐπὶ τὸ βάπτισμα αὐτοῦ (coming **for the purpose** of his baptism); Eph. 2:10: κτισθέντες ἐν Χριστῷ Ἰησοῦ ἐπὶ ἔργοις ἀγαθοῖς (having been created in Christ Jesus **for the purpose of** good works).

Κατά

5.18. *Case and frequency.* Κατά is used with the genitive and accusative cases and occurs 473 times (74 with the gen.; 399 with the acc.) in the NT.

Basic or local meaning. The basic meaning of κατά involves *movement downward.* Its antonym is ἀνά (up). This positional sense occurs with both the genitive and accusative cases. Matthew 8:32: καὶ ἰδοὺ ὥρμησεν πᾶσα ἡ ἀγέλη κατὰ τοῦ κρημνοῦ (and look, the whole herd rushed [headlong] **down** the slope); 1 Cor. 11:4: προσευχόμενος ἢ προφητεύων κατὰ κεφαλῆς ἔχων (praying or prophesying having **down upon** his head [NIV, "having his head covered"]).

Opposition (genitive). Sometimes κατά can be translated "against." Acts 24:1: ἐνεφάνισαν τῷ ἡγεμόνι κατὰ τοῦ Παύλου (they brought charges to the governor **against** Paul).

Standard or measure (genitive, accusative). Κατά can be used in various ways to point out the standard or measure for evaluating something. Galatians 3:15: κατὰ ἄνθρωπον λέγω (I speak **as a human** [by human standards]); Rev. 2:23: δώσω ὑμῖν ἑκάστῳ κατὰ τὰ ἔργα ὑμῶν (I will give to each of you **according to** your works). The genitive is also used to refer to the guarantor of an oath: Heb. 6:13: ὤμοσεν καθ᾽ ἑαυτοῦ (he swore **by** himself [Moule 59]).

Possession (accusative).[24] The notion of "according to" or "pertaining to" can suggest "belonging to." Acts 25:14: ἀνέθετο τὰ κατὰ τὸν Παῦλον (he laid out the affairs **of** Paul); Eph. 1:15: ἀκούσας τὴν καθ᾽ ὑμᾶς πίστιν (having heard **of** your faith).

---

24. Zerwick 43–44; BDF §224; Turner 268.

Distributive (accusative). Κατά can designate individual items of a group. Mark 15:6: **Κατὰ** δὲ ἑορτήν (And **at each** feast); Rev. 4:8: τὰ τέσσαρα ζῷα, ἓν **καθ'** ἓν αὐτῶν (the four living creatures, **each** one of them).

Temporal (accusative). Acts 12:1: **Κατ'** ἐκεῖνον δὲ τὸν καιρόν (And **at that** time); κατά can also refer to distributed time, as in Heb. 9:25: ὁ ἀρχιερεὺς εἰσέρχεται . . . **κατ'** ἐνιαυτόν (the high priest enters . . . **each** year).

Μετά

5.19. *Case and frequency.* Μετά is used with the genitive and accusative cases and occurs 469 times (365 with the gen.; 104 with the acc.) in the NT.

Basic or local meaning. The basic meaning of μετά seems to be *accompaniment* ("with"). With the accusative, it is only used temporally of a succession of events ("after"). Perhaps the association of events could be seen in terms of their succession. Μετά overlaps in meaning with σύν (with, together with).

Accompaniment (genitive). The notion of accompaniment can be both literal and metaphorical. Galatians 6:18: Ἡ χάρις . . . **μετὰ** τοῦ πνεύματος ὑμῶν (The grace . . . [be] **with** your spirit); Rev. 19:20: ἐπιάσθη τὸ θηρίον καὶ **μετ'** αὐτοῦ ὁ ψευδοπροφήτης (the beast was seized and **with** him the false prophet).

More figurative uses of μετά often specify *manner.* Ephesians 4:2: **μετὰ** πάσης ταπεινοφροσύνης καὶ πραΰτητος, **μετὰ** μακροθυμίας (**with** all humility and gentleness, **with** patience); Col. 1:11–12: **μετὰ** χαρᾶς, εὐχαριστοῦντες τῷ πατρὶ (**with** joy, giving thanks to the Father). Sometimes μετά occurs in contexts that suggest conflict or opposition, particularly in reference to doing battle ("against"): Rev. 11:7: ποιήσει **μετ'** αὐτῶν πόλεμον ([the beast] will make war **against** them).

Succession of time (accusative). Μετά is used in a temporal sense to signal an event that takes place after another one. Acts 10:41: **μετὰ** τὸ ἀναστῆναι αὐτὸν ἐκ νεκρῶν (**after** he rose from the dead); Rev. 19:1: **Μετὰ** ταῦτα ἤκουσα (**After** these things I heard).

Παρά

5.20. *Case and frequency.* Παρά is used with the genitive, dative, and accusative cases and occurs 194 times (82 with the gen.; 53 with the dat.; 59 with the acc.) in the NT.

Basic or local meaning. Παρά has as its local meaning *position alongside of* or *beside*. With the accusative it usually expresses movement alongside of or near: Matt. 13:1: ἐκάθητο **παρὰ** τὴν θάλασσαν (he sat **beside** the sea); Mark 4:4: ἔπεσεν **παρὰ** τὴν ὁδόν (it fell **beside** the path). It is never used with the accusative case with personal objects (Porter 166). With the genitive it entails movement *from* alongside of and is used with a personal object. Luke 1:45: τοῖς λελαλημένοις αὐτῇ **παρὰ** κυρίου (the things spoken to her **from** the Lord); John 16:27: ἐγὼ **παρὰ** τοῦ θεοῦ ἐξῆλθον (I went out **from beside** God). With the dative it implies position alongside of. This usage often carries the sense of "in the sight of" or "in the presence of." James 1:27: θρησκεία καθαρὰ καὶ ἀμίαντος **παρὰ** τῷ θεῷ (religion pure and undefiled **before** God); 1 Pet. 2:20: τοῦτο χάρις **παρὰ** θεῷ (this is grace **before** God).

Agency or source (genitive). "Movement from" often implies agency or source. See Luke 1:45 above. Ephesians 6:8: τοῦτο κομίσεται **παρὰ** κυρίου (this he/she will receive back **from** the Lord); James 1:7: λήμψεταί τι **παρὰ** τοῦ κυρίου (he/she will receive something **from** the Lord).

Comparison (accusative). This usage and the next (replacement) are probably natural outgrowths of the idea of *alongside of.* Luke 3:13: Μηδὲν πλέον **παρὰ** τὸ διατεταγμένον (nothing more **than** what is prescribed); Heb. 1:4: διαφορώτερον **παρ'** αὐτοὺς . . . ὄνομα (a more excellent name **than** theirs).

Replacement (accusative). Romans 1:25: ἐλάτρευσαν τῇ κτίσει **παρὰ** τὸν κτίσαντα (they worshiped the creation **rather than** the Creator); Gal. 1:8: εὐαγγελίζηται ὑμῖν **παρ'** ὃ εὐηγγελισάμεθα ὑμῖν (preaches a gospel to you **other than** what we preached to you).

Περί

5.21. *Case and frequency.* Περί is used with the genitive and accusative cases and occurs 333 times (294 with the gen.; 39 with the acc.) in the NT.

Basic or local meaning. The local meaning of περί is *encircling* or *around.* It is used with the accusative case (not the genitive) to communicate this notion. Matthew 3:4: ζώνην δερματίνην **περὶ** τὴν ὀσφὺν αὐτοῦ (a leather belt **around** his waist); Matt. 8:18: πολλοὺς ὄχλους **περὶ** αὐτόν (many crowds **around** him).

Temporal (accusative). Περί can be used to communicate the approximate time, the time around which something took place. Mark 6:48: **περὶ** τετάρτην φυλακὴν τῆς νυκτός (**about** the fourth watch of the night); Acts 10:9: προσεύξασθαι **περὶ** ὥραν ἕκτην (to pray **at about** the sixth hour).

Concerning or focus of attention (genitive, accusative). The concept of *surrounding* or *around* can extend to the idea of *being concerned with or about something.* First Corinthians 7:1: **Περὶ** δὲ ὧν ἐγράψατε (now **concerning** the things that you wrote); Phil. 2:23: τὰ **περὶ** ἐμέ (the things **concerning/about** me). As Moule (62) observes, this sense often occurs after verbs of speaking, thinking, feeling, and the like. John 7:13: ἐλάλει **περὶ** αὐτοῦ ([no one] spoke **concerning** him); 1 Pet. 5:7: αὐτῷ μέλει περὶ ὑμῶν (it is a care to him **concerning** you); see also Matt. 6:28.

This use can also imply *benefaction* (Young 100): something is done concerning someone, for their benefit. Luke 6:28: προσεύχεσθε περὶ τῶν ἐπηρεαζόντων ὑμᾶς (pray **for** those who mistreat you); Eph. 6:18: προσευχόμενοι . . . περὶ πάντων τῶν ἁγίων (praying . . . **concerning/for** all the saints); see also Col. 1:3.

Πρό

5.22. *Case and frequency.* Πρό is used with the genitive case and occurs 47 times in the NT.

Basic or local meaning. The basic meaning of πρό is *position before* or *in front of*. This seems to give rise to the following shades of meaning.

Location before. Acts 12:14: ἑστάναι τὸν Πέτρον **πρὸ** τοῦ πυλῶνος (Peter stood **at/before** the gate); James 5:9: ὁ κριτὴς **πρὸ** τῶν θυρῶν ἔστηκεν (the judge stands **at/before** the doors).

Temporal (prior time). John 11:55: ἀνέβησαν πολλοὶ . . . **πρὸ** τοῦ πάσχα (many went up . . . **before** the Passover); Eph. 1:4: ἐξελέξατο ἡμᾶς . . . **πρὸ** καταβολῆς κόσμου (he chose us . . . **before** the foundation of the world).

Priority (metaphorical). This usage may be difficult and sometimes unnecessary to distinguish from temporal priority. Colossians 1:17: καὶ αὐτός ἐστιν **πρὸ** πάντων (and he is **before** all things); James 5:12: **Πρὸ** πάντων δέ (and **above** all).

Πρός

5.23. *Case and frequency.* Πρός is used with the genitive, dative, and accusative cases and occurs 700 times (1 with the gen.; 7 with the dat.; 692 with the acc.) in the NT. Because the accusative case dominates, Moule (52) says that πρός "is nearly a one-case preposition."

Basic or local meaning. Πρός has as its local sense *facing toward*. It overlaps in meaning with εἰς, and its antonym is ἀπό.

Location (accusative, dative). The accusative case is usually employed to signify *motion to, direction toward*, or *destination*.

1. *Accusative.* With the accusative, πρός frequently indicates motion toward. Matthew 7:15: ἔρχονται **πρὸς** ὑμᾶς ἐν ἐνδύμασι προβάτων (they come **to** you in sheep's clothing); Mark 1:33: ἐπισυνηγμένη **πρὸς** τὴν θύραν (being gathered **at** [i.e., facing] the door); Eph. 6:12: οὐκ ἔστιν ἡμῖν ἡ πάλη **πρὸς** αἷμα καὶ σάρκα, ἀλλὰ **πρὸς** τὰς ἀρχάς, **πρὸς** τὰς ἐξουσίας, **πρὸς** τοὺς

κοσμοκράτορας τοῦ σκότους τούτου, **πρὸς** τὰ πνευματικὰ τῆς πονηρίας (our battle is not **against** blood and flesh, but **against** the rulers, **against** the authorities, **against** the powers of this darkness, **against** the spirits of evil). Porter (173) says that the idea is "facing off with adversaries."

2. *Dative.* Πρός is always used with a positional sense when used with the dative. John 20:12: ἕνα **πρὸς** τῇ κεφαλῇ καὶ ἕνα **πρὸς** τοῖς ποσίν (one at the head, and one at the feet); Rev. 1:13: περιεζωσμένον **πρὸς** τοῖς μαστοῖς ζώνην χρυσᾶν (girded with a gold belt **around** his chest). The remaining usages of πρός with the dative in the NT are Mark 5:11; Luke 19:37; John 18:16; 20:11.

Purpose (metaphorical). By extension, πρός, like εἰς, is found in some contexts to indicate purpose. Matthew 6:1: **πρὸς** τὸ θεαθῆναι αὐτοῖς (**for the purpose** of being seen by them [with the infinitive]); Eph. 4:12: **πρὸς** τὸν καταρτισμὸν τῶν ἁγίων (**for** the equipping of the saints).

Genitive. The sole occurrence of πρός with the genitive in the NT is Acts 27:34: τοῦτο γὰρ **πρὸς** τῆς ὑμετέρας σωτηρίας ὑπάρχει (Moule [54] translates it as "for this is **in the interest of** your safety").

Σύν

5.24. *Case and frequency.* Σύν is used with the dative case and occurs 128 times in the NT.

Basic or local meaning. The basic meaning of σύν concerns *association* or *being with*. It shares semantic overlap with the preposition μετά. Luke 9:32: ὁ δὲ Πέτρος καὶ οἱ **σὺν** αὐτῷ (and Peter and those **with** him); Eph. 3:18: ἐξισχύσητε καταλαβέσθαι **σὺν** πᾶσιν τοῖς ἁγίοις (you might be able to comprehend **with** all the saints). The best-known examples are those where σύν is used with reference to our union with Christ in Paul's letters, usually prefixed to verbs (the so-called σύν-compounds). Romans 6:8: εἰ δὲ ἀπεθάνομεν **σὺν** Χριστῷ (and if we died **with** Christ); Col. 2:13: συνεζωοποίησεν ὑμᾶς **σὺν** αὐτῷ (he made you alive **with** him); see also Rom. 6:4; Eph. 2:5, 6. In these instances σύν suggests our incorporation into Christ.[25] According to Harris, σύν (rather than μετά) was used by Paul because it was suited to "express[ing] intimate personal union or close fellowship."[26]

---

25. For a detailed exegetical treatment, see Campbell, *Paul and Union with Christ.*
26. Harris, *Prepositions,* 200.

Ὑπέρ

5.25. *Case and frequency.* Ὑπέρ is used with the genitive and accusative cases and occurs 149 times (130 with the gen.; 19 with the acc.) in the NT.

Basic or local meaning. Ὑπέρ has as its basic meaning *position or location above*. Its antonym is ὑπό. It is never used with this physical sense in the NT, but it has a number of related senses.

Position above or beyond (accusative). Ὑπέρ with the accusative can suggest a position beyond, surpassing, or superior to something else. Matthew 10:24: Οὐκ ἔστιν μαθητὴς **ὑπὲρ** τὸν διδάσκαλον οὐδὲ δοῦλος **ὑπὲρ** τὸν κύριον αὐτοῦ (a disciple is not **above** his teacher, nor a slave **above** his master); 1 Cor. 4:6: Μὴ **ὑπὲρ** ἃ γέγραπται (not **beyond** what is written); see also 1 Cor. 10:13.

Benefaction-advantage (genitive). Here ὑπέρ communicates that something is done on someone's behalf or for their benefit. Mark 9:40: ὃς γὰρ οὐκ ἔστιν καθ᾽ ἡμῶν, **ὑπὲρ** ἡμῶν ἐστιν (for who is not against us is **for** us); Rom. 5:6: **ὑπὲρ** ἀσεβῶν ἀπέθανεν (he died **on behalf of** the ungodly [but see below, on "Substitution"]).

Concerning, about (genitive). Philippians 1:7: τοῦτο φρονεῖν **ὑπὲρ** πάντων ὑμῶν (to think this **about** all of you).

Substitution (genitive). Ὑπέρ, like ἀντί, seems capable of a substitutionary sense. This use is disputed, especially in passages that refer to Christ's death. Harris has shown that in Classical Greek, Hellenistic Greek literature, and the papyri, ὑπέρ was used in the sense of substitution ("in the place of").[27] This is important for a number of texts that refer to the death of Christ. John 11:50: εἷς ἄνθρωπος ἀποθάνῃ **ὑπὲρ** τοῦ λαοῦ (one man might die **for** the people); 2 Cor. 5:14–15: εἷς **ὑπὲρ** πάντων ἀπέθανεν . . . καὶ **ὑπὲρ** πάντων ἀπέθανεν (one died **for** all . . . and he died **for** all); Gal. 3:13: γενόμενος **ὑπὲρ** ἡμῶν κατάρα (having become a curse **for us / in our place**). See also Rom. 5:7, 8. Even if some of these chiefly indicate benefaction or representation, the notion of substitution is still present. Christ's death benefits us by taking our place.[28] This obviously has important implications for understanding Christ's atonement.

Ὑπό

5.26. *Case and frequency.* Ὑπό is used with the genitive and accusative cases and occurs 220 times (169 with the gen.; 51 with the acc.) in the NT.

---

27. Ibid., 211–12. For this usage, see also Robertson 630–32; Dana and Mantey 111–12; Moule 64; Zerwick 30; Porter 176–77; Young 101–2; Wallace 383–89.
28. Harris, *Prepositions*, 215.

Basic or local meaning. The basic sense of ὑπό is positional *location under.* Its antonym is ὑπέρ.

Location under or beneath (accusative). The preposition ὑπό specifies position under, physically or metaphorically (e.g., "under" authority). Mark 4:21: ὑπὸ τὸν μόδιον τεθῇ ἢ ὑπὸ τὴν κλίνην (**under** the bushel basket he might place it or **under** the bed); Rom. 6:14: οὐ γάρ ἐστε ὑπὸ νόμον ἀλλὰ ὑπὸ χάριν (for you are not **under** the law but **under** grace).

Agency (personal agent) (genitive). Ὑπό is found, often with passive verb constructions, to designate the personal or direct agent of an action (see the discussion of the passive voice in chap. 7 for how it differs from διά and ἐν). Matthew 4:1: ὁ Ἰησοῦς ἀνήχθη . . . ὑπὸ τοῦ πνεύματος (Jesus was led . . . **by** the Spirit); Rev. 6:8: ὑπὸ τῶν θηρίων τῆς γῆς (**by the beasts of the earth**). The preceding items listed in Rev. 6:8 have ἐν, so John is probably distinguishing between impersonal and personal (beasts) agency with his shift to ὑπό.

For Practice

5.27. For the following passages, locate the prepositions and analyze their meanings. What sense do they convey? Then determine what the prepositional phrases modify.

²¹Νυνὶ δὲ χωρὶς νόμου δικαιοσύνη θεοῦ πεφανέρωται, μαρτυρουμένη ὑπὸ τοῦ νόμου καὶ τῶν προφητῶν, ²²δικαιοσύνη δὲ θεοῦ διὰ πίστεως Ἰησοῦ Χριστοῦ, εἰς πάντας τοὺς πιστεύοντας, οὐ γάρ ἐστιν διαστολή. ²³πάντες γὰρ ἥμαρτον καὶ ὑστεροῦνται τῆς δόξης τοῦ θεοῦ, ²⁴δικαιούμενοι δωρεὰν τῇ αὐτοῦ χάριτι διὰ τῆς ἀπολυτρώσεως τῆς ἐν Χριστῷ Ἰησοῦ· ²⁵ὃν προέθετο ὁ θεὸς ἱλαστήριον διὰ πίστεως ἐν τῷ αὐτοῦ αἵματι εἰς ἔνδειξιν τῆς δικαιοσύνης αὐτοῦ διὰ τὴν πάρεσιν τῶν προγεγονότων ἁμαρτημάτων ²⁶ἐν τῇ ἀνοχῇ τοῦ θεοῦ, πρὸς τὴν ἔνδειξιν τῆς δικαιοσύνης αὐτοῦ ἐν τῷ νῦν καιρῷ, εἰς τὸ εἶναι αὐτὸν δίκαιον καὶ δικαιοῦντα τὸν ἐκ πίστεως Ἰησοῦ. (Rom. 3:21–26)

³Εὐχαριστῶ τῷ θεῷ μου ἐπὶ πάσῃ τῇ μνείᾳ ὑμῶν ⁴πάντοτε ἐν πάσῃ δεήσει μου ὑπὲρ πάντων ὑμῶν, μετὰ χαρᾶς τὴν δέησιν ποιούμενος, ⁵ἐπὶ τῇ κοινωνίᾳ ὑμῶν εἰς τὸ εὐαγγέλιον ἀπὸ τῆς πρώτης ἡμέρας ἄχρι τοῦ νῦν, ⁶πεποιθὼς αὐτὸ τοῦτο ὅτι ὁ ἐναρξάμενος ἐν ὑμῖν ἔργον ἀγαθὸν ἐπιτελέσει ἄχρι ἡμέρας Χριστοῦ Ἰησοῦ· ⁷καθώς ἐστιν δίκαιον ἐμοὶ τοῦτο φρονεῖν ὑπὲρ πάντων ὑμῶν, διὰ τὸ ἔχειν με ἐν τῇ καρδίᾳ ὑμᾶς, ἔν τε τοῖς δεσμοῖς μου καὶ ἐν τῇ ἀπολογίᾳ καὶ βεβαιώσει τοῦ εὐαγγελίου συγκοινωνούς μου τῆς

χάριτος πάντας ὑμᾶς ὄντας· ⁸μάρτυς γάρ μου ὁ θεός, ὡς ἐπιποθῶ πάντας ὑμᾶς ἐν σπλάγχνοις Χριστοῦ Ἰησοῦ. ⁹καὶ τοῦτο προσεύχομαι ἵνα ἡ ἀγάπη ὑμῶν ἔτι μᾶλλον καὶ μᾶλλον περισσεύῃ ἐν ἐπιγνώσει καὶ πάσῃ αἰσθήσει, ¹⁰εἰς τὸ δοκιμάζειν ὑμᾶς τὰ διαφέροντα, ἵνα ἦτε εἰλικρινεῖς καὶ ἀπρόσκοποι εἰς ἡμέραν Χριστοῦ, ¹¹πεπληρωμένοι καρπὸν δικαιοσύνης τὸν διὰ Ἰησοῦ Χριστοῦ εἰς δόξαν καὶ ἔπαινον θεοῦ. (Phil. 1:3–11)

6

THE GREEK VERB SYSTEM

6.1. One of the most important yet complex features of Koine Greek is its verb system. Though Greek does not require a verb to construct a clause, most clauses do contain a verbal element. Like many other features of the Greek language, the verb is inflected to indicate important grammatical information: tense/aspect, voice, mood, person, and number. That is, the selection of a verb ending communicates a perspective on these features. The treatment of NT Greek verbs in this grammar will discuss these five features, but more attention will be given to the first three (tense, voice, and mood) since more issues surround their interpretation. A basic division to recognize is between finite and nonfinite verbs. Finite verbs are those that have endings to indicate person. Nonfinite verbs (participles and infinitives) do not. This chapter will focus on finite verb forms, verbs that are limited by a subject and take endings to indicate person. Nevertheless, much of what is said here applies to nonfinite forms as well.

Tense (Aspect)

6.2. The feature of the Greek verb system that has received the most attention lately is its tense system. For much of the twentieth century, grammarians of NT Greek understood Greek verb tenses to communicate two things: *kind of action* (known as *Aktionsart*)[1] and the *time of action* (past, present, future)

---

1. BDF §318. *Aktionsart* is a German word that means "kind [*Art*] of action [*Aktions*]."

in the indicative mood (even those who think Greek verb tenses indicate time agree that time is not a factor outside the indicative mood).[2] In other words, the verb tenses were thought to tell us both *how* an action actually took place (i.e., the kind of action) and *when* it took place (i.e., the time of action). For example, a common conception of the aorist tense was that it indicates punctiliar action (kind) in the past (time). The present tense was seen as conveying continuous action (kind) in the present (time). In some cases this is still the basic model for teaching Greek tense usage.

However, this approach has been challenged recently and is being replaced by a different model known as verbal aspect theory.[3] According to aspect theory, the Greek verb tenses do not indicate the kind or even the time of action, but *how the author chooses to conceive of or view the action.* Aspect concerns the *author's perspective* on an action. Here is a definition of verbal aspect from Stanley Porter, one of the most important advocates of this view: "Verbal aspect is defined as a semantic (meaning) category by which a speaker or writer grammaticalizes (i.e., represents a meaning by choice of a word-form) a perspective on an action by the selection of a particular tense-form in the verbal system."[4] According to another proponent, Buist Fanning, aspect is "that category in grammar of the verb which reflects the focus or viewpoint of the speaker in regard to the action or condition which the verb describes."[5] Another way of looking at aspect is that it is "perspectival."[6] By choosing a specific tense-form, the author chooses to view the action in a specific way, irrespective of when or how it actually took

2. See Dana and Mantey 177.

3. See esp. Stanley E. Porter, *Verbal Aspect in the Greek of the New Testament, with Reference to Tense and Mood,* Studies in Biblical Greek 1 (New York: Peter Lang, 1989); Buist M. Fanning, *Verbal Aspect in New Testament Greek* (Oxford: Clarendon, 1990); K. L. McKay, *A New Syntax of the Verb in New Testament Greek: An Aspectual Approach,* Studies in Biblical Greek 5 (New York: Peter Lang, 1994); Rodney J. Decker, *Temporal Deixis of the Greek Verb in the Gospel of Mark with Reference to Verbal Aspect,* Studies in Biblical Greek 10 (New York: Peter Lang, 2001); Constantine R. Campbell, *Verbal Aspect, the Indicative Mood, and Narrative: Soundings in the Greek New Testament,* Studies in Biblical Greek 13 (New York: Peter Lang, 2007). For the implementation of verbal aspect into a first-year grammar, see Rodney J. Decker, *Reading Koine Greek: An Introduction and Integrated Workbook* (Grand Rapids: Baker Academic, 2014); Stanley E. Porter, Jeffrey T. Reed, and Matthew Brook O'Donnell, *Fundamentals of New Testament Greek* (Grand Rapids: Eerdmans, 2010).

4. Porter 20–21, italics removed. Or more technically: "Greek verbal aspect is a synthetic semantic category (realized in the forms of verbs) used of meaningful oppositions in a network of tense systems to grammaticalize the author's reasoned subjective choice of conception of a process" (*Verbal Aspect,* 88).

5. Fanning, *Verbal Aspect,* 84. See Campbell, *Verbal Aspect,* 6: "Verbal aspect refers to the manner in which verbs are used to view an action or state."

6. J. W. Voelz, "Present and Aorist Verbal Aspect: A New Proposal," *Neotestamentica* 27 (1993): 157.

place. This conclusion is confirmed by noticing the variety of temporal and kind-of-action contexts in which Greek verb tenses occur (see the examples below). Time and kind of action are indicated not by the verb tense-forms but by the broader context (clauses, sentences, paragraphs). Though there is still some disagreement on the issue of whether Greek indicative verb tenses indicate time, our grammar will side with advocates of verbal aspect in the treatment of the Greek tense system.[7] But one must at least agree with Robertson (824–25) that time is but a subordinate element in Greek verb tenses.

By way of contrast, the English tense system primarily indicates time (past, present, future). However, in a more limited way even English can indicate aspect. What is the difference between these two statements?

I studied Greek last night.

I was studying Greek last night.

Both refer to the same event, the act of studying Greek, and the same time, last night. The difference is one of aspect, how the speaker chooses to portray the action: as a simple whole ("studied") or as in progress ("was studying"). The following comments are meant to further explain the theory of verbal aspect as utilized in this grammar.

6.3. There are three fundamental aspects in Greek: perfective, imperfective, and stative. As mentioned above, these three aspects are indicated by the inflected endings attached to verbs. By the choice of a tense-form, the author indicates a particular aspect, or way of viewing an action. The *perfective aspect* looks at an action as a complete whole, in its entirety, without reference to its makeup or development. It has sometimes been referred to as the "external viewpoint,"[8] a view from outside of the action. The tense-form used to communicate this aspect is the **aorist**.[9] The *imperfective aspect* looks at an action as in progress, as developing or unfolding. It has sometimes been referred to as the "internal viewpoint."[10] It is a more close-up view of the action seen from the perspective of its internal makeup. The verb tense-forms used to indicate this aspect are the **present** and **imperfect**. The *stative aspect* looks at an action as an existing state of affairs.

---

7. For a recent argument for the nontemporal nature of the Greek tense endings, see Stanley E. Porter, *Linguistic Analysis of the Greek New Testament: Studies in Tools, Methods, and Practice* (Grand Rapids: Baker Academic, 2015), chaps. 10, 11.

8. Fanning, *Verbal Aspect*, 97.

9. We will continue to use the word *tense* to refer to the tense-forms themselves, not to time.

10. Fanning, *Verbal Aspect*, 103.

The tense-forms used to communicate this aspect are the **perfect** and the **pluperfect**.

Aspect	Meaning	Tense-Form
Perfective	Action viewed as a whole, in its entirety	Aorist
Imperfective	Action viewed as in progress, as developing or unfolding	Present and Imperfect
Stative	Action viewed as an existing state	Perfect and Pluperfect

Notice the absence of the future tense. The future tense is not fully aspectual. That is, it has a unique place within the Greek tense system and does not function along with the other tense-forms as part of Greek's system of aspect. It is better treated separately from the other aspects (see below).

6.4. It is crucial to distinguish between kind of action (*Aktionsart*) and aspect. The former refers more to the *objective* nature of an action as determined where possible by the context, while aspect refers more *subjectively* to how the author chooses to view an action, irrespective of how it actually took place. Many misconceptions of the Greek tense-forms are due to a failure to distinguish aspect from *Aktionsart* (e.g., the aorist = punctiliar action; the present = continuous action). What this means is that most actions can be portrayed by most aspects; it all depends on how the author wants to view an action. In Rom. 6:4 Jesus' resurrection is referred to with the aorist tense (ἠγέρθη, was raised). However, in 1 Cor. 15:4 the same verb is used to refer to his resurrection with the perfect tense (ἐγήγερται). The same objective event, Christ's resurrection (not two different resurrections), is referred to with two different aspects that serve to provide different perspectives of the author on the action: an action viewed in its entirety versus as a state of affairs.

6.5. An important linguistic principle is that *meaning implies choice*. There are several verbs that do not offer a choice between perfective and imperfective aspects in Greek. The most obvious example is εἰμί, which exhibits only imperfective tense-forms (present and imperfect).[11] Other common verbs that do not provide a choice between aorist and present/imperfective tense-forms are κάθημαι (I sit), κεῖμαι (I lie), and φημί (I say). These verbs are what Porter (24–25) calls "aspectually vague." Also, sometimes an author may prefer a certain aspect with certain verbs. For example, in Revelation the verb ἔχω occurs exclusively in the imperfective aspect (i.e., present and imperfect tense-forms),

---

11. It does have future forms, but remember that the future is probably not fully an aspect (see below).

so the reader should not make too much of the present tense-form of ἔχω in Revelation. Therefore, the interpreter should not give weight or exegetical significance to the aspect of such verbs, since vague verbs (or an author defaulting to one aspect) do not reflect a full range of tense/aspect choices.

6.6. One of the functions of the Greek aspects is to structure the discourse[12] or lend prominence to parts of a text. No discourse is flat; discourses have certain parts that "stick out" or are more important than others. One important way that Greek can indicate levels of prominence in a discourse is through the use of verbal aspect (see chap. 13, on discourse considerations). It must be emphasized that showing prominence is *not* the meaning of the tenses. And verbal aspect *does not always* show prominence. The aspects primarily indicate the author's perspective on an action. But it is at least worth considering whether the use of aspect signals prominence (Porter 23).

How do the aspects structure a discourse? The following scheme represents a possible model for how aspect can function in the two major literary types in the NT.[13]

Narrative

Aorist	Used to summarize and narrate the main events on the main story line.
Imperfect	Used to narrate events that are remote from the main story line, often supplementary or supporting material; it can also function to draw attention to a main action.
Present	Used to draw attention to (i.e., to "foreground") significant events (the so-called historical present) or to signal the importance of an upcoming event.
Perfect	Used as another way of expressing prominence, due to the fact that the perfect tense is rare in narrative and seems to carry more meaning.

Exposition

Aorist	Used to establish background material, often past events that form the basis for more thematic material.
Imperfect	Used to highlight events over against the background aorist.

12. By "discourse" we are referring not to speech but to larger units of text beyond the sentence and even the paragraph.

13. See also Buist M. Fanning, "Greek Presents, Imperfects, and Aorists in the Synoptic Gospels: Their Contribution to Narrative Structuring," in *Discourse Studies & Biblical Interpretation: A Festschrift in Honor of Stephen H. Levinsohn*, ed. Steven E. Runge (Bellingham, WA: Logos Bible Software, 2011), 157–90.

Present   Used to indicate foreground material (material that is thematically prominent and moves the discourse forward).

Perfect   Used also to indicate action that is prominent.

For example, John 20:1–10 mixes aorist, present, imperfect, and pluperfect indicative tense-forms. The narrative begins with a string of present tenses (the so-called historical present): ἔρχεται, βλέπει, τρέχει, ἔρχεται, λέγει (vv. 1–2). The present tense-forms highlight and provide a transition to a new scene. One imperfect is found in verse 2, ἐφίλει, indicating supplementary material. Verses 3–4 switch to an aorist, ἐξῆλθεν, followed by two imperfects, ἤρχοντο and ἔτρεχον, and then more aorists: προέδραμεν, ἦλθεν. The aorists carry the story along, and the imperfects indicate supplementary material. Verse 5 begins with a present tense-form βλέπει to refer to looking into the tomb but switches to an aorist to refer to entering it (εἰσῆλθεν). Verse 6 then contains two present tense-forms: ἔρχεται brings Peter to the tomb, and θεωρεῖ is used along with the aorist of entering (εἰσῆλθεν). A pattern emerges: the aorists summarize the entering into the tomb, while the presents draw attention to what is more important: seeing what is in the tomb. Verses 8–10 end with a string of aorist forms, εἰσῆλθεν, εἶδεν, ἐπίστευσεν, ἀπῆλθον, which move the story forward by resuming the main story line. The one pluperfect form (ᾔδεισαν, v. 9) may add further supplementary material or close out this section.

In 1 John 2:12–14 the author, in repeating his threefold purpose for writing, switches from the present-tense γράφω in verses 12, 13 to the aorist of the same verb, ἔγραψα, in verse 14. Under a traditional view of Greek verb tenses, one would have to account for why the author switches from a present to a past tense: is the author referring to an earlier part of his letter or to a previous letter or writing? Some think the change is merely stylistic.[14] However, verbal aspect can make sense of the shift. Both tenses refer to the writing of the same letter in its entirety. The present tense γράφω marks the material in verses 12 and 13 as significant and makes emphatic statements as to the author's main intention in writing. Then the aorist tense in verse 14 simply summarizes the repeated assertions of his purpose for writing. According to Porter, the author "introduces a set of assertions [vv. 12, 13] with Present verbs to his three-fold audience. . . . Rather than using the more heavily marked Present to re-introduce his repeated assertions the author uses

14. See Raymond E. Brown, *The Epistles of John*, Anchor Bible 30 (Garden City, NY: Doubleday, 1982), 297.

the less heavily marked Aorist in the second set [v. 14] so as not to detract emphasis from the message itself."[15]

Again, this is not to suggest that the aspects always function this way or that this is the meaning of the aspects. But since they sometimes do function in this manner, it is worth asking whether changes in tense-forms in a passage are for the purpose of structuring the discourse or establishing prominence.

6.7. An aspectual view of verb tenses does not mean that the Greek language does not or cannot indicate time. Rather, time is primarily signaled by other elements, such as temporal adverbs or deictic (pointing) indicators (e.g., νῦν, σήμερον, πότε, ὅτε). Literary genre itself may also function to indicate time (e.g., narrative indicates past-time events). Even for those who still want to see some temporal element in the Greek verb system, it remains advisable to look at the broader context to determine the time of an action. Any given aspect can be used in past, present, future, and timeless contexts.[16]

6.8. One unique feature of this book is that it will avoid the labels that are commonly attached to verb tenses in most grammars. For example, one often finds such descriptive labels as *progressive present, iterative present, inceptive imperfect, conative imperfect, constative aorist, ingressive aorist,* and *consummative perfect.*[17] However, these labels are more appropriate for contextual information that gives evidence for the kind of action than for the aspects themselves. Furthermore, they fail to distinguish between semantics (the meaning of the tense-forms) and pragmatics (the various contexts in which the aspects are used) or between aspect (the author's viewpoint) and *Aktionsart* (the kind of action). It is illegitimate to make the verb tenses bear all of the information from the surrounding context (in the same way that all the meaning from the context should not be loaded onto a single word, a word-study fallacy). There are no such things as iterative presents, conative imperfects, or ingressive aorists. These labels are at most only descriptions, which may or may not be accurate, of actions *based on broader contextual information*; they are not the meanings of the tenses/aspects themselves. Verbal aspect simply indicates the author's perspective on the action, irrespective of the objective nature of the action. At most, it can be said that "an aorist tense-form is used in an ingressive context" when there is enough clear information in the context to indicate the beginning of an action. But the aspects of the verbs themselves do not "mean" these things or emphasize them. Often these labels reflect more the necessity of English translation. As

---

15. Porter, *Verbal Aspect*, 230.
16. McKay, *New Syntax*, 39. Porter (*Idioms*, 28–42) gives examples.
17. For use of these labels, along with definitions and descriptions, see Wallace 513–86.

Martin M. Culy says, "Simply put, Greek verb tenses do not *denote* semantic features such as ingressive, iterative, or conative; they certainly do not *emphasize* such notions; at best they *allow* for ingressive, iterative, or conative *translations*."[18] Therefore, these labels are better set aside; this grammar will not use them.

Kind of Action (*Aktionsart*)

6.9. We have argued above that it is important to distinguish between kind of action (*Aktionsart*) and aspect (viewpoint). Kind of action is usually the focus of grammars that use the terminology of iterative, continuous, punctiliar, consummative, ingressive, and such. As suggested above, these notions are not encoded in the verb tense endings. As Decker concludes, *Aktionsart* "is neither synonymous with aspect nor based on the tense-form of the verb."[19] The kind of action is determined by such factors as the meaning of the verb (its lexis), modifiers or adjuncts, and broader contextual features.

Lexis

6.10. In Mark 5:22 the act of Jairus falling (πίπτει) at Jesus' feet is an instantaneous act, but this is a matter of the meaning of the word "to fall" in this context. When Jesus tells his followers to "remain" in him (John 15:4), he may imply a continuing activity based on the meaning of μείνατε (remain), even though the tense-form of μείνατε is aorist. Other verbs such as εὑρίσκω (I find) or ἀνοίγω (I open) may suggest actions of short duration. The verb ἄρχομαι (I begin) often indicates the beginning of an action (ingressive; see Matt. 4:17).

Modifiers and Adjuncts

6.11. In Rom. 1:9 Paul makes continuous, unceasing prayer for his readers, which is indicated not by the present-tense ποιοῦμαι (I make) but by the adverb ἀδιαλείπτως (unceasingly). Likewise, Jesus' death is "once for all" in Heb. 9:28, based not on the aorist-tense προσενεχθείς (having been offered) but on the adverb ἅπαξ (once). At most the aorist allows for this understanding.

---

18. Martin M. Culy, *I, II, III John: A Handbook on the Greek Text* (Waco: Baylor University Press, 2004), xxiii.
19. Decker, *Reading Koine Greek*, 226.

In Mark 9:22 the demon-possessed man threw (ἔβαλεν, aorist) himself into the fire and into water πολλάκις (many times), a clearly repetitive action.

Context

6.12. Other contextual features can contribute to our understanding of the kind of action. The resurrection of the saints in Rev. 20:4 might be ingressive (ἔζησαν, they came to life), but this conclusion is based not on the aorist ἔζησαν but rather on the contrast between two states: being beheaded and being alive (moreover an ingressive notion is not certain). In Matt. 4:25 the plural subject ὄχλοι πολλοί (further described as people from Galilee, Decapolis, Jerusalem, and Judea) makes the act of following (ἠκολούθησαν) a repeated one over a period of time.

To summarize, in order to determine the kind of action for any given verb, the interpreter must carefully weigh a number of factors, including the lexical meaning of the verb, modifiers such as adverbs, and the broader context.

The Aspects

6.13. Following the description of each aspect below, we will give some examples of the different kinds of contexts, temporal and "kinds of action" (*Aktionsarten*), in which the aspects can be used. These are not to be confused with labels for various "kinds" of presents, or aorists, or perfects found in other grammars. What follows the description of each aspect is *only a sampling* of the kinds of *contexts* in which the tenses can be used. We will not attempt to be exhaustive, but only representative and illustrative.

Perfective Aspect: The Aorist Tense

6.14. Our treatment of the Greek tense-forms begins with the aorist since it is often regarded as the "default" tense, the tense used "unless there was special reason for using some other tense" (Robertson 831). The aorist tense views action in its entirety or as a complete whole,[20] irrespective of the duration of action or of the time of its occurrence. It is the primary tense used in narrative to summarize past events that compose the main story line. In expositional (e.g., epistolary) literature it is used of past action or of action that forms the background for more prominent material. The aorist tense can

---

20. Saying that the aorist views the action as a *complete* whole is not to be confused with saying that the action is *completed*.

be used in a variety of temporal contexts and to refer to a variety of kinds of action (*Aktionsarten*). The following descriptions should not be confused with the labels used in most grammars. The meaning of the aorist is the same: the action is conceived of as perfective.

1. *Aorist used of past-time action.* A common use of the aorist is to refer to action that is temporally past, viewing the event as complete. This view of action as a complete whole lent itself naturally and logically to being used of past-time events.[21] Such use of the aorist is the staple of narrative.

ἰδοὺ μάγοι ἀπὸ ἀνατολῶν **παρεγένοντο** εἰς Ἱεροσόλυμα (Matt. 2:1)	Look, magi from the east **arrived** in Jerusalem.
ἔτι ἁμαρτωλῶν ὄντων ἡμῶν Χριστὸς ὑπὲρ ἡμῶν **ἀπέθανεν**. (Rom. 5:8)	While we were still sinners, Christ **died** for us.
Καὶ **εἶδον** ἐπὶ τὴν δεξιὰν τοῦ καθημένου ἐπὶ τοῦ θρόνου βιβλίον (Rev. 5:1)	And **I saw** upon the right hand of the one seated upon the throne a scroll.

2. *Aorist used of present-time action.* Particularly with verbs of emotion, or verbs indicating short duration (such as throwing, βάλλω), the aorist can be used of events that occur in the present or at least extend into the present from the standpoint of the author.

ἐγὼ **ἐβάπτισα** ὑμᾶς ὕδατι, αὐτὸς δὲ βαπτίσει ὑμᾶς ἐν πνεύματι ἁγίῳ. (Mark 1:8)	I **baptize** you with water, but he will baptize you with/in the Holy Spirit.
ἔγνων τί ποιήσω (Luke 16:4)	**I know** what I will do.

This is the classic example of a present-referring aorist. Here the aorist refers to a present knowledge from the standpoint of the speaker, not to something that happened in the recent past.

21. Gary A. Long, *Grammatical Concepts 101 for Biblical Greek* (Peabody, MA: Hendrickson, 2006), 73.

| ὃν ἔπεμψα πρὸς ὑμᾶς εἰς αὐτὸ τοῦτο (Col. 4:8) | Whom **I send** to you for this very thing. |

Grammarians often label this an "epistolary aorist." The so-called epistolary aorist is usually understood to refer to the writing or sending of the letter from the standpoint of its readers, for whom it is a past event (Brooks and Winbery 102). Yet this assumes that the aorist must always carry past-time implication. Rather, from the author's perspective the aorist refers to the writing of the entire letter (Porter 36–37).

3. *Aorist used of future-time action.* Though a rare usage, the aorist can refer to a future action. This use of the aorist is usually understood to mean that the writer is presenting a future event as so certain that it is portrayed as if it has already happened.[22] Again, such an interpretation assumes that the aorist must always carry past-time implications. But when used of future time, is the aorist any more certain than the future tense or than the present? Instead, we argue that this is simply a future-referring use of the perfective aspect: a future action is viewed as a complete whole.

| Ἰδοὺ **ἦλθεν** κύριος ἐν ἁγίαις μυριάσιν αὐτοῦ (Jude 14) | Look, the Lord **is going to come** with myriads of his holy ones. |
| ἀλλ᾽ ἐν ταῖς ἡμέραις τῆς φωνῆς τοῦ ἑβδόμου ἀγγέλου, ὅταν μέλλῃ σαλπίζειν, καὶ **ἐτελέσθη** τὸ μυστήριον τοῦ θεοῦ (Rev. 10:7) | But in the days of the sound [of the trumpet] of the seventh angel, whenever he is about to sound the trumpet, and the mystery of God **will be completed.** |

The reference to ὅταν μέλλῃ σαλπίζειν suggests the future-time context for ἐτελέσθη.

| Καὶ εἶδον . . . ἀγγέλους ἑπτὰ ἔχοντας πληγὰς ἑπτὰ τὰς ἐσχάτας, ὅτι ἐν αὐταῖς **ἐτελέσθη** ὁ θυμὸς τοῦ θεοῦ. (Rev. 15:1) | And I saw . . . the seven angels holding the seven last plagues, for in them the wrath of God **will be completed.** (*since the bowls have not yet been poured out at this point*) |

22. Brooks and Winbery 103; Wallace 564.

4. *Aorist used of timeless or omnitemporal action.* The aorist can refer to
an action that can occur at any time (not at any one specific time) or to
make timeless statements (Young 124). Some have attempted to argue
that the aorist tense refers to a specific event in the past that becomes
an example for subsequent occurrences (BDF §333). Instead, the aorist is used to present the timeless or regular occurrence of an action in
its entirety. It is often used in proverbial contexts or in other universal
statements. This use of the aorist can often be translated into English
with the present tense.

Σὺ εἶ ὁ υἱός μου ὁ ἀγαπητός, ἐν σοὶ **εὐδόκησα**. (Mark 1:11)	You are my beloved Son; in you **I am pleased.**

> It is fruitless to postulate a past event at which time the Father was
> pleased with the Son (e.g., baptism). The implication is that the Father
> is always pleased with his Son, a clearly timeless use of the aorist.

οὐδεὶς γάρ ποτε τὴν ἑαυτοῦ σάρκα **ἐμίσησεν**, ἀλλὰ ἐκτρέφει καὶ θάλπει αὐτήν (Eph. 5:29)	For no one ever **hates** his/her own flesh, but nourishes and cherishes it.
ἀνέτειλεν γὰρ ὁ ἥλιος . . . καὶ **ἐξήρανεν** τὸν χόρτον, καὶ τὸ ἄνθος αὐτοῦ **ἐξέπεσεν** καὶ ἡ εὐπρέπεια τοῦ προσώπου αὐτοῦ **ἀπώλετο**· (James 1:11)	For the sun **rises** . . . and the grass **withers** and its flower **falls off** and the beauty of its appearance **passes away.**

> See also 1 Pet. 1:24.

5. *Aorist used of extended action.* The aorist can be used of action that
takes place over a more or less extended period of time but is still viewed
in its entirety. This is one of the more common usages of the aorist.
Grammarians often label this the constative or global aorist.[23]

Ἐνέμεινεν δὲ διετίαν ὅλην ἐν ἰδίῳ μισθώματι, καὶ **ἀπεδέχετο** πάντας τοὺς εἰσπορευομένους πρὸς αὐτόν (Acts 28:30)	He [i.e., Paul] **remained** there for two entire years in his own rented house, and **he welcomed** all who came to him.

> The time frame is established by the temporal indicator διετίαν ὅλην.

23. Dana and Mantey 196; BDF §332; Wallace 557–58.

ἐβασίλευσεν ὁ θάνατος ἀπὸ Ἀδὰμ μέχρι Μωϋσέως (Rom. 5:14)	Death **reigned** from Adam until Moses.
καὶ ἔζησαν καὶ **ἐβασίλευσαν** μετὰ τοῦ χριστοῦ χίλια ἔτη. (Rev. 20:4)	And they lived and **reigned** with Christ for a thousand years.

> Whether one takes "a thousand years" literally or symbolically, at the visionary level the aorist ἐβασίλευσαν encompasses a period of "one thousand years." This creates difficulties for views of the aorist as "punctiliar."

6. *Aorist used of instantaneous, onetime, or punctiliar action.* In the past this was often thought (incorrectly) to be the primary semantic force or meaning of the aorist. However, grammars now largely avoid this misunderstanding.[24] Still, the aorist *can be used* of this kind of action *when the context warrants it.* Often the lexical meaning of the verb indicates this type of action (see ἔπεσαν below).

οὐδὲ δι' αἵματος τράγων καὶ μόσχων διὰ δὲ τοῦ ἰδίου αἵματος, **εἰσῆλθεν** ἐφάπαξ εἰς τὰ ἅγια (Heb. 9:12)	Neither through the blood of goats and calves, but through his own blood he **entered** once and for all into the holy place.

> The nature of the action is established on the basis of ἐφάπαξ, not the aorist tense-form.

καὶ οἱ πρεσβύτεροι **ἔπεσαν** καὶ προσεκύνησαν. (Rev. 5:14)	And the elders **fell** and worshiped.

> Notice that the aorist προσεκύνησαν (worshiped) is not punctiliar.

7. *Aorist used of repeated action.* A series of actions that occur over a period of time can be gathered up into a single whole with the aorist tense.

---

24. See especially the important, older work of Frank Stagg, "The Abused Aorist," *Journal of Biblical Literature* 91 (1972): 222–31. After the work of Stagg, there is no excuse to perpetuate this and other misconceptions regarding the aorist tense.

| πολλάκις **προεθέμην** ἐλθεῖν πρὸς ὑμᾶς (Rom. 1:13) | Many times **I intended** to come to you. (*Πολλάκις establishes the repeated nature of the action.*) |
| Κατὰ πίστιν **ἀπέθανον** οὗτοι πάντες, μὴ λαβόντες τὰς ἐπαγγελίας (Heb. 11:13) | These all **died** in faith, not receiving the promises. |

> Here the aorist refers to a series of deaths (πάντες) in verses 1–12 that span a lengthy period of time; the aorist gathers them all up in summary fashion.

8. *Aorist used of ingressive or entry-point action.* When there are clear contextual indicators, the aorist may be said to refer to the beginning of an action, though many of the examples often considered ingressive by other grammars should be understood otherwise. For example, some grammars claim that verbs referring to states (live, know, be angry, rule)[25] indicate entry into those states when in the aorist tense. However, an aorist could just as easily refer to the entire state, not just entry into it. There must be clear clues in the context for an ingressive notion, such as a change from one state to another (though this is not always ingressive) or a meaning inherent in the lexis (ἄρχομαι). Apart from such clues, appeals to ingressive action should be avoided. The author is not emphasizing ingressive action with the aorist, and this may depend more on the necessity of English translation.

| Καὶ πάλιν **ἤρξατο** διδάσκειν παρὰ τὴν θάλασσαν. (Mark 4:1) | And again **he began** to teach by the sea. |

> An ingressive notion is clearly established by the lexical meaning of ἤρξατο.

| ὅτι δι' ὑμᾶς **ἐπτώχευσεν** πλούσιος ὤν (2 Cor. 8:9) | That though being rich, **he became poor** for your sake. |

> There is a contrast of two states, but this could still be understood in terms of Christ living in a state of poverty ("he was poor") rather than his entrance into that state.

---

25. Fanning, *Verbal Aspect*, 261–63.

καὶ **ἔζησαν** καὶ ἐβασίλευσαν
μετὰ τοῦ χριστοῦ χίλια ἔτη.
(Rev. 20:4)

And **they came to life / lived**
and reigned with Christ for a
thousand years.

The ingressive notion is possible based on the contrast between
having been beheaded (v. 3) and now living, but it is not implied by
the aorist, and the context does not focus on an ingressive notion.

Imperfective Aspect: The Present Tense

6.15. The present tense-form is the one chosen by the author to portray
an action as in progress, as developing or unfolding, irrespective of the time
or the nature of the action itself. Grammars have frequently described the
present tense as indicating action that is continuous, habitual, or repeated.[26]
However, this is a misunderstanding of the semantics of the present tense that
fits only some of the contexts in which the present is used, and it confuses
aspect with *Aktionsart* (kind of action). In contrast to the aorist tense, which
can be understood as the "external" perspective (action viewed in its entirety,
as a complete whole), the present tense represents the "internal" perspective, a
more close-up view of the action, seeing it as a process in progress or unfolding. This perspective explains its common use to refer to present-time actions,
but the present tense can be used in a variety of temporal contexts and of
more than one kind of action. Again, the following is only representative and
should not be confused with the labels used in most grammars.

1. *Present used of action in the present time.* A very common function of
   the present tense is to indicate action taking place in the present from
   the standpoint of the speaker. This usage needs little illustration.

   Θαυμάζω ὅτι οὕτως ταχέως
   μετατίθεσθε ἀπὸ τοῦ καλέσαντος
   ὑμᾶς ἐν χάριτι Χριστοῦ εἰς
   ἕτερον εὐαγγέλιον (Gal. 1:6)

   I marvel that you have so
   quickly turned from the one
   who called you in the grace of
   Christ to another gospel.

   Κακοπαθεῖ τις ἐν ὑμῖν; προσευχέ-
   σθω· (James 5:13)

   Is anyone among you **sick?** He/
   she should pray.

---

26. Mounce 135, 245, 250; Dana and Mantey 178–79, 181; Black 96.

Οἶδα ποῦ **κατοικεῖς**, ὅπου ὁ
θρόνος τοῦ Σατανᾶ, καὶ **κρατεῖς**
τὸ ὄνομά μου (Rev. 2:13)

I know where **you live**, where
the throne of Satan is, and yet
you hold on to my name.

2. *Present used of action in the past (the so-called historical present or
narrative present).* The present tense can be used of past-time action
from the standpoint of the speaker, typically in narrative contexts: a
past action is viewed as in progress. In English this will normally be
translated with a past tense.

Ἐν δὲ ταῖς ἡμέραις ἐκείναις
παραγίνεται Ἰωάννης ὁ
βαπτιστὴς κηρύσσων ἐν τῇ
ἐρήμῳ τῆς Ἰουδαίας (Matt. 3:1)

And in those days John the
Baptist **arrived**, preaching in
the desert of Judea.

καὶ **ἔρχονται** φέροντες πρὸς
αὐτὸν παραλυτικὸν αἰρόμενον
ὑπὸ τεσσάρων. (Mark 2:3)

And **they came** bringing to him
a paralyzed man, being carried
by four [people].

λέγει ἡ μήτηρ τοῦ Ἰησοῦ πρὸς
αὐτόν· Οἶνον οὐκ ἔχουσιν.
(John 2:3)

The mother of Jesus **said** to
him, "They have no wine."

καὶ ἡ οὐρὰ αὐτοῦ **σύρει** τὸ τρίτον
τῶν ἀστέρων τοῦ οὐρανοῦ, καὶ
ἔβαλεν αὐτοὺς εἰς τὴν γῆν.
(Rev. 12:4)

And his tail **dragged** a third
of the stars of heaven, and he
threw them onto the earth.

Excursus: The Historical, or Narrative, Present

There has been much discussion on the phenomenon known as the "historical present," that is, the present tense used in narrative to refer to past-time
events. This has been explained in various ways. Based on the belief that tenses
of indicative verbs in Greek always include time as part of their meaning, some
have suggested that by using the present tense the author wants to draw readers
into the past events, as if they are actually there and seeing the action unfold
before their eyes! However, this does not explain why the author sometimes
alternates between aorist and present tenses in narrative, requiring that readers
keep changing their point of reference: first past, now present, then past again!

Furthermore, it does not explain why the author selects some events but not others to be portrayed with the present tense.

Some have suggested that the present tense is reduced to a "zero aspect" (the present loses its aspectual meaning when referring to events that took place in the past). However, this incorrectly assumes that the present tense means "repeated, continuous, or progressive" action, which is hard to reconcile with some past-time actions (Wallace 508–9). A better explanation can be found in verbal aspect (Porter, *Verbal Aspect*, 189–98; Campbell, *Verbal Aspect*, 57–76). If Greek tenses do not primarily communicate time, then they can be used outside of their common temporal spheres.

The effect of using a present tense (imperfective aspect) in past time narrative that is dominated by aorists and imperfects is to make something in the discourse stick out. Sometimes certain actions or speeches are highlighted using the present. At other times the present will point forward to significant speeches or scenes, or it can function as a transition to an important event or shift in scene.

Compared to the aorist, the present is the more marked tense-form (i.e., it carries more meaning and is more unusual in narrative; Porter, *Idioms*, 31). The present tense, which looks at an action as unfolding or in progress, could be seen as slowing down the narrative in order to focus attention on an action or an upcoming element (Campbell, *Verbal Aspect*, 54). Therefore, in the example from Matt. 3:1 above, the present tense-form παραγίνεται functions to draw attention to a new character and scene. The important point is that in narrative the present tense should get us to sit up, take notice, and ask why the author has used it.

---

3. *Present used of action in the future.* It has long been recognized that the present tense can be used of action that will occur in the future from the standpoint of the speaker. This often occurs with verbs of motion, such as verbs of coming and going.[27]

Ἠλίας μὲν **ἔρχεται** καὶ ἀποκαταστήσει πάντα· (Matt. 17:11)	Elijah **is** indeed **coming**, and he will restore all things. (*Note the future tense-form that follows the present.*)
Ἰδοὺ **ἀναβαίνομεν** εἰς Ἱεροσόλυμα, καὶ ὁ υἱὸς τοῦ ἀνθρώπου παραδοθήσεται (Mark 10:33)	Look, **we are going to go up** to Jerusalem, and the Son of Man will be betrayed.

27. McKay, *New Syntax*, 41; Fanning, *Verbal Aspect*, 222, 225; Wallace 335–36.

| καὶ ἐπιθυμήσουσιν ἀποθανεῖν καὶ **φεύγει** ὁ θάνατος ἀπ᾽ αὐτῶν. (Rev. 9:6) | They will desire to die, and death **will flee** from them. (*The present tense-form follows a string of futures.*) |

4. *Present used of action that is omnitemporal or timeless.* The present tense can be used to refer to action that is unrestricted temporally; such action can occur at any time. Here the present tense is often found in proverbial or universal contexts. The difference between this and the aorist used of timeless action is verbal aspect. Regularly occurring actions can be seen from the standpoint of their development, as a process in progress, rather than as a complete whole (Porter 33).

ἱλαρὸν γὰρ δότην **ἀγαπᾷ** ὁ θεός. (2 Cor. 9:7)	For God **loves** a cheerful giver.
ἡ γὰρ κρίσις ἀνέλεος τῷ μὴ ποιήσαντι ἔλεος· **κατακαυχᾶται** ἔλεος κρίσεως. (James 2:13)	For judgment without mercy [will be] for the one who does not show mercy; mercy **triumphs** over judgment.
καὶ ἔκραξεν φωνῇ μεγάλῃ ὥσπερ λέων **μυκᾶται**. (Rev. 10:3)	And he cried out with a great voice, as a lion **roars**. (*a proverbial-type statement*)

5. *Present used of action that is durative, ongoing, or repeated.* The present tense can be used of action that continues over a period of time. Many grammars incorrectly associate this with the basic meaning of the present tense (continuous action). But once again, continuity can be communicated only by the context.

| Καὶ διὰ τοῦτο καὶ ἡμεῖς **εὐχαριστοῦμεν** τῷ θεῷ ἀδιαλείπτως, ὅτι παραλαβόντες λόγον ἀκοῆς παρ᾽ ἡμῶν τοῦ θεοῦ ἐδέξασθε οὐ λόγον ἀνθρώπων ἀλλὰ καθὼς ἀληθῶς ἐστιν λόγον θεοῦ (1 Thess. 2:13) | And for this reason **we** also **give thanks** to God continuously, for having received the word of God that you heard from us, you accepted it not as a word from humans but just as it is truly, a word from God. |

It is the adverb ἀδιαλείπτως, not the present tense itself, that establishes this as a durative, ongoing action.

128

ὁσάκις γὰρ ἐὰν **ἐσθίητε** τὸν
ἄρτον τοῦτον καὶ τὸ ποτήριον
πίνητε, τὸν θάνατον τοῦ κυρίου
καταγγέλλετε, ἄχρι οὗ ἔλθῃ.
(1 Cor. 11:26)

For as often as **you eat** this
bread and **drink** the cup, **you
proclaim** the Lord's death until
he comes.

Both ὁσάκις and ἄχρι οὗ ἔλθῃ signal the repeated nature of the
action.

Εὐχαριστοῦμεν τῷ θεῷ πατρὶ τοῦ
κυρίου ἡμῶν Ἰησοῦ Χριστοῦ
πάντοτε (Col. 1:3)

We give thanks to God, the Father of our Lord Jesus Christ,
always.

The adverb πάντοτε contributes the sense of continuation.

6. *Present used of action of short duration.* The present tense can sometimes be used of an action that is of relatively short duration or is a
specific action (e.g., λέγω can be used of things said quickly). This often
depends on the lexical meaning of the verb (see πίπτει below).

καὶ ἰδὼν αὐτὸν **πίπτει** πρὸς τοὺς
πόδας αὐτοῦ (Mark 5:22)

And seeing him, **he fell** at his
feet.

Παραγγέλλω σοι ἐν ὀνόματι
Ἰησοῦ Χριστοῦ ἐξελθεῖν ἀπ'
αὐτῆς· (Acts 16:18)

I command you in the name of
Jesus Christ to come out from
her. *(a single, not a repeated,
command)*

Ἀσπάζεται ὑμᾶς Ἀρίσταρχος ὁ
συναιχμάλωτός μου (Col. 4:10)

Aristarchus, my fellow pris-
oner, **greets** you.

7. *Present used of general action.* The present tense can be used of action
that is only general and whose duration is not specified.

Παῦλος ... ἔφη· Ἄνδρες
Ἀθηναῖοι, κατὰ πάντα ὡς
δεισιδαιμονεστέρους ὑμᾶς
θεωρῶ. (Acts 17:22)

Paul ... said, "Athenians, **I
perceive** that you are extremely
religious in respect to all
things."

Οὐ γὰρ **ἐπαισχύνομαι** τὸ
εὐαγγέλιον (Rom. 1:16)

For **I am** not **ashamed** of the
gospel.

πᾶς ὁ γεγεννημένος ἐκ τοῦ θεοῦ ἁμαρτίαν οὐ ποιεῖ... καὶ οὐ δύναται ἁμαρτάνειν (1 John 3:9)

Everyone who has been born from God **does** not **commit** sin . . . and **he/she is** not **able to sin.**

This verse has evoked much discussion, since it appears to conflict with John's earlier statement that to claim we have no sin makes God out to be a liar (1:10)! To alleviate the difficulty of the author claiming the possibility of perfection in this life in 3:9, some have concluded that the present tense should be seen as indicating continuous, habitual, or repeated (iterative) action: Christians do not "continue to sin" or "habitually sin."[28] The NIV reflects this interpretation: "No one who is born of God will continue to sin." See also the NIV's translation of 3:6b ("No one who continues to sin . . ."). However, this is a misunderstanding of the present tense and illegitimately attributes a continuous notion or repetition to the present without clear contextual clues. The present tense only looks at the action as a process in progress.[29] More likely, 1 John 3:9 is just a general reference (that person "does not sin"), with no indication of duration or repetition. The present tense is the more marked form, used to foreground and draw attention to what should not have any place in the life of Christians since they are "born of God": they should not sin!

Imperfective Aspect and Remoteness: The Imperfect Tense

6.16. Since both the present and imperfect tense-forms communicate imperfective aspect (action viewed as in progress, as developing or unfolding), the question naturally arises, What is the difference between the two? The imperfect tense-form, in addition to communicating imperfective aspect, also carries the notion of *remoteness*.[30] Remoteness is a spatial notion that is applied nonspatially to this tense-form. By "remote" we mean "remote from the author's perspective." The author's perspective on the action is not quite as immediate as it is when the present tense is used. To use the illustration of a parade, the imperfect has observers standing back and watching the parade as it passes a block away. By contrast, the present tense has observers standing on the street corner and watching it unfold right in front of them. This accounts for why the imperfect tense-form is frequently (though not exclusively) used in past-time contexts. Remote action translates easily into

28. Donald W. Burdick, *The Letters of John the Apostle: An In-Depth Commentary* (Chicago: Moody, 1985), 246.

29. See David L. Mathewson, "The Abused Present," *Bulletin for Biblical Research* 23, no. 3 (2013): 343–63.

30. Porter, *Verbal Aspect*, 207–8; Campbell, *Verbal Aspect*, 84–85.

remote time. The concept of remoteness accounts for the various ways that the imperfect tense-form is used.

1. *Imperfect used of action in the past.* The imperfect tense is often used of past-time action viewed as in progress by the author. It is commonly employed this way in narrative.

καὶ ἰδοὺ ἄγγελοι προσῆλθον καὶ διηκόνουν αὐτῷ. (Matt. 4:11)	And look, angels came and **ministered** to him.
ὅτε δὲ ἦλθον, **ὑπέστελλεν** καὶ **ἀφώριζεν** ἑαυτόν, φοβούμενος τοὺς ἐκ περιτομῆς. (Gal. 2:12)	But when they came, **he withdrew** and **separated** himself, fearing those of the circumcision.
καὶ ἐγὼ **ἔκλαιον** πολὺ ὅτι οὐδεὶς ἄξιος εὑρέθη (Rev. 5:4)	And I **wept** greatly, for no one was found worthy.

2. *Imperfect used of nonpast action.* Though commonly used in past-time contexts, the imperfect tense-form can be used in contexts that do not refer to past time.[31]

   a. *The imperfect of δεῖ (it is necessary)*

ταῦτα **ἔδει** ποιῆσαι κἀκεῖνα μὴ ἀφιέναι. (Matt. 23:23)	**It is necessary** to do these things without also neglecting the others.

   Jesus is clearly not referring to an event in the past.

   b. *The imperfect in some class 2 conditional (contrary-to-fact) sentences*

Εἰ ὁ θεὸς πατὴρ ὑμῶν **ἦν** **ἠγαπᾶτε** ἂν ἐμέ, ἐγὼ γὰρ ἐκ τοῦ θεοῦ ἐξῆλθον (John 8:42)	If God **were** your Father, you **would love** me, for I have come from God.

---

31. McKay, *New Syntax*, 45–46.

c. *The imperfect in excluded wishes (desired action that is unrealized)*

ηὐχόμην γὰρ ἀνάθεμα εἶναι   For I myself **could wish** to be
αὐτὸς ἐγὼ ἀπὸ τοῦ Χριστοῦ   cursed and cut off from Christ.
(Rom. 9:3)

3. *Imperfect used of action that is attempted (so-called conative imperfect).*
   This is the use of the imperfect in contexts where the action is only attempted or contemplated and not fully carried out. Again, indicating
   that the action is not achieved is solely a feature of the context, not
   part of the meaning of the imperfect tense, and it is more of an issue
   of English translation.

ὁ δὲ Ἰωάννης **διεκώλυεν** αὐτὸν   But John **tried to prevent** him,
λέγων· (Matt. 3:14)   saying.

καθ' ὑπερβολὴν **ἐδίωκον**   Beyond measure I was persecut-
τὴν ἐκκλησίαν τοῦ θεοῦ καὶ   ing the church of God and **was**
ἐπόρθουν αὐτήν (Gal. 1:13)   **attempting to destroy** it.

4. *Imperfect used of action that is durative or repeated.* The imperfect
   can be used, like the present, of action that is continuing, repeated, or
   customary in certain contexts.

Καὶ **ἐπορεύοντο** οἱ γονεῖς αὐτοῦ   And his parents **would go** [or
κατ' ἔτος εἰς Ἰερουσαλὴμ τῇ   "went"] each year into Jeru-
ἑορτῇ τοῦ πάσχα. (Luke 2:41)   salem on the feast of Passover.

The notion of ongoing action or repetition comes from the adjunct
κατ' ἔτος (each year).

καί τις ἀνήρ . . . , ὃν **ἐτίθουν**   And a certain man . . . , whom
καθ' ἡμέραν πρὸς τὴν θύραν τοῦ   **they set down** each day at the
ἱεροῦ (Acts 3:2)   gate of the temple.

Repetition is indicated by καθ' ἡμέραν.

καὶ **προέκοπτον** ἐν τῷ Ἰουδα-   And I **was advancing** in Judaism
ϊσμῷ ὑπὲρ πολλοὺς συνηλι-   beyond many of my contempo-
κιώτας ἐν τῷ γένει μου (Gal.   raries in my people.
1:14)

5. *Imperfect used of inceptive (ingressive) action.* The imperfect may be used of the beginning point of an action. However, this description must be used with caution. The context must be explicit; the imperfect itself does not indicate inception and certainly does not focus on it. Refer to the aorist used in ingressive contexts above.

εὐθὺς τοῖς σάββασιν **ἐδίδασκεν**   Immediately on the Sabbath
εἰς τὴν συναγωγήν. (Mark 1:21)   **he began/was teaching** in the
                                        synagogue.

> The context may suggest that Jesus began teaching since he was not doing it before. However, this is not being emphasized by or inherent in the imperfect. Mark may be referring to Jesus' entire teaching in the synagogue. When the author wants to emphasize ingression, he uses ἄρχομαι (cf. Mark 1:45).[32]

Stative Aspect: The Perfect Tense

6.17. There has been quite a bit of debate over the meaning of the perfect tense-form. The older, popular understanding of the perfect was that it depicted a past, completed action with results continuing into the present.[33] However, this understanding of the perfect does not fit numerous examples of the tense-form in the NT. Many contexts do not have a clear reference to a past action that produced the result. And many contexts cannot be understood to have results continuing into the present. Often categories of usage are created to try to deal with the problems inherent in this older approach: consummative perfects, aoristic perfects, and intensive perfects. More helpfully, McKay and Porter have argued that the meaning of the perfect tense-form is stative aspect.[34] That is, it looks at an action as an existing state of affairs. More specifically, the perfect expresses the state of the subject.[35] For example, the perfect γέγραπται suggests the idea "it is in the state of being written"; ἔγνωκαν suggests "they are in a state of knowing." Christ was "in the state of being raised" (ἐγήγερται). Furthermore, any notion of a past action that produces the state must be derived from the context and should not be seen

---

32. Rodney J. Decker, *Mark 1–8: A Handbook on the Greek Text* (Waco: Baylor University Press, 2014), 24–25.

33. Dana and Mantey 200; Moule 13; Brooks and Winbery 104. See also Wallace 573.

34. Porter 21–22; McKay, *New Syntax*, 49. See, however, Campbell (*Verbal Aspect*, 195–99), who argues that the perfect tense-form communicates imperfective aspect with heightened proximity to the action (sort of a super present). See Porter, *Linguistic Analysis*, 195–215.

35. McKay, *New Syntax*, 49.

as part of the meaning of the perfect tense itself. The perfect tense sometimes is used to lend prominence to particular actions in a discourse.

1. *The perfect used of past time.* Though not common, sometimes the perfect tense refers to a past action, envisioning a past state of affairs.

Ἰωάννης μαρτυρεῖ περὶ αὐτοῦ καὶ **κέκραγεν** λέγων· (John 1:15)	John witnessed concerning him and **cried out**, saying.
καὶ ὅτι **ἐγήγερται** τῇ ἡμέρᾳ τῇ τρίτῃ κατὰ τὰς γραφάς (1 Cor. 15:4)	And that **he was raised** on the third day according to the Scriptures.

> Preachers and commentators frequently appeal to the perfect tense here for theological capital. Thus the fact that in 1 Cor. 15:4 Jesus was raised (ἐγήγερται, perfect tense) is taken to mean that Jesus was raised in the past with consequences that continue into the present and even further.[36] He is still the risen Lord! But the tense here in itself says nothing about that fact—the context actually restricts the state indicated by the perfect ἐγήγερται to a point in the past: "the third day" (τῇ ἡμέρᾳ τῇ τρίτῃ). The broader context is abundantly clear that Jesus remains the risen Lord (an extremely important theological point that Paul goes to great pains to emphasize), but the perfect tense does not indicate it grammatically. It says only that on the third day Christ was in the state of being raised. Paul chooses the perfect tense to signal and highlight the main theme of the rest of the chapter: the resurrection.

καὶ **εἴρηκα** αὐτῷ· Κύριέ μου, σὺ οἶδας. (Rev. 7:14)	And **I said** to him, "My Lord, you know."

2. *The perfect used of present time.* The perfect tense can refer to a state of affairs in the present. Many grammars label this the "intensive perfect."

Ἐλήλυθεν ἡ ὥρα ἵνα δοξασθῇ ὁ υἱὸς τοῦ ἀνθρώπου. (John 12:23)	The hour **has come / is here** in order that the Son of Man might be glorified.

---

36. Gordon D. Fee, *1 Corinthians*, rev. ed., New International Commentary on the New Testament (Grand Rapids: Eerdmans, 2014), 806.

ἀπεθάνετε γάρ, καὶ ἡ ζωὴ ὑμῶν **κέκρυπται** σὺν τῷ Χριστῷ ἐν τῷ θεῷ· (Col. 3:3)	For you died, and your life **is hidden** with Christ in God.
Οἶδα τὰ ἔργα σου, καὶ τὸν κόπον καὶ τὴν ὑπομονήν σου (Rev. 2:2)	**I know** your works, and your labor and endurance.

3. *The perfect used of temporally unrestricted action.* The perfect tense can also be used of an action that can occur at any time, in gnomic or proverbial contexts.

ἡ γὰρ ὕπανδρος γυνὴ τῷ ζῶντι ἀνδρὶ **δέδεται** νόμῳ· ἐὰν δὲ ἀποθάνῃ ὁ ἀνήρ, **κατήργηται** ἀπὸ τοῦ νόμου τοῦ ἀνδρός. (Rom. 7:2)	For the wife **is bound** to her husband by the law while he is living. But if the husband dies, **she is freed** from the law of the husband.
κατενόησεν γὰρ ἑαυτὸν καὶ **ἀπελήλυθεν** καὶ εὐθέως ἐπελάθετο ὁποῖος ἦν. (James 1:24)	For he/she looks at himself/herself and he/she **goes away** and immediately forgets what sort [of person] he/she was.

4. *The "aoristic" perfect?* Many grammars suggest that in some cases the perfect tense has been reduced to the sense of an aorist. Especially in narrative, when the perfect is found alongside other aorists, the "existing results" or "state" do not seem to be present.[37] This suggestion is also combined by grammarians with the view that the perfect tense was becoming more confused with the aorist and starting to die out in Koine Greek.

However, this category of the perfect often appears to depend more on the fact that an existing state in the present is not reflected in English translation. The presence of the perfect and aorist in the same context does not require that they carry identical aspectual value. The fact that the perfect occurs alongside other aorists may suggest instead an intentional choice on the part of the author and a distinction in meaning. This is particularly true when the same verb occurs in both the aorist and perfect within the same context (as with Rev. 5:7 in the example below). While there probably are times where the perfect tense has been

37. Wallace 578–79; Turner 69; BDF §343; Chrys Caragounis, *The Development of Greek and the New Testament* (Grand Rapids: Baker Academic, 2006), 154–55.

reduced in meaning to an aorist, this category should not be applied uncritically. Some of these so-called aoristic perfects should be given their full stative force. They are just perfects used in past-time contexts.

τοῦτον ὁ θεὸς καὶ ἄρχοντα καὶ λυτρωτὴν **ἀπέσταλκεν** σὺν χειρὶ ἀγγέλου (Acts 7:35)	This one [i.e., Moses] God **sent** as a ruler and deliverer together with the hand of the angel.
καὶ ἦλθεν καὶ **εἴληφεν** ἐκ τῆς δεξιᾶς τοῦ καθημένου ἐπὶ τοῦ θρόνου. (Rev. 5:7)	And he came and **took** [the scroll] from the right hand of the one seated on the throne.

> But notice that the very next verb in the following verse (v. 8) is the aorist ἔλαβεν of the same verb (λαμβάνω), which suggests that the choice of the perfect in verse 7 is intentional (see a similar use of εἴληφεν in Rev. 8:5).

Stative Aspect and Remoteness: The Pluperfect Tense

6.18. As Porter (42) says, the "use of the pluperfect is restricted in the NT." It was being replaced by a periphrastic construction (see chap. 10, on participles): the imperfect of εἰμί + a perfect participle. Like the perfect, the pluperfect communicates stative aspect. In addition to this, like the imperfect tense, it also shares the feature of remoteness. The pluperfect stands in relationship to the perfect as the imperfect does to the present. Because of its remote perspective, the pluperfect is found predominantly in past-time contexts.

οἱ γὰρ μαθηταὶ αὐτοῦ **ἀπεληλύ-θεισαν** εἰς τὴν πόλιν, ἵνα τροφὰς ἀγοράσωσιν. (John 4:8)	For his disciples **had gone** into the city in order to buy food.
παρέθεντο αὐτοὺς τῷ κυρίῳ εἰς ὃν **πεπιστεύκεισαν**. (Acts 14:23)	They commended them to the Lord, in whom **they had believed**.
καὶ πάντες οἱ ἄγγελοι **εἱστήκεισαν** κύκλῳ τοῦ θρόνου καὶ τῶν πρεσβυτέρων καὶ τῶν τεσσάρων ζῴων (Rev. 7:11)	And all the angels **stood** around the throne and the elders and the four living creatures.

> The remote pluperfect form may be used so as not to distract attention from the throne or in order to portray the group of angels as more

"remote" from the throne, that is, as the outer circle of those who surround the throne.[38]

The Future Tense (Intention or Expectation)

6.19. The future tense-form seems fairly straightforward. However, there is some disagreement as to its origins and its exact meaning. Scholars have long recognized the similarity in form and function with the aorist subjunctive. Therefore, some treat it as a modal (related to a mood) similar to the subjunctive. Others treat it as a pure tense that refers to future time.[39] McKay treats it as an aspect expressing "intention,"[40] though virtually no one has followed him. Some think that it conveys future time and perfective (aorist) aspect.[41] Part of the problem is that the future does not behave like the other aspectual forms. There is no future subjunctive, imperative, or optative, and the future infinitive and participle are infrequent. Due to this, McKay concludes that the future tense-form "is something of an enigma in the ancient Greek verb system."[42] Similarly, Wallace (566n1) says that "this tense is still something of an enigma, rendering any statements less than iron-clad." And Porter (43) concludes that it "has a special and unique place in the Greek verbal system."[43] Consequently, we will tentatively treat the future as a form that expresses expectation—action that can be expected to take place.[44] The feature of expectation should usually be understood to refer to future time. It is probably the closest thing that Greek has to a true tense. Though related to the subjunctive mood, as mentioned above, the main difference is that the future tense is stronger and more certain than the subjunctive. The future can be used in at least the contexts that follow.

1. *The future tense used in future-time contexts (predictive or prospective).* This is the function that is usually associated with the future. It can be used prospectively, to predict or expect future events, and needs little illustration.

---

38. David L. Mathewson, *Verbal Aspect in the Book of Revelation: The Function of Greek Verb Tenses in John's Apocalypse*, Linguistic Biblical Studies 4 (Leiden: Brill, 2010), 131–32.
39. Fanning, *Verbal Aspect*, 122–23.
40. McKay, *New Syntax*, 34.
41. Moule 10: "'punctiliar' action in the future."
42. McKay, *New Syntax*, 34.
43. See also Zerwick 93.
44. Porter 43–44; Long, *Grammatical Concepts*, 77.

πολλοὶ ἐροῦσίν μοι ἐν ἐκείνῃ τῇ
ἡμέρᾳ· Κύριε κύριε (Matt. 7:22)

Many **will say** to me in that
day, "Lord, Lord."

καὶ πολλοὶ **ἐξακολουθήσουσιν**
αὐτῶν ταῖς ἀσελγείαις, δι'
οὓς ἡ ὁδὸς τῆς ἀληθείας
βλασφημηθήσεται· (2 Pet. 2:2)

And many **will follow** in
their debauchery, because of
which the way of truth **will be
blasphemed.**

2. *The future used in gnomic, or timeless, contexts.* The future seems to
be used of what can (or cannot) be expected to take place under certain
circumstances (BDF §349).

Οὐκ ἐπ' ἄρτῳ μόνῳ **ζήσεται** ὁ
ἄνθρωπος (Matt. 4:4)

A person **will not live** on bread
alone.

ἄρα οὖν ζῶντος τοῦ ἀνδρὸς
μοιχαλὶς **χρηματίσει** ἐὰν γένηται
ἀνδρὶ ἑτέρῳ· (Rom. 7:3)

Therefore, while her husband
is living **she will be called**
an adulteress if she becomes
[joined] to another man.

3. *The future used as a command.* The future form can be used to express
a command. Though some grammarians attribute this to Semitic influence, Porter (44) says that this usage is not unknown in secular Greek.
The imperatival future should be viewed as more semantically marked
than the imperative mood since it grammaticalizes expectation rather
than mere direction.[45]

τέξεται δὲ υἱὸν καὶ **καλέσεις** τὸ
ὄνομα αὐτοῦ Ἰησοῦν
(Matt. 1:21)

She will give birth to a son and
you shall call his name Jesus.
(*following the predictive use of
the future* τέξεται)

Ἀγαπήσεις τὸν πλησίον σου ὡς
σεαυτόν (James 2:8)

You **shall love** your neighbor as
yourself. (*in an OT quotation,
Lev. 19:18*)

4. *The deliberative use of the future.* The future can be used in questions
that express some uncertainty as to the answer.

---

45. Porter, *Verbal Aspect,* 414, 335.

ἀπεκρίθη αὐτῷ Σίμων Πέτρος· Κύριε, πρὸς τίνα **ἀπελευσόμεθα**; ῥήματα ζωῆς αἰωνίου ἔχεις (John 6:68)	Simon Peter answered him, "Lord, to whom **shall we go?** You have the words of eternal life.
τίς οὐ μὴ φοβηθῇ, κύριε, καὶ **δοξάσει** τὸ ὄνομά σου; (Rev. 15:4)	Who will not fear, Lord, and **glorify** your name? (*with the future following an aorist subjunctive*)

Traditional and Aspectual Views Compared

6.20. Now that we have discussed all the tense-forms in Greek, the following two charts compare and contrast the more traditional view of verb tenses based on time and kind of action, and the more recent verbal aspect view being advocated here.

What Is Communicated by the Greek Tenses?

Traditional	Aspectual
Refers to the kind of action taking place and to the time of the action (in the indicative mood)	Refers to how the author represents or conceives of the action (in all moods)

What Is the Meaning of the Greek Tenses?

	Traditional	Aspectual
Aorist	Punctiliar action in the past	Action viewed as a complete whole
Present	Continuous, durative action in the present	Action viewed as in progress, developing, unfolding
Imperfect	Continuous, durative action in the past	Action viewed as in progress, developing, but more remote
Perfect	A past action with present results	Action viewed as a state of affairs
Pluperfect	A past action with existing results in the past	Action viewed as a state of affairs, but more remote
Future	Future action	Future action or action expected to occur

So What?

6.21. In light of the above discussion, how should we analyze Greek verb tenses? First, we must identify the meaning of the aspect. What perspective on the action is being communicated by the author's choice of a given aspect? Verbs that provide the author with no choice (e.g., εἰμί) should not be pressed. Second, we can determine from the context, if possible, the time and kind of action to which the aspect is referring. Are there clear clues from the context as to when the action takes place or the type of action being portrayed? If not, it is safer not to press these. Third, we must ask whether the author has chosen an aspect to indicate prominence. Here the exegete will usually pay less attention to the aorist and more attention to departures from it (e.g., the present or perfect). More important than examining verb tenses in isolation is examining them over stretches of discourse to determine possible patterns or functions (see the examples of John 20 and 1 John 2 in §6.6 above).

For Practice

6.22. In the following texts from the NT, analyze the aspects of the indicative verbs according to the discussion above. Pay particular attention to how they might function to indicate prominence:

¹⁶καὶ διηγήσαντο αὐτοῖς οἱ ἰδόντες πῶς ἐγένετο τῷ δαιμονιζομένῳ καὶ περὶ τῶν χοίρων. ¹⁷καὶ ἤρξαντο παρακαλεῖν αὐτὸν ἀπελθεῖν ἀπὸ τῶν ὁρίων αὐτῶν. ¹⁸καὶ ἐμβαίνοντος αὐτοῦ εἰς τὸ πλοῖον παρεκάλει αὐτὸν ὁ δαιμονισθεὶς ἵνα μετ' αὐτοῦ ᾖ. ¹⁹καὶ οὐκ ἀφῆκεν αὐτόν, ἀλλὰ λέγει αὐτῷ· Ὕπαγε εἰς τὸν οἶκόν σου πρὸς τοὺς σούς, καὶ ἀπάγγειλον αὐτοῖς ὅσα ὁ κύριός σοι πεποίηκεν καὶ ἠλέησέν σε. ²⁰καὶ ἀπῆλθεν καὶ ἤρξατο κηρύσσειν ἐν τῇ Δεκαπόλει ὅσα ἐποίησεν αὐτῷ ὁ Ἰησοῦς, καὶ πάντες ἐθαύμαζον. ²¹Καὶ διαπεράσαντος τοῦ Ἰησοῦ ἐν τῷ πλοίῳ πάλιν εἰς τὸ πέραν συνήχθη ὄχλος πολὺς ἐπ' αὐτόν, καὶ ἦν παρὰ τὴν θάλασσαν. ²²καὶ ἔρχεται εἷς τῶν ἀρχισυναγώγων, ὀνόματι Ἰάϊρος, καὶ ἰδὼν αὐτὸν πίπτει πρὸς τοὺς πόδας αὐτοῦ ²³καὶ παρακαλεῖ αὐτὸν πολλὰ λέγων ὅτι Τὸ θυγάτριόν μου ἐσχάτως ἔχει, ἵνα ἐλθὼν ἐπιθῇς τὰς χεῖρας αὐτῇ ἵνα σωθῇ καὶ ζήσῃ. ²⁴καὶ ἀπῆλθεν μετ' αὐτοῦ. Καὶ ἠκολούθει αὐτῷ ὄχλος πολύς, καὶ συνέθλιβον αὐτόν. (Mark 5:16–24)

¹Δικαιωθέντες οὖν ἐκ πίστεως εἰρήνην ἔχομεν πρὸς τὸν θεὸν διὰ τοῦ κυρίου ἡμῶν Ἰησοῦ Χριστοῦ, ²δι' οὗ καὶ τὴν προσαγωγὴν ἐσχήκαμεν τῇ πίστει εἰς

τὴν χάριν ταύτην ἐν ᾗ ἑστήκαμεν, καὶ καυχώμεθα ἐπ᾽ ἐλπίδι τῆς δόξης τοῦ θεοῦ· ³οὐ μόνον δέ, ἀλλὰ καὶ καυχώμεθα ἐν ταῖς θλίψεσιν, εἰδότες ὅτι ἡ θλῖψις ὑπομονὴν κατεργάζεται, ⁴ἡ δὲ ὑπομονὴ δοκιμήν, ἡ δὲ δοκιμὴ ἐλπίδα. ⁵ἡ δὲ ἐλπὶς οὐ καταισχύνει· ὅτι ἡ ἀγάπη τοῦ θεοῦ ἐκκέχυται ἐν ταῖς καρδίαις ἡμῶν διὰ πνεύματος ἁγίου τοῦ δοθέντος ἡμῖν. (Rom. 5:1–5)

7

THE VERB: VOICE, PERSON, AND NUMBER

Voice

7.1. The voice system in NT Greek indicates the author's perspective on the relationship of a grammatical subject to the process expressed by the verb.[1] That is, voice indicates the role the subject of a clause plays with respect to the verb's action. Like other elements of the Greek verb (tense, mood, person, and number), voice is indicated by the inflectional endings. Koine Greek offers a choice of two or three sets of endings to designate three voices: active, passive, and middle (sometimes the same set of endings does double-duty for the passive and middle). The grammatical subject, usually indicated by a nominal form in the nominative case,[2] can be the agent of the action in the verb (i.e., the active voice), the recipient or patient of the action in the verb (i.e., the passive voice), or in some way directly involved in or participating in the action of the verb (i.e., the middle voice).[3] The passive and middle voices place particular focus on the subject, whereas the active voice does

1. Albert Rijksbaron, *The Syntax and Semantics of the Verb in Classical Greek*, 3rd ed. (Chicago: University of Chicago Press, 2002), 137.
2. Since Greek verbs are inflected for person, an explicit nominative subject is not required. Also, infinitives take their "subject" in the accusative case.
3. Historically, it appears that the active and middle voices existed first, and the passive voice was a later development.

not. Many verbs offer the choice of all three voices, but some verbs do not (so-called deponent verbs; see below). Analyzing the voice of Greek verbs is often significant for interpretation.

In discussing voice, we find it useful to distinguish the grammatical function from the semantic function of substantives or nominals related to the verb. Many verbs, called transitive, take a grammatical subject and an object; some, called intransitive, take only a subject. The subject is usually a substantive in the nominative case, and the object is usually a substantive in the accusative case (see chap. 1, on cases). Subject and object are *grammatical* categories indicated by the case endings of substantives. However, subjects and objects can also be considered from the standpoint of their *semantic* function. The *agent* is the producer or initiator of the action of the verb, while the *patient* or *goal* is the recipient of the action. Thus, when the grammatical subject plays the role of the agent, we have an active-voice verb (e.g., "The **student** studied *Greek*"). The direct object ("*Greek*"), then, plays the role of the patient or recipient of the action. However, when the grammatical subject plays the role of the patient or goal, we have a passive-voice verb (e.g., "The **buildings** were destroyed"), and the agent, if indicated, is expressed by a prepositional phrase ("The buildings were destroyed **by vandals**").

Below we have largely avoided the traditional labels for further divisions of the voices found in most grammars: simple active, causative active, reflexive active, direct middle, indirect middle, permissive middle, simple passive, divine passive, permissive passive, and the like.[4] These categories reflect more the meanings of the verbs and their function in the contexts than the meanings of the voice forms themselves.

Transitivity and Intransitivity

7.2. It is important to distinguish between transitive and intransitive verbs. Transitive verbs take two constituents, a subject and object, while intransitive verbs take only one constituent, a subject.[5] Technically, transitivity is a separate issue from voice and is concerned with the meaning of the verb itself.[6] Active- and middle-voice verbs may be either transitive or intransitive, while passive verbs are usually intransitive.

4. See Dana and Mantey 155–62; Brooks and Winbery 108–14; Wallace 408–41.
5. Rijksbaron, *Syntax and Semantics of the Verb*, 137.
6. Robertson 797; Wallace 409.

τέξεται δὲ υἱὸν καὶ **καλέσεις** τὸ ὄνομα αὐτοῦ Ἰησοῦν (Matt. 1:21)	And **she will bear** a son and **you will call** his name Jesus. (*two transitive verbs followed by direct objects in the accusative case*)
ἐν αἷς ποτε **περιεπατήσατε** κατὰ τὸν αἰῶνα τοῦ κόσμου τούτου (Eph. 2:2)	In which **you** once **walked about** according to the power of this world. (*an intransitive verb modified by prepositional phrases*)
Καὶ **ἐδόθη** μοι κάλαμος ὅμοιος ῥάβδῳ (Rev. 11:1)	And a reed like a rod **was given** to me. (*a passive intransitive verb*)

The Active Voice

7.3. The active voice indicates that the grammatical subject of the clause is the agent, the producer or initiator of the verbal process or state. The subject performs, carries out, or causes the action of the verb (causation runs from subject to verb). The active voice is the most common voice in the NT and is therefore the least semantically significant (or unmarked; Porter 63). It occurs about 20,697 times in the NT.

Στέφανος δὲ πλήρης χάριτος καὶ δυνάμεως **ἐποίει** τέρατα καὶ σημεῖα μεγάλα (Acts 6:8)	And Stephen, full of grace and power, **performed** great wonders and signs.
Τεκνία μου, ταῦτα **γράφω** ὑμῖν ἵνα μὴ **ἁμάρτητε.** (1 John 2:1)	My little children, **I am writing** these things to you in order that **you might** not **sin.** (*active-voice verbs in both the main clause and the subordinate clause*)
Καὶ ὅτε **ἤνοιξεν** τὴν πέμπτην σφραγῖδα, **εἶδον** ὑποκάτω τοῦ θυσιαστηρίου τὰς ψυχὰς τῶν ἐσφαγμένων διὰ τὸν λόγον τοῦ θεοῦ καὶ διὰ τὴν μαρτυρίαν ἣν **εἶχον.** (Rev. 6:9)	And when **he opened** the fifth seal, **I saw** beneath the altar the souls of those slain because of the word of God and the testimony that **they had.** (*all three active voice verbs are transitive*)

The Passive Voice

7.4. In the passive voice, the grammatical subject is the patient, the recipient of the action of the verb, rather than the agent, the performer of the action (as in the active voice). If agency is expressed with passive verbs in Greek, it is usually in the form of a prepositional phrase (see below). With the passive voice, emphasis is placed on the grammatical subject as the recipient of the action, and the agent is backgrounded. In comparison with the active voice, the passive occurs only about 3,933 times in the NT. The passive voice allows the author to maintain "topic continuity";[7] that is, it often functions to maintain the topic or subject of the previous clause (Young 135; see Mark 1:9 below). It is also used to foreground or highlight the introduction of a new participant into a scene that is about someone or something else (see Rev. 13:5 below).

μακάριοι οἱ πενθοῦντες, ὅτι αὐτοὶ **παρακληθήσονται.**	Blessed are those who mourn, for they **will be comforted.**
μακάριοι οἱ πεινῶντες καὶ διψῶντες τὴν δικαιοσύνην, ὅτι αὐτοὶ **χορτασθήσονται.**	Blessed are those who hunger and thirst for righteousness, for they **will be filled.**
μακάριοι οἱ ἐλεήμονες, ὅτι αὐτοὶ **ἐλεηθήσονται.**	Blessed are the merciful, for they **will be shown mercy.**
μακάριοι οἱ εἰρηνοποιοί, ὅτι αὐτοὶ υἱοὶ θεοῦ **κληθήσονται.** (Matt. 5:4–9)	Blessed are those who make peace, for they **will be called** children of God.

The passive-voice forms in the Beatitudes of Matt. 5 keep attention on the recipients of the action (αὐτοί) rather than on the agent (which in all these instances presumably is God).

ἦλθεν Ἰησοῦς ἀπὸ Ναζαρὲτ τῆς Γαλιλαίας καὶ **ἐβαπτίσθη** εἰς τὸν Ἰορδάνην ὑπὸ Ἰωάννου (Mark 1:9)	Jesus came from Nazareth of Galilee and **was baptized** in the Jordan by John.

The passive voice keeps the focus on Jesus rather than on John.

Μετανοήσατε, καὶ **βαπτισθήτω** ἕκαστος ὑμῶν (Acts 2:38)	Repent and **be baptized**, each of you.

7. Rijksbaron, *Syntax and Semantics of the Verb*, 141.

145

ἐν ᾧ καὶ **περιετμήθητε** περιτομῇ ἀχειροποιήτῳ (Col. 2:11)	In whom also you **were circumcised** with a circumcision not made by hands. (*The passive is used with an expression of impersonal agency: circumcision.*)
Καὶ **ἐδόθη** αὐτῷ στόμα λαλοῦν μεγάλα καὶ βλασφημίας, καὶ **ἐδόθη** αὐτῷ ἐξουσία ποιῆσαι μῆνας τεσσεράκοντα δύο. (Rev. 13:5)	And a mouth speaking great and blasphemous things **was given** to him, and authority **was given** to him to act for forty-two months.

7.5. Passives and accusatives. While verbs in the passive voice are usually intransitive (i.e., they do not take a direct object), a few take an object in the accusative case. These verbs are typically associated with two accusatives in the active voice (see chap. 1, on cases). When such verbs occur in the passive, one of the accusatives (the personal object) becomes the subject, and the other (the impersonal object) is retained in the accusative case (BDF §159). In English, for example, "He gave **her** *fresh flowers*" becomes "**She** was given *fresh flowers*."

καὶ κρατεῖτε τὰς παραδόσεις **ἃς** ἐδιδάχθητε (2 Thess. 2:15)	And hold on to the traditions **that** *you were taught*.

> If the relative clause were transformed into an active construction, it would be "We taught you that [i.e., the traditions]." In a passive construction, "you" (supplied by the verb ending) becomes the subject, and "that" (the traditions) remains as the direct object of the verb.

ἰδόντες ὅτι πεπίστευμαι τὸ **εὐαγγέλιον** τῆς ἀκροβυστίας (Gal. 2:7)	Seeing that *I was entrusted* [with] the **gospel** for the uncircumcision. (*from "he entrusted me [with] the gospel"*)

A number of examples seem to reveal a slightly different phenomenon. Most of these are translated in English with a preposition, such as *with* (see also the previous example).

οὐ παυόμεθα ὑπὲρ ὑμῶν προσευχόμενοι καὶ αἰτούμενοι ἵνα πληρωθῆτε **τὴν ἐπίγνωσιν** τοῦ θελήματος αὐτοῦ (Col. 1:9)	We do not cease praying for you and asking that *you might be filled* **with the knowledge** of his will.

καὶ *ἐκαυματίσθησαν* οἱ ἄνθρωποι
καῦμα μέγα· καὶ ἐβλασφήμησαν τὸ
ὄνομα τοῦ θεοῦ (Rev. 16:9)

And people *were burned* **with great heat**, and they blasphemed the name of God.

There are two ways to understand these examples. It may be that the accusatives are actually functioning as accusatives of respect: for example, "in order that you might be filled **with respect to** the knowledge of his will"; "people were burned **with respect to** great heat" (see Porter 66). Alternatively, the accusatives with the passive constructions would replace genitive or dative cases in the active counterparts: for example, "He might fill you **with the knowledge** [dative] of his will." When turned into a passive construction ("**You** might *be filled* **with the knowledge**"), the object "you" becomes the subject, and the noun "knowledge," which would be in the dative case expressing means, advances, so to speak, to the direct object slot and takes the accusative case,[8] though we should still translate it as indicating means.

7.6. Expressions of agency. In passive-voice constructions the agent, if it is expressed, usually takes the form of a prepositional phrase. The following are the most common.

1. Personal agency is often expressed by the preposition ὑπό + genitive.

ἦλθεν Ἰησοῦς . . . καὶ ἐβαπτίσθη
εἰς τὸν Ἰορδάνην **ὑπὸ Ἰωάννου.**
(Mark 1:9)

Jesus came . . . and was baptized in the Jordan **by John.**

2. Secondary or intermediate agency is often expressed by διά + genitive or ἐκ + genitive.

ἵνα πληρωθῇ τὸ ῥηθὲν ὑπὸ
κυρίου **διὰ τοῦ προφήτου**
(Matt. 2:15)

In order that what was spoken by the Lord **through** the **prophet** might be fulfilled.

Here the author seems to distinguish between the direct agent (ὑπὸ κυρίου) and the intermediate agent (διὰ τοῦ προφήτου).

3. Impersonal means is often expressed either by ἐν + dative or by the simple dative.

8. Martin M. Culy, "Double Case Constructions in Koine Greek," *Journal of Greco-Roman Christianity and Judaism* 6 (2009): 82–106.

ἐν ᾧ καὶ περιετμήθητε **περιτομῇ** In whom also you were circum-
ἀχειροποιήτῳ (Col. 2:11) cised **with a circumcision** not
  made by hands.

7.7. Agency is often left unexpressed and must be inferred from the context, although at times it may be unnecessary to speculate about the agent of a passive verb. The "divine passive," a label employed by most grammars and commentaries, should probably not be treated as a category of usage separate from that of unexpressed agency.

Καὶ **ἐδόθη** μοι κάλαμος ὅμοιος And a reed like a rod **was given**
ῥάβδῳ (Rev. 11:1) to me.

> The agent could be the one who commands John to arise and mea-
> sure, though the identity of the voice is unclear.

The Middle Voice

7.8. For many students, the middle voice will prove the most difficult to conceptualize since the English language does not exhibit a middle-voice form. Because of this, it is impossible at times to bring out its force in translation. Most grammars are now agreed that the reflexive sense, where the subject acts upon itself (it is both the agent and the patient; e.g., "he washed *himself*" in English), is not the essential or most common meaning of the middle voice in NT Greek (often called the "direct middle" in grammars), and therefore translating with a reflexive sense should generally be avoided by the Greek student unless context clearly warrants it.[9] It is best to understand the Greek middle voice semantically as expressing *"more direct participation, specific involvement, or even some form of benefit of the subject doing the action."*[10] Rutger Allan says that the semantic feature of the middle is "subject-affectedness."[11] Or as Robertson (804) says, "The middle calls special attention to the subject." Often the action of middle verbs is internally caused (with no outside agent; e.g., "I rise" in English), in contrast to active or passive verbs, which have an external agent (e.g., "he raised him" or "he was raised"). The middle is the

---

9. Wallace 416. Wallace says that this use of the middle "is quite rare." Cf. also Moule 24; Robertson 806; Dana and Mantey 158; Porter 67; Young 134.

10. Porter 67, italics original. For a similar understanding of the middle, see Wallace 414–15; Young 134.

11. Rutger J. Allan, "The Middle Voice in Ancient Greek: A Study in Polysemy" (PhD diss., University of Amsterdam, 2002), 185.

most semantically significant of the three voices. It is the least frequent in the NT, occurring about 3,500 times.

The student should maintain a fair amount of flexibility when translating the middle voice. Much of the time our English translation will not fully capture its force. Often translations for the subject such as "himself" (reflexive), "each other" (reciprocal), "to herself," "for herself," or "by himself" (intensive) will prove adequate. At other times these glosses will seem to be too much, and the middle will be translated just like an active voice. It must be remembered that the notion of the direct involvement or participation of the subject in the action of the verb is present irrespective of how we translate it.

1. *Reflexive* (though rare)

καὶ ἀπ' ἀγορᾶς ἐὰν μὴ βαπτίσωνται οὐκ ἐσθίουσιν (Mark 7:4)	And they do not eat from the market unless **they wash themselves**. (*The subjects act upon themselves.*)
καὶ σὺ **φυλάσσου**, λίαν γὰρ ἀντέστη τοῖς ἡμετέροις λόγοις. (2 Tim. 4:15)	And you **guard yourself**, for he strongly opposed our words.

2. *Intensive* (emphasizes the subject's interest in the action)

Οὗτος μὲν οὖν **ἐκτήσατο** χωρίον ἐκ μισθοῦ τῆς ἀδικίας (Acts 1:18)	Therefore, this one [i.e., Judas] **purchased** [for himself] a field with the wages of his wickedness.
ὁ δὲ Ἰησοῦς εἶπεν αὐτοῖς· Οὐκ οἴδατε τί **αἰτεῖσθε**· (Mark 10:38)	And Jesus said to them, "You do not know what **you ask**."

> The middle voice here, in contrast to the active voice referring to asking (αἰτήσωμεν) in verse 35, may draw attention to the disciples' inappropriate asking for themselves.

οὐκ ἔχετε διὰ τὸ μὴ **αἰτεῖσθαι** ὑμᾶς· **αἰτεῖτε** καὶ οὐ λαμβάνετε, διότι κακῶς **αἰτεῖσθε**, ἵνα ἐν ταῖς ἡδοναῖς ὑμῶν δαπανήσητε. (James 4:2–3)	You do not have because **you do** not **ask**; you ask and you do not receive because **you ask** wrongly, in order that you might spend [it] on your pleasures.

> In these two clauses both the middle and active forms occur, suggesting that the shift to the middle is indeed intentional. The middle, emphasizing the subject's heightened involvement in the action, seems to be used to emphasize the reasons for not receiving—not asking or asking incorrectly.

3. *Reciprocal* (when plural)

καὶ **συνεβουλεύσαντο** ἵνα τὸν Ἰησοῦν δόλῳ κρατήσωσιν καὶ ἀποκτείνωσιν· (Matt. 26:4)	And they **counseled one another** that they should cunningly seize Jesus and put him to death.

ἤδη γὰρ **συνετέθειντο** οἱ Ἰουδαῖοι ἵνα ἐάν τις αὐτὸν ὁμολογήσῃ χριστόν, ἀποσυνάγωγος γένηται. (John 9:22)	For the Jews had already **agreed with one another** that if anyone confessed him as the Christ, he/she would be expelled from the synagogue.

7.9. Often the middle voice turns a transitive verb (i.e., one that takes an object) into an intransitive one (i.e., one that does not take an object). For example, in English we "set" something on the table, or we "seat" someone (both are transitive, with direct objects), but we "sit" down (intransitive, without an object). In Greek αὐξάνω is transitive and means "to increase or grow (something)." However, the middle αὐξάνομαι is intransitive and means "to grow." The actions of such verbs are usually internally caused (e.g., "he appeared") rather than externally caused by an agent.

ἰδοὺ ἄγγελος κυρίου **φαίνεται** κατ' ὄναρ τῷ Ἰωσήφ (Matt. 2:13)	Look, an angel of the Lord **appeared** to Joseph in a dream.

> The active φαίνω has a causative meaning: "to cause to appear" or "to show." The middle emphasizes that the action is internally caused.

εἴτε δὲ προφητεῖαι, καταργηθή-	But whether prophecies, they
σονται· εἴτε γλῶσσαι, **παύσονται·**	will be done away with; whether
εἴτε γνῶσις, καταργηθήσεται.	tongues, **they will cease**; whether
(1 Cor. 13:8)	knowledge, it will be done away
	with.

> The verb παύω in the active is transitive ("to stop something"), but in the middle (παύομαι) it becomes intransitive ("to cease"). Therefore, this verse cannot be used to argue for a distinction between what happens to tongues and what happens to prophecy and knowledge, as if tongues will cease in a different way—by themselves, or they will cease themselves, or they will die off. The middle here turns a transitive verb into an intransitive one and tells us that tongues will cease, with the point being the subject's heightened participation in the process, but it does not tell us how (or when) tongues will cease.

7.10. The middle voice can also change the meaning of a verb. In the active voice, ἄρχω means "I rule," but in the middle voice, ἄρχομαι means "I begin."

Excursus: The So-Called Deponent Verb

In Koine Greek there are a number of verbs that do not appear in all three voices. A common pattern is for some verbs to have middle/passive endings but no active ones. For example, ἔρχομαι occurs with middle/passive endings, but it did not develop active endings. Another suppletive form, ἦλθον, is used for the aorist of ἔρχομαι.

This phenomenon is often labeled "deponency." This term comes from the Latin *deponere*, "to lay aside," since it was thought that the active endings had been laid aside. But it is not clear that so-called deponent verbs ever had active endings that were later laid aside, whatever this might mean. The traditional explanation of deponency in Greek is that the middle/passive endings substitute for the active endings of these verbs. Hence, "deponent" verbs are often described as "middle/passive in form, but active in meaning" (see Dana and Mantey 163; Wallace 428; Mounce 152). However, according to Constantine Campbell, "A paradigm shift is taking place in our understanding of Greek voice, with particular reference to the concept of deponency."[a]

Early on, A. T. Robertson said that the name "deponent" was "unsatisfactory" (811) and that "it should not be used at all" (332). Some scholars have followed Robertson's lead and have called into question the legitimacy of deponency as a feature of the Greek voice system for at least two primary reasons.[b] (1) This label may often reflect the English meaning and translation of these verbs with an active sense, with the attendant conclusion that the middle form must be "active in meaning." However, just because a middle-voice verb is translated with an active English voice and seems to have active meaning does not mean that semantically the Greek verb is not truly middle in meaning. (2) The appeal to "deponency" is an imposition of a category from Latin (which has no middle voice) on Greek and therefore should be avoided, since there is no evidence that Greek verbs ever had active endings that were "laid aside." We conclude that the concept of deponency is unnecessary, and what we have traditionally called deponent verbs should be seen as true middles with middle meaning.

Instead of "deponent," perhaps we should call these "middle-only verbs." Most of these verbs probably have middle forms to reflect the semantics of the verb itself: involvement, interest, or participation of the subject in the action. That is, the subject-focused meaning of certain verbs lends itself to middle forms. For example, δέχομαι (I receive, I welcome) seems to be inherently reflexive (Wallace 429). The verb ἔρχομαι (I come, I go) is usually touted as a common example of deponency, but it probably retains a middle meaning (movement of oneself in a direction, internal agency). And a verb like ἐργάζομαι (I work) may suggest the notion of acting in one's own interest. On the other hand, we should probably refrain from analyzing these verbs as if the author were drawing particular attention to or foregrounding the subject, and we should avoid giving too much interpretive weight to these middles, since the author did not have a choice among the full range of voices. Meaning implies choice!

A number of middle-only verbs appear to take passive forms when in the *aorist*: they end with -θη- and are often incorrectly called "passive deponents"[c] (e.g., ἀποκρίνομαι becomes ἀπεκρίθην, βούλομαι becomes ἐβουλήθην, and πορεύομαι becomes ἐπορεύθην). According to Chrys Caragounis, the passive was overtaking the middle voice, and the passive -θη- endings did double-duty for both the middle and passive voices.[d] Decker explains these as dual-voice forms.[e] Whatever the reason, these are not actually "passive deponents" but middle verbs with -θη- endings. When these verbs (such as those mentioned above) occur in the aorist, they take -θη- endings but should be translated and interpreted like any other middle-voice verb.

[a]Constantine R. Campbell, *Advances in the Study of Greek: New Insights for Reading the New Testament* (Grand Rapids: Zondervan, 2015), 91.

[b]See esp. Jonathan T. Pennington, "Deponency in Koine Greek: The Grammatical Question and the Lexicographical Dilemma," *Trinity Journal* 24 (2003): 55–76; Bernard A. Taylor, "Deponency and Greek Lexicography," in *Biblical Greek Language and Lexicography: Essays in Honor of Frederick W. Danker*, ed. B. A. Taylor et al. (Grand Rapids: Eerdmans, 2004), 167–76; Allan, "Middle Voice," 2n4; Campbell, *Advances*, 91–104.

[c]Young 136: "Some verbs with passive forms have active meanings."

[d]Chrys Caragounis, *The Development of Greek and the New Testament* (Grand Rapids: Baker Academic, 2006), 153.

[e]Rodney J. Decker, *Reading Koine Greek: An Introduction and Integrated Workbook* (Grand Rapids: Baker Academic, 2014), 283.

Person

7.11. Greek verbs grammaticalize three persons by their inflected endings: first, second, and third persons. All three occur in the singular and plural.

Person	Singular	Plural
First	I	we
Second	you	you[a]
Third	he/she	they

[a]Unlike English, Greek distinguishes formally between "you [sg.]" and "you [pl.]" by its endings. Some have suggested that the closest English equivalent to the second-person plural is the colloquial "you all."

There is a close relationship between the first and second person, since they refer to the author and readers. The third person indicates someone or something outside of the author-reader relationship (i.e., the author addresses the readers about an "outside" person or entity; Porter 77).

First Person

7.12. First-person forms are used when authors or speakers refer to themselves alone (in the first-person singular) or include themselves in the action (in the first-person plural).

Τοῦτο οὖν **λέγω** καὶ **μαρτύρομαι** ἐν κυρίῳ (Eph. 4:17)

Therefore, **I say** and **I witness** this in the Lord.

> The author identifies himself in the discourse as addressing his hearers. In an epistle, when the author refers to himself in the first person after introducing himself in the greeting (Eph. 1:1), the reference is usually emphatic.

Οἶδά τὰ ἔργα σου, καὶ τὸν κόπον καὶ τὴν ὑπομονήν σου (Rev. 2:2)

I know your works, and your labor and endurance.

> John is recording the words of the risen Christ, who refers to himself in the first person while addressing the church at Ephesus.

Plural first-person forms are used when the author refers to a group of participants of which the author is a part or when for some reason the author wants to include others (e.g., the readers) with himself/herself.

Εὐχαριστοῦμεν τῷ θεῷ πατρὶ τοῦ κυρίου ἡμῶν Ἰησοῦ Χριστοῦ (Col. 1:3)	**We give thanks** to God the Father of our Lord Jesus Christ.

> The plural probably refers to Paul and Timothy (see Col. 1:1).

καὶ *ἡμεῖς*, τοσοῦτον ἔχοντες περικείμενον *ἡμῖν* νέφος μαρτύρων … *τρέχωμεν* τὸν προκείμενον *ἡμῖν* ἀγῶνα (Heb. 12:1)	And *we*, having such a cloud of witnesses surrounding *us*, . . . **let us run** the race placed before *us*.

> The first-person plural includes the readers with the author, which is also supported with first-person plural pronouns.

Second Person

7.13. Second-person forms are used when the author or speaker refers to the readers/hearers.

Οὐκ **οἴδατε** ὅτι ναὸς θεοῦ **ἐστε** καὶ τὸ πνεῦμα τοῦ θεοῦ οἰκεῖ ἐν *ὑμῖν*; (1 Cor. 3:16)	**Do you** not **know** that **you are** also the temple of God and the Spirit of God dwells in *you*?
φυλάξατε ἑαυτὰ ἀπὸ τῶν εἰδώλων. (1 John 5:21)	**Guard** yourselves from idols.
πλὴν ὃ **ἔχετε κρατήσατε** ἄχρι οὗ ἂν ἥξω. (Rev. 2:25)	However, what **you have, hold on to** [it] until I come.

Third Person

7.14. Third-person forms are used when an author or speaker refers to an "outside party," that is, someone or something other than the speaker and hearers. At times the subject may be ambiguous or indefinite (BDF §130).

Ἐγένετο ἄνθρωπος ἀπεσταλμένος παρὰ θεοῦ (John 1:6)	A man **came,** sent from God.
Ἐπεφάνη γὰρ ἡ χάρις τοῦ θεοῦ σωτήριος πᾶσιν ἀνθρώποις (Titus 2:11)	For the grace of God **appeared** for salvation to all people.
ἵνα ἐκεῖ **τρέφωσιν** αὐτὴν ἡμέρας χιλίας διακοσίας ἑξήκοντα. (Rev. 12:6)	In order that there **they might nourish** her for 1,260 days.

> The subject of the verb is indefinite or impersonal and could be translated with the passive: "in order that she might be nourished."

Number

7.15. Concerning number, Greek verb endings indicate singularity and plurality.[12] All verb forms in Greek, except for the infinitive, are inflected for number. The general rule is that the number of the Greek verb ending will agree with the subject (whether the subject is specified or not). However, there are a number of exceptions to this.

Number Agreement

7.16. It is easy to find examples where the rule is followed: singular subject with singular verb ending, and plural subject with plural verb ending.

Καὶ **οἱ πατριάρχαι** ζηλώσαντες τὸν Ἰωσὴφ **ἀπέδοντο** εἰς Αἴγυπτον· (Acts 7:9)	And the **patriarchs** being jealous of Joseph, **sold** him into Egypt. (*plural subject with plural participle and indicative verb*)
ἐγὼ Παῦλος ἔγραψα τῇ ἐμῇ χειρί, ἐγὼ ἀποτίσω· (Philem. 19)	I, Paul, **write** in my own hand, I **will pay back.** (*singular subjects and verbs*)
ἀπεκρίθη **εἷς** ἐκ τῶν πρεσβυτέρων λέγων μοι· (Rev. 7:13)	**One** of the elders **answered,** saying to me.

---

12. As nearly all grammars recognize, Greek once had a dual number that died out by the time of Koine Greek.

155

Number Disagreement

7.17. However, this pattern is not always followed, and the careful reader will notice a number of exceptions.

1. The most obvious exception is when a neuter plural subject occurs with a singular verb ending, though grammars do not agree on why this is the case. Wallace says, "Since the neuter usually refers to impersonal things (including animals), the singular verb regards the plural subject as a collective whole" (399), but collective wholes can be found with plural verbs (see Mark 3:11; Luke 24:11), and persons, not just impersonal things, can also be conceived of as a collective whole with a singular verb.

καὶ τὰ ἐμὰ πάντα σά **ἐστιν** (John 17:10)	And *all my things* **are** yours.
μηκέτι ὑμᾶς περιπατεῖν καθὼς καὶ τὰ ἔθνη **περιπατεῖ** ἐν ματαιότητι τοῦ νοὸς αὐτῶν (Eph. 4:17)	You should no longer walk as *the gentiles* also **walk**, in the futility of their mind. (*a personal plural neuter subject with a singular verb*)
Καὶ ὅταν **τελεσθῇ** τὰ χίλια ἔτη, λυθήσεται ὁ Σατανᾶς ἐκ τῆς φυλακῆς αὐτοῦ (Rev. 20:7)	And whenever *the thousand years* **are completed**, Satan will be released from his prison.

Moreover, there are numerous examples where this exception is not observed and neuter plural subjects are found with plural verb endings. In contrast to Wallace's statement above, Robertson (403) has suggested that "usually a neuter plural in the NT that has a personal or collective meaning has a plural verb,"[13] though this is only a tendency.[14]

πάντα γὰρ ταῦτα τὰ ἔθνη **ἐπιζητοῦσιν·** (Matt. 6:32)	For *the gentiles* **are seeking** after all these things. (*a personal plural neuter subject with a plural verb*)

---

13. Also Turner 313.
14. For some exceptions, see Wallace 400n15.

τὰ δὲ ζιζάνιά **εἰσιν** οἱ υἱοὶ τοῦ πονηροῦ (Matt. 13:38)	*The weeds* **are** the children of the evil one.

The neuter subject is impersonal, but perhaps it was regarded as personal due to being equated metaphorically with "the children of the evil one."

καὶ τὰ δαιμόνια **πιστεύουσιν** καὶ **φρίσσουσιν.** (James 2:19)	*The demons* also **believe,** and **they shudder.**
καὶ ἑπτὰ λαμπάδες πυρὸς καιόμεναι ἐνώπιον τοῦ θρόνου, ἅ **εἰσιν** τὰ ἑπτὰ πνεύματα τοῦ θεοῦ (Rev. 4:5)	And [I saw] *seven lamps* of fire burning before the throne, *which* **are** the seven Spirits of God.

The neuter relative pronoun refers back to ἑπτὰ λαμπάδες, which are metaphorically equated with the Spirits of God.

2. Another exception is the use of singular subjects with plural verb endings. This often occurs with nouns that are collective in meaning (e.g., ὄχλος, πλῆθος).[15] Though the word *fish* in English is not always collective, it can serve as an example: "The fish in this lake *are* plentiful."

ὁ δὲ πλεῖστος ὄχλος **ἔστρωσαν** ἑαυτῶν τὰ ἱμάτια ἐν τῇ ὁδῷ (Matt. 21:8)	And *most of the crowd* **spread out** their own garments on the way.
καὶ πᾶς ὁ ὄχλος **ἐζήτουν** ἅπτεσθαι αὐτοῦ (Luke 6:19)	And *the whole crowd* **was seeking** to touch him.
φωνὴν μεγάλην ὄχλου πολλοῦ ἐν τῷ οὐρανῷ **λεγόντων·** (Rev. 19:1)	A great voice *of a great crowd* in heaven **saying.**

3. A further exception to the agreement in number between subject and verb is the use of a singular verb with multiple singular subjects (which in English we would treat together as a plural subject). There have been various explanations for this phenomenon. The two most common tendencies are (1) for the singular verb to be used when multiple subjects

15. Porter 74; Wallace 400–401; Robertson 404; Turner 311–12; K. L. McKay, *A New Syntax of the Verb in New Testament Greek: An Aspectual Approach*, Studies in Biblical Greek 5 (New York: Peter Lang, 1994), 19.

are treated as a totality or single entity[16] or (2) for a singular verb to be either at the beginning of a group of singular subjects or in between subjects but to agree with the first subject.[17] At times this may be due to the author's desire to highlight the first subject (Wallace 401). However, this does not account for all the exceptions; there are no hard-and-fast rules.

ἀμὴν γὰρ λέγω ὑμῖν, ἕως ἄν παρέλθῃ ὁ οὐρανὸς καὶ ἡ γῆ (Matt. 5:18)	For truly I tell you, until *heaven and earth* **pass away.**

Most likely heaven and earth are being treated as a totality.

Ἀβραὰμ **ἀπέθανεν** καὶ οἱ προφῆται (John 8:52)	Abraham and *the prophets* **died.**

The singular verb splits the two subjects and agrees with the first one.

καὶ **ἐβαπτίσθη** αὐτὸς καὶ οἱ αὐτοῦ πάντες παραχρῆμα (Acts 16:33)	And *he* **was baptized** *and all his family* immediately. (*the more important item, αὐτός, is the focus*)

νυνὶ δὲ **μένει** πίστις, ἐλπίς, ἀγάπη· τὰ τρία ταῦτα (1 Cor. 13:13)	Now **remains** *faith, hope, love,* these three.

It is possible that the author wants to treat these as a totality; more likely the singular has been determined by the first subject, just as in our English translation (Robertson 405; see also the KJV).

7.18. An interesting example of number disagreement is found in Rev. 9:12: ἰδοὺ ἔρχεται ἔτι δύο οὐαὶ μετὰ ταῦτα (Behold, **two** more **woes** are still **coming** after these things). While some have argued that the woe was understood as neuter, so that the neuter plural takes a singular verb, the feminine Ἡ οὐαὶ ἡ μία right before it makes this unlikely. It is possible, then, that the author treats the two woes as a totality. A further possibility, following David Aune, is that we should see δύο as multiplicative, meaning "twice."[18] If this is the

16. Robertson 405; McKay, *New Syntax*, 19.
17. Turner 313–14; Porter 75.
18. David E. Aune, *Revelation 6–16*, Word Biblical Commentary (Nashville: Nelson, 1998), 488.

case, οὐαί is considered singular (G. Mussies translates it as "there is to come yet twice a Woe").[19]

For Practice

7.19. Analyze the voice of the verbs in the following passage.

[37]Ἀκούσαντες δὲ κατενύγησαν τὴν καρδίαν, εἶπόν τε πρὸς τὸν Πέτρον καὶ τοὺς λοιποὺς ἀποστόλους· Τί ποιήσωμεν, ἄνδρες ἀδελφοί; [38]Πέτρος δὲ πρὸς αὐτούς· Μετανοήσατε, καὶ βαπτισθήτω ἕκαστος ὑμῶν ἐπὶ τῷ ὀνόματι Ἰησοῦ Χριστοῦ εἰς ἄφεσιν τῶν ἁμαρτιῶν ὑμῶν, καὶ λήμψεσθε τὴν δωρεὰν τοῦ ἁγίου πνεύματος· [39]ὑμῖν γάρ ἐστιν ἡ ἐπαγγελία καὶ τοῖς τέκνοις ὑμῶν καὶ πᾶσι τοῖς εἰς μακρὰν ὅσους ἂν προσκαλέσηται κύριος ὁ θεὸς ἡμῶν. [40]ἑτέροις τε λόγοις πλείοσιν διεμαρτύρατο, καὶ παρεκάλει αὐτοὺς λέγων· Σώθητε ἀπὸ τῆς γενεᾶς τῆς σκολιᾶς ταύτης. [41]οἱ μὲν οὖν ἀποδεξάμενοι τὸν λόγον αὐτοῦ ἐβαπτίσθησαν, καὶ προσετέθησαν ἐν τῇ ἡμέρᾳ ἐκείνῃ ψυχαὶ ὡσεὶ τρισχίλιαι. (Acts 2:37–41)

19. G. Mussies, *The Morphology of Koine Greek as Used in the Apocalypse of John: A Study in Bilingualism*, Supplements to Novum Testamentum 27 (Leiden: Brill, 1971), 217.

8

MOOD

8.1. The selection of a particular verbal mood indicates or grammaticalizes a speaker's or writer's decision regarding how to portray the relationship of a verbal idea to reality. As Porter (50) points out, "The choice of attitude [mood] is probably the second most important semantic choice by a language user in selection of a verbal element in Greek, second only to verbal aspect." When a Greek language user wants to portray a verbal idea (e.g., action, state of being) as if it were a reality, the indicative mood is selected. At the same time, it should be remembered that "the indicative is the 'unmarked' mood form" (Porter 51); that is, the indicative is the default mood, the mood used when none of the other moods is called for. Whether the action or state grammaticalized by an indicative verb form indicates objective reality or not is a matter of context, history, and the like. One may lie, employ various figures of speech (e.g., metaphor and hyperbole, which do not use language "literally"), or merely err in the indicative mood. If the indicative mood indicates reality, it is subjective reality.[1] The nonindicative, or oblique, moods are alike in that they make projections or directions rather than assertions about reality.

Assertion	Projection	Projection and Contingency	Direction
Indicative	Subjunctive	Optative	Imperative

1. This assertion is in no way intended to undermine a high view of the authority and inspiration of the Bible.

Indicative Mood

8.2. The primary use of the indicative mood in NT Greek is to make assertions about reality from the perspective of the writer or speaker, irrespective of objective reality. Nevertheless, the indicative mood may also be employed when asking questions, issuing commands, making wishes, or framing certain types of conditions. The indicative mood occurs about 15,618 times in the NT. For the tense and aspect use in the indicative mood, see chapter 6, on the Greek verb system.

Declarative

8.3. A declarative sentence makes a statement or assertion. There are thousands of declarative sentences in the NT because this is the most basic use of the indicative mood.

τότε ἤρξατο καταθεματίζειν καὶ ὀμνύειν ὅτι **Οὐκ οἶδα τὸν ἄνθρωπον**. καὶ εὐθέως ἀλέκτωρ ἐφώνησεν· (Matt. 26:74)	Then he began to curse and swear, "**I do not know the man**." And immediately a rooster crowed. (*The statement in bold is false.*)
Καὶ **ἔστιν** αὕτη ἡ ἀγγελία ἣν **ἀκηκόαμεν** ἀπ᾽ αὐτοῦ καὶ **ἀναγγέλλομεν** ὑμῖν, ὅτι ὁ θεὸς φῶς **ἐστιν** καὶ σκοτία ἐν αὐτῷ οὐκ **ἔστιν** οὐδεμία. (1 John 1:5)	And this **is** the message that **we have heard** from him and **announce** to you, that God **is** light and darkness **is not** in him at all.

Interrogative

8.4. An interrogative sentence asks a question that can be real or rhetorical.

Real

καὶ εἶπαν αὐτῷ· **Ποῦ ἐστιν ἐκεῖνος;** λέγει· Οὐκ οἶδα. (John 9:12)	And they said to him, "**Where is he / that one?**" He said, "I don't know."

Rhetorical

τί δὲ βλέπεις τὸ κάρφος τὸ ἐν τῷ ὀφθαλμῷ τοῦ ἀδελφοῦ σου, τὴν δὲ ἐν τῷ σῷ ὀφθαλμῷ δοκὸν οὐ κατανοεῖς; (Matt. 7:3)	And **why do you see** the speck that is in the eye of your brother/sister but **do not consider** the log that is in your own eye?

Command

8.5. Although the imperative is the mood most often employed for the issuing of commands, the future[2] indicative can also be used with imperatival force. This has more to do with the expectation associated with the future tense than with the indicative mood per se. Still, it bears repeating that since the indicative grammaticalizes assertion, the imperatival future carries more semantic weight (assertion + expectation) than the imperative mood (direction). See the discussion of the future tense in chapter 6.

Ἠκούσατε ὅτι ἐρρέθη· Οὐ μοιχεύσεις. (Matt. 5:27)	You have heard that it was said, "**You shall** not **commit adultery.**"
Ἔσεσθε οὖν ὑμεῖς τέλειοι ὡς ὁ πατὴρ ὑμῶν ὁ οὐράνιος τέλειός ἐστιν. (Matt. 5:48)	Therefore, **you will be** perfect as your heavenly Father is perfect.
Ὅρα γάρ, φησιν, ποιήσεις πάντα κατὰ τὸν τύπον τὸν δειχθέντα σοι ἐν τῷ ὄρει· (Heb. 8:5)	For he [i.e., God] said, "See [to it that] **you make** everything according to the pattern that was shown to you on the mountain."

The future tense of ποιήσεις here and in the LXX (Exod. 25:40) reflects a Hebrew imperative (עֲשֵׂה).

Volitive (Wish, Desire, Mild Command)

8.6. In the NT the indicative mood is used to express a wish or desire far more frequently than the optative or the hortatory subjunctive (see below for

---

2. "Greek [is] . . . a bi-temporal language (past-present) . . . rather than tri-temporal. . . . The future is . . . a unique form in Greek, similar both to the aspects and to the attitudes [moods], but fully neither, and realizing not a temporal conception but a marked and emphatic expectation toward a process" (Stanley E. Porter, *Verbal Aspect in the Greek of the New Testament, with Reference to Tense and Mood*, Studies in Biblical Greek 1 [New York: Peter Lang, 1989], 411, 414).

both). This is because most NT wishes employ verbs whose semantic ranges include desire/wish/will: θέλω (144× in the indicative),[3] βούλομαι (16× in the indicative), ἀξιόω (1× in the indicative), εὔχομαι (4× in the indicative), δοκέω (1× in the indicative), ζητέω (22× in the indicative), ἐπιθυμέω (14× in the indicative), ὀρέγω (2× in the indicative), and ἐπιποθέω (4× in the indicative). In other words, the NT authors convey the idea of wish or desire through their lexical choice rather than just through their choice of mood. We also consider here the verbs that introduce obligation or necessity: ὀφείλω (31× in the indicative) and δεῖ (93× in the indicative).

εἰς νῆσον δέ τινα **δεῖ** ἡμᾶς ἐκπεσεῖν. (Acts 27:26)	But **it is necessary** for us to / we **must** run aground on a certain island.
θέλω δὲ πάντας ἀνθρώπους εἶναι ὡς καὶ ἐμαυτόν· (1 Cor. 7:7)	But **I wish** all people to be as even I myself [am].
ἀγαπητοί, εἰ οὕτως ὁ θεὸς ἠγάπησεν ἡμᾶς, καὶ ἡμεῖς **ὀφείλομεν** ἀλλήλους ἀγαπᾶν. (1 John 4:11)	Beloved, if God so loved us, we also **ought** to / **must** love one another.

Conditional

8.7. The indicative mood is employed in the protases (*if*-clauses) of two types of conditions in the NT: class 1 and class 2 conditional sentences. For a thorough treatment of conditions and examples, see chapter 11, on clauses.

1. Class 1 conditions (more than 300 instances in the NT) use εἰ and the indicative in the protasis, and they make an assertion, for the sake of argument, that may or may not actually be true. The apodosis (*then*-clause) of a class 1 condition can have a variety of verbs forms, from indicative to imperative.

ὁ δὲ Πέτρος ἔφη αὐτῷ· Εἰ καὶ πάντες **σκανδαλισθήσονται**, ἀλλ᾽ οὐκ ἐγώ. (Mark 14:29)	And Peter said to him, " Even if all **stumble**, yet I [will] not."

Note that there is no verb in the apodosis.

---

3. θέλω occurs 208× in the NT, frequently as a participle.

εἰ δὲ ὃ οὐ **θέλω** τοῦτο **ποιῶ**, **σύμφημι** τῷ νόμῳ ὅτι καλός. (Rom. 7:16)	Now if what **I do** not **want** this **I do**, **I agree** with the law that [it is] good.
Εἴ τις **ἔχει** οὖς **ἀκουσάτω**. (Rev. 13:9)	If anyone **has** an ear, **he/she must hear.**

    Note that the verb in the apodosis is an imperative.

2. Class 2 conditions (47 instances in the NT) also use εἰ and the indicative in the protasis, with the additional refinement that the tense-forms are always secondary (aorist, imperfect, pluperfect). Apodoses of class 2 conditions usually include the particle ἄν (in 37 of the 47 instances) and draw conclusions indicating that the protases are contrary to fact from the perspective of the writer or speaker.

εἰ δὲ **ἐγνώκειτε** τί ἐστιν· Ἔλεος θέλω καὶ οὐ θυσίαν, οὐκ ἂν **κατεδικάσατε** τοὺς ἀναιτίους. (Matt. 12:7)	But if **you had known** what it is/means, "I desire mercy and not sacrifice," **you would** not **have condemned** the innocent. (*pluperfect [stative] and aorist verbs*)
εἰ δὲ ἑαυτοὺς **διεκρίνομεν**, οὐκ ἂν **ἐκρινόμεθα**· (1 Cor. 11:31)	For if **we evaluated** ourselves, **we would** not **be judged.** (*imperfect of both verbs*)
καὶ εἰ μὲν ἐκείνης **ἐμνημόνευον** ἀφ' ἧς ἐξέβησαν, **εἶχον** ἂν καιρὸν ἀνακάμψαι· (Heb. 11:15)	And if indeed **they had called to mind** that [country] from which they departed, **they would have had** opportunity to return. (*imperfect of both verbs*)

For Practice

8.8. Analyze the indicatives (in bold) in the following texts. As you perform your analyses, be sure to consult chapter 6, on the Greek verbal system.

¹⁵καὶ **εἶπεν** αὐτοῖς ὁ Ἰησοῦς· μὴ **δύνανται** οἱ υἱοὶ τοῦ νυμφῶνος πενθεῖν ἐφ' ὅσον μετ' αὐτῶν **ἐστιν** ὁ νυμφίος; **ἐλεύσονται** δὲ ἡμέραι ὅταν ἀπαρθῇ ἀπ' αὐτῶν ὁ νυμφίος, καὶ τότε **νηστεύσουσιν**. ¹⁶οὐδεὶς δὲ **ἐπιβάλλει** ἐπίβλημα

ῥάκους ἀγνάφου ἐπὶ ἱματίῳ παλαιῷ· **αἴρει** γὰρ τὸ πλήρωμα αὐτοῦ ἀπὸ τοῦ ἱματίου καὶ χεῖρον σχίσμα **γίνεται.** ¹⁷οὐδὲ **βάλλουσιν** οἶνον νέον εἰς ἀσκοὺς παλαιούς· εἰ δὲ μή γε, **ῥήγνυνται** οἱ ἀσκοὶ καὶ ὁ οἶνος **ἐκχεῖται** καὶ οἱ ἀσκοὶ **ἀπόλλυνται·** ἀλλὰ **βάλλουσιν** οἶνον νέον εἰς ἀσκοὺς καινούς, καὶ ἀμφότεροι **συντηροῦνται.** (Matt. 9:15–17)

Τί οὖν **ἐροῦμεν**; ὁ νόμος ἁμαρτία; μὴ **γένοιτο·** ἀλλὰ τὴν ἁμαρτίαν οὐκ **ἔγνων** εἰ μὴ διὰ νόμου· τήν τε γὰρ ἐπιθυμίαν οὐκ **ᾔδειν** εἰ μὴ ὁ νόμος **ἔλεγεν·** οὐκ **ἐπιθυμήσεις.** (Rom. 7:7)

Subjunctive Mood

8.9. Whereas the indicative mood is mainly concerned with assertions about reality, the subjunctive mood makes projections about reality. From the perspective of the writer or speaker, the subjunctive mood grammaticalizes contemplating or projecting actions or states. It is common to understand the subjunctive mood as the mood of probability. Dana and Mantey (170), as well as David Alan Black (98), say that it is the "mood of probability." Wallace (461) says that the subjunctive mood is *uncertain but probable* (italics original). However, we prefer to think of the subjunctive in terms of projection rather than likelihood or probability, because one can employ the mood to visualize the impossible ("If pigs had silver wings, . . .") as well as to suppose the actual ("If humans are fallen beings, . . ."). Whatever doubt,[4] if any, the subjunctive expresses must be determined in light of the context in which it occurs; it is not a feature of the subjunctive mood itself. Projection itself does not necessarily entail doubt, but it also cannot determine reality. Subjunctive verbs view verbal processes as hypotheses submitted for our contemplation (Porter 57). The action is viewed as capable of being realized.

There are only ten perfect subjunctives in the NT (all from the stative verb οἶδα), so we are basically left with a two-tense opposition. That is, the NT writers had two choices for the tense-form of most subjunctive verbs: the aorist (perfective aspect), when there was no reason to use the present; and the present (imperfective aspect), when the writer wanted to highlight the verbal process. The subjunctive mood can be found in both independent and dependent clauses.

---

4. Some grammars speak of the subjunctive as expressing uncertainty or doubt, if less so than the optative. E.g., John W. Wenham calls it "the *mood of doubtful assertion.*" See his *Elements of New Testament Greek* (Cambridge: Cambridge University Press, 1965), 160.

Independent Clauses

In independent (primary) clauses, the subjunctive is most often utilized in exhortations, deliberations, and prohibitions.

8.10. Hortatory/Volitive. Apart from a small handful (3–5) of NT uses with a singular verb, the hortatory subjunctive is a first-person plural expression that functions similarly to an imperative ("Let's . . .").[5] As Robertson (931) explains, "It was a necessity for the first person, since the imperative was deficient there." Sometimes "Let's go" is a gentle nudge to move; at other times it is a firm exhortation; at still other times it is an out-and-out command. Context, of course, will help one decide which is which.

ἢ πῶς ἐρεῖς τῷ ἀδελφῷ σου· Ἄφες **ἐκβάλω** τὸ κάρφος ἐκ τοῦ ὀφθαλμοῦ σου, καὶ ἰδοὺ ἡ δοκὸς ἐν τῷ ὀφθαλμῷ σοῦ; (Matt. 7:4)	Or how can you say to your brother/sister, "*Let me remove* the speck from your eye," and look, a log is in your [own] eye?

The first-person singular hortatory subjunctives in the NT follow either ἄφες ("allow, permit, let") or δεῦρο (an adverb meaning "come here").

ἐγείρεσθε **ἄγωμεν**· ἰδοὺ ἤγγικεν ὁ παραδιδούς με. (Matt. 26:46)	Get up, **let's go**; "Look, the one betraying me is near."
εἶπαν οὖν πρὸς ἀλλήλους· Μὴ **σχίσωμεν** αὐτόν, ἀλλὰ **λάχωμεν** περὶ αὐτοῦ τίνος ἔσται· (John 19:24)	Therefore they said to one another, "Let's not **tear** it, but let's **cast lots** for it—for whose it will be."
μηδὲ **πορνεύωμεν**, καθώς τινες αὐτῶν ἐπόρνευσαν καὶ ἔπεσαν μιᾷ ἡμέρᾳ εἴκοσι τρεῖς χιλιάδες. (1 Cor. 10:8)	Let's not **commit sexual immorality**, as some of them committed, and twenty-three thousand fell in one day.
χαίρωμεν καὶ **ἀγαλλιῶμεν**, καὶ **δώσωμεν** τὴν δόξαν αὐτῷ, ὅτι ἦλθεν ὁ γάμος τοῦ ἀρνίου καὶ ἡ γυνὴ αὐτοῦ ἡτοίμασεν ἑαυτὴν (Rev. 19:7)	Let's **rejoice** and **exult** and **give** glory to him, because the marriage of the Lamb has come, and his bride has readied herself.

---

5. Since the Greek imperative mood has only second- and third-person forms, the hortatory subjunctive can fill the first-person slot.

8.11. Deliberative. As the label suggests, deliberative subjunctives ask questions, often rhetorical questions, of oneself (first-person singular) or a group of which one is a part (first-person plural). And, to supplement Moule's observation, a deliberative subjunctive can be more than a hortatory subjunctive "merely . . . turned into a question" (22). Certainly one can turn "Let's study Greek" into "Shall we study Greek?" with no significant change in meaning. Both are projections about the study of Greek and can be viewed as mild commands. However, it seems to us that it may be helpful to distinguish between the exhortation "Let's buy bread at the store" and the true (nonrhetorical) question "Shall we buy bread at the store?" Both are still projections, but the question might be asking for a decision rather than making a tacit command.

To add another layer to our discussion, Carson has contributed the category of "pseudodeliberative" subjunctives; that is, first-person subjunctives that do not truly, or properly (within oneself or a group of which one is a part), deliberate at all.[6] In his mind, all but seven of the generally accepted deliberative subjunctives in the NT do not actually belong in the category. Commands framed as questions and questions aimed at a third party, for example, would not. Although we suspect that Carson is correct in thinking that the deliberative subjunctive is among the "grammatical categories [that] mask as much as they reveal," we will treat true examples and pseudoexamples of its use together.[7]

εἶπεν αὐτῷ· Σὺ εἶ ὁ ἐρχόμενος ἢ ἕτερον **προσδοκῶμεν**; (Matt. 11:3)	He said to him, "Are you the one coming, or **should/shall we expect** another?" (*real*)
Καὶ ἔλεγεν· Πῶς **ὁμοιώσωμεν** τὴν βασιλείαν τοῦ θεοῦ ἢ ἐν τίνι αὐτὴν παραβολῇ **θῶμεν**; (Mark 4:30)	And he said, "How **shall we compare** the kingdom of God, or by what parable **shall we illustrate** it?" (*rhetorical*)
εἶπον οὖν πρὸς αὐτόν· Τί **ποιῶμεν** ἵνα ἐργαζώμεθα τὰ ἔργα τοῦ θεοῦ; (John 6:28)	Therefore they said to him, "What **should we do** so that we may work the works of God?" (*real*)
Τί οὖν; **ἁμαρτήσωμεν**, ὅτι οὐκ ἐσμὲν ὑπὸ νόμον ἀλλὰ ὑπὸ χάριν; μὴ γένοιτο· (Rom. 6:15)	What then, **shall we sin** because we are not under law but under grace? May it not be! (*rhetorical*)

6. D. A. Carson, *Exegetical Fallacies*, 2nd ed. (Grand Rapids: Baker, 1996), 74.
7. Ibid., 75.

8.12. Prohibition (μή + aorist subjunctive). To express aorist prohibitions (i.e., commands to not do something), NT Greek employs the negated subjunctive rather than the imperative form.[8] Why this is the case is a matter for speculation: "All we can say is that (perhaps unaccountably) usage came to dictate that an *Aorist* prohibition should be expressed by the Subjunctive (not an Imperative), while a *present* prohibition should be expressed by the Imperative" (Moule 21). For examples, see the treatment of Aorist Prohibitions under the Imperative Mood below.

8.13. Emphatic negation (οὐ μή + aorist subjunctive). As indicated in the parentheses, emphatic negation is signaled by the use of two negative particles[9] with the aorist subjunctive. The construction has the strength or force of the colloquial expression "No way!" Despite Moulton's opinion that only Paul (and only 4 times) employed this construction "with its full classical emphasis,"[10] we view all of the NT uses (mostly in what Jesus is reported to have said and LXX quotations) of the doubly negated aorist subjunctive as genuinely emphatic. It is indeed possible that in places where the LXX, angels, or Jesus are quoted in the NT, οὐ μή with the aorist subjunctive is "used with a prophetic emphasis that, in addition to its classical emphatic force, carries with it divine certainty, finality, and decisiveness."[11] Such prophetic emphasis, of course, would stem from subject matter and context rather than anything inherent in the grammatical construction. In any case, in the NT, οὐ μή with the aorist subjunctive has not lost its force.

ἔσται γὰρ μέγας ἐνώπιον τοῦ κυρίου, καὶ οἶνον καὶ σίκερα *οὐ μὴ πίῃ*, καὶ πνεύματος ἁγίου πλησθήσεται ἔτι ἐκ κοιλίας μητρὸς αὐτοῦ (Luke 1:15)	For he will be great in the sight of the Lord, and *he must never drink* wine or strong liquor, and he will be filled by the Holy Spirit, even from his mother's womb.

8. The negated second-person subjunctive appears over 80 times; the negated third-person form appears 5 or 6 times.

9. Οὐ normally negates the indicative mood, and μή normally negates the oblique moods; together they form a stronger negative than either does on its own. James L. Boyer suggests that the double negative is "a form of litotes; i.e., the second negative (μή) negates the subjunctive verb . . . ; the first negative (οὐ) negates the doubtful clause introduced by μή. As a whole the clause communicates that 'there is no doubt about it; it is not an uncertain matter'" ("The Classification of Subjunctives: A Statistical Study," *Grace Theological Journal* 7, no. 1 [1986]: 6).

10. James Hope Moulton, *Prolegomena*, vol. 1 of *A Grammar of New Testament Greek*, by James Hope Moulton, Wilbert Francis Howard, and Nigel Turner, 3rd ed. (Edinburgh: T&T Clark, 1908), 190.

11. Abera Mitiku Mengestu, "The Use of *OU MH* in the New Testament: Emphatic Negation or Mild Negation?" (ThM thesis, Dallas Theological Seminary, 2005), 72.

λέγει αὐτῷ Πέτρος· *Οὐ μὴ νίψῃς*
μου τοὺς πόδας εἰς τὸν αἰῶνα.
(John 13:8)

Peter said to him, "*You will
never, ever wash* my feet.*"*

Λέγω δέ, πνεύματι περιπατεῖτε καὶ
ἐπιθυμίαν σαρκὸς *οὐ μὴ τελέσητε.*
(Gal. 5:16)

But I say, walk by the Spirit and
you will in no way carry out the
desire of the flesh.

καὶ οἱ πυλῶνες αὐτῆς *οὐ μὴ
κλεισθῶσιν* ἡμέρας, νὺξ γὰρ οὐκ
ἔσται ἐκεῖ (Rev. 21:25)

And its gates *will never be closed*
by day, for there will not be night
there.

Dependent Clauses

The following are the most common uses of the subjunctive in dependent
(secondary) clauses.

8.14. Conditional (with ἐάν). As will be discussed in more detail in chapter 11, on clauses, ἐάν with the subjunctive is used in class 3 conditions, or
conditions in which the content of the protasis (*if*-clause) is presented as a
hypothesis. Class 3 conditions imply a tentativeness that first-class conditions
(using the indicative mood) do not simply because the subjunctive mood deals
in the realm of projection rather than assertion. Hypothetical conditions then,
as now, are powerful tools in the hands of a gifted preacher or teacher. NT
authors made very good use of class 3 conditions for hortatory purposes.

ἐὰν γὰρ *εἰσέλθῃ* εἰς συναγωγὴν
ὑμῶν ἀνὴρ χρυσοδακτύλιος ἐν
ἐσθῆτι λαμπρᾷ, *εἰσέλθῃ* δὲ καὶ
πτωχὸς ἐν ῥυπαρᾷ ἐσθῆτι
(James 2:2)

For if a man **enters** your assembly
with a gold ring and splendid
clothes, and also a poor man in
filthy clothes **enters**.

> Here James begins a description of outrageous partiality. Because it is
> an almost (alas, not quite) unimaginable situation, James is able to chal-
> lenge his readers to consider their own practices without ever accus-
> ing them of the extreme acts he describes. Both James and John may
> employ hypothetical scenarios, based on sad realities, precisely to leave
> their readers the space in which to examine their own consciences. Our
> point is that the interpreter needs to do more than look at the class of
> a condition to determine its relationship to reality. Moreover, a judicious
> dose of hyperbolic case study may help cure people of very real moral ills.

ἐὰν **εἴπωμεν** ὅτι κοινωνίαν ἔχομεν μετ᾽ αὐτοῦ καὶ ἐν τῷ σκότει **περιπατῶμεν**, ψευδόμεθα καὶ οὐ ποιοῦμεν τὴν ἀλήθειαν· (1 John 1:6)	If **we say** that we have fellowship with him yet **we are walking** in the dark, we are lying and do not practice the truth.

> This is the first of a series of five class 3 conditions in the immediate context (one in each verse of 1:6–10), in which we think John frames as hypothetical what he knows some (at the very least, the false teachers who have left the church) are actually saying. In this manner, without specifically finger-pointing, he sets before those who have remained the consequences of making the outlined false claims and a tacit exhortation not to make them.[12]

μνημόνευε οὖν πῶς εἴληφας καὶ ἤκουσας καὶ τήρει, καὶ μετανόησον· ἐὰν οὖν μὴ **γρηγορήσῃς**, ἥξω ὡς κλέπτης, καὶ οὐ μὴ γνῷς ποίαν ὥραν ἥξω ἐπὶ σέ· (Rev. 3:3)	Therefore remember what you have received and heard; keep it and repent. Therefore, if **you are** not **alert**, I will come as a thief, and you will not know what time I will come to you.

> Christ, too, was a master of the hortatory third-class condition.

8.15. Purpose (telic, final) / result (ecbatic, consecutive) / content (with ἵνα). The NT employs the subjunctive after ἵνα in a variety of ways, the most frequent of which are to indicate purpose, result, and content (for a further treatment, see chap. 12). Purpose and result are naturally and logically linked, so there are ἵνα clauses in the NT that could be interpreted either way. As both Porter (234) and Wallace (472) point out, verbs expressing intention are naturally followed by purpose clauses. Result clauses are more easily distinguished from purpose clauses when the verbs on which they depend do not convey "intention, direction, or purpose" (Porter 234). Content clauses are substantival clauses that function as subjects or objects of verbs or that limit other substantives or adjectives. Although ὅτι with the indicative introduces the majority of NT content clauses, ἵνα with the subjunctive introduces a significant minority. In particular, ἵνα with the subjunctive is used with verbs of striving, wishing, permitting, beseeching, and commanding; ἵνα μή (in

---

12. Culy also notes, "The conditional construction functions as a mitigated exhortation." Martin M. Culy, *I, II, III John: A Handbook on the Greek Text* (Waco: Baylor University Press, 2004), 19.

order that not / lest) with the subjunctive is used with verbs of fearing and apprehension.[13]

Μὴ κρίνετε, ἵνα μὴ **κριθῆτε**· (Matt. 7:1)	Do not judge *so that* **you will** *not /* **lest you be judged.** (*negative purpose or result*)
καὶ ἀπὸ τότε ἐζήτει εὐκαιρίαν ἵνα αὐτὸν **παραδῷ**. (Matt. 26:16)	And from then he was seeking an opportunity *to* **betray** him. (*epexegetical content*)

The ἵνα clause explains εὐκαιρίαν in the same way an infinitive would.

καὶ ἠρώτησαν αὐτὸν οἱ μαθηταὶ αὐτοῦ λέγοντες· Ῥαββί, τίς ἥμαρτεν, οὗτος ἢ οἱ γονεῖς αὐτοῦ, ἵνα τυφλὸς **γεννηθῇ**; (John 9:2)	And his disciples asked him saying, "Rabbi, who sinned, this man or his parents, *so / with the result that* **he was born** blind?" (*result*)
μείζονα ταύτης ἀγάπην οὐδεὶς ἔχει, ἵνα τις τὴν ψυχὴν αὐτοῦ **θῇ** ὑπὲρ τῶν φίλων αὐτοῦ. (John 15:13)	Greater love than this no one has, *that* someone **lay down** his/her life for his/her friends. (*epexegetical content,*[a] *the* ἵνα *clause explains* ταύτης)

[a] Thus Max Zerwick and Mary Grosvenor, *A Grammatical Analysis of the Greek New Testament* (Rome: Biblical Institute Press, 1981), 333.

ἀλλ' ἐγὼ τὴν ἀλήθειαν λέγω ὑμῖν, συμφέρει ὑμῖν ἵνα ἐγὼ **ἀπέλθω**. (John 16:7)	But I tell you the truth, *that* **I go away** is to your benefit. (*content, subject*)
οὐκ ἐρωτῶ ἵνα **ἄρῃς** αὐτοὺς ἐκ τοῦ κόσμου ἀλλ' ἵνα **τηρήσῃς** αὐτοὺς ἐκ τοῦ πονηροῦ. (John 17:15)	I do not ask *that* **you take** them out of the world, but *that* **you keep** them from the evil one. (*content, direct object*)

Both ἵνα clauses function as object complements of ἐρωτῶ.

ἐρεῖς οὖν· Ἐξεκλάσθησαν κλάδοι ἵνα ἐγὼ **ἐγκεντρισθῶ**. (Rom. 11:19)	You will say then, "Branches were cut off *so that* I myself **could be grafted in.**" (*purpose*)

13. Boyer, "Classification of Subjunctives," 9–11.

εὐχαριστῶ ὅτι οὐδένα ὑμῶν ἐβάπτισα εἰ μὴ Κρίσπον καὶ Γάϊον, ἵνα μή τις **εἴπῃ** ὅτι εἰς τὸ ἐμὸν ὄνομα ἐβαπτίσθητε· (1 Cor. 1:14–15)

I give thanks that I baptized none of you except Crispus and Gaius, *lest* anyone / *so that no* one **say** that you were baptized in my name. (*negative result*)

καὶ διὰ τοῦτο πέμπει αὐτοῖς ὁ θεὸς ἐνέργειαν πλάνης εἰς τὸ πιστεῦσαι αὐτοὺς τῷ ψεύδει, ἵνα **κριθῶσιν** πάντες οἱ μὴ πιστεύσαντες τῇ ἀληθείᾳ ἀλλὰ εὐδοκήσαντες τῇ ἀδικίᾳ. (2 Thess. 2:11–12)

And because of this God is sending them a deluding power for them to believe the lie, *so that* all who do not believe the truth, but think well of unrighteousness, **are condemned.** (*purpose or result*)

μὴ νεόφυτον, *ἵνα μὴ* τυφωθεὶς εἰς κρίμα **ἐμπέσῃ** τοῦ διαβόλου. (1 Tim. 3:6)

Not a new convert *so that*, being conceited, **he might** not **fall under** the condemnation of the devil. (*negative purpose*)

8.16. Indefinite (most often with forms of ἄν). Because they are more tentative than their definite counterparts, indefinite clauses (relative, e.g., whoever; temporal, e.g., whenever; local, e.g., wherever) commonly use subjunctive verbs.

ὅστις γὰρ ἄν **ποιήσῃ** τὸ θέλημα τοῦ πατρός μου τοῦ ἐν οὐρανοῖς, αὐτός μου ἀδελφὸς καὶ ἀδελφὴ καὶ μήτηρ ἐστίν. (Matt. 12:50)

For *whoever* **does** the will of my Father in heaven is himself/herself my brother and sister and mother. (*relative*)

βάπτισμα δὲ ἔχω βαπτισθῆναι, καὶ πῶς συνέχομαι ἕως ὅτου **τελεσθῇ**. (Luke 12:50)

But I have a baptism to be baptized with, and how consumed I am *until* it is finished! (*temporal/relative*)

ὅταν ὁ Χριστὸς **φανερωθῇ**, ἡ ζωὴ ὑμῶν, τότε καὶ ὑμεῖς σὺν αὐτῷ φανερωθήσεσθε ἐν δόξῃ. (Col. 3:4)

Whenever Christ, your life, **appears**, then you also will appear with him in glory. (*temporal*)

Ὅταν is a contraction of ὅτε and ἄν.

πρὸς ὑμᾶς δὲ τυχὸν παραμενῶ ἢ
καὶ παραχειμάσω, ἵνα ὑμεῖς με
προπέμψητε οὗ ἐὰν **πορεύωμαι.**
(1 Cor. 16:6)

And perhaps I will stay with you
or even spend the winter, so that
you may send me *wherever* I go.
(*local*)

οὗτοι οἱ ἀκολουθοῦντες τῷ ἀρνίῳ
ὅπου ἂν **ὑπάγῃ·** (Rev. 14:4)

These are the ones who follow
the Lamb *wherever* he goes.
(*local*)

For Practice

8.17. Analyze the subjunctives (in bold) in the following verses.

ὅταν **κληθῇς** ὑπό τινος εἰς γάμους, μὴ **κατακλιθῇς** εἰς τὴν πρωτοκλισίαν,
μήποτε ἐντιμότερός σου **ᾖ** κεκλημένος ὑπ᾽ αὐτοῦ. (Luke 14:8)

εἶπεν οὖν Θωμᾶς ὁ λεγόμενος Δίδυμος τοῖς συμμαθηταῖς· Ἄγωμεν καὶ
ἡμεῖς ἵνα **ἀποθάνωμεν** μετ᾽ αὐτοῦ. (John 11:16)

ἔλεγον οὖν αὐτῷ οἱ ἄλλοι μαθηταί· Ἑωράκαμεν τὸν κύριον. ὁ δὲ εἶπεν
αὐτοῖς· Ἐὰν μὴ **ἴδω** ἐν ταῖς χερσὶν αὐτοῦ τὸν τύπον τῶν ἥλων καὶ **βάλω**
τὸν δάκτυλόν μου εἰς τὸν τύπον τῶν ἥλων καὶ **βάλω** μου τὴν χεῖρα εἰς
τὴν πλευρὰν αὐτοῦ, οὐ μὴ **πιστεύσω.** (John 20:25)

³ἔπεμψα δὲ τοὺς ἀδελφούς, ἵνα μὴ τὸ καύχημα ἡμῶν τὸ ὑπὲρ ὑμῶν **κενωθῇ**
ἐν τῷ μέρει τούτῳ, ἵνα καθὼς ἔλεγον παρεσκευασμένοι **ἦτε,** ⁴μή πως
ἐὰν **ἔλθωσιν** σὺν ἐμοὶ Μακεδόνες καὶ **εὕρωσιν** ὑμᾶς ἀπαρασκευάστους
καταισχυνθῶμεν ἡμεῖς, ἵνα μὴ **λέγωμεν** ὑμεῖς, ἐν τῇ ὑποστάσει ταύτῃ.
⁵ἀναγκαῖον οὖν ἡγησάμην παρακαλέσαι τοὺς ἀδελφούς, ἵνα **προέλθωσιν** εἰς
ὑμᾶς καὶ **προκαταρτίσωσι** τὴν προεπηγγελμένην εὐλογίαν ὑμῶν, ταύτην
ἑτοίμην εἶναι οὕτως ὡς εὐλογίαν καὶ μὴ ὡς πλεονεξίαν. (2 Cor. 9:3–5)

προσερχώμεθα οὖν μετὰ παρρησίας τῷ θρόνῳ τῆς χάριτος, ἵνα **λάβωμεν**
ἔλεος καὶ χάριν **εὕρωμεν** εἰς εὔκαιρον βοήθειαν. (Heb. 4:16)

Optative Mood

8.18. The optative occurs only 68 times in the NT. It was already in decline by
the Koine period, probably due to its having a semantic range similar to that of

the subjunctive (and perhaps due to the subjunctive's "easier" endings). Like the subjunctive, the optative mood is one of projection, but with an added element of hesitation or contingency. With Boyer, however, we maintain that "the optative implies a less distinct anticipation than the subjunctive, but not less probable."[14] The mood is used in the NT to convey wishes or prayers and in various potential (contingent) expressions. All but nine of the NT optatives are found in Luke's and Paul's writings. The semantic feature of projection with hesitancy accounts for the following usages.

Volitive (Wish, Prayer, Request)

8.19. Most (about 57 percent) of the NT optatives are volitive, and almost half of those (14× in Paul and 1× in Luke) are found in the idiomatic saying μὴ γένοιτο (May it never be!). The remaining occurrences are found in both formal and informal benedictions, requests (2×), curses (2× or 3×), and in Mary's decision (presumably an act of will rather than a wish) to accept God's will humbly and participate in the incarnation (Luke 1:38), with the positive γένοιτο.

Πέτρος δὲ εἶπεν πρὸς αὐτόν· Τὸ ἀργύριόν σου σὺν σοὶ **εἴη** εἰς ἀπώλειαν ὅτι τὴν δωρεὰν τοῦ θεοῦ ἐνόμισας διὰ χρημάτων κτᾶσθαι. (Acts 8:20)

But Peter said to him. "**May** your silver **be** for destruction [i.e., perish] with you because you thought the gift of God could be acquired with money." (*curse*)

νόμον οὖν καταργοῦμεν διὰ τῆς πίστεως; **μὴ γένοιτο**, ἀλλὰ νόμον ἱστάνομεν. (Rom. 3:31)

Therefore do we nullify the law through this faith? **May it never be**, but we establish the law. (*negative wish*)

Αὐτὸς δὲ ὁ κύριος τῆς εἰρήνης **δῴη** ὑμῖν τὴν εἰρήνην διὰ παντὸς ἐν παντὶ τρόπῳ. (2 Thess. 3:16)

And **may** the Lord of peace himself **give** you peace through everything [and] in every way. (*formal benediction*)

ναὶ ἀδελφέ, ἐγώ σου **ὀναίμην** ἐν κυρίῳ· ἀνάπαυσόν μου τὰ σπλάγχνα ἐν Χριστῷ. (Philem. 20)

Yes, brother, **may** I **benefit** from you in the Lord; refresh my heart in Christ. (*request*)

---

14. James L. Boyer, "The Classification of Optatives: A Statistical Study," *Grace Theological Journal* 9, no. 1 (1988): 129.

ἀλλὰ εἶπεν· Ἐπιτιμήσαι σοι κύριος. (Jude 9)

But he [i.e., Michael, the archangel] said, "**May** the Lord **rebuke** you." (*probably a curse*)

Potential

8.20. Both direct and indirect questions can employ the optative, as can conditional sentences. In the NT most of the potential optatives are found in questions (2 direct, 17 indirect) and are often preceded by the particle ἄν; the rest are in more or less "incomplete," class 4 conditional sentences.

καὶ προσκαλεσάμενος ἕνα τῶν παίδων ἐπυνθάνετο τί ἂν **εἴη** ταῦτα· (Luke 15:26)

And having summoned one of the servants, he inquired what these things **might be/mean**. (*indirect question*)

> The equivalent direct question is "What are these things" or "What do these things mean?"

νεύει οὖν τούτῳ Σίμων Πέτρος πυθέσθαι τίς ἂν **εἴη** περὶ οὗ λέγει. (John 13:24)

Therefore Simon Peter gestured to this man to ask who **it might be** about whom he spoke. (*indirect question*)

> The equivalent direct question is "About whom are you speaking?" This is the only optative in the Johannine corpus.

ὁ δὲ εἶπεν· Πῶς γὰρ ἂν **δυναίμην** ἐὰν μή τις ὁδηγήσει με; (Acts 8:31)

And he said, "For how **can I**, unless someone guides me?" (*direct question*)

τινὲς δὲ ἀπὸ τῆς Ἀσίας Ἰουδαῖοι, οὓς ἔδει ἐπὶ σοῦ παρεῖναι καὶ κατηγορεῖν εἴ τι **ἔχοιεν** πρὸς ἐμέ (Acts 24:19)

But [there were] some Jews from Asia for whom it was necessary to be present before you and to make an accusation if **they might have** anything against me. (*incomplete class 4 conditional; there is no ἄν + optative in the apodosis*)

For Practice

8.21. Analyze the optatives (in bold) in the following verses.

ζητεῖν τὸν θεόν, εἰ ἄρα γε **ψηλαφήσειαν** αὐτὸν καὶ **εὕροιεν**, καί γε οὐ μακρὰν ἀπὸ ἑνὸς ἑκάστου ἡμῶν ὑπάρχοντα. (Acts 17:27)

Τί οὖν ἐροῦμεν; μὴ ἀδικία παρὰ τῷ θεῷ; μὴ **γένοιτο·** (Rom. 9:14)

ὑμᾶς δὲ ὁ κύριος **πλεονάσαι** καὶ **περισσεύσαι** τῇ ἀγάπῃ εἰς ἀλλήλους καὶ εἰς πάντας, καθάπερ καὶ ἡμεῖς εἰς ὑμᾶς (1 Thess. 3:12)

Imperative Mood

8.22. Although not limited to the realm of issuing orders, the imperative mood is associated with commands and prohibitions. Imperatives direct, entreat, or impose one person's will on others, but also grant permission. Many older grammars state that the imperative is the furthest removed of the moods from reality.[15] We do not find this explanation to be helpful or even entirely accurate. Boyer is correct: "There are degrees of potentiality *within* the moods, but not *between* the moods."[16] Is direction demonstrably less likely to be realized than projection (or are projections more or less likely to be realized depending on their mood)? It may be more helpful to see the imperative mood on a scale that moves from assertion to direction or volition (see the table at the beginning of this chapter). Whereas the indicative makes an assertion and the subjunctive and optative make a projection, the imperative mood *directs the will* or *volition* of the person(s) being addressed. And unlike English, Greek imperatives can be inflected for third-person as well as for second-person addressees. Third-person imperatives, despite their usual (and, dare we say it, misleading) permissive translation ("Let him/her . . ."), are not necessarily weaker than second-person imperatives. As Gary Long says, "Greek's 3d person imperative is, however, every bit as direct as its 2d person

---

15. Dana and Mantey (165) define mood as an *"affirmation of relation* [of a verbal idea] *to reality* . . . : mood represents the way in which the matter is conceived" (italics original). In their system, the indicative is "the mood of *certainty*"; the subjunctive is "the mood of *probability*"; the optative is "the mood of *possibility*"; and the imperative is "the mood of *volition*" (168–74, italics original). The imperative "expresses neither probability nor possibility, but only intention, and is, therefore, the furthest removed from reality" (174).

16. Boyer, "Classification of Optatives," 138.

imperative,"[17] if by "direct" he means "directive." We make this distinction because, as Decker points out, third-person imperatives are often indirect (they are addressed to him/her/it to get "you" to do something) and can be addressed to a third party, instead of to "you," to soften a direct command.[18]

Along with its relationship to reality, tense usage in the imperative mood has been a matter of debate. Therefore, although verbal aspect is discussed more fully in chapter 6, it is necessary to revisit it here. In the NT the imperative, like the subjunctive, is confined almost exclusively to two tense-forms, or two aspects.[19] Aorist imperatives view their verbal processes as complete wholes, and present imperatives view their verbal processes as in progress. In a system in which opposition between aorist and present plays a key role, the aorist is the "default" tense, and the present is chosen for special emphasis.[20] As Boyer states, "It is contrary to the basic significance of the aorist to make it special in any way."[21] A common scheme found in many grammars is that aorist imperatives communicate specific, ingressive, or urgent actions; presents communicate habitual, repeated, or characteristic actions. The aorist prohibitions are seen as warnings not to begin an action ("Don't ever"), present prohibitions as commands to stop an action already in progress ("Stop"; Dana and Mantey 299–302). However, the variety of contexts in which imperatives and prohibitions occur simply do not bear this out. This also confuses aspect and *Aktionsart*. Neither aspectual choice indicates the kind of action (*Aktionsart*) in view; only context can do this. Aorist commands are neither necessarily urgent nor punctiliar or specific; present commands need not be general and do not themselves imply continuity or repetition. By the same token, aorist prohibitions do not necessarily warn against starting something, and present prohibitions often do not mean "Stop!"[22] Before turning to the particular uses of the imperative mood, we implore our readers, "the

17. Gary A. Long, *Grammatical Concepts 101 for Biblical Greek* (Peabody, MA: Hendrickson, 2006), 80.

18. Rodney J. Decker, *Reading Koine Greek: An Introduction and Integrated Workbook* (Grand Rapids: Baker Academic, 2014), 490–91.

19. There are ten perfect subjunctives in the NT (all from the stative verb οἶδα) and four or five perfect imperatives (two or three from οἶδα, one as a standard, if stative, greeting [Acts 15:29] and one that seems stative by choice [Mark 4:39]).

20. In the NT, unlike secular Greek, present imperatives outnumber their aorist counterparts.

21. James L. Boyer, "The Classification of Imperatives: A Statistical Study," *Grace Theological Journal* 8, no. 1 (1987): 45.

22. For an examination of all of the prohibitions in the NT with specific reference to whether they are cessative or ingressive, durative or punctiliar, and general or specific, see Douglas S. Huffman, *Verbal Aspect Theory and the Prohibitions in the Greek New Testament*, Studies in Biblical Greek 16 (New York: Peter Lang, 2014).

temptation to standardize the translation of the various imperatival usages should be resisted."[23]

Commands and Prohibitions

8.23. Just over 80 percent of NT imperatives can be classified as positive commands (1,169) to do something or negative prohibitions (188) against doing something.[24] This is in keeping with the mood's essential expression of direction. The following chart illustrates our understanding of verbal aspect in the imperative mood.

Two Aspects in Second-Person Commands and Prohibitions

Aspect	Command	Prohibition (with μή)
Present (Imperfective): Used to highlight a verbal process by viewing it as in progress *(with no necessary expectation of continuous action)	Do it!	Don't do it!
	*(Be doing it!)	*(Don't be doing it!)
Aorist (Perfective): Used to indicate a verbal process as a complete whole	Do it!	Don't do it! (*with the subjunctive*)

1. Present-tense commands

a. *Second person*

ἀσθενοῦντας **θεραπεύετε**, νεκροὺς **ἐγείρετε**, λεπροὺς **καθαρίζετε**, δαιμόνια **ἐκβάλλετε**· δωρεὰν ἐλάβετε, δωρεὰν δότε. (Matt. 10:8)	**Heal** those who are sick, **raise** the dead, **cleanse** the lepers, **throw out** demons. Freely you received, freely *give*.

All of these commands are general, as is the aorist δότε.

ὁ δὲ εἶπεν· **Φέρετέ** μοι ὧδε αὐτούς. (Matt. 14:18)	And he said, "**Bring** them [the loaves and fish] to me here."

The context indicates neither continuity nor repetition; the command is specific.

---

23. Boyer, "Classification of Imperatives," 35.
24. Ibid., 36.

παρακαλοῦμεν δὲ ὑμᾶς, ἀδελφοί, **νουθετεῖτε** τοὺς ἀτάκτους, **παραμυθεῖσθε** τοὺς ὀλιγοψύχους, **ἀντέχεσθε** τῶν ἀσθενῶν, **μακροθυμεῖτε** πρὸς πάντας. (1 Thess. 5:14)	And we exhort you, brothers and sisters, **admonish** the irresponsible, **encourage** the discouraged, **help** the weak, **be patient** toward all. (*general*)
Καὶ νῦν, τεκνία, **μένετε** ἐν αὐτῷ (1 John 2:28)	And now, little children, **remain** in him. (*continuous [implied by the verb's lexis], general*)
Καὶ ἡ φωνὴ ἣν ἤκουσα ἐκ τοῦ οὐρανοῦ πάλιν λαλοῦσαν μετ' ἐμοῦ καὶ λέγουσαν· Ὕπαγε **λάβε** τὸ βιβλίον τὸ ἠνεῳγμένον ἐν τῇ χειρὶ τοῦ ἀγγέλου τοῦ ἑστῶτος ἐπὶ τῆς θαλάσσης καὶ ἐπὶ τῆς γῆς. (Rev. 10:8)	And the voice that I heard from heaven speaking with me again and saying/said, "**Go,** *take* the open scroll in the hand of the angel standing on the sea and the earth." (*specific, as is the aorist imperative immediately following it*)

All imperative forms of ὑπάγω in the NT are in the present tense.

b. *Third person*

Ὅταν δὲ ἴδητε τὸ βδέλυγμα τῆς ἐρημώσεως ἑστηκότα ὅπου οὐ δεῖ, ὁ ἀναγινώσκων **νοείτω**, τότε οἱ ἐν τῇ Ἰουδαίᾳ **φευγέτωσαν** εἰς τὰ ὄρη (Mark 13:14)	But whenever you see the abomination of desolation standing where it should not be, the one reading **must understand**, then those in Judea **should flee** to the mountains. (*specific*)
πάντα ὑμῶν ἐν ἀγάπῃ **γινέσθω**. (1 Cor. 16:14)	Your everything / all you do **must be done** in love. (*general*)

Remember that neuter plural subjects often take a singular verb.

Ἡ φιλαδελφία **μενέτω**. (Heb. 13:1)	Brotherly love **must continue**. (*general, continuous*)

Κακοπαθεῖ τις ἐν ὑμῖν; προσευχέσθω· εὐθυμεῖ τις; ψαλλέτω. (James 5:13)

Is anyone among you suffering? **He/she should pray.** Is anyone happy? **He/she should sing psalms.** (*general*)

καὶ τὸ πνεῦμα καὶ ἡ νύμφη λέγουσιν· Ἔρχου· καὶ ὁ ἀκούων εἰπάτω· Ἔρχου· καὶ ὁ διψῶν ἐρχέσθω, ὁ θέλων λαβέτω ὕδωρ ζωῆς δωρεάν. (Rev. 22:17)

And the Spirit and the bride say, "Come." And the one hearing *must say,* "Come." And the one thirsting **must come;** the one desiring *must take* the water of life as a gift. (*general, as are the aorist imperatives in the verse*)

All imperatives of ἔρχομαι in Revelation are present. There is one aorist form in John 4:16.

2. Aorist-tense commands

a. *Second person*

σὺ δὲ νηστεύων ἄλειψαί σου τὴν κεφαλὴν καὶ τὸ πρόσωπόν σου νίψαι (Matt. 6:17)

And you, when fasting, **anoint** your head and **wash** your face. (*general*)

καὶ φέρετε τὸν μόσχον τὸν σιτευτόν, θύσατε, καὶ φαγόντες εὐφρανθῶμεν (Luke 15:23)

And *bring* the fattened calf, **kill** it, and let's celebrate with feasting. (*specific, as is the present-tense φέρετε*)

ἠγοράσθητε γὰρ τιμῆς· δοξάσατε δὴ τὸν θεὸν ἐν τῷ σώματι ὑμῶν. (1 Cor. 6:20)

For you were bought with a price; therefore, **glorify** God in your body. (*general*)

Διὸ τὰς παρειμένας χεῖρας καὶ τὰ παραλελυμένα γόνατα ἀνορθώσατε (Heb. 12:12)

Therefore **strengthen** your drooping hands and your weakened knees. (*general*)

ἐγὼ ὅσους ἐὰν φιλῶ ἐλέγχω καὶ παιδεύω· ζήλευε οὖν καὶ μετανόησον. (Rev. 3:19)

I rebuke and discipline whomever I love. Therefore *be zealous* and **repent.** (*general, as is the present-tense ζήλευε*)

b. *Third person*

ὁ δὲ ἔφη· Τί γὰρ κακὸν ἐποίησεν; οἱ δὲ περισσῶς ἔκραζον λέγοντες· **Σταυρωθήτω.** (Matt. 27:23)	And he said, "For what evil has he done?" But they were shouting all the more, saying, "**He must be crucified.**" (*specific*)

Note the use of the aorist active in Mark 15:13 (Σταύρωσον αὐτόν) and the present active in Luke 23:21 (Σταύρου σταύρου αὐτόν).

Ἔλεγεν δὲ πρὸς πάντας· Εἴ τις θέλει ὀπίσω μου ἔρχεσθαι, **ἀρνησάσθω** ἑαυτὸν καὶ **ἀράτω** τὸν σταυρὸν αὐτοῦ καθ᾽ ἡμέραν καὶ **ἀκολουθείτω** μοι. (Luke 9:23)	And he was saying to all, "If anyone wishes to come after me **he/she must deny** him/herself and **take up** his/her cross daily and *follow* me." (*general, as is the present-tense ἀκολουθείτω*)
τὸ ἐπιεικὲς ὑμῶν **γνωσθήτω** πᾶσιν ἀνθρώποις. ὁ κύριος ἐγγύς· (Phil. 4:5)	Your gentleness **should be known** to all people. The Lord is near. (*general*)
ἀσθενεῖ τις ἐν ὑμῖν; **προσκαλεσάσθω** τοὺς πρεσβυτέρους τῆς ἐκκλησίας, καὶ **προσευξάσθωσαν** ἐπ᾽ αὐτὸν ἀλείψαντες αὐτὸν ἐλαίῳ ἐν τῷ ὀνόματι τοῦ κυρίου· (James 5:14)	Is anyone among you weak/sick? **He/she should call** the elders of the church, and **they should pray** over him/her, anointing him/her in the name of the Lord. (*general, as are the present imperatives in the previous verse*)
Εἴ τις ἔχει οὖς **ἀκουσάτω.** (Rev. 13:9)	If anyone has an ear, **he/she must hear.** (*general*)

3. **Present-tense prohibitions**

a. *Second person*

Μὴ **κρίνετε**, ἵνα μὴ κριθῆτε· (Matt. 7:1)	Do *not judge*, lest you / so that you not be judged. (*general; "stop judging" is not required by the context*)

Μὴ οὖν βασιλευέτω ἡ ἁμαρτία ἐν τῷ θνητῷ ὑμῶν σώματι εἰς τὸ ὑπακούειν ταῖς ἐπιθυμίαις αὐτοῦ, μηδὲ **παριστάνετε** τὰ μέλη ὑμῶν ὅπλα ἀδικίας τῇ ἁμαρτίᾳ, ἀλλὰ παραστήσατε ἑαυτοὺς τῷ θεῷ (Rom. 6:12–13)

Therefore, sin *must not rule* in your mortal body so that you obey its desires, and *do not present* your members to sin as instruments of unrighteousness, but *present* yourselves to God. (*general*)

These present imperatives are frequently taken as expressing prohibitions against the already ongoing act of sinning: "stop letting sin rule," "stop presenting your members." The aorist παραστήσατε is then given an ingressive meaning: "start to present" (after they have stopped the former).[25] However, this reflects a misunderstanding of the tense-forms and incorrectly assumes, apart from any clear contextual evidence, that the readers are already engaged in the action (which they are told to stop). Instead, the present-tense prohibitions are used to draw attention to the theme begun in 6:1 of freedom from the reign of sin. The aorist command simply summarizes the positive counterpart.

τὸ αὐτὸ εἰς ἀλλήλους φρονοῦντες, μὴ τὰ ὑψηλὰ φρονοῦντες ἀλλὰ τοῖς ταπεινοῖς συναπαγόμενοι. μὴ **γίνεσθε** φρόνιμοι παρ' ἑαυτοῖς. (Rom. 12:16)

Be of the same mind with one another. Do not set your minds on high things, but associate with the humble. *Do not be* wise in your own estimation. (*general; "stop being wise" is not required by the context*)

ἐκνήψατε δικαίως καὶ μὴ **ἁμαρτάνετε**, ἀγνωσίαν γὰρ θεοῦ τινες ἔχουσιν, πρὸς ἐντροπὴν ὑμῖν λαλῶ. (1 Cor. 15:34)

Come to your senses rightly / as you ought, and *stop sinning*, for some are ignorant about God, I say to your shame. (*general; "stop" is warranted by the context*)

25. Cf. David L. Mathewson, "Verbal Aspect in Imperatival Constructions in Pauline Ethical Injunctions," *Filologia Neotestamentaria* 9 (1996): 21–35.

τῇ ἐλευθερίᾳ ἡμᾶς Χριστὸς
ἠλευθέρωσεν· στήκετε οὖν
καὶ μὴ πάλιν ζυγῷ δουλείας
ἐνέχεσθε. (Gal. 5:1)

For freedom Christ set us free.
Therefore *stand* and **do not**
again **be subject** to the yoke of
slavery. (*general; "stop being
subject" is made impossible
by* πάλιν)

καὶ εἷς ἐκ τῶν πρεσβυτέρων
λέγει μοι· *Μὴ κλαῖε·* ἰδοὺ
ἐνίκησεν ὁ λέων ὁ ἐκ τῆς
φυλῆς Ἰούδα, ἡ ῥίζα Δαυίδ,
ἀνοῖξαι τὸ βιβλίον καὶ τὰς ἑπτὰ
σφραγῖδας αὐτοῦ. (Rev. 5:5)

And one of the elders said to
me, "*Stop crying*; look, the
Lion of the tribe of Judah, the
Root of David, has conquered
in order to open the scroll
and its seven seals." (*specific;
"stop" is legitimate, based
on the preceding verse where
John is already crying*)

b. *Third person*

ὁ οὖν ὁ θεὸς συνέζευξεν
ἄνθρωπος μὴ *χωριζέτω.*
(Mark 10:9)

Therefore what God has
joined together, a person **must
not separate.** (*general; "stop
separating" is not required by
the context*)

Μὴ οὖν *βασιλευέτω* ἡ ἁμαρτία
ἐν τῷ θνητῷ ὑμῶν σώματι εἰς
τὸ ὑπακούειν ταῖς ἐπιθυμίαις
αὐτοῦ (Rom. 6:12)

Therefore, sin **must** not **rule** in
your mortal body so that you
obey its desires. (*general; see
above*)

Τοῖς δὲ λοιποῖς λέγω ἐγώ,
οὐχ ὁ κύριος· εἴ τις ἀδελφὸς
γυναῖκα ἔχει ἄπιστον, καὶ αὕτη
συνευδοκεῖ οἰκεῖν μετ' αὐτοῦ,
μὴ ἀφιέτω αὐτήν· (1 Cor. 7:12)

But to the rest I say, not the
Lord, if a certain brother has
an unbelieving wife and she
consents to live with him, **he
must** not **divorce** her. (*general;
"stop divorcing" is impossible
in the context*)

| ὁ κλέπτων μηκέτι **κλεπτέτω,** μᾶλλον δὲ κοπιάτω ἐργαζόμενος ταῖς ἰδίαις χερσὶν τὸ ἀγαθόν, ἵνα ἔχῃ μεταδιδόναι τῷ χρείαν ἔχοντι. (Eph. 4:28) | The thief **must** no longer **steal / must stop stealing,** but rather he/she must labor, doing something good with his/her own hands, so that he/she has something to share with one having need. (general; "stop" is implied by μηκέτι) |

| εἰ δὲ ὡς Χριστιανός, μὴ **αἰσχυνέσθω,** δοξαζέτω δὲ τὸν θεὸν ἐν τῷ ὀνόματι τούτῳ. (1 Pet. 4:16) | But if [anyone suffers] as a Christian, **he/she should** not **be ashamed** but should glorify God for this name. (general; "stop being ashamed" is not required by the context) |

4. Aorist-tense prohibitions

a. *Second person* (see above, on subjunctive prohibitions). Since some grammars indicate that aorist prohibitions tend to be specific (in both type and time of action),[26] all but a couple of examples we have chosen to use below are general in their scope.[27]

| ὑμεῖς δὲ μὴ **κληθῆτε·** Ῥαββί, εἷς γάρ ἐστιν ὑμῶν ὁ διδάσκαλος, πάντες δὲ ὑμεῖς ἀδελφοί ἐστε· (Matt. 23:8) | But you, **do** not **be called** Rabbi, for you have / yours is one teacher, and you all are brothers and sisters. |

| καὶ ἀπὸ τοῦ αἴροντός σου τὸ ἱμάτιον καὶ τὸν χιτῶνα μὴ **κωλύσῃς.** (Luke 6:29) | And from the one who takes your coat, **do** not **withhold** your shirt either. |

| μὴ **θαυμάσῃς** ὅτι εἶπόν σοι Δεῖ ὑμᾶς γεννηθῆναι ἄνωθεν. (John 3:7) | **Do** not **marvel** that I said to you, "It is necessary for you to be born again / from above." |

> This example cannot be "don't start to marvel," since the context is pretty clear that Nicodemus is already astonished at what Jesus is saying.

26. See BDF §335; Buist M. Fanning, *Verbal Aspect in New Testament Greek* (Oxford: Clarendon, 1990), 327; Mounce 317.

27. Aorist prohibitions are about evenly split between general and specific by Huffman's reckoning (*Verbal Aspect Theory,* 176–96).

ὑμεῖς δέ, ἀδελφοί, μὴ ἐγκακήσητε καλοποιοῦντες. (2 Thess. 3:13)	But you, brothers and sisters, *do not lose heart* in doing good.
μὴ *ἀποβάλητε* οὖν τὴν παρρησίαν ὑμῶν, ἥτις ἔχει μεγάλην μισθαποδοσίαν (Heb. 10:35)	Therefore *do not throw away* your confidence, which has a great reward.
Σφράγισον ἃ ἐλάλησαν αἱ ἑπτὰ βρονταί, καὶ μὴ αὐτὰ *γράψης*. (Rev. 10:4)	Seal what things the seven thunders said and *do not write* them *down*.

This seems to be an example where "don't start to write" works, since John says he was about to write these things down in the first part of the verse.

b. *Third person.* There are only eight aorist prohibitions in the NT that use imperative forms; all occur in the Gospels, half of them in parallel passages. All are specific according to Huffman and can be understood as prohibiting an action from ever occurring.[28]

σοῦ δὲ ποιοῦντος ἐλεημοσύνην μὴ *γνώτω* ἡ ἀριστερά σου τί ποιεῖ ἡ δεξιά σου (Matt. 6:3)	But when you are doing something charitable, your left hand *must not know* what your right hand is doing.
ὁ ἐπὶ τοῦ δώματος μὴ *καταβάτω* μηδὲ *εἰσελθάτω* τι ἆραι ἐκ τῆς οἰκίας αὐτοῦ (Mark 13:15)	The one on the housetop *must not go down* or *enter* to take anything from his/her house.

Entreaty (Request)

8.24. Although entreaties, or requests, might well be treated as a subcategory under commands, we have chosen to highlight them here. All that makes an imperative an entreaty rather than a command is context; therefore, special attention must be paid to context. In general, social or vocational inferiors do not command their superiors, and superiors do not entreat inferiors. But, with Wallace (488), we recognize that since we are dealing with written documents, we cannot determine by tone of voice, gesture, or tacit "please" when this general rule is broken. At the same time, we can state with confidence,

28. Ibid., 200.

based on his character, that Jesus *asked* the woman at the well for water rather than *ordering* her. We can also assume that Jesus taught his disciples to make humble requests of God rather than to place arrogant demands on him. It should go without saying that ontological inferiors ought not to command their superior; that is, people should not command God. Not surprisingly, most of the NT imperatives of entreaty are found in prayers, and most (80 percent) of the entreaties are in the aorist tense-form. Unfortunately, Boyer explains this predominance of aorists, which is out of keeping with the overall NT preference for present imperatives, with the observation that it "is in accord with usual Greek practice and reflects the tendency of requests and prayers to be occasional and specific."[29] Since both present and aorist imperatives are used for both general and specific commands, prohibitions, and entreaties,[30] "it is best to regard the aorist as grammaticalizing the entirety of the request; that is, when we pray, we normally commit the whole matter to God" (Young 144–45).

Οὕτως οὖν *προσεύχεσθε* ὑμεῖς·
Πάτερ ἡμῶν ὁ ἐν τοῖς οὐρανοῖς·
ἁγιασθήτω τὸ ὄνομά σου
(Matt. 6:9)

Therefore, you *pray* this way,
"Our Father who is in heaven, **let
your name be sanctified.**"

Jesus commands or entreats (present, general) his disciples to entreat (aorist, general and viewed as a whole) God.

καὶ προσελθόντες οἱ μαθηταὶ
αὐτοῦ ἠρώτουν αὐτὸν λέγοντες·
Ἀπόλυσον αὐτήν, ὅτι κράζει
ὄπισθεν ἡμῶν. (Matt. 15:23)

And having approached, his disciples requested of him, saying, "**Send** her **away**, because she is crying behind us."

ἡ δὲ ἐλθοῦσα προσεκύνει αὐτῷ
λέγουσα· Κύριε, **βοήθει** μοι.
(Matt. 15:25)

But the woman who came knelt before him, saying, "Lord, **help me.**"

Though it is in the present tense, we understand this entreaty as urgent and specific.

29. Boyer, "Classification of Imperatives," 37.
30. See, e.g., Young 142–43; Huffman, *Verbal Aspect Theory*; Porter 224–26; Mathewson, "Verbal Aspect," 21–35.

λέγει πρὸς αὐτὸν ἡ γυνή· Κύριε,
δός μοι τοῦτο τὸ ὕδωρ, ἵνα μὴ
διψῶ μηδὲ διέρχωμαι ἐνθάδε
ἀντλεῖν. (John 4:15)

The woman said to him, " Sir,
give me this water so that I am
not thirsty and do not have to
come here to draw water."

Λέγει ὁ μαρτυρῶν ταῦτα· Ναί·
ἔρχομαι ταχύ. Ἀμήν· **ἔρχου**, κύριε
Ἰησοῦ. (Rev. 22:20)

The one testifying to these things
says, "Yes, I am coming quickly."
Amen, **come**, Lord Jesus.

Permission

8.25. Some imperatives grant permission or consent rather than give explicit direction. "Rather than an appeal to the will, this category involves a response to the will of another."[31] Again, this depends on the context. Of the 27 classified in this way by Boyer, 17 are in the second person.[32] Perhaps this will further dispel the notion that third-person imperatives must have a permissive sense in Greek.

καὶ ἀποκριθεὶς ὁ Ἰησοῦς εἶπεν
πρὸς αὐτόν· Σίμων, ἔχω σοί τι
εἰπεῖν. ὁ δέ· Διδάσκαλε, **εἰπέ**,
φησίν. (Luke 7:40)

And answering, Jesus said to him,
"Simon, I have something to say
to you." And he said, "Teacher,
speak."

Peter isn't entreating Jesus but rather indicating that he is willing to hear what Jesus has to say.

ὅτε οὖν εἶδον αὐτὸν οἱ ἀρχιερεῖς
καὶ οἱ ὑπηρέται ἐκραύγασαν
λέγοντες· Σταύρωσον σταύρωσον.
λέγει αὐτοῖς ὁ Πιλᾶτος· **Λάβετε**
αὐτὸν ὑμεῖς καὶ **σταυρώσατε**, ἐγὼ
γὰρ οὐχ εὑρίσκω ἐν αὐτῷ αἰτίαν.
(John 19:6)

Therefore when they saw him, the
chief priests and officers shouted,
saying, "*Crucify, crucify.*" Pilate
said to them, "**Take** him and you
crucify [him], for I find no case
against him."

Against his better judgment, Pilate is granting permission.

31. Boyer, "Classification of Imperatives," 37.
32. Ibid.

εἰ δὲ ὁ ἄπιστος χωρίζεται,
χωριζέσθω· οὐ δεδούλωται ὁ
ἀδελφὸς ἢ ἡ ἀδελφὴ ἐν τοῖς
τοιούτοις, ἐν δὲ εἰρήνῃ κέκληκεν
ὑμᾶς ὁ θεός. (1 Cor. 7:15)

But if the unbelieving spouse
separates, **let him/her separate.**
The brother or sister is not bound
in such situations. God has called
you to peace.

ὁ ἀδικῶν **ἀδικησάτω** ἔτι, καὶ ὁ
ῥυπαρὸς **ῥυπανθήτω** ἔτι, καὶ ὁ
δίκαιος δικαιοσύνην **ποιησάτω** ἔτι,
καὶ ὁ ἅγιος **ἁγιασθήτω** ἔτι.
(Rev. 22:11)

Let the unjust person **be unjust**
still and the filthy **be filthy** still,
and the just **do** righteousness still
and the holy **be sanctified/holy**
still.

Not only do all four aorist imperatives grant permission, but they also
are made durative by ἔτι.

Condition

8.26. In certain contexts, imperatival clauses act similarly to protases of
conditional sentences. An imperative followed by καί and a future indicative
("Do *x*, and *y* will happen") creates an idiomatic construction that can be
understood as pragmatically if not formally equivalent to a condition. At the
same time, Porter's caution is valid: "Contextually the first verb may express a
condition or supposition for the second process, but formally the Imperative
is nothing but an Imperative and its [+ direction] semantic force is present."[33]
The presence of the semantic force of the imperative in the twenty or so un-
disputed conditional imperatives in the NT is clear enough: "The imperative
expresses the desire of the speaker/writer to fulfill the condition."[34] John
2:19, however, raises a question; it fits the imperative + καί + future indicative
pattern, but in what sense is Jesus directing the Jews to destroy the temple?
Alternately, Eph. 4:26 would make a great deal of sense as a conditional construction ("If you are angry, don't sin . . ."), but it does not fit the pattern,
involving as it does an imperative followed by καί and a prohibition.[35]

33. Porter, *Verbal Aspect*, 353.
34. Joseph D. Fantin, *The Greek Imperative Mood in the New Testament*, Studies in Biblical
Greek 12 (New York: Peter Lang, 2010), 306.
35. For more discussion, see Daniel B. Wallace, "Ὀργίζεσθε in Ephesians 4:26: Command or
Condition?," *Criswell Theological Review* 3 (1989): 353–72; Fantin, *Greek Imperative*, 303–6.

Ταῦτα αὐτοῦ λαλοῦντος αὐτοῖς
ἰδοὺ ἄρχων εἷς ἐλθὼν προσεκύνει
αὐτῷ λέγων ὅτι Ἡ θυγάτηρ μου
ἄρτι ἐτελεύτησεν· ἀλλὰ ἐλθὼν
ἐπίθες τὴν χεῖρά σου ἐπ᾽ αὐτήν, **καὶ**
ζήσεται. (Matt. 9:18)

While he was saying these things
to them, look, a leader having
come, kneeled before him saying,
"My daughter has just now died.
But having come, [if you] **lay** your
hand on her, **and she will live."**

διὰ τοῦτο λέγω ὑμῖν, πάντα
ὅσα προσεύχεσθε καὶ αἰτεῖσθε,
πιστεύετε ὅτι ἐλάβετε, **καὶ ἔσται**
ὑμῖν. (Mark 11:24)

Therefore I say to you, all things
that you pray and ask, [if you] believe that you receive [them], **and**
they will be yours.

ταπεινώθητε ἐνώπιον κυρίου, **καὶ**
ὑψώσει ὑμᾶς. (James 4:10)

[If you] **humble yourselves** before
the Lord, **and he will lift** you.

Greeting and Interjection

8.27. The imperative mood also came to be used in certain greetings and
exclamations. These are idiomatic uses that do not carry the imperative's
normal directive force. In the latter two examples below, the interjections
(singular imperatives in form) are addressed to a plural audience.

καὶ εὐθέως προσελθὼν τῷ
Ἰησοῦ εἶπεν· **Χαῖρε,** ῥαββί· καὶ
κατεφίλησεν αὐτόν. (Matt. 26:49)

And immediately, having come
to Jesus, he said, "**Greetings,**
Rabbi," and he kissed him.

Ἴδε ἐγὼ Παῦλος λέγω ὑμῖν ὅτι ἐὰν
περιτέμνησθε Χριστὸς ὑμᾶς οὐδὲν
ὠφελήσει. (Gal. 5:2)

Look, I, Paul, say to you that if
you become circumcised, Christ is
no benefit to you.

Ἄγε νῦν οἱ πλούσιοι, κλαύσατε
ὀλολύζοντες ἐπὶ ταῖς ταλαιπωρίαις
ὑμῶν ταῖς ἐπερχομέναις.
(James 5:1)

Come now, rich people, weep,
wailing because of the miseries
that are coming upon you.

Other Ways to Express a Command

8.28. The following summarizes a handful of other ways that commands
can be expressed in the NT with constructions other than with the imperative mood.

1. *Verbs of volition (in the indicative; see above).* Verbs of exhorting and commanding, with the infinitive.

Παρακαλῶ οὖν ὑμᾶς . . . ἀξίως περιπατῆσαι τῆς κλήσεως ἧς ἐκλήθητε (Eph. 4:1)	Therefore **I exhort** you . . . to walk worthily of the calling with which you were called.

2. *Infinitives*

χαίρειν μετὰ χαιρόντων, **κλαίειν** μετὰ κλαιόντων. (Rom. 12:15)	**Rejoice** with those who rejoice, **weep** with those who weep.

3. *Participles.* See chapter 10, on participles.

4. *Future indicative*

Ἠκούσατε ὅτι ἐρρέθη τοῖς ἀρχαίοις· Οὐ **φονεύσεις·** (Matt. 5:21)	You have heard that it was said to those of old, "**You shall** not **murder!**"

For Practice

8.29. Analyze the imperatives (in bold) in the following texts. Be sure to consider tense-form usage.

ἔφη αὐτῷ ὁ Ἰησοῦς· εἰ θέλεις τέλειος εἶναι, **ὕπαγε** πώλησόν σου τὰ ὑπάρχοντα καὶ **δὸς** τοῖς πτωχοῖς, καὶ ἕξεις θησαυρὸν ἐν οὐρανοῖς, καὶ δεῦρο **ἀκολούθει** μοι. (Matt. 19:21)

τότε λέγει αὐταῖς ὁ Ἰησοῦς· μὴ **φοβεῖσθε·** **ὑπάγετε ἀπαγγείλατε** τοῖς ἀδελ-φοῖς μου ἵνα ἀπέλθωσιν εἰς τὴν Γαλιλαίαν, κἀκεῖ με ὄψονται. (Matt. 28:10)

⁶ὁ δὲ Ἰησοῦς ἐπορεύετο σὺν αὐτοῖς. ἤδη δὲ αὐτοῦ οὐ μακρὰν ἀπέχοντος ἀπὸ τῆς οἰκίας ἔπεμψεν φίλους ὁ ἑκατοντάρχης λέγων αὐτῷ· Κύριε, μὴ **σκύλλου**, οὐ γὰρ ἱκανός εἰμι ἵνα ὑπὸ τὴν στέγην μου εἰσέλθῃς· ⁷διὸ οὐδὲ ἐμαυτὸν ἠξίωσα πρὸς σὲ ἐλθεῖν· ἀλλὰ **εἰπὲ** λόγῳ, καὶ **ἰαθήτω** ὁ παῖς μου· ⁸καὶ γὰρ ἐγὼ ἄνθρωπός εἰμι ὑπὸ ἐξουσίαν τασσόμενος, ἔχων ὑπ᾽ ἐμαυτὸν στρατιώτας, καὶ λέγω τούτῳ· **Πορεύθητι**, καὶ πορεύεται, καὶ ἄλλῳ· **Ἔρχου**, καὶ ἔρχεται, καὶ τῷ δούλῳ μου· **Ποίησον** τοῦτο, καὶ ποιεῖ. (Luke 7:6–8)

[11]Παράγγελλε ταῦτα καὶ **δίδασκε**. [12]μηδείς σου τῆς νεότητος **καταφρονείτω**, ἀλλὰ τύπος **γίνου** τῶν πιστῶν ἐν λόγῳ, ἐν ἀναστροφῇ, ἐν ἀγάπῃ, ἐν πίστει, ἐν ἁγνείᾳ. (1 Tim. 4:11–12)

[8]**ἐγγίσατε** τῷ θεῷ, καὶ ἐγγιεῖ ὑμῖν. **καθαρίσατε** χεῖρας, ἁμαρτωλοί, καὶ **ἁγνίσατε** καρδίας, δίψυχοι. [9]**ταλαιπωρήσατε** καὶ **πενθήσατε** καὶ **κλαύσατε**· ὁ γέλως ὑμῶν εἰς πένθος **μετατραπήτω** καὶ ἡ χαρὰ εἰς κατήφειαν· (James 4:8–9)

[1]Καὶ τῷ ἀγγέλῳ τῆς ἐν Σάρδεσιν ἐκκλησίας **γράψον**· Τάδε λέγει ὁ ἔχων τὰ ἑπτὰ πνεύματα τοῦ θεοῦ καὶ τοὺς ἑπτὰ ἀστέρας· Οἶδά σου τὰ ἔργα ὅτι ὄνομα ἔχεις ὅτι ζῇς, καὶ νεκρὸς εἶ. [2]**γίνου** γρηγορῶν καὶ **στήρισον** τὰ λοιπὰ ἃ ἔμελλον ἀποθανεῖν, οὐ γὰρ εὕρηκά σου τὰ ἔργα πεπληρωμένα ἐνώπιον τοῦ θεοῦ μου· [3]**μνημόνευε** οὖν πῶς εἴληφας καὶ ἤκουσας καὶ **τήρει**, καὶ **μετανόησον**· ἐὰν οὖν μὴ γρηγορήσῃς, ἥξω ὡς κλέπτης, καὶ οὐ μὴ γνῷς ποίαν ὥραν ἥξω ἐπὶ σέ· (Rev. 3:1–3)

9

INFINITIVES

9.1. Like the participle, the infinitive is a nonfinite verb form. While participles are classified as verbal adjectives, infinitives are generally classified as indeclinable verbal nouns. As verbs they have tense/aspect and voice, but no person or mood (in parsing, "infinitive" is used to fill the mood slot; e.g., λέγειν: to speak/speaking, present active infinitive of λέγω). As nouns they are singular in number (even with a plural "subject," e.g., ἐν τῷ λέγειν αὐτούς), neuter in gender (which is obvious only when they are preceded by the nominative or accusative article), can take an article, and though indeclinable themselves, may be considered to have case when they are articular (e.g., ἐν τῷ λέγειν). None of these attributes of nouns (gender, number, and case) are included in the parsing of an infinitive, however. The substantival properties of infinitives become clear when we begin to examine their usage. Infinitives can be subjects, direct objects, or complements of verbs; objects of prepositions; appositives; or adjectival modifiers. Not surprisingly, infinitives also have some verbal and adverbial functions. It is worth stressing with Robertson that although "in this or that example the substantival or verbal aspect of the hybrid form may be dominant," an infinitive "is not just a substantive, nor just a verb, but both at the same time" (1057).

Like finite verbs and participles, infinitives are found in all three aspects (imperfective in the present tense-form, perfective in the aorist tense-form, stative in the perfect tense-form. In addition there are five aspectually vague, future infinitives in the NT). Aorist forms, which view actions/states as complete wholes, make up the majority (1,241) of NT infinitives; present forms, viewing actions/states as unfolding, follow (996); and perfect forms, focusing on existing states of affairs, occur only 49 times. All four tense-forms of the infinitive may often be translated as "to . . ."; the future infinitive does indicate expectation, however, and the perfect could be translated as "to have _____ed" in certain contexts. Thus it is especially important for the interpreter to identify the aspect of an infinitive, because, though it will affect meaning, that meaning may be impossible to bring out in translation. Overall, interpreters must be flexible in how they translate infinitives.

The "Subject" of the Infinitive

9.2. Because infinitives are nonfinite verbs, they do not have personal endings. Therefore, there is some debate regarding whether or not they can have subjects at all. Strictly speaking, they cannot; that is, infinitives are not limited by grammatical subjects, "the doer[s] of the action or the possessor[s] of the condition expressed by the infinitive."[1] They do, however, have logical "subjects." Much of the time (about 48 percent in the NT), the nominative subject of the main verb in the sentence in which an infinitive is found is also the logical "subject" of the infinitive.

Διὸ καὶ ἐνεκοπτόμην τὰ πολλὰ τοῦ ἐλθεῖν πρὸς ὑμᾶς· (Rom. 15:22)	For this reason also I was many times prevented from coming / prevented to come to you.

Paul (I) is the "subject" of "prevented" and "coming / to come."

Moreover, there are a significant number of datives (indirect objects and datives of reference) that function as the logical subjects of infinitives.[2] There are numerous occasions when the logical subject of an infinitive is not in the accusative case. For example, the nominative subject of the main verb and the subject of the infinitive may be the same or the subject of the infinitive may also be a direct object (but not accusative), indirect object, or some other part of speech. However, when the subject of the infinitive is not the same as that of the main verb, a very common phenomenon is to find the subject of the infinitive expressed in the accusative case. There is debate as to whether this

---

1. James L. Boyer, "The Classification of Infinitives: A Statistical Study," *Grace Theological Journal* 6, no. 1 (1985): 20.
2. Ibid., 21.

is a true subject or an accusative of reference (i.e., the action of the infinitive happens "with reference to someone," which is to say that they perform the action). We will simply refer to the accusative as functioning as the subject of the infinitive.

Some of the time, the logical subject of the infinitive is also the direct object (in either the accusative or genitive case) of its governing verb. However, when a noun or pronoun other than the accusative direct object of the main verb is "explicitly stated within the infinitive clause"[3] as the producer of the action or state of the infinitive (608× in NT), it is always in the accusative case (e.g., Τί οὖν οἱ γραμματεῖς λέγουσιν ὅτι Ἠλίαν δεῖ ἐλθεῖν πρῶτον; "Why then do the scribes say that it is necessary for **Elijah** to come first / that **Elijah** come first?" [Matt. 17:10]). At this point it probably is good to mention that in cases where the infinitive has both a subject and a direct object in the accusative case, word order is helpful in determining which is which: in about 70 percent of NT occurrences, the first accusative is the subject. With the verb εἶναι (to be), the same considerations we discussed in chapter 1 must be kept in mind.

Two Main Functions of the Infinitive

9.3. Our division and discussion of infinitives will take as its point of departure the common description of infinitives as "verbal nouns." Therefore, we will discuss their substantival and verbal functions.

Substantival Function

Here we examine those uses of the infinitive in which their substantival, or nominal, character is paramount.

9.4. Subject. An infinitive or infinitive clause may be the subject of a verb.

1. *With personal verbs*

ταῦτά ἐστιν τὰ κοινοῦντα τὸν ἄνθρωπον, τὸ δὲ ἀνίπτοις χερσὶν **φαγεῖν** οὐ κοινοῖ τὸν ἄνθρωπον. (Matt. 15:20)	These are the things that defile a person, but **to eat / eating** with unwashed hands does not defile a person.

---

3. Ibid., 22.

τὸ δὲ **καθίσαι** ἐκ δεξιῶν μου ἢ
ἐξ εὐωνύμων οὐκ ἔστιν ἐμὸν
δοῦναι, ἀλλ' οἷς ἡτοίμασται.
(Mark 10:40)

But **to sit** *at my right or left* is
not mine to give, but [it is for
those] for whom it is prepared.

> "To sit" is the simple subject of the verb "is"; the infinitive clause
> "to sit at my right or left" is the complete subject, or nominal clause.

2. *With impersonal verbs.* Infinitives usually follow δεῖ and ἔξεστιν, but
regardless of word order, they could also be understood as grammatical subjects ("*to boast* is necessary"), even though they make sense as
complements ("it is not lawful *to have*"; Wallace 601). The verb γίνομαι
is also sometimes used with infinitives when it is found in the introduc-
tory formula "It came to pass / it happened . . ." ("*to stay* came to pass /
staying happened").

ἔλεγεν γὰρ αὐτῷ ὁ Ἰωάννης·
Οὐκ **ἔξεστίν** σοι **ἔχειν** αὐτήν·
(Matt. 14:4)

Because John had said to him,
"For you **to have** her *is* not
lawful."

ἐγένετο δὲ ἡμέρας ἱκανὰς **μεῖναι**
ἐν Ἰόππῃ παρά τινι Σίμωνι
βυρσεῖ. (Acts 9:43)

And *it happened* that **he stayed**
for some days in Joppa with a
certain Simon, a tanner.

> Another rendering that reflects the Greek syntax more closely is,
> "**Staying** for some days in Joppa with a certain Simon, a tanner,
> *happened.*"

Εἰ **καυχᾶσθαι** δεῖ, τὰ τῆς
ἀσθενείας μου καυχήσομαι.
(2 Cor. 11:30)

If **to boast** *is necessary* / *it is
necessary* to boast, I will boast
in the things that show / of my
weakness.

9.5. Predicate complement. The infinitive can function as the predicate
complement of a linking verb (e.g., εἰμί).

καὶ τὸν λόγον ἐκράτησαν πρὸς   And they kept the word to
ἑαυτοὺς συζητοῦντες τί ἐστιν τὸ   themselves, discussing *what* it is
ἐκ νεκρῶν **ἀναστῆναι**.   **to be raised** from the dead.
(Mark 9:10)

> This rather wooden translation preserves the Greek structure: "what"
> is the subject, and "to be raised" the predicate complement.

9.6. Complement. The infinitive can function as the complement of a verb
in a number of ways.

1. *Direct object*

νυνὶ δὲ καὶ **τὸ ποιῆσαι** *ἐπιτελέ-*   But now also *finish* **doing** [it],
σατε, ὅπως καθάπερ ἡ προθυμία   so that just as [is] your eager-
τοῦ θέλειν οὕτως καὶ τὸ ἐπιτε-   ness to want [to do it], so also
λέσαι ἐκ τοῦ ἔχειν. (2 Cor. 8:11)   [may be] the completion from
                                         what you have.

> According to Boyer, τὸ ποιῆσαι is one of two or three true direct
> object uses.[4] Consider how Paul uses the other infinitives in the verse
> as you continue to read this chapter.

2. *Catenative/complementary (after certain verbs).* Complementary infinitives can also be considered as direct objects. Certain Greek verbal ideas
   (as well as their cognate nouns and adjectives) are frequently completed
   by infinitives. To put it slightly differently, some verbs leave us hanging
   and require a complement. Other verbs need a complement in certain
   contexts. Because complementary infinitives do not always immediately
   follow (and may occasionally precede; e.g., 2 Thess. 1:3) the verbs they
   complete, we offer the following chart. Whenever one encounters one
   of these verbs, it is well worth a few seconds to skim the rest of the sentence in search of an infinitive. For example, in 1 John 2:6 the infinitive
   περιπατεῖν, which completes ὀφείλει, is the last word in the sentence:
   ὁ λέγων ἐν αὐτῷ μένειν ὀφείλει καθὼς ἐκεῖνος περιεπάτησεν καὶ αὐτὸς
   περιπατεῖν, "The one claiming to remain in him *ought* also himself/
   herself **to walk** just as that one walked."

4. Ibid., 9.

196

Verbs Often (at Least 20 Times) Followed by Complementary Infinitives

ἄρχομαι	I begin	ζητέω	I seek/try
βούλομαι	I want/desire	θέλω	I wish/will
δύναμαι	I am able	μέλλω	I am about to
ἔχω	I have	ὀφείλω	I ought

καὶ ζητοῦντες αὐτὸν **κρατῆσαι** ἐφοβήθησαν τοὺς ὄχλους, ἐπεὶ εἰς προφήτην αὐτὸν εἶχον. (Matt. 21:46)

And *seeking* **to arrest** him, they were afraid of the crowds, since they regarded him as a prophet.

ἰδοὺ *μέλλει* **βάλλειν** ὁ διάβολος ἐξ ὑμῶν εἰς φυλακὴν (Rev. 2:10)

Look, the devil *is about* **to throw** [some] of you into prison.

3. *Indirect discourse.* In indirect discourse, certain verbs of verbal or mental communication or perception are completed by infinitives. Because these infinitives express the content of speech (either spoken or heard), thought, belief, or feeling, they may also be viewed as introducing direct-object clauses. Another chart may be helpful.

Verbs Followed (at Least 10 Times) by Infinitives in Indirect Discourse

δοκέω	I think	κρίνω	I judge
ἐλπίζω	I hope	λέγω	I say/claim
ἐρωτάω	I ask	νομίζω	I think
κελεύω	I order/command	παρακαλέω	I urge/exhort

καὶ διεστείλατο αὐτοῖς πολλὰ ἵνα μηδεὶς γνοῖ τοῦτο, καὶ *εἶπεν* **δοθῆναι** αὐτῇ φαγεῖν. (Mark 5:43)

And he strictly ordered them that no one should know this and *said* **to give** her [something] to eat.

In direct discourse, Jesus said, "Give her something to eat."

περισσοτέρως δὲ *παρακαλῶ* τοῦτο **ποιῆσαι**, ἵνα τάχιον ἀποκατασταθῶ ὑμῖν. (Heb. 13:19)

And *I* strongly *urge* [you] **to do** this, so that I may be restored to you more/very quickly.

9.7. Appositive. Most of the appositional infinitives in the NT define demonstrative pronouns.

ὁ δὲ θεός ἃ προκατήγγειλεν διὰ στόματος πάντων τῶν προφητῶν **παθεῖν** τὸν χριστὸν αὐτοῦ ἐπλήρωσεν οὕτως. (Acts 3:18)

But *what* God predicted through the mouth of all the prophets, his Messiah [was] **to suffer**, he fulfilled thus. (*"what" is in apposition to "to suffer"*)

Μηκέτι οὖν ἀλλήλους κρίνωμεν· ἀλλὰ *τοῦτο* κρίνατε μᾶλλον, **τὸ μὴ τιθέναι** πρόσκομμα τῷ ἀδελφῷ ἢ σκάνδαλον. (Rom. 14:13)

Therefore let's no longer judge one another, but rather decide *this*, not **to place** an obstacle or stumbling block in a brother or sister's way. (*"this" is in apposition to "not to place"*)

With Prepositions (Preposition + Article + Infinitive)

9.8. We have placed the use of infinitives with prepositions between the more obviously substantival and the more obviously verbal uses simply because we think they fit this in-between spot. Objects of prepositions are substantives; thus, when infinitives act as prepositional objects, they are in one sense substantival.[5] They also take an article when used with prepositions. However, infinitives are still verbal forms, and when they occur in prepositional phrases, they often must be translated as finite verbs in English. Finally, the prepositional *phrases* in which infinitives occur fill an adverb slot. But it must be stressed that it is the entire prepositional phrase, not just the infinitive, that functions adverbially. Thus the Greek infinitive construction (preposition + articular infinitive) that is least like any English infinitive construction is also the most multifaceted (substantival, verbal, and adverbial). The following chart summarizes the primary categories of infinitives in prepositional phrases.

Prepositions with Infinitives

Time	μετὰ τό + infinitive: "after"
	ἐν τῷ + infinitive: "as, when, while"
	πρὸ τοῦ (πρὶν, πρὶν ἤ) + infinitive: "before"

5. In the NT, when an infinitive is the object of a preposition, it is articular in all but eleven occurrences, and these exceptions are when the infinitive follows the improper prepositions πρὶν and πρὶν ἤ. This further strengthens our argument for viewing the infinitive as a substantive in this construction (contra Wallace 589).

Purpose/Result	εἰς τό + infinitive: "so that"
	πρὸς τό + infinitive: "so that"
Cause/Reason	διὰ τό + infinitive: "because"
Means	ἐν τῷ + infinitive: "by"

1. Time (subsequent, simultaneous, and antecedent)

μαρτυρεῖ δὲ ἡμῖν καὶ τὸ πνεῦμα τὸ ἅγιον, μετὰ γὰρ τὸ **εἰρηκέναι**· Αὕτη ἡ διαθήκη ἣν διαθήσομαι πρὸς αὐτοὺς μετὰ τὰς ἡμέρας ἐκείνας (Heb. 10:15–16)

And the Holy Spirit also testifies to us, for *after* **saying,** "This is the covenant that I will make with them after those days." (*subsequent time*)

καὶ *ἐν τῷ* **κατηγορεῖσθαι** αὐτὸν ὑπὸ τῶν ἀρχιερέων καὶ πρεσβυτέρων οὐδὲν ἀπεκρίνατο. (Matt. 27:12)

And *while* he **was being accused** by the high priests and elders, he answered nothing. (*simultaneous time*)

καὶ νῦν δόξασόν με σύ, πάτερ, παρὰ σεαυτῷ τῇ δόξῃ ᾗ εἶχον *πρὸ τοῦ* τὸν κόσμον **εἶναι** παρὰ σοί. (John 17:5)

And now you glorify me, Father, in your presence with the glory that I had with you *before* the world **was.** (*antecedent time*)

2. Purpose/result

βαλοῦσα γὰρ αὕτη τὸ μύρον τοῦτο ἐπὶ τοῦ σώματός μου *πρὸς τὸ* **ἐνταφιάσαι** με ἐποίησεν. (Matt. 26:12)

For she, pouring this ointment on my body, did [it] *in order* to **prepare** me for burial.

μετανοήσατε οὖν καὶ ἐπιστρέψατε *πρὸς τὸ* **ἐξαλειφθῆναι** ὑμῶν τὰς ἁμαρτίας (Acts 3:19)

Therefore, repent and turn back *so that* your sins **are erased.**

3. Cause/reason

ἡλίου δὲ ἀνατείλαντος ἐκαυματίσθη καὶ *διὰ τὸ μὴ* **ἔχειν** ῥίζαν ἐξηράνθη. (Matt. 13:6)

And the sun having risen, they were scorched, and *because* they **had** no root, they were dried out.

4. *Means*

> ἐν τῷ γὰρ **ὑποτάξαι** τὰ
> πάντα οὐδὲν ἀφῆκεν αὐτῷ
> ἀνυπότακτον. (Heb. 2:8)

> For *in/by* **subjecting** all things
> he left nothing not subjected to
> him.

5. *Substitution*. This category is not listed in the table above because there is only one NT example.

> **ἀντὶ** τοῦ **λέγειν** ὑμᾶς· Ἐὰν ὁ
> κύριος θελήσῃ, καὶ ζήσομεν
> καὶ ποιήσομεν τοῦτο ἢ ἐκεῖνο.
> (James 4:15)

> *Instead of* your **saying**, "If the
> Lord wills, we will both live
> and do this or that."[a]

[a] Scot McKnight, *The Letter of James*, NICNT (Grand Rapids: Eerdmans, 2011), 374.

Verbal Function

The infinitive can sometimes modify a verbal element or even act as a finite verb.

9.9. Adverbial. Infinitives may modify verbs directly, with the conjunctions ὡς and ὥστε, after articles, or, as we saw above, in prepositional phrases.

1. *With verbs*. The simple (anarthrous and without conjunction) infinitive indicates the purpose or result of a verb, most often in the NT with ἔρχομαι and its compounds and with ἀποστέλλω. The genitive articular infinitive along with ὡς and ὥστε also indicates purpose or result.

> πολλοὺς γὰρ ἐθεράπευσεν,
> **ὥστε ἐπιπίπτειν** αὐτῷ ἵνα αὐτοῦ
> ἅψωνται ὅσοι εἶχον μάστιγας.
> (Mark 3:10)

> For he healed many *so that* as
> many as had afflictions **pressed
> in** on him in order to touch /
> that they could touch him.

> Πνεῦμα κυρίου ἐπ᾿ ἐμέ, οὗ εἵνε-
> κεν ἔχρισέν με **εὐαγγελίσασθαι**
> πτωχοῖς, ἀπέσταλκέν με, **κηρύξαι**
> αἰχμαλώτοις ἄφεσιν καὶ τυ-
> φλοῖς ἀνάβλεψιν, **ἀποστεῖλαι**
> τεθραυσμένους ἐν ἀφέσει
> (Luke 4:18)

> The Spirit of the Lord is on
> me, on account of which *he
> anointed* me **in order to / to
> spread good news** to the poor;
> *he sent* me **to proclaim** freedom
> to the captives and recovery of
> sight to the blind, **to set** the op-
> pressed at liberty.

καὶ ἀπέστειλεν ἀγγέλους πρὸ προσώπου αὐτοῦ. καὶ πορευ- θέντες εἰσῆλθον εἰς κώμην Σαμαριτῶν, ὡς **ἑτοιμάσαι** αὐτῷ· (Luke 9:52)

And he sent messengers ahead of him, and, having gone, they entered a Samaritan village *so as* **to prepare** for him.

ἦλθεν γὰρ ὁ υἱὸς τοῦ ἀνθρώπου **ζητῆσαι** καὶ **σῶσαι** τὸ ἀπολωλός. (Luke 19:10)

For the Son of Man *came* in order to / to seek and to save the lost.

τότε διήνοιξεν αὐτῶν τὸν νοῦν **τοῦ συνιέναι** τὰς γραφάς (Luke 24:45)

Then he opened their mind[s] **to understand** / **so they could understand** the Scriptures.

οὐκ ἔσχηκα ἄνεσιν τῷ πνεύματί μου τῷ μὴ **εὑρεῖν** με Τίτον τὸν ἀδελφόν μου, ἀλλὰ ἀποτα- ξάμενος αὐτοῖς ἐξῆλθον εἰς Μακεδονίαν. (2 Cor. 2:13)

I had no rest in my spirit **because I did** not **find** Titus my brother, but taking leave from them I departed for Macedonia.

According to Boyer, this is the only "infinitive without a preposition functioning in the adverbial sense of cause" in the NT.[6]

καὶ ἐξελεύσεται **πλανῆσαι** τὰ ἔθνη τὰ ἐν ταῖς τέσσαρσι γωνίαις τῆς γῆς (Rev. 20:8)

And *he will go out* **in order to** / **to deceive** the nations that are in the four corners of the earth.

2. *With adjectives.* Infinitives modify adjectives about 40 times in the NT.[7] In more than half of these instances, the adjectives are cognates of verbs that can govern complementary infinitives (e.g., δυνατός and ἄξιος).

καὶ πληροφορηθεὶς ὅτι ὃ ἐπήγγελται *δυνατός ἐστιν* καὶ **ποιῆσαι.** (Rom. 4:21)

And fully convinced that what he [i.e., God] promised he was *able* also **to do.**

ἀναγκαῖον οὖν ἡγησάμην **παρακαλέσαι** τοὺς ἀδελφούς (2 Cor. 9:5)

Therefore I deemed it *necessary* **to urge** the brothers.

6. Boyer, "Classification of Infinitives," 14.
7. Ibid., 17.

λέγοντες φωνῇ μεγάλῃ· Ἄξιόν
ἐστιν τὸ ἀρνίον τὸ ἐσφαγμένον
λαβεῖν τὴν δύναμιν καὶ πλοῦτον
καὶ σοφίαν καὶ ἰσχὺν καὶ τιμὴν
καὶ δόξαν καὶ εὐλογίαν.
(Rev. 5:12)

Saying with a loud voice, "*Worthy* is the slaughtered Lamb
to receive power and wealth
and wisdom and strength and
honor and glory and praise."

9.10. Verbal

1. *Imperatival*. Rarely in the NT (it did occur in Classical Greek), and not
without dispute, the infinitive can issue commands or exhortations.[8]
Imperatival infinitives are to be found only in clauses with no main verb.
That is, they fill the main-verb slot in a sentence. Wallace (608) follows
BDF in finding only three, all of which occur in two verses.

χαίρειν μετὰ χαιρόντων, **κλαίειν**
μετὰ κλαιόντων. (Rom. 12:15)

Rejoice with those rejoicing;
cry with those crying.

 These seem to be legitimate commands/exhortations after the imperatives in verse 14.

πλὴν εἰς ὃ ἐφθάσαμεν, τῷ αὐτῷ
στοιχεῖν. (Phil. 3:16)

Only, to what we have reached,
let's / we must walk in it.

 Again, this infinitive could be either a command or an exhortation,
but it is probably the latter in light of verse 15.

2. *Absolute*. Like the genitive absolute, the infinitive absolute is grammatically independent of the main clause to which it is loosely attached. The
infinitive absolutes in the NT primarily function as interjections and are
all forms of the verb χαίρω, the imperatives of which were also used in
greetings.

Κλαύδιος Λυσίας τῷ κρατίστῳ
ἡγεμόνι Φήλικι **χαίρειν**.
(Acts 23:26)

Claudius Lysias, to the most
excellent [i.e., His Excellency]
governor Felix: **Greetings!**

---

8. Boyer (ibid., 15) thinks the "so-called imperatival infinitives should be considered
elliptical and assigned to the complementary or indirect discourse categories."

Adjectival (Epexegetical)

9.11. Infinitives that modify nouns do not impress us as being either more substantival or more verbal; they simply limit or restrict nouns, especially nouns of power, authority, ability, desire, obligation, need, and time.[9] As we saw with adverbial infinitives that modify adjectives, the most commonly occurring adjectival infinitives (88, by Boyer's count) may restrict nouns whose cognate verbs govern complementary infinitives (most notably ἐξουσία).[10] Adjectival infinitives may be either arthrous—with the genitive or, less frequently, accusative article—or anarthrous.[11]

ὁ δὲ Ἰωάννης διεκώλυεν αὐτὸν λέγων· Ἐγὼ χρείαν ἔχω ὑπὸ σοῦ **βαπτισθῆναι**, καὶ σὺ ἔρχῃ πρός με; (Matt. 3:14)

But John tried to prevent him saying, "I have *need* **to be baptized** by you, yet you come to me?"

καὶ *ἐξουσίαν* ἔδωκεν αὐτῷ κρίσιν **ποιεῖν**, ὅτι υἱὸς ἀνθρώπου ἐστίν. (John 5:27)

And he gave him *authority* **to pass** judgment, because he is the Son of Man.

νυνὶ δὲ μηκέτι τόπον ἔχων ἐν τοῖς κλίμασι τούτοις, *ἐπιποθίαν* δὲ ἔχων **τοῦ ἐλθεῖν** πρὸς ὑμᾶς ἀπὸ ἱκανῶν ἐτῶν (Rom. 15:23)

And now no longer having a place in these parts, but having a *desire* **to come** to you for many years.

ἢ μόνος ἐγὼ καὶ Βαρναβᾶς οὐκ ἔχομεν *ἐξουσίαν* μὴ **ἐργάζεσθαι**; (1 Cor. 9:6)

Or do only Barnabas and I not have *the right* not **to work**?

καὶ τὰ ἔθνη ὠργίσθησαν, καὶ ἦλθεν ἡ ὀργή σου καὶ ὁ *καιρὸς* τῶν νεκρῶν **κριθῆναι** καὶ **δοῦναι** τὸν μισθὸν τοῖς δούλοις σου τοῖς προφήταις καὶ τοῖς ἁγίοις καὶ τοῖς φοβουμένοις τὸ ὄνομά σου, τοὺς μικροὺς καὶ τοὺς μεγάλους, καὶ **διαφθεῖραι** τοὺς διαφθείροντας τὴν γῆν. (Rev. 11:18)

And the nations were enraged, and your wrath has come and the *time* for the dead **to be judged** and **to give** the reward to your servants, the prophets and the saints and those fearing your name, the small and the great, and **to destroy** those destroying the earth.

9. Ibid., 17.
10. Ibid., 16.
11. Adjectival infinitives in the NT are arthrous 15 times and anarthrous 73 times.

For Practice

9.12. Analyze the infinitives (in bold) in the following texts.

[17]Ἐγένετο δὲ μετὰ ἡμέρας τρεῖς **συγκαλέσασθαι** αὐτὸν τοὺς ὄντας τῶν Ἰουδαίων πρώτους· συνελθόντων δὲ αὐτῶν ἔλεγεν πρὸς αὐτούς· Ἐγώ, ἄνδρες ἀδελφοί, οὐδὲν ἐναντίον ποιήσας τῷ λαῷ ἢ τοῖς ἔθεσι τοῖς πατρῴοις δέσμιος ἐξ Ἱεροσολύμων παρεδόθην εἰς τὰς χεῖρας τῶν Ῥωμαίων, [18]οἵτινες ἀνακρίναντές με ἐβούλοντο **ἀπολῦσαι** διὰ τὸ μηδεμίαν αἰτίαν θανάτου **ὑπάρχειν** ἐν ἐμοί· [19]ἀντιλεγόντων δὲ τῶν Ἰουδαίων ἠναγκάσθην **ἐπικαλέσασθαι** Καίσαρα οὐχ ὡς τοῦ ἔθνους μου ἔχων τι **κατηγορεῖν**. [20]διὰ ταύτην οὖν τὴν αἰτίαν παρεκάλεσα ὑμᾶς **ἰδεῖν** καὶ **προσλαλῆσαι**, ἕνεκεν γὰρ τῆς ἐλπίδος τοῦ Ἰσραὴλ τὴν ἅλυσιν ταύτην περίκειμαι. (Acts 28:17–20)

[10]Ἐχάρην δὲ ἐν κυρίῳ μεγάλως ὅτι ἤδη ποτὲ ἀνεθάλετε τὸ ὑπὲρ ἐμοῦ **φρονεῖν**, ἐφ᾽ ᾧ καὶ ἐφρονεῖτε, ἠκαιρεῖσθε δέ. [11]οὐχ ὅτι καθ᾽ ὑστέρησιν λέγω, ἐγὼ γὰρ ἔμαθον ἐν οἷς εἰμι αὐτάρκης **εἶναι**· [12]οἶδα καὶ **ταπεινοῦσθαι**, οἶδα καὶ **περισσεύειν**· ἐν παντὶ καὶ ἐν πᾶσιν μεμύημαι, καὶ **χορτάζεσθαι** καὶ **πεινᾶν** καὶ **περισσεύειν** καὶ **ὑστερεῖσθαι**. (Phil. 4:10–12)

10

PARTICIPLES

10.1. "We now come to one of NT Greek's favorite parts of speech, the versatile participle, whose use serves to illustrate the genius of the language."[1] According to Wallace, "Mastery of the syntax of participles is mastery of Greek syntax" (613). The participle is a "heavily worked" form in the Greek NT, occurring 6,662 times. Therefore, the ability to analyze it is essential for interpreting virtually any NT text. The participle is frequently described as a verbal adjective, "part adjective, part verb" (Robertson 1101), possessing characteristics of both. As a verbal form it has aspect and voice, and it can take adverbial modifiers and direct objects. It can even function like a main verb in a sentence in a few instances. As an adjective, it takes case, gender, and number, and it can modify a substantive or act as one. The participle is a nonfinite form; that is, like the infinitive, it is not limited by person, nor does it possess mood.

All grammarians realize that participles do not indicate absolute time (past, present, future) but relative time (see below, on participles and time). As with finite verbs, the key feature of participles is not time but verbal aspect, or how the author chooses to represent an action:[2] aorist participles convey perfective aspect; present participles convey imperfective aspect; perfect participles

---

1. Warren F. Dicharry, *Greek without Grief: An Outline Guide to New Testament Greek* (Chicago: Loyola, 1989), 84.
2. Stanley E. Porter, *Verbal Aspect in the Greek of the New Testament, with Reference to Tense and Mood*, Studies in Biblical Greek 1 (New York: Peter Lang, 1989), 377–88; Constantine R. Campbell, *Verbal Aspect and Non-indicative Verbs*, Studies in Biblical Greek 13 (New York: Peter Lang, 2008), 13–47.

convey stative aspect. The rare future participle (only 13 in the NT) conveys action that is expected to take place. No matter what the function of the participle (see below), it still always communicates verbal aspect.[3]

A key to determining how a participle is being utilized is the presence or absence of the article (with which, if present, the participle agrees in gender, number, and case). If a participle is preceded by an article, it is adjectival—functioning either as an attributive modifier (if it stands in relation to another nominal in the same case, gender, and number) or as a substantive (if it does not modify another nominal). If it does not have an article, the participle usually functions adverbially—and possibly as complementary to another verb in periphrastic constructions or, in a few instances, as a main verb. However, though the presence of the article guarantees that a participle is adjectival, the absence of the article does not guarantee that it is adverbial; some anarthrous participles (i.e., those without the article) are still employed adjectivally. When no article is present, one must pay special attention to the context to determine how a participle is functioning. (Participles that are nominative and lack an article are usually adverbial.) Based on the above discussion, it is important to distinguish the *form* of a participle (a participle is a participle is a participle!) from the variety of ways it can *function* (as a substantive; attributive or adverbial modifier; predicate; etc.).

Though there are multiple ways of classifying participles,[4] given their description as "verbal adjectives," we will discuss them according to their adjectival functions (as attributive modifiers, as predicate adjectives, and as substantives) and according to their verbal functions (as adverbial modifiers, supplementary to verbs, as predicates—used as a finite verb). We will also discuss two additional uses: genitive absolutes and periphrastic constructions. One way in which this grammar departs from many previous ones is in its treatment of the adverbial participle. Most grammars subcategorize adverbial participles into at least eight different categories: temporal, causal, concessive, manner, conditional, means, attendant circumstances, purpose, and result.[5] However, for reasons to be discussed below, we will avoid using those labels for the participles themselves.

---

3. Contra Wallace (615–16), who thinks the aspect is sometimes reduced.
4. James L. Boyer, "The Classification of Participles: A Statistical Study," *Grace Theological Journal* 5, no. 2 (1984): 163.
5. Wallace 623; Black 123–24.

Adjectival Uses of the Participle

Attributive (Noun Modifier)

10.2. A participle can function like an adjective to modify another substantive in a clause by restricting it in some way. This is one of the most common uses of the participle. What distinguishes an adjectival participle from an adjective is that participles provide us with the bonus features of aspect and voice (Porter 186). An attributive participle agrees in case, gender, and number with the substantive it modifies. It may have an article or be anarthrous. Though attributive participles are usually translated as relative clauses ("who . . ."; "which . . ."; "that . . ."), it would be incorrect to conclude that they simply replace relative clauses. They still maintain their distinctives as participles.

Τοῦτό ἐστιν τὸ αἷμά μου τῆς διαθήκης τὸ **ἐκχυννόμενον** ὑπὲρ πολλῶν. (Mark 14:24)	This is my blood of the covenant, **which is poured out** for many.
καὶ οἱ μάρτυρες ἀπέθεντο τὰ ἱμάτια αὐτῶν παρὰ τοὺς πόδας νεανίου **καλουμένου** Σαύλου. (Acts 7:58)	And the witnesses laid their garments before the feet of a young man **named** Saul. (*an attributive participle without the article*)
εἰς ἔνδειξιν τῆς δικαιοσύνης αὐτοῦ διὰ τὴν πάρεσιν τῶν **προγεγονότων** ἁμαρτημάτων (Rom. 3:25)	For a display of his righteousness because of the passing over of sins **previously committed**.
Εὐλογητὸς ὁ θεὸς καὶ πατὴρ τοῦ κυρίου ἡμῶν Ἰησοῦ Χριστοῦ, ὁ κατὰ τὸ πολὺ αὐτοῦ ἔλεος **ἀναγεννήσας** ἡμᾶς (1 Pet. 1:3)	Blessed is the God and Father of our Lord Jesus Christ, **who gave** us **new birth** according to his great mercy.
καὶ οἱ λοιποὶ ἀπεκτάνθησαν ἐν τῇ ῥομφαίᾳ τοῦ καθημένου ἐπὶ τοῦ ἵππου τῇ **ἐξελθούσῃ** ἐκ τοῦ στόματος αὐτοῦ (Rev. 19:21)	And the rest died by the sword **that comes out of** the mouth of the one seated upon the horse.

Predicate Adjective

10.3. The participle can occur (infrequently) with or without a linking verb as a predicate adjective. It will also be anarthrous.

Ζῶν γὰρ ὁ λόγος τοῦ θεοῦ καὶ ἐνεργὴς (Heb. 4:12)

For the word of God is **living** and effective.

ἐὰν ἀδελφὸς ἢ ἀδελφὴ γυμνοὶ ὑπάρχωσιν καὶ **λειπόμενοι** τῆς ἐφημέρου τροφῆς (James 2:15)

If a brother or sister is naked and **lacking** food for the day.

καὶ ἐγενόμην νεκρὸς καὶ ἰδοὺ **ζῶν** εἰμι (Rev. 1:18)

And I was dead and look, I am **living**.

The participle is parallel to the predicate adjective νεκρός in the previous clause.

Substantive

10.4. The participle can also function as (i.e., fill the slot of) a substantive in a clause. In this case, it does not modify another nominal but acts as one itself (e.g., "the one believing"). A substantival participle can be employed in virtually any way a noun can: subject, direct object, indirect object, object of a preposition, and the like. The article usually accompanies this usage of the participle.[6]

Ποῦ ἐστιν ὁ **τεχθεὶς** βασιλεὺς τῶν Ἰουδαίων; (Matt. 2:2)

Where is the **one born** king of the Jews?

The participle functions as the subject of the verb ἐστίν.

φωνὴ **βοῶντος** ἐν τῇ ἐρήμῳ· (Mark 1:3)

The voice **of one crying** in the desert.

The genitive participle cannot modify φωνή as an attributive ("a voice crying") but functions as a substantive, with the genitive showing possession.

6. K. L. McKay, *A New Syntax of the Verb in New Testament Greek: An Aspectual Approach*, Studies in Biblical Greek 5 (New York: Peter Lang, 1994), 61.

Ἀδύνατον γὰρ τοὺς ἅπαξ φω-
τισθέντας γευσαμένους . . . καὶ
. . . γενηθέντας . . . καὶ . . . γευσαμένους . . . καὶ παραπεσόντας,
πάλιν ἀνακαινίζειν εἰς μετάνοιαν
(Heb. 6:4–6)

For it is impossible to renew again
to repentance **those who have**
once **been enlightened, who have**
tasted . . . and . . . **who have be-**
come . . . and . . . **who have tasted**
. . . and **who have fallen away.**

The accusative participles all function as the direct objects of the infinitive ἀνακαινίζειν.

χάρις ὑμῖν καὶ εἰρήνη ἀπὸ ὁ ὢν καὶ
ὁ ἦν καὶ ὁ **ἐρχόμενος** (Rev. 1:4)

Grace to you and peace from the
one who is and who was and **who**
is coming.

The participles are the objects of a preposition. Notice the grammatical
incongruity with the nominative used after the preposition ἀπό (we would
expect the genitive). This incongruity is likely intentional on the part of
the author and is meant to get the readers to sit up and take notice. This
is probably because the author wants to draw attention to the nature of
this expression as a title and its OT antecedent (Exod. 3:14).[7]

καὶ ὅταν δώσουσιν τὰ ζῷα δόξαν
καὶ τιμὴν καὶ εὐχαριστίαν τῷ
καθημένῳ ἐπὶ τῷ θρόνῳ (Rev. 4:9)

And whenever the living creatures
give glory and honor and thanksgiving to the **one seated** upon the
throne. (*indirect object*)

ὁ δράκων ὁ μέγας, ὁ ὄφις ὁ
ἀρχαῖος, ὁ **καλούμενος** Διάβολος
καὶ ὁ Σατανᾶς (Rev. 12:9)

The great dragon, the ancient serpent, the **one called** the devil and
Satan. (*in apposition to* δράκων)

10.5. The category of the participle often labeled as a "predicate" use
(Wallace 618) or as a "complementary" use (BDF §§414–16) probably belongs here as a substantival usage instead. This is the use of the participle
along with another nominal in the accusative case, after verbs of perception:
thinking, considering, hearing, and seeing. In these instances the participle
could be attributive, modifying an accusative nominal. However, it could
also be substantival, acting as the complement in a double accusative object-
complement construction (see chap. 1, on cases).[8] The noun or noun substitute

7. David L. Mathewson, *Revelation: A Handbook on the Greek Text* (Waco: Baylor University Press, 2016), 4.
8. Martin M. Culy, "Double Case Constructions in Koine Greek," *Journal of Greco-Roman*
Christianity and Judaism 6 (2009): 82–106.

is the object and the participle the complement. In "I saw him studying," the pronoun "him" is the object, and the participle "studying" is the complement following the verb "saw."

εἶδεν πνεῦμα θεοῦ **καταβαῖνον** ὡσεὶ περιστεράν (Matt. 3:16)	I saw the *Spirit* of God [object] **coming down** [complement] as a dove.

> It is possible to analyze this as an attributive use of the participle: "I saw the Spirit of God that was coming down as a dove." However, this could more easily be seen as the complement in a double accusative object-complement construction.

ἐν τούτῳ γινώσκετε τὸ πνεῦμα τοῦ θεοῦ· πᾶν πνεῦμα ὃ ὁμολογεῖ Ἰησοῦν Χριστὸν ἐν σαρκὶ **ἐληλυθότα** ἐκ τοῦ θεοῦ ἐστιν (1 John 4:2)	By this we know the Spirit of God: every spirit that confesses *Jesus Christ* [object] **having come** [complement] in flesh is from God.

> Again, it is possible to analyze this as an attributive use of the participle: "Every spirit that confesses *Jesus Christ* who **has come** in flesh is from God." Yet, we prefer to understand it as the complement in a double-accusative object-complement construction in indirect discourse (in direct speech: "Every spirit that confesses, 'Jesus Christ has come in flesh,' is from God").

εἶδον ἄγγελον ἰσχυρὸν **κηρύσσοντα** ἐν φωνῇ μεγάλῃ· (Rev. 5:2)	I saw a strong *angel* [object] **proclaiming** [complement] with a great voice.

> There are a number of examples of this construction in Revelation (see also 7:1, 2; 10:1).

Adverbial Use of the Participles

Verbal Modifier (Circumstantial)

10.6. Like an adverb, the participle can modify another verbal element in the sentence. This usage will never have an article, though the absence of an article is no guarantee that a participle is adverbial. It will also usually be in the nominative case, since the subject of the participle is usually identical with the subject of the main verb; that is, the participle maintains a connection to the subject of the main verb, whether explicit or implied, from which it gets its case, gender, and number.[9] The adverbial participle simply *specifies the circumstances* (hence "circumstantial") *under which the action of the verb it modifies takes place*.[10]

Most grammars subcategorize adverbial participles as temporal, causal, concessive, manner, conditional, means, purpose, and result. Some actually see these as eight different *kinds* of adverbial participles. Grammatical analysis, then, consists of fitting a given participle into one of these categories. However, we are not convinced that this is the best way to approach adverbial participles. As most grammars admit, these meanings are heavily dependent on the wider context, if they are present at all.[11] But the participles themselves do not bear these meanings. If the author wanted unambiguously to indicate time, cause, manner, purpose, condition, or other ideas, there were very clear means of doing so: for example, a ὅτι-clause (cause), a ἵνα-clause (purpose or result), or a clause beginning with ὅτε (time) or ἐάν (condition). The point is that participles are ambiguous and, by themselves, do not indicate such refinements of meaning. They are marked not for these meanings but only for tense, voice, gender, number, and case. Rather, these meanings, if present at all, are context driven. It is not that such nuances are not present; it is just that the participles do not indicate or emphasize them. In other words, a participle seems to be the ideal construction to use when the author does not want to commit to any specific adverbial meaning (cause, manner, condition, etc.). It is therefore probably better to avoid these labels as descriptions of the participle.

So what *is* the function of the adverbial participle? A helpful way of analyzing adverbial participles is to observe the spatial relationship of the participle to the main verb. Does the participle *precede* or *follow* the main verb?

10.7. If the participle *precedes* the main verb, it usually communicates background or prerequisite action to the main verb, especially when it is in the aorist tense-form. The participle signals information that is of secondary importance to the action of the main verb, so that more attention is placed on

9. Dana and Mantey 226: "Its adjectival force is retained and relates it intimately with the noun as well as the verb." Adverbial participles that modify an infinitive, however, can agree with their accusative "subject" (cf. Matt. 13:2).

10. Brooks and Winbery 145; Robertson 1124; Chrys Caragounis, *The Development of Greek and the New Testament* (Grand Rapids: Baker Academic, 2006), 175. For this reason we prefer the term "circumstantial" to encompass all the ways an adverbial participle can function.

11. Robertson 1124: "It must be distinctly noted, the participle does not express time, manner, cause, purpose, condition or concession. These ideas are not in the participle, but are merely suggested by the context, if at all." Though written in the 1930s, Robertson's advice has not always been heeded.

the main verb.[12] The participle could as well be seen as a step to accomplishing the goal of the main verb (Young 158).

We would also include what most grammarians label "attendant circumstances" under this construction.[13] In this "use" of the participle, the action of the participle occurs in close proximity to that of the main verb and is usually construed as a coordinate finite verb connected to the main verb it modifies; an "and" is supplied by the translator. Both the participle and the main verb occur in the aorist tense. For example, in Matt. 28:19 (πορευθέντες οὖν μαθητεύσατε πάντα τὰ ἔθνη) the aorist participle (πορευθέντες) that precedes the main verb (the aorist imperative μαθητεύσατε) is often labeled a participle of attendant circumstances and is translated as an imperative: "Go and make disciples." While this may be a valid *translation*, it overlooks the fact that the participle is still *subordinate* to and modifies the main verb, irrespective of how we translate it.[14] Here πορευθέντες, though it may pick up some of the imperatival force of the main verb, depicts action that is prerequisite to or a step to the goal of the action of the main verb (Young 158). It communicates action backgrounded to that of the main verb, with the primary focus being on the imperative, "make disciples."[15] The action of the participle is closely associated with or occurs in close proximity to the action of the main verb but is not necessarily simultaneous with it. This so-called usage is often found in narrative.

Participle → Main Verb

Τότε Ἡρῴδης λάθρᾳ **καλέσας** τοὺς μάγους ἠκρίβωσεν παρ᾽ αὐτῶν τὸν χρόνον τοῦ φαινομένου ἀστέρος (Matt. 2:7)	Then Herod, **having called** the magi secretly, ascertained from them the time of the appearing of the star.

The action of calling is prerequisite to, or the background to, the main focus of attention, which is the main verb, "ascertained."

---

12. Stephen H. Levinsohn, *Discourse Features of New Testament Greek: A Coursebook*, 2nd ed. (Dallas: Summer Institute of Linguistics, 2000), 183: "This means that the information they convey is of secondary importance vis-à-vis that of the nuclear clause."

13. This is sometimes confusingly labeled by grammars as the "circumstantial participle."

14. Wallace 640; Young 158.

15. Stanley E. Porter, *Linguistic Analysis of the Greek New Testament: Studies in Tools, Methods, and Practice* (Grand Rapids: Baker Academic, 2015), 245.

καθίσας δὲ ἐκ τοῦ πλοίου ἐδίδα- | And **sitting** in the boat, he taught
σκεν τοὺς ὄχλους. (Luke 5:3) | the crowds.

> The NIV translates this with two coordinate verbs: "Then he *sat down*
> and *taught* the people." While this may be a valid translation, it obscures
> the fact that the first verb form is a participle that is subordinate to and
> indicates action prerequisite to the main verb, "taught."

ἐν ᾧ καὶ **πιστεύσαντες** ἐσφραγί- | In whom also **having believed**,
σθητε τῷ πνεύματι τῆς ἐπαγγελίας | you were sealed with the Holy
τῷ ἁγίῳ (Eph. 1:13) | Spirit of promise.

> The two actions either are simultaneous or occur in close proximity.

Ἀποθέμενοι οὖν πᾶσαν κακίαν καὶ | Therefore, **having put off** all evil
πάντα δόλον . . . ὡς ἀρτιγέννητα | and all guile . . . , as newborn ba-
βρέφη τὸ λογικὸν ἄδολον γάλα | bies, desire the pure milk of the
ἐπιποθήσατε (1 Pet. 2:1–2) | word.

> Though it may pick up some of the imperatival force of the main verb,
> the participle ἀποθέμενοι is a prerequisite and backgrounded to the
> action of the imperative ἐπιποθήσατε.

καὶ **ἐπιστρέψας** εἶδον ἑπτὰ λυχνίας | And **having turned**, I saw seven
χρυσᾶς (Rev. 1:12) | golden lampstands.

10.8. When the participle *follows* the main verb, it tends to further explain
or describe in some way what is entailed in the action of the main verb. This
is especially true with present-tense participles. That is, "they elaborate the
action of the main verb, often providing more specific explanation of what
is meant by the main action."[16]

Main Verb → Participle

---

16. Steven E. Runge, *Discourse Grammar of the Greek New Testament: A Practical Introduction for Teaching and Exegesis* (Peabody, MA: Hendrickson, 2010), 262. What Wallace labels the participle of means describes this use of the participle: "In some sense, the participle of means almost always defines the action of the main verb. . . . The participle of means could be called an *epexegetical* participle in that it *defines* or *explains* the action of the controlling verb" (629, italics original).

πορευθέντες οὖν μαθητεύσατε
πάντα τὰ ἔθνη, **βαπτίζοντες** αὐτοὺς
εἰς τὸ ὄνομα τοῦ πατρὸς καὶ τοῦ
υἱοῦ καὶ τοῦ ἁγίου πνεύματος,
διδάσκοντες αὐτοὺς τηρεῖν πάντα
ὅσα ἐνετειλάμην ὑμῖν·
(Matt. 28:19–20)

Therefore, having gone [go], make
disciples of all nations, **baptizing**
them in the name of the Father
and the Son and the Holy Spirit,
teaching them to keep all that I
have commanded you.

> The two present participles (βαπτίζοντες, διδάσκοντες) define further
> what it means to make disciples: baptizing and teaching.

κρίμα ἑαυτῷ ἐσθίει καὶ πίνει μὴ
διακρίνων τὸ σῶμα. (1 Cor. 11:29)

He/she eats and drinks judgment
upon himself/herself, not **discern-
ing** the body.

Τῇ προσευχῇ προσκαρτερεῖτε,
γρηγοροῦντες ἐν αὐτῇ ἐν
εὐχαριστίᾳ (Col. 4:2)

Devote [yourselves] to prayer,
being watchful in it with
thanksgiving.

Ἄγε νῦν οἱ πλούσιοι, κλαύσατε
ὀλολύζοντες ἐπὶ ταῖς ταλαιπωρίαις
ὑμῶν ταῖς ἐπερχομέναις.
(James 5:1)

Come now, rich people, weep,
wailing because of the miseries
that are coming upon you.

καὶ ἔβαλον χοῦν ἐπὶ τὰς κεφαλὰς
αὐτῶν καὶ ἔκραξαν **κλαίοντες** καὶ
πενθοῦντες (Rev. 18:19)

And they threw dust on their
heads and cried out, **weeping** and
mourning. (*further specifying
what the "crying out" is*)

10.9. This kind of analysis, we suggest, is more important than assigning
the traditional labels found in most grammars (time, cause, manner, conditional, etc.). The participle is "unmarked" for those kinds of meanings, and
the student should not feel compelled to assign one. Rather, the participle is
used to prioritize verbal actions in relationship to that of the main verb. As
Runge states, "The most important thing to understand about the participle
is the idea of *prioritization of action*."[17] That is, certain actions (conveyed
through participles) play a subordinate, modifying role over against the main
verb, which is the primary focus. Participles either provide background or
prerequisite information, or they further explain and describe in more detail
the action of the main verb. Nevertheless, the adverbial participle can occur

17. Runge, *Discourse Grammar*, 247, italics original.

in *contexts* that indicate various adverbial nuances (time, cause, concession, manner, condition, purpose, means, etc.). Rather than saying, "This is a causal participle," it is more accurate, though more cumbersome, to say, "This is an adverbial participle used in a context that indicates a causal relationship to the main verb," if the evidence in the context points to such a conclusion. Even then, this is not the most important thing communicated by the participle. But in the absence of clear contextual indicators, most of the time "it may simply be better not to specify the relation between the participle and the other elements of the construction" (Porter 191). Many are ambiguous and could fit more than one category. Below are some examples of the participle functioning in different types of contexts.

1. *Cause.* The participle can be used in a context that may suggest cause.

Δικαιωθέντες οὖν ἐκ πίστεως εἰρήνην ἔχομεν πρὸς τὸν θεόν (Rom. 5:1)	Therefore, **having been justified** [since we have been justified] by faith, we have peace with God.

2. *Manner.* The participle can be used in a context that may suggest manner.

παραγίνεται Ἰωάννης ὁ βαπτιστὴς **κηρύσσων** ἐν τῇ ἐρήμῳ τῆς Ἰουδαίας (Matt. 3:1)	John the Baptist came, **preaching** in the desert of Judea.

3. *Time.* The participle can be used in a context that may suggest time (see the section on participles and time below).

καὶ ἔκραξαν **βλέποντες** τὸν καπνὸν τῆς πυρώσεως αὐτῆς (Rev. 18:18)	And they cried out, **seeing** [when they saw] the smoke from its burning. (*though this could also suggest cause*)

4. *Concession.* The participle can be used in a context that may suggest concession ("in spite of, although").

εἰ γὰρ ἐχθροὶ **ὄντες** κατηλλά-
γημεν τῷ θεῷ διὰ τοῦ θανάτου
τοῦ υἱοῦ αὐτοῦ (Rom. 5:10)

For if **being** [although we were]
enemies we were reconciled to
God through the death of his
Son. (*though this could also
suggest time*)

See also Heb. 5:8, where the concessive force of the participle ὤν
is made clear by the particle καίπερ (although).

5. *Instrument.* The participle can be used in a context that may suggest
instrument or means.

ἀλλὰ ἑαυτὸν ἐκένωσεν μορφὴν
δούλου **λαβών** (Phil. 2:7)

But he emptied himself, [by]
taking on the form of a slave.

6. *Purpose or result.* The participle can be used in a context that may suggest purpose or result.

Καὶ ἰδοὺ νομικός τις ἀνέστη
ἐκπειράζων αὐτὸν (Luke 10:25)

And look, a certain lawyer stood
up, **testing** [in order to test] him.

7. *Condition.* The participle can be used in a context that may express a
condition ("if").

πῶς ἡμεῖς ἐκφευξόμεθα
τηλικαύτης **ἀμελήσαντες**
σωτηρίας; (Heb. 2:3)

How shall we escape, **ignoring**
[if we ignore] such a great salvation? (*could be causal*)

Participles and Time

10.10. There has been ample discussion on the relationship between participles and time. Though participles in and of themselves indicate verbal
aspect rather than time, it is commonly accepted that they do have a temporal relationship within the context (Zerwick 129). That is, they indicate
time relative to that of the main verb. However, the temporal relationship is
not always clear. A very influential proposal is that *aorist participles* indicate
antecedent (past) time in relationship to the main verb, *present participles*
indicate time simultaneous (contemporaneous) with that of the main verb,
and *future participles* indicate action subsequent (future) to the main verb.[18]

18. Dana and Mantey 229–30; Wallace 623–27.

This is natural, since action that is conceived of as perfective, grammaticalized with the aorist participle, lends itself to being used of action that is complete and thus preceding another action. The present tense, since it conceives of the action as developing or unfolding, lends itself to portraying an action that overlaps (is simultaneous) with another one.

οἱ ἀρχιερεῖς **ἐμπαίζοντες** μετὰ τῶν γραμματέων καὶ πρεσβυτέρων ἔλεγον· (Matt. 27:41)	The chief priests with the scribes and elders, **mocking**, were saying. (*the present tense used of simultaneous action*)
ἀκούσας τὴν καθ᾽ ὑμᾶς πίστιν ἐν τῷ κυρίῳ Ἰησοῦ . . . , οὐ παύομαι εὐχαριστῶν (Eph. 1:15–16)	**Having heard** of your faith in the Lord Jesus . . . , I do not stop giving thanks. (*the aorist participle used of antecedent action*)
ζῶντες ἐβλήθησαν οἱ δύο εἰς τὴν λίμνην τοῦ πυρός (Rev. 19:20)	**While living**, the two (beasts) were thrown into the lake of fire. (*the present participle used of simultaneous action*)

While there are plenty of examples of this, there are also numerous exceptions to this so-called rule. A more promising proposal is that word order plays a role in indicating temporal relationship. When the participle precedes the main verb, it tends to indicate action prior (antecedent) to the action of the main verb; when the participle follows the main verb, it tends to indicate action that is simultaneous or subsequent to the action of the main verb. As Porter says, this is only a generalization, but it is one that often holds true.[19]

10.11. Antecedent action. In the following examples of the participle preceding the main verb, the action of the participle appears to be antecedent to that of the verb.

ἐληλακότες οὖν ὡς σταδίους εἴκοσι πέντε ἢ τριάκοντα θεωροῦσιν τὸν Ἰησοῦν (John 6:19)	Therefore, **having rowed** about twenty-five or thirty stadia, they beheld Jesus.

> Here the rowing a distance (expressed with the perfect participle) seems to temporally precede the seeing.

---

19. Porter 188; and Porter, *Verbal Aspect*, 380–85. See also James Hope Moulton, *Prolegomena*, vol. 1 of *A Grammar of New Testament Greek*, by James Hope Moulton, Wilbert Francis Howard, and Nigel Turner, 3rd ed. (Edinburgh: T&T Clark, 1908), 131; Young 147.

ἓν οἶδα ὅτι τυφλὸς ὢν ἄρτι βλέπω.   One thing I know, that [once]
(John 9:25)   **being** blind, now I see.

The present participle is used for antecedent action.

ἐν ᾧ καὶ ὑμεῖς **ἀκούσαντες** τὸν   In whom you also—**having heard**
λόγον τῆς ἀληθείας, τὸ εὐαγγέλιον   the word of truth, the gospel of
τῆς σωτηρίας ὑμῶν, ἐν ᾧ καὶ   your salvation, in which **having**
πιστεύσαντες ἐσφραγίσθητε τῷ   also **believed**—were sealed with
πνεύματι (Eph. 1:13)   the Spirit.

Though it is possible that the action of the participles is antecedent to
that of the main verb, "were sealed," the idea may be that the actions
are closely related.

10.12. Simultaneous action. In the following examples of the participle
following the main verb, the action of the participle appears to be contemporaneous with (occurring at the same time as) the action of the verb. When
the aorist participle is used of simultaneous action, the main verb is usually
also in the aorist tense-form.

Εἰ πνεῦμα ἅγιον ἐλάβετε   Did you receive the Holy Spirit
πιστεύσαντες; (Acts 19:2)   **when you believed?**

The aorist participle seems to indicate action that takes place at the same
time as, or closely associated with, the main verb "receive," which is also
aorist (see Eph. 1:13 above, where the aorist participle "having believed"
precedes the main verb and indicates antecedent action).

συνεζωοποίησεν ὑμᾶς σὺν αὐτῷ·   He made you alive together with
χαρισάμενος ἡμῖν πάντα τὰ   him, **forgiving** us all our tres-
παραπτώματα (Col. 2:13)   passes. (*an aorist participle fol-
                                           lowing an aorist main verb*)

The forgiving seems to be simultaneous with the act of making alive
rather than a temporally subsequent event.

καὶ ἔκραξαν **κλαίοντες** καὶ   And they cried out, **weeping** and
πενθοῦντες λέγοντες· (Rev. 18:19)   **mourning, saying.** (*present par-
                                           ticiples following an imperfect
                                           main verb*)

10.13. Subsequent action. In the following examples of the participle following the main verb, the action of the participle appears to be subsequent to (occurring after) that of the verb.

ἰδοὺ νομικός τις ἀνέστη **ἐκπειράζων** αὐτὸν **λέγων**· (Luke 10:25)	Look, a certain lawyer got up, **testing** him, **saying**.

> Both present participles are subsequent (future) in relation to the act of getting up.

Ἀγρίππας ὁ βασιλεὺς καὶ Βερνίκη κατήντησαν εἰς Καισάρειαν **ἀσπασάμενοι** τὸν Φῆστον. (Acts 25:13)	Agrippa the king and Bernice arrived in Caesarea, **greeting** Festus.
εἰσῆλθεν ἐφάπαξ εἰς τὰ ἅγια, αἰωνίαν λύτρωσιν **εὑράμενος**. (Heb. 9:12)	He entered once for all into the holy place, **finding** an eternal redemption.

> Most likely the action of finding takes place subsequent to the entrance into the holy place (Porter 190).

There are obviously some examples in the NT that resist this scheme (e.g., ἀποκριθεὶς εἶπεν, "answering, he said": the answering does not come before the saying).[20] As seen above, sometimes the position of the participle indicates prioritizing of action. But at least the above demonstrates that the aspects of the participle can all be used in different temporal contexts. Ultimately, the safest procedure is to examine each participle in its broader context, along with its verbal aspect and its position in relationship to the main verb, in order to determine the temporal relationship between the participle and the verb that it modifies.

Complementary (Supplementary)

10.14. The participle sometimes completes the meaning of a finite verb. It occurs with verbs of ceasing or continuing and verbs that express emotion.[21]

---

20. Robert E. Picirilli, "Order and Relative Time in the Participles of the Greek New Testament," *Journal of the Evangelical Theological Society* 57, no. 1 (2014): 99–110, though not all of Picirilli's examples to the contrary are convincing.

21. BDF §§414–16; McKay, *New Syntax*, 65.

Καὶ ἐγένετο ὅτε ἐτέλεσεν ὁ Ἰησοῦς διατάσσων τοῖς δώδεκα μαθηταῖς αὐτοῦ (Matt. 11:1)

And it came about, when Jesus finished **instructing** his twelve disciples.

ὁ δὲ Πέτρος ἐπέμενεν **κρούων·** (Acts 12:16)

But Peter continued **knocking.**

Διὰ τοῦτο . . . οὐ παυόμεθα ὑπὲρ ὑμῶν **προσευχόμενοι** καὶ **αἰτούμενοι** (Col. 1:9)

For this reason . . . we do not cease **praying** on behalf of you and **asking.**

The main verb is completed by two participles (see also Eph. 1:16).

ὑμεῖς δέ, ἀδελφοί, μὴ ἐγκακήσητε **καλοποιοῦντες.** (2 Thess. 3:13)

But you, brothers and sisters, do not lose heart in **doing good.**

Here the participle complements an aorist prohibition.

Predicate (Independent)

10.15. Although this usage is sometimes questioned and is rare, the participle can function as a finite verb; that is, it does not modify another verb (the adverbial modifier above), but it fills the slot of and acts as a finite verb. In these instances it is also possible that the participle completes an assumed or elided verb εἰμί.

οὐ μόνον δέ, ἀλλὰ καὶ **καυχώμενοι** ἐν τῷ θεῷ (Rom. 5:11)

And not only [this], but also we **boast** in God.

καὶ **ἔχων** ἐν τῇ δεξιᾷ χειρὶ αὐτοῦ ἀστέρας ἑπτά, καὶ ἐκ τοῦ στόματος αὐτοῦ ῥομφαία δίστομος ὀξεῖα **ἐκπορευομένη** (Rev. 1:16)

And **he has** in his right hand seven stars, and from his mouth **proceeds** a sharp two-edged sword.

Here both participles seem to function as finite verbs in clauses that contain no finite verb forms. Revelation may have a number of other examples of the participle used as a finite verb (as possibilities, see 4:2, 4, 7, 8; 6:2; 9:17; 10:2, 8; 14:1; 19:12; 21:12, 14).[22]

There may also be some examples in the NT of the participle acting as an imperative verb. Again, this is fairly rare, but there is no reason to assume

22. David E. Aune, *Revelation 1–5*, Word Biblical Commentary (Waco: Word, 1997), cc.

a "missing" verb that the participle supposedly modifies.[23] The participle is simply taking the place of an imperative verb. Some think that this has been influenced by Hebrew idiom, where a Hebrew participle can function as a finite verb. However, James Moulton has demonstrated that this occurs in secular Greek outside of the NT.[24]

Ἡ ἀγάπη ἀνυπόκριτος. ἀποστυγοῦντες τὸ πονηρόν, κολλώμενοι τῷ ἀγαθῷ· (Rom. 12:9)	Love [should be] without hypocrisy. **Hate** the evil; **cling** to the good.

For other possible examples, see Rom. 12:10, 11, 13, 16, 17, 18, 19; 2 Cor. 8:24; 1 Pet 2:18; 3:7.

Two Further Uses of the Participle

Genitive Absolute

10.16. As the name "absolute" suggests, this use of the participle is grammatically unconnected (though it is conceptually related) to something in the main clause. (Contrast this with the use of the participle as a verbal modifier or attributive modifier above.) In Greek this construction consists of a genitive participle, usually accompanied by a genitive substantive that functions as the subject of the participle. There are two other identifying features of the genitive absolute. First, the subject of the participle (when there is one, it is in the genitive case) is *not* the same as the subject of the verb in the main clause (e.g., "Kara *having eaten* her lunch, *he arrived* at the bank": the person doing the action of the participle, "having eaten," is not the same as the person performing the action of the verb in the main clause, "arrived"). By contrast, in adverbial participles the subject of the participle is the same as that of the main verb (e.g., "While eating lunch, she studied for her exam"). Second, the genitive absolute usually occurs at the beginning of the sentence. Especially in narrative, the genitive absolute is used to indicate a transition from one topic or scene to another, a "switch reference."[25] The genitive absolute is more common in narrative than in the Epistles.

23. As does Boyer, "Classification of Participles," 173.
24. Moulton, *Prolegomena*, 180–83, 223–25.
25. Levinsohn, *Discourse Features*, 182. By "switch reference" he refers to "a natural way of highlighting the introduction to an existing scene of participants who perform significant actions that change the direction of the story, etc."

Τοῦ δὲ Ἰησοῦ γεννηθέντος ἐν Βηθλέεμ τῆς Ἰουδαίας . . . , ἰδοὺ μάγοι ἀπὸ ἀνατολῶν παρεγένοντο (Matt. 2:1)

Now **Jesus being born** in Bethlehem of Judea . . . look, magi from the east arrived.

Note that the person involved in the act of being born (Jesus, the subject) is different from the subject of arriving (the magi). The genitive absolute provides a transition to a new subject: the magi and their arrival.

Τελευτήσαντος δὲ τοῦ Ἡρῴδου ἰδοὺ ἄγγελος κυρίου φαίνεται κατ᾿ ὄναρ τῷ Ἰωσὴφ ἐν Αἰγύπτῳ (Matt. 2:19)

And **Herod having died**, look, an angel of the Lord appeared in a dream to Joseph in Egypt.

The genitive absolute closes the previous section on Herod (2:16–18) by referring to his death in order to transition to a new scene and actor: the angel who appears to Joseph.

ἐξελθόντος αὐτοῦ ἐκ τοῦ πλοίου εὐθὺς ὑπήντησεν αὐτῷ ἐκ τῶν μνημείων ἄνθρωπος ἐν πνεύματι ἀκαθάρτῳ (Mark 5:2)

When he came out of the boat, immediately a man with an unclean spirit from the tombs met him.

ἐποικοδομηθέντες ἐπὶ τῷ θεμελίῳ τῶν ἀποστόλων καὶ προφητῶν, **ὄντος** ἀκρογωνιαίου αὐτοῦ **Χριστοῦ Ἰησοῦ** (Eph. 2:20)

Having been built upon the foundation of the apostles and prophets, **Jesus Christ** himself **being** the chief cornerstone.

Note that those who have been built upon the foundation are distinguished from the one who is the cornerstone. The most intriguing feature is that the genitive absolute construction comes at the end of the sentence, after the main clause. This probably has the effect of highlighting Jesus as the main stone in the building.

Χριστοῦ οὖν **παθόντος** σαρκὶ καὶ ὑμεῖς τὴν αὐτὴν ἔννοιαν ὁπλίσασθε (1 Pet. 4:1)

Therefore, **Christ having suffered** in the flesh, you also, arm yourselves with the same mind.

Here the genitive absolute functions to switch the topic from the suffering of Christ, which was the topic of 3:18–22, to its implications for the readers.

Periphrastic Constructions

10.17. A periphrastic construction consists of a form of an auxiliary verb (εἰμί or perhaps γίνομαι) and a participle. A periphrastic participle is a roundabout way of expressing what could be expressed with a normal finite verb form.[26] According to Porter (45), the auxiliary (εἰμί or γίνομαι) contributes the mood, person, and number, while the participle contributes the verbal aspect and voice to the construction. The following combinations are found in the NT.

Auxiliary Verb	Participle	Parallel Indicative Form
present tense of εἰμί	present participle	present indicative

καὶ καλέσουσιν τὸ ὄνομα αὐτοῦ Ἐμμανουήλ· ὅ **ἐστιν** **μεθερμηνευόμενον** Μεθ᾽ ἡμῶν ὁ θεός. (Matt. 1:23)	And they will call his name Emmanuel, which **is interpreted,** "God with us."
καθὼς καὶ ἐν παντὶ τῷ κόσμῳ **ἐστὶν** **καρποφορούμενον** καὶ **αὐξανόμενον** (Col. 1:6)	Just as also in all the world **it is bearing fruit** and **growing.**

Auxiliary Verb	Participle	Parallel Indicative Form
imperfect tense of εἰμί	present participle	imperfect indicative

καὶ **ἦν διδάσκων** αὐτοὺς ἐν τοῖς σάββασιν· (Luke 4:31)	And **he was teaching** them on the Sabbath.
ἤμην δὲ **ἀγνοούμενος** τῷ προσώπῳ ταῖς ἐκκλησίαις (Gal. 1:22)	But **I was unknown** by face to the churches.

Auxiliary Verb	Participle	Parallel Indicative Form
future tense of εἰμί	present participle	future indicative

καὶ **ἔσεσθε μισούμενοι** ὑπὸ πάντων διὰ τὸ ὄνομά μου. (Mark 13:13)	And **you will be hated** by everyone because of my name.

See also Mark 13:25: **ἔσονται** ἐκ τοῦ οὐρανοῦ **πίπτοντες**.

---

26. English, e.g., uses periphrastic constructions frequently: "I am going," "I am reading," "She was studying."

| Μὴ φοβοῦ· ἀπὸ τοῦ νῦν ἀνθρώπους **ἔσῃ ζωγρῶν.** (Luke 5:10) | Do not fear; from now on **you will be catching** people. |

Auxiliary Verb	Participle	Parallel Indicative Form
present tense of εἰμί	perfect participle	perfect indicative

| Πολλὰ . . . ἄλλα σημεῖα ἐποίησεν ὁ Ἰησοῦς . . . , ἃ οὐκ **ἔστιν γεγραμμένα** ἐν τῷ βιβλίῳ τούτῳ· (John 20:30) | Many . . . other signs Jesus did . . . which **are** not **written** in this scroll. |

| καὶ **ἐστὲ** ἐν αὐτῷ **πεπληρωμένοι** (Col. 2:10) | And **you are full/complete** in him. |

Auxiliary Verb	Participle	Parallel Indicative Form
imperfect tense of εἰμί	perfect participle	pluperfect indicative

The pluperfect periphrastic construction has basically displaced the pluperfect indicative form in the NT.

| ὅτε ἦμεν νήπιοι, ὑπὸ τὰ στοιχεῖα τοῦ κόσμου **ἤμεθα δεδουλωμένοι·** (Gal. 4:3) | When we were infants, **we were enslaved** by the elements of the world. |

| καὶ ἡ γυνὴ **ἦν περιβεβλημένη** πορφυροῦν καὶ κόκκινον (Rev. 17:4) | And the woman **was clothed** with purple and scarlet. |

Auxiliary Verb	Participle	Parallel Indicative Form
future tense of εἰμί	perfect participle	future perfect indicative

| καὶ ὃ ἐὰν δήσῃς ἐπὶ τῆς γῆς **ἔσται δεδεμένον** ἐν τοῖς οὐρανοῖς, καὶ ὃ ἐὰν λύσῃς ἐπὶ τῆς γῆς **ἔσται λελυμένον** ἐν τοῖς οὐρανοῖς. (Matt. 16:19) | Whatever you bind upon the earth **will be bound** in heaven, and whatever you loose upon the earth **will be loosed** in heaven. |

This is probably the most famous example of a future perfect periphrastic in the NT and perhaps the most problematic; there is significant debate as to how to interpret this construction. Based on an understanding of the perfect tense as indicating a past action with ongoing results, the future perfect is understood as indicating a future binding and loosing that is determined by a past act: what is bound on earth has already been bound in the past in heaven. However, based on verbal aspect, the perfect tense indicates an existing state, so that we should see it as simply a future state of binding and loosing with no necessary reference to a past event that produced the state. Most likely it refers to the binding and loosing as a future state of affairs. But this does not logically entail that heavenly decisions are contingent on earthly decisions (i.e., that heaven ratifies the decisions that are first made on earth). How one interprets these participles carries important theological implications.[27]

καὶ πάλιν· Ἐγὼ ἔσομαι πεποιθὼς ἐπ᾽ αὐτῷ· (Heb. 2:13)   And again, "I **will trust** in him."

10.18. One natural question concerns the difference between a normal indicative verb form and a periphrastic construction. Are they merely synonymous, or is there a distinction in meaning? Why might an author choose a periphrastic construction? Though it is difficult to tell why someone might use one construction over another, an author might use a periphrastic construction because it replaces a verb form that is dying out or has died out (like the pluperfect or future perfect) or for stylistic variation from standard verb forms. Additionally, as Porter suggests, "grammarians who wish to stress that the periphrastic is more emphatic or significant" are likely correct.[28]

For Practice

10.19. Analyze the participles (in bold) in the following sections of texts based on the preceding discussion. Particularly notice their positions in relationship to the main verbs and what those indicate about their function and status vis-à-vis the main verbs.

¹Τοῦ δὲ Ἰησοῦ **γεννηθέντος** ἐν Βηθλέεμ τῆς Ἰουδαίας ἐν ἡμέραις Ἡρῴδου τοῦ βασιλέως, ἰδοὺ μάγοι ἀπὸ ἀνατολῶν παρεγένοντο εἰς Ἱεροσόλυμα ²**λέγοντες**· Ποῦ ἐστιν ὁ **τεχθεὶς** βασιλεὺς τῶν Ἰουδαίων; εἴδομεν γὰρ αὐτοῦ τὸν ἀστέρα ἐν τῇ ἀνατολῇ καὶ ἤλθομεν προσκυνῆσαι αὐτῷ. ³**ἀκούσας** δὲ ὁ βασιλεὺς Ἡρῴδης ἐταράχθη καὶ πᾶσα Ἱεροσόλυμα μετ᾽ αὐτοῦ, ⁴καὶ

---

27. See Stanley E. Porter, "Vague Verbs, Periphrastics, and Matt. 16.19," *Filologia Neotestamentaria* 1 (1988): 155–73.
28. Porter 46; cf. Young 161.

συναγαγὼν πάντας τοὺς ἀρχιερεῖς καὶ γραμματεῖς τοῦ λαοῦ ἐπυνθάνετο παρ' αὐτῶν ποῦ ὁ χριστὸς γεννᾶται. ⁵οἱ δὲ εἶπαν αὐτῷ· Ἐν Βηθλέεμ τῆς Ἰουδαίας· οὕτως γὰρ γέγραπται διὰ τοῦ προφήτου· ⁶Καὶ σύ, Βηθλέεμ γῆ Ἰούδα, οὐδαμῶς ἐλαχίστη εἶ ἐν τοῖς ἡγεμόσιν Ἰούδα· ἐκ σοῦ γὰρ ἐξελεύσεται **ἡγούμενος**, ὅστις ποιμανεῖ τὸν λαόν μου τὸν Ἰσραήλ. ⁷Τότε Ἡρῴδης λάθρᾳ **καλέσας** τοὺς μάγους ἠκρίβωσεν παρ' αὐτῶν τὸν χρόνον τοῦ **φαινομένου** ἀστέρος, ⁸καὶ **πέμψας** αὐτοὺς εἰς Βηθλέεμ εἶπεν· Πορευθέντες ἐξετάσατε ἀκριβῶς περὶ τοῦ παιδίου· ἐπὰν δὲ εὕρητε, ἀπαγγείλατέ μοι, ὅπως κἀγὼ **ἐλθὼν** προσκυνήσω αὐτῷ. (Matt. 2:1–8)

⁸νῦν δὲ φῶς ἐν κυρίῳ· ὡς τέκνα φωτὸς περιπατεῖτε, ⁹ὁ γὰρ καρπὸς τοῦ φωτὸς ἐν πάσῃ ἀγαθωσύνῃ καὶ δικαιοσύνῃ καὶ ἀληθείᾳ, ¹⁰**δοκιμάζοντες** τί ἐστιν εὐάρεστον τῷ κυρίῳ· ¹¹καὶ μὴ συγκοινωνεῖτε τοῖς ἔργοις τοῖς ἀκάρποις τοῦ σκότους, μᾶλλον δὲ καὶ ἐλέγχετε, ¹²τὰ γὰρ κρυφῇ **γινόμενα** ὑπ' αὐτῶν αἰσχρόν ἐστιν καὶ λέγειν· ¹³τὰ δὲ πάντα **ἐλεγχόμενα** ὑπὸ τοῦ φωτὸς φανεροῦται, ¹⁴πᾶν γὰρ τὸ **φανερούμενον** φῶς ἐστιν. διὸ λέγει· Ἔγειρε, ὁ **καθεύδων**, καὶ ἀνάστα ἐκ τῶν νεκρῶν, καὶ ἐπιφαύσει σοι ὁ Χριστός. ¹⁵Βλέπετε οὖν ἀκριβῶς πῶς περιπατεῖτε, μὴ ὡς ἄσοφοι ἀλλ' ὡς σοφοί, ¹⁶**ἐξαγοραζόμενοι** τὸν καιρόν, ὅτι αἱ ἡμέραι πονηραί εἰσιν. ¹⁷διὰ τοῦτο μὴ γίνεσθε ἄφρονες, ἀλλὰ συνίετε τί τὸ θέλημα τοῦ κυρίου· ¹⁸καὶ μὴ μεθύσκεσθε οἴνῳ, ἐν ᾧ ἐστιν ἀσωτία, ἀλλὰ πληροῦσθε ἐν πνεύματι, ¹⁹**λαλοῦντες** ἑαυτοῖς ψαλμοῖς καὶ ὕμνοις καὶ ᾠδαῖς πνευματικαῖς, **ᾄδοντες** καὶ **ψάλλοντες** τῇ καρδίᾳ ὑμῶν τῷ κυρίῳ, ²⁰**εὐχαριστοῦντες** πάντοτε ὑπὲρ πάντων ἐν ὀνόματι τοῦ κυρίου ἡμῶν Ἰησοῦ Χριστοῦ τῷ θεῷ καὶ πατρί, ²¹**ὑποτασσόμενοι** ἀλλήλοις ἐν φόβῳ Χριστοῦ. (Eph. 5:8–21)

11

CLAUSES, CONDITIONAL CLAUSES, AND RELATIVE CLAUSES

Three Clause Types

11.1. Up to this point most of our discussion of grammar has taken place at the word or word-group level. The remaining chapters will branch out to consider grammar at the level of the clause and even larger units of discourse. In NT Greek, the basic grammatical unit for analysis is the clause. A clause can be described as a group of words that contains a verb phrase (a verb and any modifiers that go with it),[1] though Greek does not require a verb to form a clause. Clauses usually contain a subject as well, but Greek does not require an explicit subject since it is a built-in feature of the verb's personal ending. Greek exhibits at least three types of clauses: (1) primary, (2) secondary, and (3) embedded clauses. The following provides a brief description of these three types of clauses.

1. *Primary clause*. A primary clause is not dependent on another clause but stands on its own and usually contains a finite verb. Often known

1. Peter James Silzer and Thomas John Finley, *How Biblical Languages Work: A Student's Guide to Learning Hebrew and Greek* (Grand Rapids: Kregel, 2004), 120.

as an independent or main clause, a primary clause can be a statement, question, or command.

2. *Secondary clause.* A secondary clause modifies another clause, is usually introduced by a conjunction (e.g., ὅτι, ἵνα, ἐάν, or with the relative pronoun ὅς), and contains a finite verb. It is often called a dependent or subordinate clause; it cannot stand alone.

3. *Embedded clause.* An embedded clause functions as a component within a larger clause (e.g., as subject, direct object, adverbial adjunct) and usually includes a nonfinite verb form (a participle or infinitive). Some embedded clauses appear with a conjunction and finite verb and fill the slot of a noun element (e.g., relative clauses acting as noun or content clauses).

11.2. The different clause types play different roles within a discourse. The primary clauses serve to move the discourse forward or advance the story, while the secondary and embedded clauses further define, add to, elaborate, or supplement the information in the primary clauses.

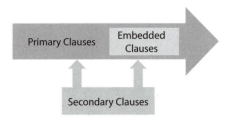

| ὃς ἐὰν οὖν λύσῃ μίαν τῶν ἐντολῶν τούτων τῶν ἐλαχίστων καὶ διδάξῃ οὕτως τοὺς ἀνθρώπους, ἐλάχιστος κληθήσεται ἐν τῇ βασιλείᾳ τῶν οὐρανῶν· (Matt. 5:19) | Therefore, *whoever breaks one of the least of these commandments and teaches people [to do] likewise* will be called least in the kingdom of heaven. |

This indefinite relative clause is an embedded clause that functions as the subject of the verb κληθήσεται.

καὶ δαιμόνια πολλὰ ἐξέβαλλον, καὶ ἤλειφον ἐλαίῳ πολλοὺς ἀρρώστους καὶ ἐθεράπευον. (Mark 6:13)

And *they cast out many demons,* and *they anointed many sick people with oil,* and *they healed [them].* (*three primary clauses connected by* καί)

A sentence with two or more primary (independent) clauses joined together like this is sometimes called a compound sentence. A single primary clause is often called a simple sentence.

[1] Δικαιωθέντες οὖν ἐκ πίστεως **εἰρήνην ἔχομεν** πρὸς τὸν θεὸν διὰ τοῦ κυρίου ἡμῶν Ἰησοῦ Χριστοῦ, [2] δι᾽ οὗ καὶ τὴν προσαγωγὴν ἐσχήκαμεν τῇ πίστει εἰς τὴν χάριν ταύτην [3] ἐν ᾗ ἑστήκαμεν. (Rom. 5:1–2)

Therefore, [1] *having been justified by faith,* **we have peace** with God through our Lord Jesus Christ, [2] *through whom also we have access by faith into this grace* [3] *in which we stand.*

This sentence contains a primary clause ("we have peace"), an embedded participle clause (1), and two secondary clauses (2, 3) consisting of two relative clauses. The first is an embedded participle clause that functions as an adverbial modifier of the main verb (ἔχομεν). The second clause is a relative clause that also modifies a previous group of words ("Lord Jesus Christ"), while the third clause modifies an element in the previous secondary clause ("grace").[2]

ἐὰν εἴπωμεν ὅτι οὐχ ἡμαρτήκαμεν, **ψεύστην ποιοῦμεν αὐτόν** (1 John 1:10)

If we say that we have not sinned, **we make him a liar.** (*a secondary clause introduced by* ἐάν)

The Construction of Clauses

11.3. How are clauses put together? As seen above, a typical clause in Greek has a *verbal* element that indicates a process (though not all Greek clauses have a verb). Clauses can also (but need not) contain a *subject*, usually in the form of a noun or substantive in the nominative case.

Subject (implied or specified)   Verb

2. A primary (independent) clause modified by one or more secondary (independent) clauses is sometimes called a complex sentence.

Greek clauses can also include a *complement*, such as a direct object and/ or indirect object or, following a linking verb such as εἰμί, a predicate nominative. Direct objects are often expressed by substantives in the accusative case, while indirect objects are expressed by substantives in the dative case. The complement of εἰμί is expressed by a substantive in the nominative case.

Subject   Verb   Complement

These elements can also be conceptualized as different "slots" in a sentence that can be filled by various grammatical means. In the sentence "Jordan drives a Mustang," the subject slot is filled with the noun "Jordan," and the verb slot is filled with "drives." The complement slot is filled with the noun "Mustang." But these slots, especially those of the subject and complement, can also be filled with larger units, such as embedded clauses (see above), like a substantival participle clause, an infinitive, or a relative clause (as in "*Whoever finds my keys* will receive a reward").[3] In addition to the subject, verb, and complement, linguists also often refer to the *adverbial adjunct*. An adjunct is a part of the clause that indicates the circumstances of the verbal process: for example, time, manner, location, and means.[4] In other words, it also is a modifier. Common adjuncts are adverbs or prepositional phrases: "Jordan drove his car *down the road*" (location) or "The teacher resigned her job *after the first week*" (time). Adjuncts are also expressed by adverbial participles or infinitive clauses that constitute embedded clauses.[5] This brings up an important distinction: adverbial clauses introduced by a conjunction (e.g., ὅτι, ἵνα, ἐάν) with a finite verb form are secondary adverbial clauses, whereas those adverbial clauses with a nonfinite verb—a participle or infinitive—fill the slot of the adverbial adjunct as embedded clauses.

Subject   Verb   Complement   Adverbial Adjunct

---

3. These are often discussed throughout this grammar under the "substantival" or "noun" use of these grammatical forms.

4. John Lyons, *Introduction to Theoretical Linguistics* (Cambridge: Cambridge University Press, 1968), 344–46.

5. Most grammars treat adverbial participles and adverbial infinitives as secondary clauses that modify the verb.

Primary Clauses: Clause Types

11.4. Primary clauses can also be subdivided according to the broader functional roles they play in language:

- statements/declarations
- questions
- commands

Statements basically provide information, whereas *questions* require information. *Commands* require a response (a question can function as a tacit command: "Will you please bring me my tea?"). If I say, "I enjoy learning Greek," I am giving information. But if I say, "Who took my book?" I am demanding information. If I say, "Give me the book!" I am demanding a response. In Greek, statements or declarations are usually communicated with verbs in the indicative mood. Questions may be expressed in any of the moods and are sometimes introduced by an interrogative word (e.g., τίς).[6] Though there are other ways of expressing a command in Greek (e.g., a future-tense verb; see chap. 8, on moods), using the imperative mood is the most common.

θεὸν οὐδεὶς ἑώρακεν πώποτε· (John 1:18)	No one has ever seen God. (*statement*)
Νεκρώσατε οὖν τὰ μέλη τὰ ἐπὶ τῆς γῆς, πορνείαν ἀκαθαρσίαν πάθος ἐπιθυμίαν κακήν (Col. 3:5)	Put to death, therefore, the members that are on the earth: sexual immorality, impurity, passion, evil desire. (*command*)
Τίς ἄξιος ἀνοῖξαι τὸ βιβλίον καὶ λῦσαι τὰς σφραγῖδας αὐτοῦ; (Rev. 5:2)	Who is worthy to open the scroll and to loose its seals? (*question*)

More on Questions

11.5. Greek can form questions in different ways. The three most popular, up-to-date editions of the Greek NT today—UBS[5], SBLGNT, and NA[28]—punctuate questions with the equivalent of an English semicolon (;). The original manuscripts contained no punctuation, so the punctuation in the

---

6. Not all questions in Greek require information. Deliberative questions (see below) are used to express hesitation or doubt, not necessarily to ask for information.

present editions of the Greek NT is the reasoned decision of the editors of the text, and there is some room for disagreement. Nevertheless, their punctuation provides a good starting point. The deciding factor, however, must always be context. There are three helpful indicators of a question: (1) if a sentence taken as a statement contradicts the other clear statements in the text; (2) if a sentence presents a set of alternatives; (3) if a sentence begins with an interrogative pronoun or adverb (e.g., τίς, ποῦ, πῶς, ποῖος, πόσος).[7]

11.6. True questions. These questions expect an answer, usually in the form of information. They may or may not be introduced with an interrogative particle or pronoun.

Ποῦ ἐστιν ὁ τεχθεὶς βασιλεὺς τῶν Ἰουδαίων; (Matt. 2:2)	Where is the one born king of the Jews?
ἁμαρτήσωμεν ὅτι οὐκ ἐσμὲν ὑπὸ νόμον ἀλλὰ ὑπὸ χάριν; (Rom. 6:15)	Shall we sin because we are not under the law but under grace?

> This would make no sense in Paul's argument if taken as a statement or exhortation.

11.7. Deliberative questions. Some questions in Greek express deliberation and uncertainty even when they seek an answer. These more often occur with a verb in the first person and the subjunctive mood but may also employ the future indicative (see chap. 8, on moods).

Τί ποιήσω; (Luke 16:3)	What shall I do?
πῶς δὲ ἀκούσωσιν χωρὶς κηρύσσοντος; (Rom. 10:14)	How will they hear without one preaching? (*a rhetorical question that demands a response rather than an answer*)

11.8. Negated questions. Some questions are negated, and how they are negated indicates the kind of response they expect. When a question is negated by οὐ, it usually expects a positive answer; but when a question is negated by μή, a negative answer is normally expected.

---

7. For these first two, see Porter 276.

μὴ δύναται εἰς τὴν κοιλίαν
τῆς μητρὸς αὐτοῦ δεύτερον
εἰσελθεῖν . . . ; (John 3:4)

[A person] is **not** able to enter into his/her mother's womb a second time, **is he/she?** (*No, a person cannot!*)

οὐχ ὁ θεὸς ἐξελέξατο τοὺς πτωχοὺς
τῷ κόσμῳ . . . ; (James 2:5)

Has God **not** chosen the poor in the world? (*Yes, he has!*)

Verbless Clauses

11.9. The NT also contains examples of clauses that are formed without a verbal element. Commonly these clauses contain only a subject and predicate nominative without a linking verb (εἰμί). Such a pattern is sometimes understood as an example of an elided verb (i.e., a verb that has dropped out), which the reader must supply. However, the phenomenon can also be explained by the fact that Greek is able to form clauses without a verbal element, or predicate. Because this seems odd to English speakers, our translations often supply a form of the verb *to be*.

Μακάριοι οἱ πτωχοὶ τῷ πνεύματι
(Matt. 5:3)

Blessed [are] the poor in spirit.

τίς δὲ συμφώνησις Χριστοῦ πρὸς
Βελιάρ, ἢ τίς μερὶς πιστῷ μετὰ
ἀπίστου; (2 Cor. 6:15)

And what accord [is there] of Christ with Beliar, or what share [is there] in a believer with an unbeliever?

καὶ ὁ καθήμενος ὅμοιος ὁράσει
λίθῳ ἰάσπιδι καὶ σαρδίῳ, καὶ ἶρις
κυκλόθεν τοῦ θρόνου ὅμοιος
ὁράσει σμαραγδίνῳ. (Rev. 4:3)

And the one seated on the throne [was] like a jasper and ruby stone in appearance, and [there was] a rainbow around the throne like an emerald in appearance.

The focus of the rest of this chapter and the next is on secondary and embedded clauses. Before moving on, we need to briefly mention two issues related to verbs in clauses. First, secondary and embedded clauses can contain a verb in the indicative or in two nonindicative (i.e., subjunctive or optative) moods. The author's choice of mood indicates the perspective on the action as it relates to reality. Second, verb tenses in these clauses designate verbal aspect, or the author's view of the process, and not time (see chap. 6, on the Greek verb system).

Conditional Clauses

11.10. The two clause types treated below could be covered in the next chapter, on dependent (secondary) clauses. However, we have chosen to treat them separately here due to their complexity and the number of important interpretive issues involved. Despite their apparent simplicity, conditional constructions are some of the most important to understand in NT Greek and have been subject to much misunderstanding. The following section will attempt to make sense of the different conditional constructions in the NT.

Recall that conditions consist of two elements: the *protasis* (the "if" part of the construction, usually introduced in Greek with εἰ or ἐάν), which is the secondary or subordinate clause, and the *apodosis* (the "then" part, though "then" is not necessarily expressed in Greek or English), which is the primary or independent clause. In the sentence, "If she studies Greek diligently, she will receive an A," the protasis is "if she studies Greek diligently," and the apodosis is "she will receive an A." In other words, the fulfillment of the apodosis (receiving an A) is consequent upon the fulfillment of the protasis (studying diligently). Whether she is actually studying or will study cannot be determined by the conditional construction but only by broader contextual factors (if at all). All that conditionals do is set up a supposition and its consequence: "if this . . . then that." As Brooks and Winbery (183) explain, "The statement in the apodosis becomes a reality only when the conditions stated in the protasis are met." The apodosis can be in the form of a statement, a command, or a question.

Greek exhibits several different conditional constructions that grammarians have divided into at least four types: class 1, class 2, class 3, and class 4 conditionals. Some grammars have typically added a number of further labels to characterize or classify conditional sentences: "more vivid," "future probable," "future less probable," "present general," and the like. However, this scheme depends on the perceived levels of certainty or the time of the fulfillment of the protasis (the "if" part), which can be determined only by contextual and other factors, not the form of the condition itself.

Richard A. Young has attempted to classify conditionals according to speech-act theory (how speakers actually do things with words; e.g., "I pronounce you husband and wife").[8] Applied to conditional sentences, one cannot stop with the surface form (i.e., the class) of the conditions but must explore their underlying semantic functions. Young suggests the following

---

8. Richard A. Young, "A Classification of Conditional Sentences Based on Speech Act Theory," *Grace Theological Journal* 10, no. 1 (1989): 29–49.

eight functions as a way of classifying conditionals: they can serve to rebuke, lament, argue, request, assert, manipulate, exhort, and mock.

While there is obvious value in considering the various tasks conditionals can perform in different contexts, this scheme ignores the fact that the author still had a choice from among up to four different conditional constructions. The existence of the different forms must mean something; otherwise, why use them? It seems that the clearest and easiest means of classifying conditional sentences is based on the *mood* of the verb in the protasis, that is, whether the verb is indicative or nonindicative. According to Robertson and Davis, "It is not the conjunction, but the mode that determines the conditional statement."[9] Therefore, we will stick with a common scheme of classifying conditionals according to four classes, though the first two classes actually belong together formally.

In the normal clause order for conditional constructions, the protasis ("if") comes first, followed by the apodosis ("then"). The reason for this is that the protasis of the conditional clause provides a frame of reference for interpreting the main clause (the "then" part), since the protasis indicates the condition under which the main clause is true. When the order is reversed, there is a more marked construction, and the protasis gains greater prominence.

Class 1 Condition

11.11. This class of conditional employs εἰ with a verb in the *indicative mood* in the protasis; the verb in the apodosis can be in any mood. It is the most common conditional construction in the NT, occurring about 300 times, and could be considered the default condition. According to Robertson and Davis, "It is the normal condition unless there is reason for using one of the others."[10] The class 1 conditional makes an assertion for the sake of argument[11] without reference to whether the condition is in reality fulfilled or not (Zerwick 102). Actual fulfillment can be determined, if at all, only by the context. An older approach to class 1 conditionals proposed that because they use the indicative mood in the protasis, they portray the action as a reality, and therefore the εἰ can or should be translated as "since."[12] However, this approach is being abandoned because there are far too many examples in the NT where this understanding simply does not work. It also

9. A. T. Robertson and W. Hersey Davis, *A New Short Grammar of the Greek Testament*, 10th ed. (Grand Rapids: Baker, 1977), 350.

10. Ibid. Dana and Mantey (287) call it the "simple condition."

11. Porter 256; D. A. Carson, *Exegetical Fallacies*, 2nd ed. (Grand Rapids: Baker, 1996), 7.

12. BDF §§371–72; Turner 115.

incorrectly assumes that the indicative mood requires that the action be a reality. One body of research[13] has suggested that 63 percent of all class 1 conditionals are either obviously false (12 percent) or undetermined as to whether true or false (51 percent). Only 37 percent were deemed to be true based on the context. If these statistics are even close to accurate, the class 1 conditional cannot mean that the action in the protasis is true and εἰ should not be translated with "since." Only the context can determine this, and often the context is ambiguous. In fact, class 1 conditionals can be used back to back to assert opposite things (see Matt. 12:27–28 below); they both cannot be true.

Other descriptions of the class 1 condition to be avoided are "real condition" or "determined as fulfilled," found in some grammars, since they could imply that the protasis is real or even thought to be real. Nor is it always accurate to call them "assumed true for the sake of argument."[14] To say that the author assumes the truth of the condition or expects his readers to do so might at times be too strong (e.g., when the author knows that something asserted is false). Class 1 conditions assert something only for the sake of argument. The force of the class 1 conditional is captured in the following expanded paraphrase: "If—and whether it is indeed true or not can be concluded based only on context; it is only being asserted for the sake of the argument—. . . , then . . ." Such an approach may be less exciting exegetically, but we think it is more accurate.

καὶ λέγει αὐτῷ· Εἰ υἱὸς εἶ τοῦ θεοῦ, βάλε σεαυτὸν κάτω· (Matt. 4:6)	And he said to him, "If you are the Son of God, throw yourself down."

The class 1 condition does not communicate whether Satan does or does not believe Jesus is the Son of God. It only makes an assertion for the sake of argument.

13. James L. Boyer, "First Class Conditions: What Do They Mean?," *Grace Theological Journal* 2, no. 1 (1981): 75–114.

14. This is probably the most common description of class 1 conditionals in the grammars. See Black 144; Wallace 692.

εἰ ἐγὼ ἐν Βεελζεβοὺλ ἐκβάλλω τὰ δαιμόνια, οἱ υἱοὶ ὑμῶν ἐν τίνι ἐκβάλλουσιν; . . . εἰ δὲ ἐν πνεύματι θεοῦ ἐγὼ ἐκβάλλω τὰ δαιμόνια, ἄρα ἔφθασεν ἐφ' ὑμᾶς ἡ βασιλεία τοῦ θεοῦ. (Matt. 12:27–28)

If I cast out demons by Beelzebul, by whom do your children cast them out? . . . But if I cast out demons by the spirit of God, then the kingdom of God has come upon you.

This classic example of class 1 conditionals demonstrates that "since" cannot be the meaning of εἰ in class 1 protases. Both protases cannot be true, because they make opposite assertions.

εἰ δὲ ἐκ θεοῦ ἐστιν, οὐ δυνήσεσθε καταλῦσαι αὐτούς· (Acts 5:39)

But if it is from God, you will not be able to overthrow them.

νυνὶ δὲ ἀποκατήλλαξεν . . . παραστῆσαι ὑμᾶς ἁγίους καὶ ἀμώμους . . ., εἴ γε ἐπιμένετε τῇ πίστει (Col. 1:22–23)

But now he has reconciled . . . to present you holy and blameless . . . , if indeed you remain in the faith.

The protasis follows the apodosis for emphasis.

εἰ γὰρ ἀποφυγόντες τὰ μιάσματα τοῦ κόσμου . . . τούτοις δὲ πάλιν ἐμπλακέντες ἡττῶνται, γέγονεν αὐτοῖς τὰ ἔσχατα χείρονα τῶν πρώτων. (2 Pet. 2:20)

For if having escaped the defilements of the world . . . and again having become entangled in these they are overpowered, the last state has become worse for them than the first.

εἴ τις εἰς αἰχμαλωσίαν, εἰς αἰχμαλωσίαν ὑπάγει· (Rev. 13:10)

If anyone [is to go] into captivity, into captivity they will go.

11.12. In our judgment, even when the context indicates that the protasis is indeed true, it is still not advisable to translate εἰ as "since." First of all, Greek had the resources available for the author to say "since": ἐπεί, ἐπειδή. Second, translating class 1 conditions with "since" obscures the rhetorical effect of the conditional. The function of the class 1 conditional is to leave the judgment as to its truthfulness up to the reader or hearer so that they will draw the appropriate conclusion.[15] Sometimes, when the context makes it clear that the condition is true, the class 1 condition can become a "tool

---

15. Boyer, "First Class Conditions," 82.

of persuasion" to move readers to agree with what is stated in the apodosis (Wallace 692).

Εἰ οὖν συνηγέρθητε τῷ Χριστῷ, τὰ ἄνω ζητεῖτε (Col. 3:1)

Therefore, **if** you have been raised with Christ, seek the things above.

> The preceding context (2:9–15) makes it clear that the readers have in fact died with Christ and have been raised with Christ, so they should draw the appropriate conclusion and carry out the command to seek the things above.

Class 2 Condition

11.13. The class 2 conditional should actually be seen as a subset of the class 1 conditional, since they both contain an indicative verb in the protasis. The class 2 conditional construction is marked in the protasis by εἰ with an *indicative-mood* verb in the *imperfect, aorist,* or *pluperfect tense-form* and in the apodosis by the particle ἄν with a verb in the imperfect, aorist, or pluperfect tense-form. This is also known as the contrary-to-fact condition, since what is stated in the protasis is asserted by the speaker or writer to be contrary to what is true for the sake of argument. The apodosis ("then") states what would have been a reality if the protasis ("if") had been true. In English, if we say "If you had studied, you would have received an A," what is stated in the protasis ("if you had studied") is stated as untrue or contrary to fact. And if the protasis is contrary to fact, then the apodosis remains unfulfilled. The force of the class 2 conditional can be illustrated in this expanded paraphrase: "If you had studied (and it is being asserted that you didn't), you would have received an A (but you did not, because you did not study)." Class 2 conditionals can function as a mild rebuke (Young 230). "If you had studied, you would have received an A" is a way of saying, "You should have studied."

Οὗτος εἰ ἦν προφήτης, ἐγίνωσκεν ἄν τίς καὶ ποταπὴ ἡ γυνὴ (Luke 7:39)

If this one were a prophet, he **would** know what manner of woman she is. (*both the protasis and apodosis are true, but the speaker assumes otherwise*)

εἰ ἦς ὧδε οὐκ ἂν ἀπέθανεν ὁ ἀδελφός μου· (John 11:21)	If you had been here, my brother **would** not have died. (*functions as a rebuke; see John 5:46*)
εἰ γὰρ ἔγνωσαν, οὐκ ἂν τὸν κύριον τῆς δόξης ἐσταύρωσαν· (1 Cor. 2:8)	For **if** they had known, they **would** not have crucified the Lord of glory.
εἰ γὰρ ἐξ ἡμῶν ἦσαν, μεμενή-κεισαν ἂν μεθ᾽ ἡμῶν· (1 John 2:19)	For **if** they were from us, they **would** have remained with us.

We have translated ἄν as "would" in the above examples, but that is not its *meaning*.

Class 3 Condition

11.14. The class 3 conditional construction uses ἐάν and a verb in the *subjunctive mood* in the protasis.[16] The verb in the apodosis can be in any mood. There are around 277 instances of the class 3 condition in the NT. Based on its use of the subjunctive mood, this condition is often treated as if it implies a greater likelihood of fulfillment than the class 4 conditional, though lacking the "certainty" of the class 1 condition. Therefore, some grammars label it the "more probable" condition;[17] the fulfillment of the protasis is seen as likely or probable. The problem is that the label fails to account for most instances of the class 3 conditionals in the NT. James Boyer, whose 1982 work is often cited, estimated that only 23 percent of all class 3 conditionals in the NT are probable based on the context.[18] This means that there is no built-in "probability" or "likelihood" to class 3 conditionals. How (im)probable or (un)likely it is that the condition will be fulfilled can be determined only by the context, if at all, since many times the context itself is unclear. Even Wallace (696), who says the class 3 conditions are uncertain but still likely to be fulfilled, recognizes that there are many exceptions, because some seem unlikely. Instances that most clearly demonstrate that probability cannot be the main semantic feature are those where class 3 conditions are used back to back to

---

16. There are a few examples of the particle εἰ with the subjunctive in the protasis rather than ἐάν. See, e.g., Rev. 11:5b: καὶ εἴ τις θελήσῃ αὐτοὺς ἀδικῆσαι, οὕτως δεῖ αὐτὸν ἀποκτανθῆναι ("And **if** anyone desires to harm them, thus it will be necessary for him/her to be put to death"). Since the class of conditional is determined by the mood of the verb in the protasis, these should be treated as class 3 conditionals.

17. Dana and Mantey 290; Brooks and Winbery 121; Black 145.

18. James L. Boyer, "Third (and Fourth) Class Conditions," *Grace Theological Journal* 3, no. 2 (1982): 163–75. See Carson, *Exegetical Fallacies*, 78.

make opposing suppositions. They cannot both be more probable (see Matt. 6:14–15 below). The most satisfying definition of the class 3 condition, based on the use of the subjunctive mood in the protasis, is Porter's: "A third class conditional . . . , in distinction to a first class conditional, is more tentative and simply projects some action or event for hypothetical consideration."[19] Only the context can tell why the author chooses to be more tentative and merely project an action. At times class 3 conditionals can serve a hortatory purpose, as mitigated exhortations: "If you forgive one another" can convey "You should forgive one another." See also chapter 8, on moods.

Some grammarians distinguish between "future probable conditions" and "present general conditions" under the umbrella of class 3 conditions.[20] However, there are no formal criteria for this distinction (both have ἐάν with the subjunctive in the protasis, and there is little consistency in the tense-forms that appear), so the interpreter must judge whether the condition seems to be generic (present general) or specific (future probable; Wallace 697). Therefore, these labels will not be used in this discussion. As Boyer observes, these two "types" of class 3 conditions are more an issue of subject matter than of grammar.[21]

ἐὰν γὰρ ἀφῆτε τοῖς ἀνθρώποις τὰ παραπτώματα αὐτῶν, ἀφήσει καὶ ὑμῖν ὁ πατὴρ ὑμῶν ὁ οὐράνιος· ἐὰν δὲ μὴ ἀφῆτε τοῖς ἀνθρώποις, οὐδὲ ὁ πατὴρ ὑμῶν ἀφήσει τὰ παραπτώματα ὑμῶν. (Matt. 6:14–15)	For if you forgive people their trespasses, your heavenly Father will also forgive you; but if you do not forgive people, neither will your Father forgive your trespasses.

These two class 3 conditions make opposite statements; they cannot both be more probable.

---

19. Porter 262, italics removed. Moule (150) says that the subjunctive mood in conditional sentences marks them as "hypothetical or uncertain." Cf. Turner 113.

20. Wallace 696–97; William Watson Goodwin, *Greek Grammar*, rev. Charles Burton Gulick (Boston: Ginn, 1930), 295, 298. K. L. McKay, *A New Syntax of the Verb in New Testament Greek: An Aspectual Approach*, Studies in Biblical Greek 5 (New York: Peter Lang, 1994), 167–73, distinguishes between "Particular Conditional Protases" and "General Conditional Protases" but does not limit them to class 3 conditionals. Zerwick (109–13) uses the terms "Eventual" and "Universal."

21. Boyer, "Third (and Fourth) Class Conditions," 175.

Περιτομὴ μὲν γὰρ ὠφελεῖ **ἐὰν**
νόμον πράσσῃς· **ἐὰν** δὲ παραβάτης
νόμου ᾖς, ἡ περιτομή σου
ἀκροβυστία γέγονεν. (Rom. 2:25)

For on the one hand circumcision
is of benefit **if** you practice the
law. But **if** you are a transgressor
of the law, your circumcision has
become uncircumcision.

The first protasis follows one main verb, and the second precedes the
next main verb. The two conditions make opposite suppositions, which
cannot both be more probable.

ἐὰν τις ἐν ὑμῖν πλανηθῇ ἀπὸ τῆς
ἀληθείας καὶ ἐπιστρέψῃ τις αὐτόν,
γινωσκέτω ὅτι ὁ ἐπιστρέψας
ἁμαρτωλὸν . . . σώσει ψυχὴν αὐτοῦ
. . . καὶ καλύψει πλῆθος ἁμαρτιῶν.
(James 5:19–20)

If anyone among you is led astray
from the truth and someone turns
him/her, he/she should know that
the one who turns a sinner . . .
will save his/her soul . . . and will
cover a multitude of sins.

ἐὰν φανερωθῇ ὅμοιοι αὐτῷ
ἐσόμεθα (1 John 3:2)

If he is revealed, we will be like
him.

The appearance of Christ is not being portrayed as more probable or
likely; it is certain.

κινήσω τὴν λυχνίαν σου ἐκ τοῦ
τόπου αὐτῆς, **ἐὰν** μὴ μετανοήσῃς
(Rev. 2:5)

I will remove your lampstand
from its place, **if** you do not
repent.

This is probably an implicit exhortation: they should repent. Notice that
the protasis follows the apodosis to emphasize the need for repentance.

Class 4 Condition

11.15. The class 4 conditional construction is marked by εἰ and a verb in the
optative mood in the protasis, and the particle ἄν and a verb in the optative
mood in the apodosis. In this conditional construction, the protasis is more
uncertain, vague, or hesitant than the class 3 conditional.[22] As virtually all
grammars recognize, there are no complete examples of this construction in
the NT. The following are often cited as partial constructions:

22. Robertson says, "There is less mist over the subj[unctive] than the opt[ative]" (1005).

οὓς ἔδει ἐπὶ σοῦ παρεῖναι καὶ
κατηγορεῖν **εἴ** τι **ἔχοιεν** πρὸς ἐμέ
(Acts 24:19)

For whom it was necessary to be
present before you and to make an
accusation, **if** anyone **might have**
anything against me.

Here the imperfect is used in the apodosis. This might be the closest we
have to a full class 4 conditional sentence in the NT.

εἰ καὶ **πάσχοιτε** διὰ δικαιοσύνην,
μακάριοι. (1 Pet. 3:14)

If you **should** also **suffer** because of righteousness, [you are]
blessed. (*with a verbless apodosis;
see also 3:17*)

Caragounis says that if the author had finished the conditional sentence,
he would have written μακάριοι ἂν εἴητε (you would be blessed).[23]

The following table summarizes the different conditional constructions.

Class of Condition	Protasis	Apodosis
Class 1	εἰ + verb in the indicative mood	verb in any tense or mood
Class 2	εἰ + verb in the indicative mood in a secondary tense (imperfect, aorist, pluperfect)	ἄν + verb in the indicative mood in a secondary tense (imperfect, aorist, pluperfect)
Class 3	ἐάν + verb in the subjunctive mood	verb in any tense and mood
Class 4	εἰ + verb in the optative mood	ἄν + verb in the optative mood

For Practice

11.16. Analyze the conditional clauses in the following texts.

[12]Εἰ δὲ Χριστὸς κηρύσσεται ὅτι ἐκ νεκρῶν ἐγήγερται, πῶς λέγουσιν ἐν
ὑμῖν τινες ὅτι ἀνάστασις νεκρῶν οὐκ ἔστιν; [13]εἰ δὲ ἀνάστασις νεκρῶν
οὐκ ἔστιν, οὐδὲ Χριστὸς ἐγήγερται· [14]εἰ δὲ Χριστὸς οὐκ ἐγήγερται, κενὸν
ἄρα τὸ κήρυγμα ἡμῶν, κενὴ καὶ ἡ πίστις ὑμῶν. . . . [17]εἰ δὲ Χριστὸς οὐκ
ἐγήγερται, ματαία ἡ πίστις ὑμῶν, ἔτι ἐστὲ ἐν ταῖς ἁμαρτίαις ὑμῶν. . . .
[19]εἰ ἐν τῇ ζωῇ ταύτῃ ἐν Χριστῷ ἠλπικότες ἐσμὲν μόνον, ἐλεεινότεροι
πάντων ἀνθρώπων ἐσμέν. (1 Cor. 15:12–19)

23. Chrys Caragounis, *The Development of Greek and the New Testament* (Grand Rapids:
Baker Academic, 2006), 187.

⁸ἐὰν εἴπωμεν ὅτι ἁμαρτίαν οὐκ ἔχομεν, ἑαυτοὺς πλανῶμεν καὶ ἡ ἀλήθεια οὐκ ἔστιν ἐν ἡμῖν. ⁹ἐὰν ὁμολογῶμεν τὰς ἁμαρτίας ἡμῶν, πιστός ἐστιν καὶ δίκαιος ἵνα ἀφῇ ἡμῖν τὰς ἁμαρτίας καὶ καθαρίσῃ ἡμᾶς ἀπὸ πάσης ἀδικίας. ¹⁰ἐὰν εἴπωμεν ὅτι οὐχ ἡμαρτήκαμεν, ψεύστην ποιοῦμεν αὐτὸν καὶ ὁ λόγος αὐτοῦ οὐκ ἔστιν ἐν ἡμῖν. ²·¹Τεκνία μου, ταῦτα γράφω ὑμῖν ἵνα μὴ ἁμάρτητε. καὶ ἐάν τις ἁμάρτῃ, παράκλητον ἔχομεν πρὸς τὸν πατέρα Ἰησοῦν Χριστὸν δίκαιον. . . . ³Καὶ ἐν τούτῳ γινώσκομεν ὅτι ἐγνώκαμεν αὐτόν, ἐὰν τὰς ἐντολὰς αὐτοῦ τηρῶμεν. (1 John 1:8–2:3)

Relative Clauses

11.17. A relative clause is introduced with a relative pronoun, which usually is related to another clause through an antecedent or "head." When the pronoun is linked like this to an antecedent, it functions as a modifier. However, sometimes the relative pronoun does not have an antecedent in the immediate context, and its clause functions as an embedded clause, usually filling a substantive slot (like subject or direct object) within a larger clause. That is, a relative clause can function in two ways: a secondary or subordinate clause functioning as an adjective, and an embedded clause functioning as a substantive. An example of the former would be "I saw the book *that* was lying on the table." The relative pronoun "that" modifies its antecedent, "book," in the main clause. But if we say "*Whoever* studies Greek daily will receive an A," the relative pronoun "whoever" (which also lacks an antecedent) introduces a clause that fills the slot of the subject of "will receive." When functioning as a modifier, relative clauses normally follow their antecedent. According to Porter, they do this over 80 percent of the time in the Greek NT.[24] This is because relative clauses usually add new information to the already established information in the clauses they modify.

Some grammars distinguish between *restrictive* and *descriptive* relative clauses (see Young 231). Restrictive relative clauses identify their antecedents, whereas descriptive relative clauses attribute a quality to their antecedents. However, since this is not strictly a grammatical issue but depends on understanding from the context, the line between these two is not always clear.

24. Porter 244. For similar statistics, see James L. Boyer, "Relative Clauses in the Greek New Testament: A Statistical Study," *Grace Theological Journal* 9, no. 2 (1988): 244.

Relative Clause as a Modifier (Secondary Clause)

11.18. This is the most common function of the relative clause: it modifies another clause to which it is connected by its antecedent. Sometimes the modifying relative pronoun is the object of a preposition in its own clause. For issues relating to the agreement between the relative pronoun and its antecedent, see chapter 2, on pronouns.

οἱ μαθηταί σου θεωρήσουσιν σοῦ τὰ ἔργα ἃ ποιεῖς· (John 7:3)	Your disciples will behold your *works* **that** you do.
τῆς διαθήκης ἧς διέθετο ὁ θεὸς πρὸς τοὺς πατέρας ὑμῶν (Acts 3:25)	*The covenant* **that** God decreed with your fathers.
τῆς βασιλείας τοῦ θεοῦ, ὑπὲρ ἧς καὶ πάσχετε (2 Thess. 1:5)	*The kingdom* of God, on behalf of **which** also you suffer.

The relative pronoun is the object of a preposition within its clause.

πόσῳ μᾶλλον τὸ αἷμα τοῦ Χριστοῦ, ὃς διὰ πνεύματος αἰωνίου ἑαυτὸν προσήνεγκεν (Heb. 9:14)	How much more the blood *of Christ*, **who** through the eternal Spirit offered himself.
Ἀποκάλυψις Ἰησοῦ Χριστοῦ, ἣν ἔδωκεν αὐτῷ ὁ θεός (Rev 1:1)	The *revelation* of Jesus Christ, **which** God gave to him.

Relative Clause as a Substantive (Embedded Clause)

11.19. Occasionally, the relative clause does not have an antecedent in another clause, but the entire relative clause functions as a noun element embedded within another clause. When it does, it usually appears as the subject or direct object of a sentence.

1. *Subject of the sentence*

Ὃς ἔχει ὦτα ἀκούειν ἀκουέτω. (Mark 4:9)	*Who has ears to hear* should listen.

The relative clause is the subject of ἀκουέτω (see also Matt. 7:24).

2. *Direct object of the sentence*

γράψον οὖν ἃ εἶδες καὶ ἃ εἰσὶν
καὶ ἃ μέλλει γίνεσθαι μετὰ
ταῦτα. (Rev. 1:19)

Therefore, write ***what*** *you see*
and ***what*** *is and* ***what*** *is about*
to take place after these things.

The relative pronouns are the subjects or direct objects within their
own clauses, but each entire relative clause functions as the direct
object of γράψον (see also Rev. 3:11, κράτει ὃ ἔχεις).

3. *Object of a preposition*

ἔμαθεν ἀφ’ ὧν ἔπαθεν τὴν
ὑπακοήν (Heb. 5:8)

He learned obedience *from*
what *he suffered.*

The relative ὧν is the object of the preposition ἀπό, and the entire
prepositional phrase modifies ἔμαθεν (see also Matt. 10:11, εἰς ἣν
δ’ ἂν πόλιν ἢ κώμην εἰσέλθητε).

Other Functions of the Relative Clause

11.20. Relative clauses may also perform a variety of other semantic roles.
They can sometimes indicate condition, purpose, concession, reason, or ground.[25]
It must be recognized that these are not grammatical categories but semantic
ones that depend on the function of the relative clause within its context.[26]

1. *Condition*

ὃς ἂν θέλῃ ἐν ὑμῖν εἶναι
πρῶτος, ἔσται πάντων δοῦλος·
(Mark 10:44)

Whoever desires to be first [i.e.,
if anyone desires to be first]
among you, [he/she] shall be a
servant of all.

2. *Purpose*

Ἰδοὺ ἐγὼ ἀποστέλλω τὸν
ἄγγελόν μου πρὸ προσώπου σου,
ὃς κατασκευάσει τὴν ὁδόν σου.
(Matt. 11:10)

Look, I am sending my mes-
senger before you, **who** will prepare your way [i.e., *in order that*
he might prepare your way].

---

25. These categories come from Young 231–33.
26. The following NT examples are also taken from Young 231–33.

3. Concession

ὃς ἐν νόμῳ καυχᾶσαι, διὰ τῆς παραβάσεως τοῦ νόμου τὸν θεὸν ἀτιμάζεις; (Rom. 2:23)	You **who** boast in the law [i.e., *although* you boast in the law], through transgression of the law do you dishonor God?

4. Reason-result

Διὸ παρέδωκεν αὐτοὺς ὁ θεός . . . , **οἵτινες** μετήλλαξαν τὴν ἀλήθειαν τοῦ θεοῦ ἐν τῷ ψεύδει (Rom. 1:24–25)	Therefore God gave them over . . . **who** exchanged the truth of God [i.e., *because* they exchanged the truth of God] for the lie.

5. Grounds-conclusion

οἵτινες ἀπεθάνομεν τῇ ἁμαρτίᾳ, πῶς ἔτι ζήσομεν ἐν αὐτῇ; (Rom. 6:2)	We **who** have died to sin [i.e., *since* we have died to sin], how shall we still live in it?

For Practice

11.21. Analyze the relative clauses in the following texts from Matthew and Colossians according to their function; also, identify the antecedent of the pronouns.

ὃς δ᾽ ἂν φονεύσῃ, ἔνοχος ἔσται τῇ κρίσει. . . . ὃς δ᾽ ἂν εἴπῃ τῷ ἀδελφῷ αὐτοῦ· Ῥακά, ἔνοχος ἔσται τῷ συνεδρίῳ· ὃς δ᾽ ἂν εἴπῃ· Μωρέ, ἔνοχος ἔσται εἰς τὴν γέενναν τοῦ πυρός. (Matt. 5:22)

ἀλλ᾽ **ὅστις** σε ῥαπίζει εἰς τὴν δεξιὰν σιαγόνα, στρέψον αὐτῷ καὶ τὴν ἄλλην· (Matt. 5:39)

οἶδεν γὰρ ὁ πατὴρ ὑμῶν **ὧν**[27] χρείαν ἔχετε πρὸ τοῦ ὑμᾶς αἰτῆσαι αὐτόν. (Matt. 6:8)

---

27. Can you explain why the relative is in the genitive case? Hint: look up χρείαν (need) in BDAG.

Προσέχετε ἀπὸ τῶν ψευδοπροφητῶν, **οἵτινες** ἔρχονται πρὸς ὑμᾶς ἐν ἐνδύμασι προβάτων. (Matt. 7:15)

[10]καὶ ἐστὲ ἐν αὐτῷ πεπληρωμένοι, **ὅς** ἐστιν ἡ κεφαλὴ πάσης ἀρχῆς καὶ ἐξουσίας, [11]ἐν **ᾧ** καὶ περιετμήθητε περιτομῇ ἀχειροποιήτῳ ἐν τῇ ἀπεκδύσει τοῦ σώματος τῆς σαρκός, ἐν τῇ περιτομῇ τοῦ Χριστοῦ, [12]συνταφέντες αὐτῷ ἐν τῷ βαπτισμῷ, ἐν **ᾧ** καὶ συνηγέρθητε διὰ τῆς πίστεως τῆς ἐνεργείας τοῦ θεοῦ τοῦ ἐγείραντος αὐτὸν ἐκ νεκρῶν· (Col. 2:10–12)

[5]Νεκρώσατε οὖν τὰ μέλη τὰ ἐπὶ τῆς γῆς, πορνείαν, ἀκαθαρσίαν, πάθος, ἐπιθυμίαν κακήν, καὶ τὴν πλεονεξίαν **ἥτις** ἐστὶν εἰδωλολατρία, [6]δι' **ἃ** ἔρχεται ἡ ὀργὴ τοῦ θεοῦ ἐπὶ τοὺς υἱοὺς τῆς ἀπειθείας· [7]ἐν **οἷς** καὶ ὑμεῖς περιεπατήσατέ ποτε ὅτε ἐζῆτε ἐν τούτοις· (Col. 3:5–7)

12

DEPENDENT CLAUSES AND CONJUNCTIONS

Dependent Clauses

12.1. As we saw in the previous chapter, there are three basic clause types in Greek: primary (independent), secondary (dependent), and embedded. We have already examined two types of clauses that fall under the latter two categories of secondary and embedded: conditional and relative clauses. These two clause types exhibit a number of important interpretive features that warranted a separate treatment. In this chapter we examine some other types of secondary and embedded clauses. We also consider several major conjunctions and particles and their functions. The following classification presents a fairly standard way of dividing the types of clauses. Our primary focus is on secondary and embedded clauses that contain a finite verb form. We have also included mention of the most common conjunctions that introduce these clauses.

Temporal Clauses

12.2. A temporal clause is a secondary clause that indicates a temporal relationship with the clause it modifies. The most common conjunctions used in such clauses are ὅτε, ὅταν, ἕως, ἄχρι, and μέχρι. The first two (ὅτε, ὅταν) indicate "time when"; the last three (ἕως, ἄχρι, μέχρι) indicate "time up to which." Expressions of time occur mainly with verbs in the indicative and subjunctive moods. Sometimes participles are used in a clause that indicates a temporal notion (see chap. 10, on participles). Also, infinitives may be used with prepositions to indicate temporal relationships (see chap 9, on infinitives). This section focuses on clauses introduced by a conjunction.

ἰῶτα ἓν ἢ μία κεραία οὐ μὴ παρέλθῃ ἀπὸ τοῦ νόμου, **ἕως ἂν** πάντα γένηται. (Matt. 5:18)	Not one iota or one stroke will pass away from the law, **until** all things have taken place.
ὅτε δὲ ἀνέβησαν ἐκ τοῦ ὕδατος, πνεῦμα κυρίου ἥρπασεν τὸν Φίλιππον (Acts 8:39)	And **when** they came up out of the water, the Spirit of the Lord carried away Philip.
εἶτα τὸ τέλος, **ὅταν** παραδιδῷ τὴν βασιλείαν τῷ θεῷ καὶ πατρί, **ὅταν** καταργήσῃ πᾶσαν ἀρχὴν καὶ πᾶσαν ἐξουσίαν καὶ δύναμιν. (1 Cor. 15:24)	Then the end [comes], **whenever** he gives the kingdom over to the God and Father, **whenever** he destroys every ruler and every authority and power.
μέχρι καταντήσωμεν οἱ πάντες εἰς τὴν ἑνότητα τῆς πίστεως καὶ τῆς ἐπιγνώσεως τοῦ υἱοῦ τοῦ θεοῦ (Eph. 4:13)	**Until** we all reach the unity of the faith and of the knowledge of the Son of God.
καὶ **ὅταν** δώσουσιν τὰ ζῷα δόξαν καὶ τιμὴν καὶ εὐχαριστίαν τῷ καθημένῳ ἐπὶ τῷ θρόνῳ . . . πεσοῦνται οἱ εἴκοσι τέσσαρες πρεσβύτεροι (Rev. 4:9–10)	And **whenever** the living creatures give glory and honor and thanksgiving to the one seated on the throne . . . , the twenty-four elders will fall.

This is an example of ὅταν used with a future indicative rather than a subjunctive. The entire construction in verses 9–10 functions as a conditional-like clause: the falling down of the elders (v. 10) is conditioned upon whenever the worship of the four living creatures expressed in the ὅταν clause occurs (v. 9). There is much debate as to the referent of the temporal clause—whether it is fulfilled in Rev. 4, 5, or elsewhere in the book and whether it refers to a definite or repeated occurrence.

Locative (Local) Clauses

12.3. A locative clause is a secondary clause that indicates where something in the clause it modifies is located or where an action takes place (including metaphorical location). In other words, such clauses usually answer the spatial question "Where?" Locative clauses are commonly introduced by ὅπου, ὅθεν, or οὗ.[1] The indicative and, less frequently, the subjunctive (usually with ἄν or ἐάν) moods are used in locative clauses.

ἐλθὼν ἐστάθη ἐπάνω **οὗ** ἦν τὸ παιδίον. (Matt. 2:9)	Having come, it stood above **where** the child was.
Μὴ θησαυρίζετε ὑμῖν θησαυροὺς ἐπὶ τῆς γῆς, **ὅπου** σὴς καὶ βρῶσις ἀφανίζει, καὶ **ὅπου** κλέπται διορύσσουσιν καὶ κλέπτουσιν· (Matt. 6:19)	Do not lay up for yourself treasures on earth, **where** moth and corrosion destroy and **where** thieves break in and steal.
Μωϋσεῖ λελάληκεν ὁ θεός, τοῦτον δὲ οὐκ οἴδαμεν **πόθεν** ἐστίν. (John 9:29)	God has spoken to Moses, but we do not know **from where** this man [i.e., Jesus] is.
τὰ ἄνω ζητεῖτε, **οὗ** ὁ Χριστός ἐστιν ἐν δεξιᾷ τοῦ θεοῦ καθήμενος· (Col. 3:1)	Seek the things above, **where** Christ is seated at the right hand of God.

> The locative οὗ functions like a relative clause, modifying the substantive τὰ ἄνω.

Οἶδα **ποῦ** κατοικεῖς, **ὅπου** ὁ θρόνος τοῦ Σατανᾶ (Rev. 2:13).	I know **where** you live, **where** the throne of Satan is.

> The local adverb ὅπου stands in apposition to ποῦ. The ποῦ introduces a clause that functions as the content of οἶδα (embedded clause).

Causal Clauses

12.4. A secondary clause can indicate the basis or reason for the clause it modifies. That is, it signals a cause-effect relationship (Porter 237). Cause can also be indicated by a preposition with a pronoun (διὰ τοῦτο, see below) or infinitive (διά + article + infinitive). However, we will focus on causal clauses with finite verbs that are introduced by conjunctions: ὅτι, διότι, and ἐπεί are the most common (γάρ usually introduces a main clause). Causal clauses, as well as the following two types of clauses, purpose and result, frequently

---

1. This last one is actually a neuter genitive form of a relative pronoun meaning "where."

come after the main clause they modify (Turner 344–45). When they are clause initial (come first), more attention is drawn to them.

Οὐκ ἔξεστιν βαλεῖν αὐτὰ εἰς τὸν κορβανᾶν, ἐπεὶ τιμὴ αἵματός ἐστιν· (Matt. 27:6)	It is not lawful to put them in the temple treasury, **since** it is blood money.
συνεχύθη, **ὅτι** ἤκουον εἷς ἕκαστος τῇ ἰδίᾳ διαλέκτῳ λαλούντων αὐτῶν· (Acts 2:6)	They were confused, **because** each one heard them speaking in their own dialect.
καὶ ἀδημονῶν **διότι** ἠκούσατε ὅτι ἠσθένησεν. (Phil. 2:26)	And being distressed **because** you heard that he was sick.
Μακάριος ἀνὴρ ὃς ὑπομένει πειρασμόν, **ὅτι** δόκιμος γενόμενος λήμψεται τὸν στέφανον τῆς ζωῆς (James 1:12)	Blessed is the person who endures trial, **because** when he/she has been tested, he/she will receive the crown of life.
ἀγγέλους ἑπτὰ ἔχοντας πληγὰς ἑπτὰ τὰς ἐσχάτας, **ὅτι** ἐν αὐταῖς ἐτελέσθη ὁ θυμὸς τοῦ θεοῦ. (Rev. 15:1)	The seven angels have the seven last plagues, **because** in them the wrath of God is completed. (*explaining why they are the seven last plagues*)

Purpose Clauses

12.5. A purpose clause is a secondary clause that indicates the intention of the verbal process in the clause that it modifies. According to Dana and Mantey, "the function of the purpose clause is to express the aim of the action denoted by the main verb" (282). Such clauses are sometimes referred to as "final" or "telic" clauses (Moule 138). A common means of showing purpose is with an infinitive with or without a preposition and/or genitive article (e.g., Matt. 2:2: ἤλθομεν **προσκυνῆσαι** αὐτῷ, "We have come **in order to worship** him"). Again, this section focuses on purpose clauses with a finite verb introduced by conjunctions. Common conjunctions are ἵνα and (less commonly) ὅπως, followed by a verb in the subjunctive mood, though on a few occasions ἵνα is followed by a future-tense verb (Moule 139; cf. John 7:3: ἵνα . . . θεωρήσουσιν).

ἐκείνοις δὲ τοῖς ἔξω ἐν παραβολαῖς τὰ πάντα γίνεται, **ἵνα**
βλέποντες βλέπωσι καὶ μὴ ἴδωσιν,
καὶ ἀκούοντες ἀκούωσι καὶ μὴ
συνιῶσιν (Mark 4:11–12)

But to those outside all things are
in parables, **in order that / so that**
seeing they might see but not perceive, and hearing they might hear
but not understand.

> The use of ἵνα here is disputed. Though some have proposed result as
> the meaning of ἵνα, others have argued for purpose (BDF §369[1]), sug-
> gesting a strong predestinarian notion: the reason Jesus spoke in parables
> was to obscure his message from some. Moule (143) thinks that the use
> of ἵνα here is an instance of the blurring of purpose and result.

οὗτος ἦλθεν εἰς μαρτυρίαν, **ἵνα**
μαρτυρήσῃ περὶ τοῦ φωτός, **ἵνα**
πάντες πιστεύσωσιν δι᾽ αὐτοῦ.
(John 1:7)

This one came as a witness **in
order that** he might witness concerning the light, **in order that** all
might believe through him.

> The second ἵνα clause modifies the first one.

λαὸς εἰς περιποίησιν, **ὅπως** τὰς
ἀρετὰς ἐξαγγείλητε τοῦ ἐκ σκότους
ὑμᾶς καλέσαντος εἰς τὸ θαυμαστὸν
αὐτοῦ φῶς· (1 Pet. 2:9)

A people as a possession, **in order
that** you might proclaim the vir-
tues of the one who called you
out of darkness into his marvel-
ous light.

ἡμεῖς οὖν ὀφείλομεν ὑπολαμβά-
νειν τοὺς τοιούτους, **ἵνα** συνεργοὶ
γινώμεθα τῇ ἀληθείᾳ. (3 John 8)

Therefore, we ought to support
such people, **in order that** we
might be fellow workers in the
truth.

ἐδόθη αὐτῷ θυμιάματα πολλὰ **ἵνα**
δώσει ταῖς προσευχαῖς τῶν ἁγίων
πάντων (Rev. 8:3).

Much incense was given to him **in
order that** *he will offer* it with the
prayers of all the saints.

> This is one of the few instances where ἵνα is followed by a verb in the
> future tense-form (see also Rev. 22:14). If the choice of the future is
> intentional, Porter suggests that "where a choice is offered between
> the Subjunctive and the Future, the Future is the more heavily marked
> semantically," indicating what can be expected to take place.[2]

---

2. Stanley E. Porter, *Verbal Aspect in the Greek of the New Testament, with Reference to Tense and Mood*, Studies in Biblical Greek 1 (New York: Peter Lang, 1989), 414.

Result Clauses

12.6. A result clause is a secondary clause that designates the result or outcome of the action of the clause it modifies and is often labeled a consecutive clause. Quite often, result clauses are difficult to distinguish from purpose clauses in meaning (and in form, since both can be introduced by ἵνα). Porter (234) says that result clauses may occur with verbs that do not suggest intention or direction and do not express actions that come about by some motivating force. Purpose clauses focus on the intention of the action, while result clauses focus on the outcome of the action.[3] The most common conjunctions introducing result clauses are ὥστε (usually followed by an infinitive) and ἵνα (with the subjunctive).

Οὕτως γὰρ ἠγάπησεν ὁ θεὸς τὸν κόσμον **ὥστε** τὸν υἱὸν τὸν μονογενῆ ἔδωκεν, ἵνα πᾶς ὁ πιστεύων εἰς αὐτὸν μὴ ἀπόληται ἀλλὰ ἔχῃ ζωὴν αἰώνιον. (John 3:16)	For God so loved the world **so that** he gave his only Son, in order that everyone who believes in him may not perish but have eternal life. (*with both a result clause and a purpose [ἵνα] clause*)
τοῦτο δὲ ἐγένετο ἐπὶ ἔτη δύο, **ὥστε** πάντας τοὺς κατοικοῦντας τὴν Ἀσίαν ἀκοῦσαι τὸν λόγον τοῦ κυρίου· (Acts 19:10)	And this happened in two years, **so that** all who live in Asia might hear the word of the Lord.
ὑμεῖς δέ, ἀδελφοί, οὐκ ἐστὲ ἐν σκότει, **ἵνα** ἡ ἡμέρα ὑμᾶς ὡς κλέπτης καταλάβῃ (1 Thess. 5:4)	But you, brothers and sisters, are not in darkness **so that** the day overtakes you as a thief.
θεὸν τὸν ἐγείραντα αὐτὸν ἐκ νεκρῶν καὶ δόξαν αὐτῷ δόντα, **ὥστε** τὴν πίστιν ὑμῶν καὶ ἐλπίδα εἶναι εἰς θεόν. (1 Pet. 1:21)	God who raised him from the dead and gave him glory, **so that** your faith and hope might be in God.

---

3. Wallace 677; Zerwick 122: "A consecutive [result] clause declares the end which in the nature of things is reached by something, whereas a final [purpose] clause declares the end which someone intends to reach."

| καὶ ποιεῖ σημεῖα μεγάλα, ἵνα καὶ πῦρ ποιῇ ἐκ τοῦ οὐρανοῦ καταβαίνειν εἰς τὴν γῆν (Rev. 13:13) | And he performed great signs, **so that / in order that / that** he also might make fire come down from heaven upon the earth. |

Is this an example of purpose or result? It is possible that it is neither and that the ἵνα clause is a content (embedded) clause that is epexegetical to σημεῖα μεγάλα, further describing what the great signs are (see below, on content clauses).[4]

Comparative Clauses

12.7. A comparative clause is a secondary clause that provides the basis on which the clause it modifies is compared.[5] Hence, it functions to elucidate the clause it modifies by way of a comparison. It often expresses the *manner* in which the action of the clause it modifies takes place. Common conjunctions introducing comparative clauses are ὡς, καθώς, καθάπερ, ὥσπερ, and ὡσεί.

δίδαξον ἡμᾶς προσεύχεσθαι, **καθὼς** καὶ Ἰωάννης ἐδίδαξεν τοὺς μαθητὰς αὐτοῦ. (Luke 11:1)	Teach us to pray, **just as** John also taught his disciples.
Εὐθύνατε τὴν ὁδὸν κυρίου, **καθὼς** εἶπεν Ἠσαΐας ὁ προφήτης. (John 1:23)	Prepare the way of the Lord, **just as** Isaiah the prophet spoke.
καθάπερ καὶ Δαυὶδ λέγει τὸν μακαρισμὸν τοῦ ἀνθρώπου ᾧ ὁ θεὸς λογίζεται δικαιοσύνην χωρὶς ἔργων· (Rom. 4:6)	**Just as** David also pronounces a blessing on the person to whom God credits righteousness without works.
ἀλλὰ καλούμενος ὑπὸ τοῦ θεοῦ, **καθώσπερ** καὶ Ἀαρών. (Heb. 5:4)	But being called by God, **just as** also Aaron.
Καὶ εἶδον . . . ἀρνίον ἑστηκὸς **ὡς** ἐσφαγμένον (Rev. 5:6)	And I saw . . . a Lamb standing **as** slain.

---

4. David L. Mathewson, *Revelation: A Handbook on the Greek Text* (Waco: Baylor University Press, 2016), 179–80.

5. Steven E. Runge, *Discourse Grammar of the Greek New Testament: A Practical Introduction for Teaching and Exegesis* (Peabody, MA: Hendrickson, 2010), 233.

Content Clauses

12.8. A content clause indicates the substance of another grammatical unit, such as the subject or direct object, or the content of a verb of perception (speaking, seeing, hearing, believing, confessing, etc.) in direct discourse. In other words, they are *embedded* clauses rather than secondary clauses. When they are the content of a verb of perception, they function as the direct object or *clausal complement* of the verb, giving the substance of what was said, heard, seen, believed, and the like. When modifying substantives or adjectives, the content clause stands in apposition to or is epexegetical to them (Wallace 678). Content clauses are most commonly introduced by ὅτι and ἵνα. The use of ἵνα to introduce content clauses is due to ἵνα beginning to take over some of the functions of infinitives in Koine Greek.[6]

Ἐμὸν βρῶμά ἐστιν **ἵνα** ποιήσω τὸ θέλημα τοῦ πέμψαντός με (John 4:34)	My food is **that** I do the will of the one who sent me.

> The content clause is the predicate complement of ἐστίν.

διανοίγων καὶ παρατιθέμενος **ὅτι** τὸν χριστὸν ἔδει παθεῖν καὶ ἀναστῆναι ἐκ νεκρῶν, καὶ **ὅτι** οὗτός ἐστιν ὁ χριστός (Acts 17:3)	Explaining and demonstrating **that** it was necessary for Christ to suffer and be raised from the dead and **that** this one is the Messiah.
οὐ παυόμεθα . . . προσευχόμενοι καὶ αἰτούμενοι **ἵνα** πληρωθῆτε τὴν ἐπίγνωσιν τοῦ θελήματος αὐτοῦ (Col. 1:9)	We do not cease . . . praying and asking **that** you might be filled with the knowledge of his will.

> The ἵνα clause indicates the content of praying and asking, not the purpose.

οὐ χρείαν ἔχετε **ἵνα** τις διδάσκῃ ὑμᾶς· (1 John 2:27)	You do not have need **that** anyone teach you. (*epexegetical to "need"*)

6. K. L. McKay, *A New Syntax of the Verb in New Testament Greek: An Aspectual Approach*, Studies in Biblical Greek 5 (New York: Peter Lang, 1994), 135.

αὕτη ἐστὶν ἡ μαρτυρία, **ὅτι** ζωὴν
αἰώνιον ἔδωκεν ὁ θεὸς ἡμῖν
(1 John 5:11)

This is the testimony, **that** God
gave us eternal life.

The ὅτι is epexegetical to αὕτη.

ἀλλὰ ἔχω κατὰ σοῦ **ὅτι** τὴν
ἀγάπην σου τὴν πρώτην ἀφῆκες.
(Rev. 2:4)

But I have against you **that** you
have left your first love.

Indirect Discourse

12.9. Clauses can be used to report indirectly the content of a speech or
thought with verbs of communication and perception. Indirect discourse is
a specific type of content clause (see the preceding section). It is helpful to
recognize the difference between direct and indirect discourse. In both cases,
what is spoken or thought fills the slot of the direct object of a verb of perception (speaking, thinking, etc.), but how they record the speech is different. In
direct discourse, we report directly (with the original speaker's words): "The
student said, 'I really want to take a Greek course.'" The quotation "I really
want to take a Greek course" functions as the direct object (i.e., the content)
of the verb "said." The first-person pronoun *I* identifies the original speaker
of the words. However, in indirect discourse the same speech is recorded
from the perspective of the person recording the speech or thought. To use
the example from above, we would say, "The student said *that he really wants
to take a Greek course.*" Notice the transfer from the first-person "I want"
(direct discourse) to the third-person "he wants" (indirect discourse) in the
words spoken. A key to recognizing indirect discourse is agreement between
the person(s) doing the communicating or perceiving ("the student" in our
example) and the pronoun(s) used to refer to them in the content clause (Porter
269; "he" in our example). Both are in the third person. In direct discourse
the persons do not agree: "student" and "I." Since there were no quotation
marks in Koine Greek, the context ultimately must determine whether a sentence records direct or indirect discourse. Two common ways of expressing
indirect discourse are with clauses introduced by a conjunction (especially
ὅτι and ἵνα) or by an infinitive.

In Greek, unlike English, indirect discourse is reported in the same tense/
aspect and mood as would have been used by the original speaker when the
statement was made, even if it is now past from the standpoint of the one

who is recording it.[7] This is despite the fact that other changes may take place in the transfer from direct to indirect speech, such as person (see above). Galatians 2:14: εἶδον ὅτι οὐκ **ὀρθοποδοῦσιν** πρὸς τὴν ἀλήθειαν τοῦ εὐαγγελίου, "I saw that they **did** not **act rightly** toward the truth of the gospel." Notice that the present tense of the verb is retained from when Paul originally made the observation; in English we translate it as past. The following examples contain indirect discourse introduced by a conjunction.

Εἰ υἱὸς εἶ τοῦ θεοῦ, εἰπὲ **ἵνα** οἱ λίθοι οὗτοι ἄρτοι γένωνται. (Matt. 4:3)	If you are the Son of God, say **that** these stones become bread [i.e., tell these stones to become bread].

> The original speech would have included an imperative, "Become bread!"

ἐλθόντες οἱ πρῶτοι ἐνόμισαν **ὅτι** πλεῖον λήμψονται· (Matt. 20:10)	And having come, the first group thought **that** they would receive more.

> Notice the agreement in person (third) between the ones doing the perceiving (the first group) and the subject of the content clause ("they"). The original thought would have been, "We will receive more."

Ὑμεῖς λέγετε **ὅτι** ἐγώ εἰμι. (Luke 22:70)	You say **that** I am.

> The original speech would be "You are. . . ."

The following examples contain indirect discourse introduced by an infinitive (see chap. 9, on infinitives).

ὁ λέγων μὴ **μοιχεύειν** μοιχεύεις; (Rom. 2:22)	The one who says not **to commit** adultery, do you commit adultery?

> The original speech would have been a prohibition: "Do not commit adultery!"

Εἴ τις δοκεῖ θρησκὸς **εἶναι** (James 1:26)	If anyone thinks he/she **is** religious.

> The original thought would have been, "I am religious."

---

7. Brooks and Winbery 184; Porter 269.

τῶν λεγόντων ἑαυτοὺς Ἰουδαίους
εἶναι (Rev. 3:9)

Those claiming themselves **to be**
Jews.

The original speech would have been "We are Jews" (see also Rev. 2:9;
3:9; 10:9: λέγων αὐτῷ δοῦναί μοι).

For Practice

12.10. In the following passages, analyze the types of dependent clauses
according to the discussion above.

²⁰προσεύχεσθε δὲ ἵνα μὴ γένηται ἡ φυγὴ ὑμῶν χειμῶνος μηδὲ σαββάτῳ·
²¹ἔσται γὰρ τότε θλῖψις μεγάλη οἵα οὐ γέγονεν ἀπ' ἀρχῆς κόσμου ἕως τοῦ
νῦν οὐδ' οὐ μὴ γένηται. ²²καὶ εἰ μὴ ἐκολοβώθησαν αἱ ἡμέραι ἐκεῖναι,
οὐκ ἂν ἐσώθη πᾶσα σάρξ· διὰ δὲ τοὺς ἐκλεκτοὺς κολοβωθήσονται αἱ
ἡμέραι ἐκεῖναι. ²³τότε ἐάν τις ὑμῖν εἴπῃ· Ἰδοὺ ὧδε ὁ χριστός, ἤ· Ὧδε, μὴ
πιστεύσητε· ²⁴ἐγερθήσονται γὰρ ψευδόχριστοι καὶ ψευδοπροφῆται, καὶ
δώσουσιν σημεῖα μεγάλα καὶ τέρατα ὥστε πλανῆσαι εἰ δυνατὸν καὶ τοὺς
ἐκλεκτούς· ²⁵ἰδοὺ προείρηκα ὑμῖν. ²⁶ἐὰν οὖν εἴπωσιν ὑμῖν· Ἰδοὺ ἐν τῇ
ἐρήμῳ ἐστίν, μὴ ἐξέλθητε· Ἰδοὺ ἐν τοῖς ταμείοις, μὴ πιστεύσητε· ²⁷ὥσπερ
γὰρ ἡ ἀστραπὴ ἐξέρχεται ἀπὸ ἀνατολῶν καὶ φαίνεται ἕως δυσμῶν, οὕτως
ἔσται ἡ παρουσία τοῦ υἱοῦ τοῦ ἀνθρώπου· ²⁸ὅπου ἐὰν ᾖ τὸ πτῶμα, ἐκεῖ
συναχθήσονται οἱ ἀετοί. (Matt. 24:20–28)

⁵Καὶ ἔστιν αὕτη ἡ ἀγγελία ἣν ἀκηκόαμεν ἀπ' αὐτοῦ καὶ ἀναγγέλλομεν
ὑμῖν, ὅτι ὁ θεὸς φῶς ἐστιν καὶ σκοτία ἐν αὐτῷ οὐκ ἔστιν οὐδεμία. ⁶ἐὰν
εἴπωμεν ὅτι κοινωνίαν ἔχομεν μετ' αὐτοῦ καὶ ἐν τῷ σκότει περιπατῶμεν,
ψευδόμεθα καὶ οὐ ποιοῦμεν τὴν ἀλήθειαν· ⁷ἐὰν δὲ ἐν τῷ φωτὶ περιπατῶμεν ὡς αὐτός ἐστιν ἐν τῷ φωτί, κοινωνίαν ἔχομεν μετ' ἀλλήλων
καὶ τὸ αἷμα Ἰησοῦ τοῦ υἱοῦ αὐτοῦ καθαρίζει ἡμᾶς ἀπὸ πάσης ἁμαρτίας.
(1 John 1:5–7)

Some Major Conjunctions and Their Functions

12.11. Conjunctions, or connectors, are small, indeclinable words (function
words) that join and relate various words or groups of words to each other,
from single words to clauses and larger units of discourse. They "make explicit

implicit relations between clauses."[8] Therefore, conjunctions are one of the clearest indications of how a discourse is to be "put together" by the reader. By linking various units of discourse together, conjunctions also give it cohesion. Conjunctions are sometimes combined to form a single construction (like ἄρα οὖν) or to form a single word (e.g., τοιγαροῦν, 1 Thess. 4:8; Heb. 12:1). Greek exhibits a rather detailed system of conjunctions. To help make sense of them, we can employ two modes of classification.

First, they can be divided into those that indicate a relationship between elements of equal status (*paratactic* conjunctions) and those that indicate a relationship between a subordinate clause and the clause on which it depends (*hypotactic* conjunctions). These are sometimes referred to as coordinating and subordinating conjunctions, respectively. In the sentence "She needed to buy fruit, *but* she bought ice cream instead," the conjunction *but* joins two clauses of equal status in paratactic relationship. However, if we say, "She bought ice cream, *so that* she was not able to buy fruit," the conjunction *so that* joins a clause that is in hypotactic relationship to the first clause: the "so that" clause is subordinate to the first clause (She bought ice cream). The following common Greek conjunctions introduce paratactic (coordinating) and hypotactic (subordinating) relationships:

Paratactic: καί, δέ, οὖν, οὕτως, δίο, γάρ, ἀλλά, τέ, οὐδέ, μηδέ, ἤ, μέν

Hypotactic: ὅτι, ἵνα, ὅπως, εἰ, ἐάν, ὅτε, ὅταν, ἕως, ὡς, καθώς, ὥσπερ, ὅπου, ἀχρί

When clauses are joined together without the aid of a conjunction, it is known as *asyndeton* ("not bound together"). "Asyndeton means that the writer did not feel compelled to specify a relation."[9] There may still be a semantic relationship between the clauses, but the author has chosen not to indicate it grammatically.

Χαίρετε ἐν κυρίῳ πάντοτε· πάλιν ἐρῶ, χαίρετε. τὸ ἐπιεικὲς ὑμῶν γνωσθήτω πᾶσιν ἀνθρώποις. ὁ κύριος ἐγγύς· (Phil. 4:4, 5)	Rejoice in the Lord always; again I say, rejoice. Your gentleness should become known to all people. The Lord is near.

Notice the lack of conjunctions coordinating or subordinating.

8. Alexandra Georgakopoulou and Dionysis Goutsos, *Discourse Analysis: An Introduction*, 2nd ed. (Edinburgh: Edinburgh University Press, 2004), 91.
9. Runge, *Discourse Grammar*, 20.

Second, the conjunctions in Greek can be organized according to their adverbial and logical functions. The *adverbial* usages of the conjunctions have already been explored in the above discussion of adverbial clauses and the conjunctions that introduce them: temporal, locative, causal, purpose, result, comparative, and content. Conjunctions can also perform a number of *logical* tasks. The following list includes the most common conjunctions involved in these functions, but is not exhaustive (Wallace 761).

1. Continuative: καί, δέ (and, also)
2. Explanatory: γάρ, καί (for, namely)
3. Adversative: δέ, ἀλλά, πλήν, εἰ μή, μενοῦν (but, however, rather)
4. Summarizing: οὖν, οὕτως (thus, in conclusion)
5. Alternation: ἤ (or)
6. Correlation: μὲν . . . δέ (on the one hand . . . on the other hand), καὶ . . . καί and καὶ . . . τε (both . . . and)
7. Inferential: οὖν, ἄρα, δίο, οὕτως (therefore)

While this list enumerates the clause types in which these conjunctions commonly occur, these labels probably reflect more the necessity of translating the conjunctions into English in their contexts. But we should not analyze the meaning of conjunctions based on the best way to *translate* them. Another complicating factor is that several conjunctions appear in more than one category (e.g., καί, δέ, οὖν). This raises a number of questions: What are the meanings of the conjunctions themselves? What is the difference between them if some can signal the same logical relationship? How should the reader understand the types of clauses they introduce?

The goal of this section is not to exhaustively discuss or classify all the conjunctions; instead, it will treat several of the more common, major conjunctions found in the NT. You have already been introduced to some conjunctions in the above explanations of the various secondary adverbial clauses and of conditional clauses in the previous chapter. We will consider five additional conjunctions that introduce a paratactic relationship: καί, δέ, ἀλλά, οὖν, γάρ, and μὲν . . . δέ. These have been selected due to their frequency and/or the significant roles that they can play in exegesis.

Καί

12.12. This conjunction is treated first because, along with δέ, it is the most commonly used conjunction in the NT, occurring over 8,000 times. Καί is used to connect just about any grammatical unit, such as words, phrases, clauses, and paragraphs. It can occur at the very beginning of a sentence or somewhere within it. Despite its frequency, καί has proved difficult to classify precisely because it is used in such a wide variety of ways. Wallace (761) classifies καί as ascensive ("also, even"), connective ("and, also"), contrastive ("but"), correlative ("both . . . and"), and explanatory ("that is, namely"). Young (188–89) lists fourteen different "meanings" of καί![10] Furthermore, the usage of καί apparently overlaps with other conjunctions: δέ, ἀλλά, and γάρ. The diversity in the use of καί, along with its apparent overlap with other conjunctions, raises the question of its basic meaning. We suggest that such notions as contrast, concession, purpose, and the like are conveyed by the contexts in which καί occurs rather than belonging to the meaning of καί itself. For example, just because we can *translate* καί as "but" in some contexts does not necessitate the creation of the *semantic* category "adversative καί."

It is more useful to understand the meaning of καί in terms of what it says about the relationship between the clauses it connects. Καί functions to add or associate clauses, connecting them closely together. "When καί introduces a new sentence or paragraph it indicates a close thematic relation to the preceding sentence or paragraph."[11] It could be seen as the "default" conjunction used when the author simply wants to link words or clauses together. There may be a semantic relationship between the clauses, such as contrast, purpose, concession, explanation, and the like. But this belongs to the context, not to the meaning of καί. What καί does is tell us that the author wants to associate clauses closely together.

Καὶ εὐθὺς ἠνάγκασεν τοὺς μαθητὰς αὐτοῦ ἐμβῆναι εἰς τὸ πλοῖον (Mark 6:45)	**And** immediately he compelled his disciples to get into the boat.
Ἐγὼ ἤμην ἐν πόλει Ἰόππῃ προσευχόμενος **καὶ** εἶδον ἐν ἐκστάσει ὅραμα (Acts 11:5)	I was in the city, Joppa, praying, **and** in a trance I saw a vision.
ἐρρύσατο ἡμᾶς ἐκ τῆς ἐξουσίας τοῦ σκότους **καὶ** μετέστησεν εἰς τὴν βασιλείαν τοῦ υἱοῦ τῆς ἀγάπης αὐτοῦ (Col. 1:13)	He rescued us from the authority of darkness **and** transferred [us] into the kingdom of his beloved Son.

10. They are addition (which includes ascensive and adjunctive), emphasis, reason, contrast, purpose, condition, consequence, concession, time, relative, conclusion, and comparison.

11. Martin M. Culy, *I, II, III John: A Handbook on the Greek Text* (Waco: Baylor University Press, 2004), 5.

Καὶ ἐπέστρεψα βλέπειν τὴν
φωνὴν ἥτις ἐλάλει μετ' ἐμοῦ· **καὶ**
ἐπιστρέψας εἶδον ἑπτὰ λυχνίας
χρυσᾶς (Rev. 1:12)

And I turned to see the voice that
was speaking with me; **and** having turned I saw seven golden
lampstands.

The conjunction καί can also be used adverbially, in which case it is emphatic.
This is often called the *ascensive* use of καί and can be translated "also,"
"even," or "indeed." It calls special attention to what follows it. The key to
identifying this usage is to notice its position. It usually occurs in postposi-
tion (i.e., it is not the first word of the clause) when it functions adverbially.[12]

οὐ περὶ τῶν ἡμετέρων δὲ μόνον
ἀλλὰ **καὶ** περὶ ὅλου τοῦ κόσμου.
(1 John 2:2)

And not concerning ours only,
but **also** concerning the entire
world's.

Ἐγένοντο δὲ **καὶ** ψευδοπροφῆται
ἐν τῷ λαῷ (2 Pet. 2:1)

And false prophets **also** came
about among the people.

Δέ

12.13. The postpositive conjunction δέ occurs just under 3,000 times in the
NT and is frequently considered to have significant overlap with καί. Therefore, it is classed both as a continuative conjunction ("and") and as a contrastive one ("but"; Dana and Mantey 244). Wallace (761) treats it as ascensive
("even"), connective, explanatory, and transitional.[13] Dana and Mantey (244)
add "emphatic" ("indeed"). Again, while these may be appropriate ways to
translate δέ in different contexts, they do not determine its actual meaning.
In contrast to καί, which links clauses and paragraphs in close relationship,[14]
δέ seems to "represent *a new step or development in the author's story or
argument.*"[15] That is, the clause introduced by δέ "represents the writer's
choice to explicitly signal that what follows is a new, distinct development in
the story or argument, based on how the writer conceived of it."[16] While καί

12. Kermit Titrud, "The Function of καί in the Greek New Testament and an Application
to 2 Peter," in *Linguistics and New Testament Interpretation: Essays on Discourse Analysis*,
ed. David Alan Black et al. (Nashville: Broadman, 1992), 245.
13. See also Young (183–84), who treats it under the categories of contrast, addition, transition, explanation, emphasis.
14. Titrud, "The Function of καί," 250.
15. Stephen H. Levinsohn, *Discourse Features of New Testament Greek: A Coursebook*,
2nd ed. (Dallas: Summer Institute of Linguistics, 2000), 72, italics original.
16. Runge, *Discourse Grammar*, 31.

indicates continuity, δέ signals discontinuity. This explains its common use in adversative contexts: that it indicates a new or distinct development lends itself to signaling contrast. In its various contexts δέ should be understood as signaling a new step or development in an argument (e.g., a new topic, character, or focus).

ἦν δὲ ἐκεῖ πρὸς τῷ ὄρει ἀγέλη χοίρων μεγάλη (Mark 5:11)	**And** there was there on the mountain a large herd of pigs.

> Δὲ indicates that the subject has changed from an unclean spirit (Legion) to "pigs."

τὸ δοκίμιον ὑμῶν τῆς πίστεως κατεργάζεται ὑπομονήν· ἡ δὲ ὑπομονὴ ἔργον τέλειον ἐχέτω.... Εἰ δέ τις ὑμῶν λείπεται σοφίας, αἰτείτω παρὰ ... θεοῦ· ... αἰτείτω δὲ ἐν πίστει (James 1:3–6)	The testing of your faith produces endurance; **and** endurance should have its perfect work. . . . **And** if anyone of you lacks wisdom, he/she should ask God. . . . **But** he/she should ask in faith.

> Δὲ indicates each new step or development in James's chain of argument.

ἡ δὲ κεφαλὴ αὐτοῦ καὶ αἱ τρίχες λευκαὶ ὡς ἔριον λευκόν (Rev. 1:14)	**And** his head and hair were white as white wool.

> The δέ shifts the focus of attention to a particular aspect of the vision of Christ, his head.

Ἀλλά

12.14. According to Dana and Mantey (240), ἀλλά "is a strong adversative conjunction" but is also "clearly emphatic in several passages" (with the sense of "certainly, in fact"; cf. Porter 205). But other conjunctions can also be used in clauses that indicate contrast (δέ, πλήν). So what is the contribution of ἀλλά to specifying the relationships between the clauses it connects? The conjunction ἀλλά can be seen to provide a correction to the preceding clause or section with which it stands in contrast. "The constraint that it brings to bear is 'correction' of some aspect in the preceding context."[17]

---

17. Ibid., 56.

οὐκ ἦλθον καταλῦσαι . . . ἀλλὰ πληρῶσαι· (Matt. 5:17)	I have not come to abolish [the Law or the Prophets] **but** to fulfill [them].
οὐκέτι ἐστὲ ξένοι καὶ πάροικοι, ἀλλὰ ἐστὲ συμπολῖται τῶν ἁγίων (Eph. 2:19)	You are no longer strangers and aliens, **but** you are fellow citizens of/with the saints.
οὐδείς μοι παρεγένετο, ἀλλὰ πάντες με ἐγκατέλιπον (2 Tim. 4:16)	No one has stood by me, **but** all have abandoned me.

At times ἀλλά can be translated with an emphatic nuance: "indeed, certainly" (Dana and Mantey 240–41).

οἱ δὲ πρὸς αὐτόν· Ἀλλ᾽ οὐδ᾽ εἰ πνεῦμα ἅγιον ἔστιν ἠκούσαμεν. (Acts 19:2)	And they said to him, "**Indeed** we have not heard that there is a Holy Spirit."
ἀλλὰ ἀπολογίαν, ἀλλὰ ἀγανάκτησιν, ἀλλὰ φόβον, ἀλλὰ ἐπιπόθησιν, ἀλλὰ ζῆλον, ἀλλὰ ἐκδίκησιν· (2 Cor. 7:11)	**Indeed** defense, **indeed** indignation, **indeed** fear, **indeed** longing, **indeed** zeal, **indeed** vengeance.

Οὖν

12.15. Οὖν is an important postpositive conjunction in the Greek NT. According to Porter (214), its "inferential sense is predominant." It draws a conclusion or inference from what precedes. Other possible senses have been suggested: it can be transitional, responsive, emphatic, and even contrastive (Dana and Mantey 253–56). But as with other conjunctions, this wide diversity of "senses" probably belongs to the context and not the meaning of οὖν. Itself, οὖν indicates a further development that draws an inference or conclusion from what comes before it. It continues the main line of argument or narrative. Sometimes it signals a resumption when the main line of discourse has been interrupted, usually by supporting or explanatory material (sometimes introduced by γάρ).[18] Thus it can pick up a main thread of thought that was interrupted.

18. Levinsohn, *Discourse Features*, 126; BDF §451: "After parenthetical remarks οὖν indicates a return to the main theme (resumptive)."

ἀσφαλῶς **οὖν** γινωσκέτω πᾶς
οἶκος Ἰσραὴλ (Acts 2:36)

Therefore, all the house of Israel
should know beyond a doubt.

Οὖν draws a conclusion from Peter's previous speech.

Παρακαλῶ **οὖν** ὑμᾶς ἐγώ (Eph. 4:1)

Therefore, I exhort you.

Ἔχοντες **οὖν**, ἀδελφοί, παρρησίαν
εἰς τὴν εἴσοδον τῶν ἁγίων ἐν τῷ
αἵματι Ἰησοῦ (Heb. 10:19)

Therefore, brothers and sisters,
having confidence of access to the
sanctuary by the blood of Jesus.

This use of οὖν resumes the call to the readers to take advantage of
their access to heaven in 4:14–16 after a long intervening argument for
Christ's superior priesthood in 7:1–10:18.

Γάρ

12.16. The postpositive conjunction γάρ is often viewed as a causal conjunction. Robertson (1190) says that its primary sense is "explanatory." Porter
(207) also mentions an inferential sense. And Dana and Mantey (243) think
that it can be used emphatically and suggest the translations "really, certainly,
indeed." A more comprehensive understanding is that it serves "to strengthen
some aspect of a previous assertion."[19] Therefore, γάρ does not advance the
main line of the discourse or move it forward. Instead, it "introduces explanatory material that strengthens or supports what precedes."[20] Material
introduced by γάρ can support by way of explanation, reason or cause, inference, or clarification.

Μετανοεῖτε, ἤγγικεν **γὰρ** ἡ
βασιλεία τῶν οὐρανῶν. (Matt. 3:2)

Repent, **for** the kingdom of
heaven is near.

Ἀδὰμ **γὰρ** πρῶτος ἐπλάσθη, εἶτα
Εὕα· (1 Tim. 2:13)

For Adam was created first, then
Eve.

The precise nature of the connection is disputed. Is it causal, explanatory,
or illustrative?

Ἀδύνατον **γὰρ** . . . πάλιν ἀνακαινίζειν εἰς μετάνοιαν (Heb. 6:4–6)

For it is impossible . . . to renew
again to repentance.

19. Levinsohn, *Discourse Features*, 91.
20. Runge, *Discourse Grammar*, 54.

Μὲν . . . δέ

12.17. The postpositive particle μέν introduces a clause that is often (but not always) followed by another clause introduced by δέ. The conjunctions stand in a correlative relationship and are often translated "on the one hand . . . on the other." More specifically, the μέν anticipates and points forward to the clause introduced by δέ. In other words, "the particle μέν . . . is anticipatory in nature, creating the expectation that another related point will follow."[21] The "related point," then, is often introduced by δέ (less frequently by τε or καί). Therefore, one should read the construction this way: μέν (anticipates an important, corollary point coming up) . . . δέ (here is the related, corollary point). The two units often stand in contrast to one another. The information introduced by δέ is more prominent than that introduced by μέν, since it is anticipated by the latter.

τὸ **μὲν** πνεῦμα πρόθυμον ἡ **δὲ** σὰρξ ἀσθενής. (Mark 14:38)	**On the one hand** the spirit is willing, **but on the other hand** the flesh is weak.
ἅτινά ἐστιν λόγον **μὲν** ἔχοντα σοφίας ἐν ἐθελοθρησκίᾳ καὶ ταπεινοφροσύνῃ καὶ ἀφειδίᾳ σώματος, οὐκ ἐν τιμῇ τινι πρὸς πλησμονὴν τῆς σαρκός. (Col. 2:23)	Which **on one hand** have the appearance of wisdom in false worship and humility and severe treatment of the body, [but] not in any value against the indulgence of the flesh. (*with no following δέ*)

The syntax of this verse is difficult. For a reading similar to the one proposed here, see the NRSV, NIV, ESV. Although there is no following δέ, the clause introduced by μέν still seems to anticipate the clause "not in any value against the indulgence of the flesh."

ὑπὸ ἀνθρώπων **μὲν** ἀποδεδοκι- μασμένον παρὰ **δὲ** θεῷ ἐκλεκτὸν ἔντιμον (1 Pet. 2:4)	**On the one hand** rejected by people, **but on the other hand** chosen and valuable before God.

---

21. Ibid., 74.

Some Additional Common Conjunctions and Particles

12.18. The following section is meant to briefly summarize and illustrate a handful of other common particles and conjunctions in the NT. A couple of entries are not technically conjunctions or particles but seem to function as such in the NT.

Ἄν

12.19. This particle adds an element of uncertainty, contingency, or indefiniteness to the word or clause within which it occurs. It can be used with other words (e.g., a relative pronoun) or as part of a clause (e.g., the apodosis of a class 2 condition). It usually occurs with a verb in the subjunctive mood.

ὃς δ' ἂν εἴπῃ κατὰ τοῦ πνεύματος τοῦ ἁγίου, οὐκ ἀφεθήσεται αὐτῷ (Matt. 12:32)	But who**ever** speaks against the Holy Spirit, he/she will not be forgiven.

See also 1 Cor. 4:5 (ἕως ἂν ἔλθῃ), where ἄν is used with a temporal particle (ἕως) to mean "until whenever he comes."

Ἄρα

12.20. This is an inferential particle that is often combined with οὖν, perhaps to indicate a more emphatic conclusion or inference.[22]

ἄρα οὖν, ἀδελφοί, στήκετε (2 Thess. 2:15)	**Therefore**, brothers and sisters, stand firm.

See also Matt. 7:20, ἄρα γε.

Γε

12.21. This postpositive particle lends emphasis to the word or phrase with which it occurs and is often translated "indeed," "even," "at least," "in fact" (Young 199). According to Robertson, it serves "to bring into prominence the particular word with which it occurs" (1147). It often occurs in combination with other conjunctions or particles such as ἀλλά, ἄρα, εἰ, and καί.

---

22. Margaret E. Thrall, *Greek Particles in the New Testament*, New Testament Tools and Studies 3 (Grand Rapids: Eerdmans, 1962), 10.

καί γε οὐ μακρὰν ἀπὸ ἑνὸς   And **indeed**, he is not far away
ἑκάστου ἡμῶν ὑπάρχοντα.   from each one of us.
(Acts 17:27)

See also Col. 1:23.

Διό

12.22. This inferential conjunction introduces a conclusion and is perhaps slightly stronger than οὖν.

Διό, πολλὴν ἐν Χριστῷ παρρησίαν   **Therefore**, having much confi-
ἔχων (Philem. 8)   dence in Christ.

See also Luke 1:35.

Ἰδού, Ἴδε

12.23. These are markers of attention or prominence, drawing attention to something that follows. Their use is common in narrative and in John's Apocalypse.

καὶ εἶδον, καὶ **ἰδοὺ** ἵππος λευκός   And I saw, and **look**, a white
(Rev. 6:2)   horse.

See also Matt. 9:2.

Τότε

12.24. This important adverb can be employed as a connector in narrative, appearing especially in the Gospel of Matthew.[23] It also highlights sequential events in narrative. According to Levinsohn, it can be used at subsections or in the concluding events of a story.[24]

τότε λέγει αὐτῷ ὁ Ἰησοῦς. . . . τότε   **Then** Jesus said to him. . . . **Then**
ἀφίησιν αὐτὸν ὁ διάβολος (Matt.   the devil left him.
4:10–11)

See also Matt. 24:30.

---

23. Levinsohn, *Discourse Features*, 95. See BDF §459(2).
24. Levinsohn, *Discourse Features*, 95.

For Practice

12.25. Analyze the conjunctions and particles in the following two texts in light of our discussion above. Pay careful attention to what they say about the way the discourse develops and how the clauses are related to each other. Can you explain the alternation between καί and δέ in these verses? Also, what is the function of τότε in Matt. 2:7?

¹ἰδοὺ μάγοι ἀπὸ ἀνατολῶν παρεγένοντο εἰς Ἱεροσόλυμα ²λέγοντες· Ποῦ ἐστιν ὁ τεχθεὶς βασιλεὺς τῶν Ἰουδαίων; εἴδομεν γὰρ αὐτοῦ τὸν ἀστέρα ἐν τῇ ἀνατολῇ καὶ ἤλθομεν προσκυνῆσαι αὐτῷ. ³ἀκούσας δὲ ὁ βασιλεὺς Ἡρῴδης ἐταράχθη καὶ πᾶσα Ἱεροσόλυμα μετ᾽ αὐτοῦ, ⁴καὶ συναγαγὼν πάντας τοὺς ἀρχιερεῖς καὶ γραμματεῖς τοῦ λαοῦ ἐπυνθάνετο παρ᾽ αὐτῶν ποῦ ὁ χριστὸς γεννᾶται. ⁵οἱ δὲ εἶπαν αὐτῷ· Ἐν Βηθλέεμ τῆς Ἰουδαίας· οὕτως γὰρ γέγραπται διὰ τοῦ προφήτου· ⁶Καὶ σύ, Βηθλέεμ γῆ Ἰούδα, οὐδαμῶς ἐλαχίστη εἶ ἐν τοῖς ἡγεμόσιν Ἰούδα· ἐκ σοῦ γὰρ ἐξελεύσεται ἡγούμενος, ὅστις ποιμανεῖ τὸν λαόν μου τὸν Ἰσραήλ. ⁷Τότε Ἡρῴδης λάθρᾳ καλέσας τοὺς μάγους ἠκρίβωσεν παρ᾽ αὐτῶν τὸν χρόνον τοῦ φαινομένου ἀστέρος, ⁸καὶ πέμψας αὐτοὺς εἰς Βηθλέεμ εἶπεν· Πορευθέντες ἐξετάσατε ἀκριβῶς περὶ τοῦ παιδίου· ἐπὰν δὲ εὕρητε, ἀπαγγείλατέ μοι, ὅπως κἀγὼ ἐλθὼν προσκυνήσω αὐτῷ. ⁹οἱ δὲ ἀκούσαντες τοῦ βασιλέως ἐπορεύθησαν, καὶ ἰδοὺ ὁ ἀστὴρ ὃν εἶδον ἐν τῇ ἀνατολῇ προῆγεν αὐτούς, ἕως ἐλθὼν ἐστάθη ἐπάνω οὗ ἦν τὸ παιδίον. ¹⁰ἰδόντες δὲ τὸν ἀστέρα ἐχάρησαν χαρὰν μεγάλην σφόδρα. (Matt. 2:1–10)

⁴Διαιρέσεις δὲ χαρισμάτων εἰσίν, τὸ δὲ αὐτὸ πνεῦμα· ⁵καὶ διαιρέσεις διακονιῶν εἰσιν, καὶ ὁ αὐτὸς κύριος· ⁶καὶ διαιρέσεις ἐνεργημάτων εἰσίν, ὁ δὲ αὐτὸς θεός, ὁ ἐνεργῶν τὰ πάντα ἐν πᾶσιν. ⁷ἑκάστῳ δὲ δίδοται ἡ φανέρωσις τοῦ πνεύματος πρὸς τὸ συμφέρον. ⁸ᾧ μὲν γὰρ διὰ τοῦ πνεύματος δίδοται λόγος σοφίας, ἄλλῳ δὲ λόγος γνώσεως κατὰ τὸ αὐτὸ πνεῦμα, ⁹ἑτέρῳ πίστις ἐν τῷ αὐτῷ πνεύματι, ἄλλῳ χαρίσματα ἰαμάτων ἐν τῷ ἑνὶ πνεύματι, ¹⁰ἄλλῳ ἐνεργήματα δυνάμεων, ἄλλῳ προφητεία, ἄλλῳ διακρίσεις πνευμάτων, ἑτέρῳ γένη γλωσσῶν, ἄλλῳ ἑρμηνεία γλωσσῶν· ¹¹πάντα δὲ ταῦτα ἐνεργεῖ τὸ ἓν καὶ τὸ αὐτὸ πνεῦμα, διαιροῦν ἰδίᾳ ἑκάστῳ καθὼς βούλεται. ¹²Καθάπερ γὰρ τὸ σῶμα ἕν ἐστιν καὶ μέλη πολλὰ ἔχει, πάντα δὲ τὰ μέλη τοῦ σώματος πολλὰ ὄντα ἕν ἐστιν σῶμα, οὕτως καὶ ὁ Χριστός· ¹³καὶ γὰρ ἐν ἑνὶ πνεύματι ἡμεῖς πάντες εἰς ἓν σῶμα ἐβαπτίσθημεν. .... (1 Cor. 12:4–13)

13

DISCOURSE CONSIDERATIONS

13.1. It has become increasingly common for Greek grammars to include a section on discourse analysis.[1] Discourse analysis, or text-linguistics, is a burgeoning area of interest in biblical studies, though NT scholarship has tended to lag behind OT scholarship in this area.[2] There is not "one method" of discourse analysis, and it is not the purpose of this section to provide a full-blown discussion of it or a method for its use. Rather, this chapter will attempt merely to be suggestive and to demonstrate and illustrate how Greek grammar can be used in analyzing discourse. Much of the discussion in the previous chapters has tried to keep discourse considerations in mind. Therefore, some of the material that follows will synthesize material from previous chapters.

1. Porter 298–307; Young 247–66; Gary A. Long, *Grammatical Concepts 101 for Biblical Greek* (Peabody, MA: Hendrickson, 2006), 211–23; David Alan Black, *Linguistics for Students of New Testament Greek*, 2nd ed. (Grand Rapids: Baker, 1995), 170–98. For an attempt to address grammar more extensively in light of discourse analysis, see Steven E. Runge, *Discourse Grammar of the Greek New Testament: A Practical Introduction for Teaching and Exegesis* (Peabody, MA: Hendrickson, 2010). This trend is in response to the call of Stanley E. Porter and Jeffrey T. Reed, "Greek Grammar since BDF: A Retrospective and Prospective Analysis," *Filologia Neotestamentaria* 4 (1991): 143–64.

2. Stanley E. Porter and D. A. Carson, eds., *Discourse Analysis and Other Topics in Biblical Greek*, JSNTSup 113 (Sheffield: Sheffield Academic, 1995); Stanley E. Porter and Jeffrey T. Reed, *Discourse Analysis and the New Testament: Approaches and Results*, JSNTSup 170 (Sheffield: Sheffield Academic, 1999); Stanley E. Porter, *Linguistic Analysis of the Greek New Testament: Studies in Tools, Methods, and Practice* (Grand Rapids: Baker Academic, 2015), 88–92, 133–43.

Discourse analysis is nothing less than the recognition that texts are the record of an act of communication in a given context.[3] Discourse "refers to texts (meaningful combinations of language units) which serve various communicative purposes and perform various acts in situational, social, and cultural contexts."[4] One of the main tenets of discourse analysis is that language should be examined beyond the level of just the sentence or clause.[5] Traditionally, most grammatical analysis of the NT has taken place at the level of the word, phrase, and sentence, but discourse analysis ranges beyond this to observe larger stretches of text, extending to an entire NT book. Words make up phrases, and phrases make up clauses. Clauses make up paragraphs, and paragraphs compose entire discourses. This requires that our analysis move beyond the sentence level to larger units. Grammar plays an important role in indicating how the discourse is structured, how it coheres, how information is presented, and the role that various actors or participants play in the text. A discourse approach to grammar supplements more traditional approaches rather than replacing them. It simply asks what discourse task is performed by various grammatical constructions.

The goal of this section is to introduce the student to several important features of discourse analysis and, in the process, to encourage the Greek student to move away from playing "pin the label on the grammatical construction" to actually analyzing Greek grammar. We urge students to pay more attention to how grammar functions in relationship to other features in discourse, how it functions over longer stretches of discourse, and to consider important patterns of usage. The remainder of this chapter examines just four important features of discourse analysis, looking at how they contribute to grammatical analysis and how grammar performs discourse level tasks. These four features have been chosen because they commonly figure in discourse studies of the NT. The following sections synthesize information from a number of works on discourse analysis.

Cohesion

13.2. Most discourses, at some level, are meant to be coherent. We assume that the NT authors were trying to make sense and communicate something

---

3. Gillian Brown and George Yule, *Discourse Analysis*, Cambridge Textbooks in Linguistics (Cambridge: Cambridge University Press, 1983), 1–26.
4. Alexandra Georgakopoulou and Dionysis Goutsos, *Discourse Analysis: An Introduction*, 2nd ed. (Edinburgh: Edinburgh University Press, 2004), 27.
5. Jeffrey T. Reed, "Discourse Analysis," in *A Handbook to the Exegesis of the New Testament*, ed. Stanley E. Porter (Leiden: Brill, 2002), 190–91; Porter 298.

to readers and that the various units that make up their discourses are meant to be related in some way (in other words, discourses are understandable, as opposed to being a string of unrelated, jumbled statements that make no sense).[6] *Cohesion* refers to the linguistic elements that an author uses to weave a discourse together. Cohesion links something in the text to something that has come before it. These linguistic elements provide signals for readers, showing how the discourse has been constructed and how readers should put it together. According to Young, "cohesion is the glue that holds a discourse together" (254). Various means are used in the NT to provide cohesion.

Organic Ties

13.3. One of the clearest means of creating cohesion is through what can be called *organic ties*. This refers simply to the system of conjunctions and connectors in a language that establish various kinds of relationships.[7] Conjunctions make up the logical system of the Greek language (see chap. 12, on dependent clauses).[8] They are important clues as to how a particular discourse is organized. For example, notice the following: "First, you pour all the ingredients into a large bowl. Then you stir them together until well mixed. Then you pour the entire mixture over the cake. After that, you place the cake and mixture in the oven." The connectors "first," "then," and "after that" serve to create cohesion by indicating a sequence.

13.4. Mark 6:1–29. In this section of Mark, cohesion is provided largely through the repetition of καί, which introduces main clauses and links them together. In verses 14–20 the conjunctions δέ and γάρ predominate, providing further developmental material and explanation. The author then returns to καί to introduce and link clauses but uses his well-known καὶ εὐθύς in verse 27 to draw attention to the main turning point in the story, the beheading of John the Baptist (Porter 305).

13.5. Colossians. The various units of Col. 2:6–4:1 are linked with the inferential conjunction οὖν (2:6, 16; 3:1, 5, 12), which gives cohesion to this section. The conjunction οὖν also establishes boundaries in the discourse.

13.6. Hebrews 10:19–30. The author begins with οὖν, which draws an inference from the preceding argument (5:1–10:18). Within 10:19–25 clauses are linked together by καί, with γάρ providing supporting material for one of the exhortations in verse 23. Verses 26–30 are linked to verses 19–25 with

---

6. Georgakopoulous and Goutsos, *Discourse Analysis*, 56.
7. Ibid., 91.
8. Reed, "Discourse Analysis," 205.

γάρ, which suggests that this section provides supporting material giving a reason for the exhortations in verses 19–25.[9]

Cohesive Ties

13.7. Another way of creating cohesion is through what are known as *cohesive ties.*[10] These refer to the words an author uses to form relationships between different words in the discourse. A "chain of reference" can be built up in a discourse by words that refer to the same person or entity.

13.8. Repetition. The repetition of the same lexical item can create cohesion in discourse. This is a common cohesive device. The repetition of the lexical items σάρξ and πνεῦμα throughout Rom. 8:1–30 creates cohesion in that section.

13.9. Pronouns (reference). Cohesion can be created through pronouns that refer to something mentioned in the discourse. In the sentence "**Jim** purchased the **bike** in the store; then **he** decided to ride **it** home," the pronoun "it" refers back to the noun "bike" so that "it" cannot be understood apart from its referent, "bike." The personal pronoun "he" refers back to "Jim." In Col. 2:8–13 cohesion is created by a series of personal and relative pronouns that refer back to Christ in verses 9 and 11: Χριστόν (v. 8) . . . ἐν αὐτῷ (v. 9) . . . ἐν αὐτῷ . . . ὅς ἐστιν (v. 10) . . . ἐν ᾧ . . . τοῦ Χριστοῦ (v. 11) . . . αὐτῷ . . . ἐν ᾧ . . . αὐτὸν (v. 12) . . . σὺν αὐτῷ (v. 13). A similar series of pronouns appears in Eph. 2:20–22.

13.10. Substitution. This occurs when one noun substitutes for another while still referring to the same person or entity. So when we say, "**Jesus** then addressed the crowd. . . . When the **Lord** had finished saying these things . . . ," the word *Jesus* is replaced by *Lord*. Or when we say, "The man across the street bought a **bike**. His wife bought **one** too," the word *one* is substituted for the word *bike*. By substituting one word with another, sentences can be linked together to form cohesion.

---

9. Cynthia Long Westfall, *A Discourse Analysis of the Letter to the Hebrews: The Relationship between Form and Meaning*, Library of New Testament Studies 297 (London: T&T Clark, 2005), 244–45.

10. Robert A. Dooley and Stephen H. Levinsohn, *Analyzing Discourse: A Manual of Basic Concepts* (Dallas: Summer Institute of Linguistics, 2001), 27.

Εἶπεν δέ· Ἄνθρωπός τις εἶχεν
δύο υἱούς. καὶ εἶπεν ὁ νεώτερος
αὐτῶν τῷ πατρί· Πάτερ, δός μοι
τὸ ἐπιβάλλον μέρος τῆς οὐσίας· ὁ
δὲ διεῖλεν αὐτοῖς τὸν βίον. (Luke
15:11–12)

And he said, "**A certain man** had
two sons. And the younger of
them said to **the father**, 'Father,
give me the share of the property that belongs to me.' And he
divided his belongings between
them."

The word τῷ πατρί (father) substitutes for the designation ἄνθρωπός
τις (a certain man) at the beginning of the parable.

13.11. Ellipsis. A further important cohesive device is ellipsis. This occurs
when the repetition of a word, group of words, or clause can be left out
because it is understood to be carried over from a previous clause. To give
another English example, if a person answers "Five" to the question "How
many deer did you see?" the answer has elided, or left unexpressed, the words
"I saw _____ deer." These words are assumed from the question "How
many deer did you see?"

οὐ μόνον δέ,[a] ἀλλὰ καὶ καυχώμεθα
ἐν ταῖς θλίψεσιν, εἰδότες ὅτι ἡ
θλῖψις ὑπομονὴν κατεργάζεται, ἡ
δὲ ὑπομονὴ δοκιμήν, ἡ δὲ δοκιμὴ
ἐλπίδα. (Rom. 5:3–4)

And not only [do we boast in the
hope in God's glory], but we also
boast in tribulations, knowing
that tribulation produces endurance, and endurance [produces]
proven character, and proven
character [produces] hope.

[a] Some ancient manuscripts insert τοῦτο here.

The elements that have been left out and understood as carried over
from the preceding context are placed in brackets at the appropriate
place in the English translation.

Repetition of Grammatical Elements

13.12. Cohesion can also be indicated by the repetition of various grammatical forms, such as verbal aspect, mood, or other grammatical features
such as an anaphoric article.

13.13. Ephesians 4:25–6:20. Cohesion in this section is indicated by both
tense-form and mood: a series of present-tense imperatives.

13.14. Revelation 5. This chapter introduces two new elements into John's
visionary narrative: the scroll and the Lamb. Both are referred to the first

time without an article (i.e., they are anarthrous): βιβλίον (v. 1); ἀρνίον (v. 6). Subsequent mentions of the scroll (vv. 2, 3, 4, 5, 8, 9) and the Lamb (vv. 12, 13) have the article (i.e., they are arthrous), which functions anaphorically (see chap. 4, on the article) to refer back to their first mention in verse 1 and verse 6, creating cohesion in this section.

Boundaries and Units

13.15. The term *boundaries* refers to the means by which language indicates where one unit begins and another one ends. That is, "there should be a point at which the shift from one topic to the next is marked."[11] In written English, boundaries are usually indicated by the indentation that begins a new paragraph (although this can sometimes just be for eye appeal, since reading an entire page without a paragraph break is difficult),[12] by the use of paragraph headings, or even by chapter titles. For Koine Greek, in the absence of punctuation, indentation, or paragraph headings in the original manuscripts, we must rely on other means to determine boundaries and units within a discourse.[13]

Boundaries are often signaled by a shift in such things as person, mood, number, or verbal aspect. Vocatives (e.g., ἀδελφοί) and conjunctions (e.g., δέ, οὖν, διὰ τοῦτο) also indicate boundaries in discourse, introducing new sections. In narrative, a change in time or place, a new cast of characters, or new roles for existing characters can indicate a shift to a new unit.[14] A *unit*, or "grouping," may be created by the clustering of patterns of repeated grammatical or lexical items.[15] Units or groupings are ways an author organizes the material into manageable pieces. According to Dooley and Levinsohn, "humans typically process large amounts of information in CHUNKS, somewhat like we eat a meal in bites."[16] Again, grouping can be achieved through the repetition of such features as verbal aspect, mood, person, and lexical items.

11. Brown and Yule, *Discourse Analysis*, 95.
12. Ibid.
13. The paragraph divisions in your Greek NT (the most common editions are the NA[28], UBS[5], and SBLGNT) are the decisions of the editorial committee. While they are often helpful, they are not always accurate or based on clear linguistic criteria. Therefore, they should be regarded as only suggestions.
14. Levinsohn, *Discourse Features*, 278–79.
15. Westfall, *Discourse Analysis*, 37.
16. Dooley and Levinsohn, *Analyzing Discourse*, 36.

Καὶ ὅτε ἐγγίζουσιν εἰς Ἱεροσόλυμα εἰς Βηθφαγὴ καὶ Βηθανίαν πρὸς τὸ Ὄρος τῶν Ἐλαιῶν, ἀποστέλλει δύο τῶν μαθητῶν αὐτοῦ καὶ λέγει αὐτοῖς· Ὑπάγετε εἰς τὴν κώμην τὴν κατέναντι ὑμῶν (Mark 11:1–2)

And when they drew near to Jerusalem in Bethpage and Bethany near the Mount of Olives, he sent two of his disciples and said to them, "Go into the village that is ahead of you."

> These verses begin a new unit where the author shifts from aorist tense-forms and an imperfect form in the previous verses (10:48–52). The author introduces the unit with the use of narrative present tense-forms (ἐγγίζουσιν, ἀποστέλλει, λέγει) in verses 1–2, and also a shift to a different location (v. 1).

Romans 5:12–21 is marked off from the previous section (5:1–11) and the following one (6:1–11) by the διὰ τοῦτο that begins 5:12 and by the οὖν and shift to rhetorical questions that begin the next unit (6:1). That 5:12–21 constitutes a unit is also indicated by tense/aspect and person. Aorist tense-forms dominate in 5:12–21. Also, the entire unit is marked by the predominance of the third person. This stands in contrast to the previous unit (5:1–11), which is marked by first-person plural forms and contains a number of perfect and present tense-forms. The following unit (6:1–11) returns to first-person plural forms (ἐροῦμεν, ἐπιμένωμεν, ἀπεθάνομεν, ζήσομεν, πιστεύομεν) and present and perfect forms (ἐπιμένωμεν, ἀγνοεῖτε, γεγόναμεν, δεδικαίωται, πιστεύομεν, ἀποθνῄσκει, κυριεύει, λογίζεσθε in the midst of aorists). The first person plural and the present and perfect tenses also highlight 5:1–11 and 6:1–11 as the more prominent sections.

Ἀγαπητοί, μὴ παντὶ πνεύματι πιστεύετε, ἀλλὰ δοκιμάζετε τὰ πνεύματα εἰ ἐκ τοῦ θεοῦ ἐστιν (1 John 4:1)

Beloved, do not believe every spirit, but test the spirits [to see] if they are from God.

> Along with the switch to the imperative, the vocative ἀγαπητοί serves as a discourse boundary to mark off a new paragraph (4:1–6). The vocative ἀγαπητοί with the hortatory subjunctive in 4:7 serves as another boundary marker. Throughout 1 John the vocative often functions in this way.[17]

---

17. Robert E. Longacre, "Towards an Exegesis of 1 John Based on the Discourse Analysis of the Greek Text," in *Linguistics and New Testament Interpretation: Essays on Discourse Analysis*, ed. David Alan Black et al. (Nashville: Broadman, 1992), 271–86.

In Rev. 4–5 the repetition of the lexical item θρόνος (throne) indicates a unit: 4:2, 3, 4, 5, 6, 9, 10; 5:1, 6, 7, 11, 13. A different set of images dominates in Rev. 6 (e.g., horses, plagues), with a shift in location from heaven to earth and new characters (e.g., horses and their riders) or new roles for already-existing characters (the Lamb, four living creatures).

Prominence

13.16. This is one of the most important aspects of discourse analysis.[18] "Prominence" refers to the way that certain parts of a discourse stick out and are more important than other parts. For example, speech is boring if it is delivered with a monotone voice. Variation in tone, volume, or speed of delivery (as well as hand and body gestures) can be used to highlight parts of an oral delivery. The same is true of written discourse, though it must use other, textual means of indicating prominence. For our purposes, prominence refers to the linguistic means that an author uses to highlight or make some part(s) of the text stand out in some way.[19] Some features of a discourse are foregrounded, while others play a background role.[20] Once again, there are various grammatical means of indicating this. Often prominence is established when an author departs from a normal grammatical pattern; that is, when there is discontinuity from what has gone before in the discourse.[21] The following are just some of the ways that prominence can be indicated by grammatical choice. The interpreter can be the most confident that prominence is being indicated when several of the following indicators converge.

18. Stanley E. Porter, "Prominence: An Overview," in *The Linguist as Pedagogue: Trends in the Teaching and Linguistic Analysis of the Greek New Testament*, ed. Stanley E. Porter and Matthew Brook O'Donnell, New Testament Monographs 11 (Sheffield: Sheffield Phoenix, 2009), 45–74.

19. Cf. Kathleen Callow, *Discourse Considerations in Translating the Word of God* (Grand Rapids: Zondervan, 1974), 50. As Reed says, prominence is "the semantic and grammatical elements of discourse that serve to set aside certain subjects, ideas or motifs of the author as more or less semantically and pragmatically significant than others." Jeffrey T. Reed, *Discourse Analysis of Philippians: Method and Rhetoric in the Debate over Literary Integrity*, JSNTSup 136 (Sheffield: Sheffield Academic, 1997), 106, italics removed.

20. S. Wallace, "Figure and Ground: The Interrelationships of Linguistic Categories," in *Tense-Aspect: Between Semantics and Pragmatics*, ed. P. Hopper, Typological Studies in Language 1 (Amsterdam: Benjamins, 1982), 201–33.

21. "Signals of continuity followed by variation are the primary indicators of discourse shifts as well as prominence" (Westfall, *Discourse Analysis*, 77).

Verbal Aspect

13.17. One important indicator of prominence is verbal aspect. By indicating the author's perspective on a process, variations in aspect can serve to indicate levels of prominence.[22] As we saw in chapter 6 above, on aspect, in narrative the aorist tense-form provides the backbone and summarizes the primary events on the main story line. The imperfect tense fills in background information, and the present tense foregrounds important information in the discourse. The perfect tense-form, being rare in narrative, is a further means of highlighting material and placing it in the foreground. In epistolary literature the aorist provides the background or grounding for the more important thematic material found in the present tense. The perfect tense may also sometimes indicate highlighted information. This does not mean that verbal aspect always indicates relative prominence, that this is the main thing it does or that this is the meaning of the aspects themselves. Yet it is one important way that aspect can function in certain contexts. For examples of its indicating prominence, recall the discussions of John 20 and 1 John 2 in §6.6. Only two further illustrations are given here.

In Rev. 5 the aorist tense is used throughout to summarize the main events of the narrative and carry the story along. The imperfect tense is used in verse 4 (ἔκλαιον) to indicate supplementary actions off the main story line and in verse 14 (ἔλεγον) to conclude the narrative. The present tense, then, is used to highlight significant speeches throughout the chapter (λέγει, v. 5; ᾄδουσιν, v. 9) and the command not to weep (κλαῖε, v. 5). The present-tense λέγει in verse 5 contrasts with the imperfect ἔκλαιον in verse 4. The off-line imperfect is used to describe John's response to the dilemma of not finding anyone worthy to open the scroll, while the present tense-form is used to draw attention to the answer. The perfect tense is then used in the midst of aorists to mark the most crucial act of the scene, the transference of the scroll from the hand of God to the Lamb in verse 7 (εἴληφεν).[23]

πάντες γὰρ **ἥμαρτον** καὶ **ὑστεροῦν**- ται τῆς δόξης τοῦ θεοῦ (Rom. 3:23)	For all **have sinned** and **fall short** of the glory of God.

> The aorist-tense ἥμαρτον signals background information, summarizing what the readers already know from the author's argument in Rom.

---

22. Porter 302–3; Porter, "Prominence," 58–61.

23. For more detail, see David L. Mathewson, *Verbal Aspect in the Book of Revelation: The Function of Greek Verb Tenses in John's Apocalypse*, Linguistic Biblical Studies 4 (Leiden: Brill, 2010), 123–29.

1:18–3:20—all are under sin. The present-tense ὑστεροῦνται is fore-grounded, introducing new information—the latter further defines what the sinning entails: it is falling short of God's glory.

Word and Clause Order

13.18. The order in which words are arranged in clauses tends to follow established patterns. When there is deviation from them, the "dislocated" word is usually foregrounded. For example, the normal position of a noun in the genitive is after its head term (the noun it modifies). Departure from this indicates that the word in the genitive is prominent. Also, when a subject of a clause is expressed, "it is often used either to draw attention to the subject of discussion or to mark a shift in the topic, perhaps signaling that a new person or event is the center of focus" (Porter 296–97). When the subject is placed at the beginning of the clause, it serves to "mark this emphasis or shift from the outset of the clause" (Porter 297). In discourse the primary clauses are the most salient, since they serve to move the discourse forward. Secondary and embedded clauses play a backgrounding or supporting role. As seen in our earlier discussion of clauses (chap. 11), some secondary clauses (e.g., conditional clauses) normally precede the main clause, while others (e.g., purpose, cause, and relative clauses) tend to follow. When this pattern is broken (e.g., when the conditional clause comes at the end), the information in the secondary clause is likely to be prominent.[24]

καὶ εἶπεν αὐτῷ· Ταῦτά σοι πάντα δώσω, ἐὰν πεσὼν προσκυνήσῃς μοι. (Matt. 4:9)

And he [i.e., Satan] said to him [i.e., Jesus], "All these things I will give to you, *if, falling down, you worship me.*"

The placing of the protasis ("if . . .") after the apodosis gives it promi-nence. Notice the usual order with the first two conditional sentences in verses 3 and 6.

---

24. Porter, "Prominence: An Overview," 73.

Encoding

13.20. Since Greek is an inflected language, it does not always need to encode (i.e., refer explicitly to) the participant in the form of an expressed nominal subject. When an entity is introduced for the first time or reintroduced after an absence in the discourse or when there is a need to avoid ambiguity, an explicit reference to the subject is usually necessary (see below, on participants). When not required, a specific reference to the subject is "often used either to draw attention to the subject of discussion or to mark a shift in the topic" (Porter 295–96). Furthermore, any "expansion with more marked cases or participial and prepositional phrases increases the focus on the new participant."[27] This is because more information is given than is necessary (overspecification).

μακάριοι οἱ πενθοῦντες, ὅτι **αὐτοὶ** παρακληθήσονται. (Matt. 5: 4)	Blessed are those who mourn, for **they** will be comforted.

The pronoun is not necessary since the subject is clear from the preceding clause. Its inclusion draws attention to "those who mourn."

Ἀνὴρ δέ τις ἐν Καισαρείᾳ ὀνόματι Κορνήλιος, **ἑκατοντάρχης** ἐκ σπείρης τῆς καλουμένης Ἰταλικῆς, **εὐσεβὴς** καὶ **φοβούμενος** τὸν θεὸν σὺν παντὶ τῷ οἴκῳ αὐτοῦ, **ποιῶν** ἐλεημοσύνας πολλὰς τῷ λαῷ καὶ **δεόμενος** τοῦ θεοῦ διὰ παντός (Acts 10:1–2)	And there was a certain man in Caesarea by the name Cornelius, **a centurion** of the Italian cohort, **devout** and **fearing** God along with all his household, **giving** much alms to the people and **beseeching** God in everything.

The introduction of Cornelius undergoes heavy expansion in the form of adjectives and participles; by providing this fuller description, the author draws special attention to the introduction of this new participant in the narrative.

Τούτου χάριν **ἐγὼ** Παῦλος ὁ **δέσμιος** τοῦ Χριστοῦ Ἰησοῦ ὑπὲρ ὑμῶν τῶν ἐθνῶν (Eph. 3:1)	For this reason, **I**, Paul, the **prisoner** of Christ Jesus in behalf of you gentiles.

After the full mention of the author in the introduction (1:1), there is no need to keep referring to himself in the first person. The reference to Paul with the personal pronoun ἐγώ, which is expanded both by his

---

27. Westfall, *Discourse Analysis*, 60.

name and by the phrase ὁ δέσμιος τοῦ Χριστοῦ Ἰησοῦ in apposition, adds prominence to this section.

καὶ ἐβλήθη ὁ δράκων ὁ μέγας, ὁ ὄφις ὁ ἀρχαῖος, ὁ **καλούμενος** Διάβολος καὶ ὁ Σατανᾶς, ὁ πλανῶν τὴν οἰκουμένην ὅλην—ἐβλήθη εἰς τὴν γῆν (Rev. 12:9)	And he was thrown, the great dragon, the ancient **serpent**, the **one called the devil** and Satan, the one **who deceived** the entire inhabited world—he was thrown to earth.

The piling up of phrases in apposition to ὁ δράκων makes the dragon a highly prominent participant in this chapter of Revelation.

Attention Markers and Deictic Markers

13.21. The Greek of the NT uses a number of forms that grab the reader's attention and point out important features in the discourse. The most important attention markers are ἰδού, ἴδε, and ἄγε. The marker ἰδού is sometimes used to indicate a main participant in narrative.[28] The demonstratives οὗτος and ὧδε can also function as important deictic (pointing) devices that point to something in close proximity and hence are emphatic.

Ἀναχωρησάντων δὲ αὐτῶν **ἰδού** ἄγγελος κυρίου φαίνεται κατ᾽ ὄναρ τῷ Ἰωσὴφ λέγων· (Matt. 2:13)	And when they had departed, **look**, an angel of the Lord appeared in a dream to Joseph, saying.

The marker ἰδού emphasizes the appearance of the angelic being, which is also supported by the use of the narrative present tense-form.

Ἀκούετε. **ἰδού** ἐξῆλθεν ὁ σπείρων σπεῖραι. (Mark 4:3)	Listen! **Look**, a sower came to sow.

This is doubly emphatic, with an imperative call to hear followed by ἰδού, which draws attention to the sower and probably the entire parable.

---

28. Robert A. Dooley, "Let Me Direct Your Attention: Attention Management and Translation," in *Discourse Studies & Biblical Interpretation: A Festschrift in Honor of Stephen H. Levinsohn*, ed. Steven E. Runge (Bellingham, WA: Logos Bible Software, 2011), 76.

εἴ τις εἰς αἰχμαλωσίαν, εἰς αἰχμαλωσίαν ὑπάγει· εἴ τις ἐν μαχαίρῃ ·
ἀποκτανθῆναι αὐτὸν ἐν μαχαίρῃ
ἀποκτανθῆναι. ὧδέ ἐστιν ἡ ὑπομονὴ καὶ ἡ πίστις τῶν ἁγίων. (Rev.
13:10)

If anyone [is to go] into captivity, into captivity he/she goes; if
anyone is to die by the sword, he/
she is to be put to death by the
sword. **Here** is the endurance and
the faith of the saints.

> The presence of ὧδε draws attention to the first part of the verse and
> also foregrounds the hortatory nature of chapter 13 as a call for endur-
> ance and faithfulness.

Expansion

13.22. One way of indicating prominence is through significant expansion of elements in the main clause. When an author is using sentences of a
certain length and then changes the length of sentences through significant
expansion, this often indicates prominence.[29] That is, the expanded section
sticks out from the surrounding context. Expansion usually occurs through
pronounced modification (adjectives, adverbs, participles, subordinate clauses,
prepositional phrases, etc.).

Εἴ τις οὖν παράκλησις ἐν Χριστῷ,
εἴ τι παραμύθιον ἀγάπης, εἴ
τις κοινωνία πνεύματος, εἴ
τις σπλάγχνα καὶ οἰκτιρμοί,
πληρώσατέ μου τὴν χαρὰν ἵνα
τὸ αὐτὸ φρονῆτε, τὴν αὐτὴν
ἀγάπην ἔχοντες, σύμψυχοι, τὸ ἓν
φρονοῦντες, μηδὲν κατ᾽ ἐριθείαν
μηδὲ κατὰ κενοδοξίαν, ἀλλὰ
τῇ ταπεινοφροσύνῃ ἀλλήλους
ἡγούμενοι ὑπερέχοντας ἑαυτῶν,
μὴ τὰ ἑαυτῶν ἕκαστοι σκοποῦντες,
ἀλλὰ καὶ τὰ ἑτέρων ἕκαστοι.
(Phil. 2:1–4)

If [there is], therefore, any en-
couragement in Christ, if any
comfort from love, if any fellowship of the Spirit, if any compas-
sion and mercy, **fill** my joy by
thinking the same thing, having
the same love, united in soul,
being of one mind, [doing] nothing according to selfish ambition
nor according to conceit, but in
humility regarding each other as
more important than yourselves,
not looking to your own interests
but each to those of others.

> The expansion of the main verb πληρώσατε, through considerable
> modification preceding and following the imperative, gives prominence

29. Long (*Grammatical Concepts*, 217–18) refers to this as "Quantity of Information."

to Paul's appeal to the Philippians; notice the four verbless protases (*if*-clauses) of class 1 conditions that precede the main verb.

Καὶ εἶδον ἐν μέσῳ τοῦ θρόνου καὶ τῶν τεσσάρων ζῴων καὶ ἐν μέσῳ τῶν πρεσβυτέρων **ἀρνίον** ἑστηκὸς ὡς ἐσφαγμένον, ἔχων κέρατα ἑπτὰ καὶ ὀφθαλμοὺς ἑπτά, οἵ εἰσιν τὰ ἑπτὰ πνεύματα τοῦ θεοῦ, ἀπεσταλμένοι εἰς πᾶσαν τὴν γῆν. (Rev. 5:6)	And I saw in the midst of the throne and of the four living creatures and in the midst of the elders a **Lamb** standing as slain, having seven horns and seven eyes, which are the seven spirits of God, sent into all the earth.

The reference to the Lamb (ἀρνίον) as the key participant is made prominent through significant modification by means of spatial prepositional phrases, participle clauses, and a relative clause. Even the modifiers get modified ("eyes," "spirits").

καὶ αὐτὸς πατεῖ τὴν ληνὸν **τοῦ οἴνου τοῦ θυμοῦ τῆς ὀργῆς τοῦ θεοῦ τοῦ παντοκράτορος.** (Rev. 19:15)	And he tramples the winepress **of the wine of the anger of the wrath of God the Almighty.**

Expansion occurs through the piling up of genitives, which serves to draw attention to God's wrath and judgment. Noticing the expansion is more important than just labeling each genitive (e.g., as possession, source, objective).

Participants

13.23. The participants of a discourse are the actors associated with the processes, which are expressed with verbs. They are usually the subjects and complements (the direct objects and indirect objects) of the verbs. Participants in discourse, especially in narrative, identify "who is doing what to whom."[30] How the participants are referred to is significant for determining the role they play, or their status.

13.24. When a participant is introduced for the first time, it is usually with full coding, as a noun and any modifiers that go with it. Sometimes in narrative a participant will be introduced with a verbless clause or a verb of being like εἰμί: "*There was* a certain man from Jerusalem named . . ." (cf. Acts 9:10). Once the participant has been introduced, subsequent references

---

30. Dooley and Levinsohn, *Analyzing Discourse*, 111.

will usually have reduced coding; that is, the participant will continue to be referred to not with a full noun phrase but with pronouns (he, she, it, they) or simply with the inflected verb ending (zero coding), when it is the subject. In other words, as long as a participant is active in the discourse, less coding is necessary to refer to that participant. However, if there is any potential for ambiguity (who is doing what to whom?), such as multiple participants, or if a participant has been inactive for some time and needs to be reactivated in the discourse or if there is any other possibility for confusion, the author might use a full reference again. A full reference is usually needed when there is a change in the subject of a sentence.[31] Full reference can also indicate the beginning of a new unit or a change in scene.[32] Use of a full noun phrase to identify a participant when a reduced form of reference (e.g., a pronoun or verb ending) is all that is needed can (1) highlight a contrast with another participant or (2) indicate prominence (in order to bring the participant back into the foreground).[33]

An analogy might be helpful. In a play, an actor must enter the stage for the first time and usually is the focus at that point: this is like full coding. As long as that actor is on the stage, there is no need to keep reintroducing him or her: this is like reduced coding. An actor who has left the stage for some time will need to be reactivated, brought back onstage (full coding again). Or if the stage is crowded with several people at the same time who need to be distinguished from each other, full coding is needed. Also, when the lights go off and the curtain comes down between acts, the actor will need to reenter the stage to begin a new act (full coding). When the actor is already onstage and enters into an important dialog with another character at a crucial point in the play, or when a spotlight is on the character center stage, the character is the focus of attention (full coding, perhaps with expansion).

13.25. Another important consideration is the grammatical role that participants play in clauses.

1. Are they the subjects of verbs or only their (direct or indirect) objects? That is, do they play a role in the discourse of doing and performing actions, or are they only acted upon?
2. Are they found in primary clauses or only secondary or embedded clauses? If they are primarily subjects of the main verbs in primary clauses, they generally play a more important role.

31. Levinsohn, *Discourse Features*, 136.
32. Georgakopoulou and Goutsos, *Discourse Analysis*, 99.
33. Reed, *Discourse Analysis of Philippians*, 103.

3. Are they "nested" within clauses?[34] Does a participant only modify something else in the clause in the form of a genitive case or as the object of a preposition? Are they modifiers of modifiers? Are they only embedded in the speech of another character, so that they don't actually advance the story or discourse themselves (they are only spoken about)?

4. If participants are the subjects of the main verbs, in what kind of verbal processes do they engage? Are they the subjects of verbs of action (e.g., run, fight, push, take, do, create, throw, eat, touch), verbs of perception (e.g., speak, see, believe, know), or verbs of being (εἰμί, γίνομαι)? Verbs that communicate an action tend to move the discourse forward. Verbal processes are important indicators of the status and role of participants in the discourse.

All of this requires that we analyze participants beyond the limited level of designating subjects or objects of verbs, as in traditional grammatical analysis. We must also observe them across larger stretches of discourse to determine the roles they play.

Matthew 2:1–12

13.26. Two main participants are referred to in this well-known story: the magi and King Herod. Both are *subjects of the main verbs* in the narrative ("all Jerusalem" has a brief role to play in v. 3; the "priests and scribes" also play only a brief role in vv. 5–6 to introduce an OT quotation; Jesus is the subject of a genitive absolute participle in v. 1, is spoken about in vv. 2, 4, 9, is in a secondary clause in v. 9, and is the object of a verb [εἶδον] in v. 11). The main participants, the magi and Herod, are referred to with a full reference the first time they are activated: μάγοι (v. 1), ὁ βασιλεὺς Ἡρῴδης (v. 3). Although Herod is mentioned in verse 1, he is given full reference in verse 3, since the *subject* shifts from the magi to him. After he is introduced in verse 3, and as long as he is the subject of each main clause, Herod receives zero coding, being referred to only with verb endings in verse 4. He receives another full reference (Ἡρῴδης) in verse 7, when the subject of the main verb switches back to him as he interacts again with the magi. He is referred to only in the verb endings in verse 8, since he remains the subject of the main verb in each clause. With another subject shift to the magi, full coding occurs with a participle phrase in verse 9 (οἱ δὲ ἀκούσαντες). Since they remain the

---

34. Matthew Brook O'Donnell, *Corpus Linguistics and the Greek of the New Testament* (Sheffield: Sheffield Phoenix, 2005), 421.

subjects of the rest of the main verbs in verses 10–12, they receive zero coding, being referred to only with verb endings.

Καὶ μετὰ τὸ παραδοθῆναι τὸν Ἰωάννην ἦλθεν ὁ Ἰησοῦς εἰς τὴν Γαλιλαίαν κηρύσσων τὸ εὐαγγέλιον τοῦ θεοῦ (Mark 1:14)	And after John was handed over, **Jesus** came into Galilee preaching the gospel of God.

Jesus is introduced with a full reference (Ἰησοῦς) back in 1:9a but is referred to with pronouns or in verb endings throughout verses 9b–13. The full reference (ὁ Ἰησοῦς) in 1:14, then, introduces a new scene.

Revelation 12

13.27. The three main participants in this chapter are the woman, the child, and the dragon. Michael and his angels play very brief roles (v. 7), as do a couple of other minor participants (two wings, a battle, the earth). The woman is introduced in verses 1–2a with full reference (γυνή) and expansion in the form of participles and descriptive verbless clauses. Then she is referred to simply in the verb ending (κράζει) in the next main clause (v. 2b), since she is still the subject.

In verse 3, the dragon is also introduced with a full reference (δράκων), with an adjective, participles, and mention of significant features (heads, horns). The dragon receives a full reference again (ὁ δράκων) in verse 4, since he becomes the subject again after a reference to the tail at the beginning of the verse. The child is introduced in verse 4 (τέκνον) and receives heavy coding as he is referred to in the next clause in verse 5 as a son (υἱόν), which in turn is expanded with a noun in apposition (ἄρσεν) and a relative clause that identifies his function. Topic continuity is retained by the passive verb (ἡρπάσθη) in verse 5, so that the focus remains on the child as the subject. The next full reference to the child (τὸ τέκνον) is probably necessary to avoid confusion (the son, not the woman, is snatched up). Though prominent here, the son only plays the role of the recipient of the action—he is the direct object of verbs and the subject of a passive verb.

In verse 5 the woman is referred to with the verb ending of ἔτεκεν, since it is obvious who is giving birth. And because the subject switches back to her again in verse 6, the woman receives another full reference (ἡ γυνή). In verse 7 the dragon and his angels get full coding, probably to contrast them with Michael and his angels. The dragon and his angels receive full reference because they become the subject of the verb at the end of verse 7. The dragon, still the subject in verse 8, is then referred to in reduced form in the verb ending of ἴσχυσεν. The explicit subject of ἐβλήθη in verse 9 (ὁ δράκων) is made more prominent by its significant expansion in the form of appositional phrases. This overspecification of the subject (dragon) adds prominence and signals the dragon as a focal participant.

When the narrative resumes in verse 13 after an interruption, the dragon merits a new full reference followed by zero coding (ἐδίωξεν). The dragon (the serpent) is the subject again in verse 15, after a switch to "wings of an eagle" in verse 14, and thus is given a full reference (ὁ ὄφις). His final full reference comes in verse 17 (ὁ δράκων), where he is the subject of the verb (the earth was the subject in v. 16), after which verb endings (ἀπῆλθεν, ἐστάθη) in verses 17–18 suffice to identify him as still being the subject. In verses 13–17 the woman is the object or indirect object of verbs in the main clauses or the object of prepositions.

It is instructive to compare the grammatical roles of the participants. As we have already seen, the son, though important, is merely the recipient of activities. The woman is the subject of just three verbs in main clauses: κράζει, ἔτεκεν, ἔφυγεν. Otherwise, she is the complement of verbs (she is acted upon). By contrast, the dragon is the subject of thirteen verbs in main clauses. This indicates that the dragon is the focal point of the scene, driving the action, while the woman and son play more passive or secondary roles.

Conclusion

13.28. Among other things, discourse analysis is a way of analyzing texts in terms of how they are organized, how information is presented, what sections or elements stand out as more prominent, and what role the different participants play. According to Runge, an author needs to do several things in constructing a discourse:

- Make clear who is doing what to whom.
- Clearly communicate changes in time, place, or participants.
- Provide some indication of how the events relate to one another.
- Decide what information to group together in a single sentence [or paragraph] and what to break into separate sentences [or paragraphs].
- Decide which part is the climax and use the appropriate signals to communicate this.
- Choose when to attract extra attention to significant details along the way.[35]

35. Runge, *Discourse Grammar*, 6–7, with slight modifications.

One of the functions of grammar is to accomplish these tasks.

The discussion above has only briefly considered some of the ways grammar can be understood in light of discourse considerations. We hope that the student will be encouraged to move beyond analyzing grammar at the word level, and even the clause and sentence levels, to considering how grammar contributes to interpreting larger units of discourse.

PRINCIPAL PARTS OF VERBS OCCURRING FIFTY TIMES OR MORE IN THE NEW TESTAMENT

Meaning	First (pres. act./mid.)	Second (fut. act./mid.)	Third (aor. act./mid.)	Fourth (perf. act.)	Fifth (perf. mid./ pass.)	Sixth (aor. pass.)
love	ἀγαπάω	ἀγαπήσω	ἠγάπησα	ἠγάπηκα	ἠγάπημαι	ἠγαπήθην
lead	ἄγω	ἄξω	ἤγαγον	ἦχα	ἦγμαι	ἤχθην
take up	αἴρω	ἀρῶ	ἦρα	ἦρκα	ἦρμαι	ἤρθην
ask	αἰτέω	αἰτήσω	ᾔτησα	ᾔτηκα	ᾔτημαι	ᾐτήθην
follow	ἀκολουθέω	ἀκολουθήσω	ἠκολούθησα	ἠκολούθηκα		
hear	ἀκούω	ἀκούσω	ἤκουσα	ἀκήκοα	ἤκουσμαι	ἠκούσθην

Meaning	First (pres. act./mid.)	Second (fut. act./mid.)	Third (aor. act./mid.)	Fourth (perf. act.)	Fifth (perf. mid./pass.)	Sixth (aor. pass.)
go up	ἀναβαίνω	ἀναβήσομαι	ἀνέβην	ἀναβέβηκα		ἀνεβήθην
rise/raise	ἀνίστημι	ἀναστήσω	ἀνέστησα	ἀνέστηκα	ἀνέστημαι	ἀνεστάθην
open	ἀνοίγω	ἀνοίξω	ἀνέῳξα	ἀνέῳγα	ἀνέῳγμαι	ἀνεῴχθην
depart	ἀπέρχομαι	ἀπελεύσομαι	ἀπῆλθον	ἀπελήλυθα		
die	ἀποθνῄσκω	ἀποθανοῦμαι	ἀπέθανον	ἀποτέθνηκα		
answer	ἀποκρίνομαι	ἀποκρινοῦμαι	ἀπεκρινάμην			ἀπεκρίθην
kill	ἀποκτείνω	ἀποκτενῶ	ἀπέκτεινα			ἀπεκτάνθην
destroy	ἀπόλλυμι	ἀπολέσω	ἀπώλεσα	ἀπόλωλα		
release	ἀπολύω	ἀπολύσω	ἀπέλυσα	ἀπολέλυκα	ἀπολέλυμαι	ἀπελύθην
send	ἀποστέλλω	ἀποστελῶ	ἀπέστειλα	ἀπέσταλκα	ἀπέσταλμαι	ἀπεστάλην
begin/rule (active)	ἄρχομαι	ἄρξομαι	ἠρξάμην			
greet	ἀσπάζομαι	ἀσπάσομαι	ἠσπασάμην			
forgive	ἀφίημι	ἀφήσω	ἀφῆκα	ἀφεῖκα	ἀφέωμαι	ἀφέθην
throw	βάλλω	βαλῶ	ἔβαλον	βέβληκα	βέβλημαι	ἐβλήθην
baptize	βαπτίζω	βαπτίσω	ἐβάπτισα		βεβάπτισμαι	ἐβαπτίσθην
see	βλέπω	βλέψω	ἔβλεψα			
beget	γεννάω	γεννήσω	ἐγέννησα	γεγέννηκα	γεγέννημαι	ἐγεννήθην
be/become	γίνομαι	γενήσομαι	ἐγενόμην	γέγονα	γεγένημαι	ἐγενήθην

Meaning	First (pres. act./mid.)	Second (fut. act./mid.)	Third (aor. act./mid.)	Fourth (perf. act.)	Fifth (perf. mid./ pass.)	Sixth (aor. pass.)
know	γινώσκω	γνώσομαι	ἔγνων	ἔγνωκα	ἔγνωσμαι	ἐγνώσθην
write	γράφω	γράψω	ἔγραψα	γέγραφα	γέγραμμαι	ἐγράφην
it is necessary	δεῖ					
receive	δέχομαι	δέξομαι	ἐδεξάμην		δέδεγμαι	ἐδέχθην
teach	διδάσκω	διδάξω	ἐδίδαξα	δεδίδαχα	δεδίδαγμαι	ἐδιδάχθην
give	δίδωμι	δώσω	ἔδωκα	δέδωκα	δέδομαι	ἐδόθην
think/seem	δοκέω	δόξω	ἔδοξα	δεδόκηκα	δεδόκημαι	ἐδοκήθην
glorify	δοξάζω	δοξάσω	ἐδόξασα	δεδόξακα	δεδόξασμαι	ἐδοξάσθην
able	δύναμαι	δυνήσομαι	ἠδυνάμην		δεδύνημαι	ἠδυνήθην
rise	ἐγείρω	ἐγερῶ	ἤγειρα	ἐγήγερκα	ἐγήγερμαι	ἠγέρθην
be/exist	εἰμί	ἔσομαι	ἤμην			
enter / go in	εἰσέρχομαι	εἰσελεύσομαι	εἰσῆλθον	εἰσελήλυθα		
throw out	ἐκβάλλω	ἐκβαλῶ	ἐξέβαλον	ἐκβέβληκα	ἐκβέβλημαι	ἐξεβλήθην
exit / go out	ἐξέρχομαι	ἐξελεύσομαι	ἐξῆλθον	ἐξελήλυθα		
ask (for)	ἐπερωτάω	ἐπερωτήσω	ἐπηρώτησα	ἐπηρώτηκα	ἐπηρώτημαι	ἐπηρωτήθην
go/come	ἔρχομαι	ἐλεύσομαι	ἦλθον	ἐλήλυθα		
ask	ἐρωτάω	ἐρωτήσω	ἠρώτησα	ἠρώτηκα	ἠρώτημαι	ἠρωτήθην
eat	ἐσθίω	φάγομαι	ἔφαγον	ἐδήδοκα	ἐδήδεσμαι	

Meaning	First (pres. act./mid.)	Second (fut. act./mid.)	Third (aor. act./mid.)	Fourth (perf. act.)	Fifth (perf. mid./pass.)	Sixth (aor. pass.)
evangelize	εὐαγγελίζω	εὐαγγελίσω	εὐηγγέλισα	εὐηγγέλικα	εὐηγγέλισμαι	εὐηγγελίσθην
find	εὑρίσκω	εὑρήσω	εὗρον	εὕρηκα	εὕρημαι	εὑρέθην
have	ἔχω	ἕξω	ἔσχον	ἔσχηκα	ἔσχημαι	
live	ζάω	ζήσω	ἔζησα			
seek	ζητέω	ζητήσω	ἐζήτησα	ἐζήτηκα		ἐζητήθην
wish	θέλω	θελήσω	ἠθέλησα	ἠθέληκα		ἠθελήθην
look at	θεωρέω	θεωρήσω	ἐθεώρησα			
stand	ἵστημι	στήσω	ἔστησα	ἕστηκα	ἕσταμαι	ἐστάθην
sit	κάθημαι	καθήσομαι				
call	καλέω	καλέσω	ἐκάλεσα	κέκληκα	κέκλημαι	ἐκλήθην
go down	καταβαίνω	καταβήσομαι	κατέβην	καταβέβηκα		κατεβήθην
proclaim	κηρύσσω	κηρύξω	ἐκήρυξα	κεκήρυχα	κεκήρυγμαι	ἐκηρύχθην
cry out	κράζω	κράξω	ἔκραξα	κέκραγα		
grasp/control	κρατέω	κρατήσω	ἐκράτησα	κεκράτηκα	κεκράτημαι	
judge	κρίνω	κρινῶ	ἔκρινα	κέκρικα	κέκριμαι	ἐκρίθην
speak	λαλέω	λαλήσω	ἐλάλησα	λελάληκα	λελάλημαι	ἐλαλήθην
receive	λαμβάνω	λήμψομαι	ἔλαβον	εἴληφα	εἴλημμαι	ἐλήμφθην
say	λέγω	ἐρῶ	εἶπον	εἴρηκα	εἴρημαι	ἐρρέθην

Meaning	First (pres. act./mid.)	Second (fut. act./mid.)	Third (aor. act./mid.)	Fourth (perf. act.)	Fifth (perf. mid./pass.)	Sixth (aor. pass.)
testify	μαρτυρέω	μαρτυρήσω	ἐμαρτύρησα	μεμαρτύρηκα	μεμαρτύρημαι	ἐμαρτυρήθην
be about to	μέλλω	μελλήσω	ἐμέλλησα			
remain	μένω	μενῶ	ἔμεινα	μεμένηκα		
know	οἶδα	εἰδήσω	ᾔδειν			
see	ὁράω	ὄψομαι	εἶδον, ὠψάμην	ἑώρακα	ἑώραμαι	ὤφθην
owe	ὀφείλω	ὀφειλήσω	ὠφείλησα	ὠφείληκα		ὠφειλήθην
give / hand over / betray	παραδίδωμι	παραδώσω	παρέδωκα	παραδέδωκα	παραδέδομαι	παρεδόθην
exhort/comfort	παρακαλέω	παρακαλέσω	παρεκάλεσα	παρακέκληκα	παρακέκλημαι	παρεκλήθην
persuade	πείθω	πείσω	ἔπεισα	πέποιθα	πέπεισμαι	ἐπείσθην
send	πέμπω	πέμψω	ἔπεμψα	πέπομφα	πέπεμμαι	ἐπέμφθην
walk/live	περιπατέω	περιπατήσω	περιεπάτησα	περιπεπάτηκα		
drink	πίνω	πίομαι	ἔπιον	πέπωκα	πέπομαι	ἐπόθην
fall	πίπτω	πεσοῦμαι	ἔπεσον	πέπτωκα		
believe	πιστεύω	πιστεύσω	ἐπίστευσα	πεπίστευκα	πεπίστευμαι	ἐπιστεύθην
fill/fulfill	πληρόω	πληρώσω	ἐπλήρωσα	πεπλήρωκα	πεπλήρωμαι	ἐπληρώθην
do/make	ποιέω	ποιήσω	ἐποίησα	πεποίηκα	πεποίημαι	ἐποιήθην
go/proceed	πορεύομαι	πορεύσομαι	ἐπορευσάμην		πεπόρευμαι	ἐπορεύθην
approach	προσέρχομαι	προσελεύσομαι	προσῆλθον	προσελήλυθα		

Meaning	First (pres. act./mid.)	Second (fut. act./mid.)	Third (aor. act./mid.)	Fourth (perf. act.)	Fifth (perf. mid./ pass.)	Sixth (aor. pass.)
pray	προσεύχομαι	προσεύξομαι	προσηυξάμην			
worship	προσκυνέω	προσκυνήσω	προσεκύνησα	προσκεκύνηκα		
gather together	συνάγω	συνάξω	συνήγαγον	συνῆχα	συνῆγμαι	συνήχθην
save	σῴζω	σώσω	ἔσωσα	σέσωκα	σέσῳσμαι	ἐσώθην
keep/guard	τηρέω	τηρήσω	ἐτήρησα	τετήρηκα	τετήρημαι	ἐτηρήθην
put	τίθημι	θήσω	ἔθηκα	τέθεικα	τέθειμαι	ἐτέθην
depart	ὑπάγω	ὑπάξω	ὑπήγαγον	ὑπῆχα	ὑπῆγμαι	ὑπήχθην
be/exist	ὑπάρχω	ὑπάρξομαι	ὑπηρξάμην			
carry	φέρω	οἴσω	ἤνεγκα	ἐνήνοχα	ἐνήνεγμαι	ἠνέχθην
say	φημί	φήσω	ἔφην			
fear	φοβέομαι	φοβήσομαι	ἐφοβησάμην		πεφόβημαι	ἐφοβήθην
rejoice	χαίρω	χαρήσομαι			κεχάρημαι	ἐχάρην

INDEX OF SCRIPTURE REFERENCES

INDEX OF SUBJECTS